DETROIT ROCK CITY

BOOKS BY STEVE MILLER

A Slaying in the Suburbs:
The Tara Grant Murder

Touch and Go: The Complete Hardcore
Punk Zine '79–'83, editor

Girl, Wanted:
The Chase for Sarah Pender

Commando: The Johnny Ramone Autobiography, co-editor

Nobody's Women: The Crimes and Victims of
Anthony Sowell, the Cleveland Serial Killer

DETROIT
ROCK
CITY

*The Uncensored History
of Rock 'n' Roll in
America's Loudest City*

Steve Miller

DA CAPO PRESS
A Member of the Perseus Books Group

Designed by Timm Bryson
Set in 10.75 point Adobe Jenson Pro by The Perseus Books Group

Thanks to the following publishers and writers for granting permission to use original interviews and material previously published for this book:

+ Ron and Scott Asheton interviews by Brian Bowe, pages 42–55, used by permission of Brian Bowe.
+ Ron Asheton, page 49, courtesy of Long Gone John, Sympathy For The Record Industry, Sympathyrecords.com, SFTRI 163.
+ Bob Seger interview, page 77, by John Morthland, July 1977, courtesy of *Creem* magazine.
+ Bob Seger interview, page 124, by Lowell Cauffiel, August 1976, courtesy of *Creem* magazine.

Library of Congress Cataloging-in-Publication Data
Miller, Steve
  Detroit rock city : the uncensored history of rock 'n' roll in America's loudest city / Steve Miller.—First Da Capo Press edition.
    pages cm
  Includes bibliographical references.
  ISBN 978-0-306-82065-6 (pbk.)—ISBN 978-0-306-82184-4 (e-book) 1. Rock music—Michigan—Detroit—History and criticism. 2. Rock musicians—Michigan—Detroit. I. Title.
  ML3534.3.M59 2013
  781.6609774'34—dc23
                                                                    2013004433

Published by Da Capo Press
A Member of the Perseus Books Group
www.dacapopress.com

Da Capo Press books are available at special discounts for bulk purchases in the U.S. by corporations, institutions, and other organizations. For more information, please contact the Special Markets Department at the Perseus Books Group, 2300 Chestnut Street, Suite 200, Philadelphia, PA 19103, or call (800) 810-4145, ext. 5000, or e-mail special.markets@perseusbooks.com.

10 9 8 7 6 5 4 3 2 1

CONTENTS

Photos follow page 154

INTRODUCTION

This book, like so many others, starts in a bar. In winter 2002 a musician I knew in Lansing, Michigan, approached me as I sat at a table alone.

"Hey, you're a journalist or something, right?" he asked.

Yes, I nodded; few of my friends knew what I did for a living. I lived at the time in Washington, DC, a world away. I was a national reporter, covering things and events that would affect their lives in ways they couldn't perceive. But they didn't care. I was still the guy who liked good music and drank with them and went to the after-parties and had some good stories about early hardcore and touring the states before there was a network of clubs and crash palaces.

"So why hasn't anyone ever written a book about Detroit's rock scene and the influence it's had on rock and roll?" my pal asked.

I had no answer. Detroit was just part of growing up. Did I take it for granted?

My dad was a copy editor at the *Detroit News* in 1967, commuting from our apartment in East Lansing, eighty miles west of Detroit, where he was getting his doctorate at Michigan State University. One steamy night that year we drove to Tiger Stadium to catch the White Sox play the Tigers, watching the gun-toting National Guard troops on the rooftops. The riots were two weeks prior.

In the fall of 1968 I was wandering across a park in East Lansing and heard what sounded like a sonic explosion, a cacophony of thud and high-end screech coming from a small, brick community center. I ran to the doors to check into what was causing this heavenly noise. Locked. I went around to the rear of the building, where an open window was giving everyone a free listen to the soundcheck of the MC5. Looking inside—the amps draped with the American flags, the buckskin jackets, and the wild hair—for an eleven-year-old, it was a life-giving experience I have never forgotten.

We started going to big shows in Detroit, national acts that hit Detroit at every chance—Aerosmith, Black Sabbath, Lou Reed, and Roxy Music—at great venues like the Michigan Palace, Cobo Center, and Masonic Auditorium. Detroit was The Show.

We all read *Creem* magazine in high school, learning about the real deal in a way that effete bullshit like *Rolling Stone* could never conceive of. *Creem* was Detroit; the rest were from, well, somewhere else. *Creem* wrote about the Stooges more than anyone else. When it came down to Mick Jagger vs. Iggy Pop in the rock-star idolatry sweepstakes, Iggy came out on top every time. He was Detroit. I would puff furiously on my Newport at the notion that anyone outside Iggy could be any more badass. Starting at age fifteen, we listened to the Stooges as we drove in cars on back roads and cradled bottles of Mad Dog 20–20.

"So why hasn't anyone ever written a book about Detroit's rock scene and the influence it's had on rock and roll?"

The question was a killer. I had no answer, but this is the response, eleven years later. Along the way to making this happen, I confirmed a number of my beliefs about music. Number one is that Detroit is the most influential rock-and-roll city on earth—not New York, not Los Angeles, not London, and not San Francisco. It's incontrovertible.

Another is that Detroit's fade as a city was part of the natural order, an ebbing of power for a city that held half of the US auto-making jobs. Wayne Kramer, his mind finely honed, told me as we sat in his Los Angeles studio in 2011 that the MC5 "were like a barometer for Detroit. Unearths an interesting question, the one of free will. Which I am more and more convinced does not exist. We think we're making decisions, but our options are so affected by our surroundings. If you're born in the wrong family, wrong neighborhood, you're not going to make it. You can't be rich someday. You ain't the kid who found out about computers like Bill Gates. He was in a unique situation. So the decline of the MC5 and the parallel decline of Detroit is not a mystery to me, the things we were going through; we were not alone. A lot of other people were in desperate situations as well. And some of them had guns."

Man, that's a Darwinian downer.

Detroit pulses with the same energy that captivated me as a kid. Detroit won't change, because that would have happened billions of dollars and many years ago. That's what so good about it—the purity of its character. On a given night you can see some great music and maybe get jacked while you pump gas a few blocks down. Detroit is Alphabet City circa 1977 squared. The Rock and Roll Hall of Fame isn't in Detroit because that would taint the city with the greedy mindlessness of the Establishment. Detroit is way past such institutions. It's the Rock City. And that's enough.

Black Sheep
(1965–1972)

Respect

Dan Carlisle (*WABX, WRIF, DJ*): How many places in the US had all the forces of immigration come together in just a twenty-five-year period? It was because of the auto money. In Detroit we had Okies, folks from Tennessee and Kentucky, black people from Georgia and other parts of the Deep South. We had people from Germany and Poland and Jewish people, and so on the radio you had Polish music, German music, gospel on Sundays, hearing all this music in this one city. Mitch Ryder made all these records composed of these sounds; the MC5 heard all this and put it together. The so-called San Francisco and Los Angeles scenes didn't have that, and you'd find most people out there were from places like Ohio or Wisconsin. We had the real thing, working-class music.

Russ Gibb (*Grande Ballroom, promoter*): We were called factory rats when I was growing up. I worked in the DeSoto plant, which was part of Chrysler, on Wyoming and Ford Road. I put hubcaps on the DeSotos. Most of the cabs in New York at one time were DeSoto. The big thing on that car was it had a shield that went over the headlights.

Mitch Ryder (*Mitch Ryder and the Detroit Wheels, Detroit, solo, vocalist*): My dad got me a job working in the factory before I started getting serious about music. It was a tool-and-die factory that did outsourcing for GM. We did gear shift levers. I was fifteen.

Stirling Silver (*scenester*): I worked for General Motors on the Cadillac line. One of my high school friend's mom was the head of personnel at Plant 21, which was a Fisher Body plant. They made fifteen Cadillac limousines a day. At the same time the Lordstown, Ohio, factory was kicking out Chevy Vegas at a hundred per hour.

There was a big union thing because it was too fast a line. The average line was running sixty to seventy cars per hour, so that'd give you a relative frame of reference. The Fisher Body line was making an average of fifteen a day, and if they're really busy, seventeen or eighteen a day. So the line can move like this minute hand on a watch. You couldn't see it move, but if you look over there and then look back, you could see that it had moved.

VC Lamont Veasey (*Black Merda bassist, vocalist*): My father worked at Ford. I was born in Mississippi. I didn't actually live in the inner city of Detroit until I was thirteen almost fourteen, but my parents, they took me to Ecorse, Michigan, until I was thirteen, and then we moved to inner-city Detroit. It was like a culture shock to me because where I was at, it was like semirural and the people were like from the South.

Robin Sommers (*designer,* Creem *magazine, scenester*): I went to art school and then went to San Francisco in 1966, but there were no jobs; all the hippies had them. So I got back and I went to work at Ford. I was working on the assembly line, the merry-go-round, as a spot welder. I welded a whole side of a car. We made '67 Mustangs and Cougars. It was horrible.

Ron Cooke (*Detroit, Gang War, Sonic's Rendezvous Band bassist*): My dad emigrated from Canada in 1922. He was a boiler operator man. A big oil refinery deal, he was a stationary engineer. I went in and out of the ironworkers union in Detroit in the midsixties. I did about two and a half years in the apprenticeship there.

Don Was (*Was (Not Was) bassist, vocalist; Traitors vocalist, producer, Rolling Stones, Bob Dylan, Bonnie Raitt, Iggy Pop*): The one thing you don't wanna do the Detroit way is to head to the factory when you're looking for work.

Mark Norton (*Ramrods, 27 vocalist, journalist,* Creem *magazine*): I started working at the Ford plant when I got out of high school. It was deadly, just going in there every day. The money was great, though. This is why so many people came to rely on that for a living—easy work, no education needed, and the money was great.

Hiawatha Bailey (*Stooges roadie, Cult Heroes, vocalist*): I was born in Columbus, Georgia, in 1948. The thing was, Detroit was an industrial complex. My grandfather worked for the railroad; he was a Pullman porter working on the railroad when they were settling from the East Coast to the West Coast. He knew there were better things to be had up North. My parents decided they wanted to hit it. My dad got a job at Chevrolet Gear and Axle in Hamtramck. I won a record player through this contest by General Motors called, "Why I'm Glad My Dad Works for General Motors." I made that crap up that I wrote; I can't even remember why I said I was glad. Because he can buy me stuff and I can get out of the house? Me and my friend Carl Grimes would take turns going through this rack of old 45s at the store and finding all this off-the-wall stuff, and we'd go down and we'd play it on the record player that I won.

Mark Norton: In Detroit either you go to college or you go work in a factory. Give a bottle of whiskey to the foreman and you got a job on the line. My dad's friend knew somebody who ran the line, and that's where I ended up. I met this guy named Willie who'd been in the paint department for twenty-three years. When I came in, it was "Hi Willie, how you doing, what's going on, Willie?" He was painting cars. "Willie, how long you been wearing a respirator?" And the guys doing the pinstriping down the cars, they came in to work just about half-assed bombed because to hold a paintbrush and have the car go by you on the line, and they're doing that thing. Man, they were ripped to the tits doing the pinstripes on the car. I used to pick up shifts shoveling silicon sand into the furnaces that melted down the engine blocks; it would be like 125 degrees in there. Everyone was working in a factory; that's what it was, nothing special.

Brian Pastoria (*producer*): Because of the auto industry, you didn't have to speak English or have a degree but could get a great job with benefits. And with American popular music and the auto industry also taking off, it spawned this wild community made of people from other places. The younger people wanted to escape. They didn't want to end up working on the line. And when Elvis and the Beatles hit, they realized things could be different for them. They could play music. And that was the way out, so they played anywhere they could.

Tom Morwatts (*Mutants, guitarist*): There were these teen clubs, and there were about five of 'em in the Metro area. Dave Leone ran one near my house on the east side. He eventually started Diversified Management Agency, DMA, which was the biggest booking agency in the Midwest. We ended up signing with them later. Dave Leone, when I was a kid, had all those teen clubs, drawing kids from about fourteen to eighteen. Bob Seger, Amboy Dukes, Rationals—they were playing at those places all the time.

Stirling Silver: There was also Fries Auditorium, over by Grosse Pointe, where I was from. I saw Bob Seger do "Hey Jude" by himself on the piano that was in that room. The song had just come out.

Russ Gibb: I started teaching in a little town called Howell, Michigan, and my salary was $2,200 a year. Howell was a two-hour drive from Detroit at the time. They didn't allow dancing, and later on the town became the center for the John Birch Society. They thought that was the work of the devil. I also worked part time in a radio station, so I knew the kids loved music. I thought "Well, gee, I knew the guy at some of these record hops, Robin Seymour, who was a local DJ." There were a few others doing this. So I put this show on. I think I spent $25 to rent out a Saturday night at the Elk's Club or the Moose Club or some club up on Grand River in Howell. I spent $10 to have mimeographed fliers put out. I gave them to certain kids I knew and said, "So and so is going to be here," and I got a hold of Bob Maxwell, who was a big radio guy back then. Not rock music—he was more pop. So he advertised it a couple of times that he was going to be up in Howell. He got $50 for coming up. So I spent $25 for the hall and $10 for the flyers, and after I paid Maxwell, I was way ahead of the game in money terms. Because I made in one night more than what I could in about two weeks of teaching. It wasn't a lot of money, but it was back then. Now I knew how to make money on rock things, and I was still working part time at the radio station. I got a reputation for knowing how to make record hops work.

Tom Morwatts: But even cooler than the record hops was the high school I went to, Notre Dame High School in Harper Woods. It was legendary for its dances. They were so needy for money, it was kind of a new school, and they had college-level sports facilities, and they needed to raise money. This one priest, Father Bryson, turned out to be a natural promoter, so they assigned him to the job. He had started out doing, just like every other high school, teen dances. But his teen dances, because they had a bigger facility, turned into concerts. He got the Supremes and the Temptations, Shadows of Knight. Bob Seger. People would come from all over the Metro area, from the west side, from all the suburbs, because of the acts that were playing there.

Jerry Bazil (*Dark Carnival, drummer*): We had these great bands playing at our high schools. Teegarden & Van Winkle, the SRC, the Up, Third Power—they all played at high school dances at places like Mercy High School and Catholic Central. This was the late sixties, early seventies.

Jaan Uhelszki (*journalist,* Creem *magazine*): The Who played at Southfield High School in 1967. I don't think that the people who showed up were necessarily students.

Pete Cavanaugh (*WTAC, DJ*): I was on the air at WTAC in Flint, and we were doing sock hops all over Michigan, and we could promote them on WTAC because our signal went so far. Punch Andrews, who went on to manage Bob Seger, was doing the Hideout. And there was the Hullabaloo franchise. Sock hops moved into live bands. It had to happen that way. Mark Farner's first band or Don Brewer's band—these were just starting, and now they had a place to play. Seger got his start that way. I'd have sock hops, and Seger would play afterward.

Robin Seymour (*CKLW/WKNR, DJ, host of* Swingin' Time *TV show*): Bob Seger did one of his first big live things at the Roostertail, where I was puting on events. He had his Beatles haircut, a little cap on, and he walked on the stage and had to walk right off; he was so nervous he had to go throw up. I went over to Punch Andrews, his manager, and I said, "Get him out of here, I won't have anybody doing my shows on drugs." Punch says, "He doesn't touch drugs. He's nervous, he's scared to death."

Pete Cavanaugh: After a while you would have bands, and the only time records would be played was between bands. The sound was shitty. No one knew any better. Question Mark and the Mysterians got their first gig there at one of our places, Mt. Holly, south of Flint. We got everybody: Bob Seger, the Rationals, Dick Wagner and the Bossmen. At the same time Jeep Holland and A-Square Production in Ann Arbor were doing things. Jeep put his bands at Mt. Holly and booked the whole year in advance at one point.

Scott Morgan (*Rationals, Sonic's Rendezvous Band, guitarist, vocalist*): Jeep was also our manager. He was like the Svengali of the Rationals: produce, find us songs, book us—you know, anything you can think of. We had this Dodge van with the Rationals logo printed on the side. You could see us coming from a mile away. Jeep was also a really bad driver, and one night he was driving the van to a show in Lansing and I was in another car behind them. Jeep was cutting in and out of traffic and eating pizza and drinking a Coke all at the same time, not paying attention to what he's doing. He passes this car in front of him and just keeps going up the side of the road, down the embankment, rolls the van three times. My brother was in the van, in the passenger seat. When it rolled and the top came off, they just got thrown off on the ground. My brother was hardly hurt at all. Jeep was a little banged up. He did everything else pretty well. Just not driving.

Deniz Tek (*Australia's Radio Birdmen, guitarist, vocalist*): The Rationals were doing this British Invasion thing, just before everything happened. They would play high schools. Pretty soon bands moved from the schools and would play TV shows, like Robin Seymour's *Swingin' Time*. He was a DJ and he also had a TV show.

Robin Seymour: We found the Rationals. Art Cervi was my talent coordinator; he later became Bozo the Clown. He was the best Bozo in the country. We discovered them and played their first record.

Then they did a cover of the song "Respect" in 1966, and it looked like they were going to take off. Jerry Wexler at Atlantic Records called me when the record was taking off, and I connected him with Jeep Holland.

Scott Morgan: Jeep turned us on to "Respect," and he just played it one time and we said, "Well, yeah. I'd like to do that song." It came out and it was a hit in Detroit.

Robin Seymour: Jeep called me and said they asked Wexler for $5,000 up front and Atlantic said, "Heck no, we won't pay it." Wexler called me back and said, "What's with these kids?" An unknown by the name of Aretha Franklin signed with Atlantic a week later, and her first hit was "Respect." That would have put them on the map. The Rationals sold fifty thousand copies of "Respect" in Michigan alone. It was frustrating.

Scott Morgan: Doing "Respect"—first it was Otis Redding in 1965, us in 1966, and Aretha Franklin in 1967. I think Aretha decided that if we could do it, she could do it better. Of course, she did.

Scott Richardson (*SRC, Chosen Few vocalist*): In Detroit it was fall of '67, and acid set it off like a bomb. Changed everything, all the music.

Deniz Tek: Once the wave of high energy hit, in '68 or '69, I was seeing most of the bands at outdoor concerts in the summer time. In Ann Arbor in 1968 that was at West Park, this leafy green park where people might take their kids to throw a Frisbee. The place had a little concert shell, and I saw the MC5 play there one weekend. It got shut down because of noise, and the shows moved to Gallup

Park, which was over by the river. That was when it got pretty big; you'd have six or seven bands on a Sunday and sometimes have a national on the bill. I saw Janis Joplin there and I saw Johnny Winter.

Steve Forgey (*scenester*): Everyone was in Detroit by 1968 because it was really cranking out better music than anywhere else in the US. You had jazz in New York, hippy music in San Francisco, peaceful rock-country in LA. In Detroit it was all upside down. I was living in Jackson, about forty-five miles west of Detroit for a while, and they had these shows in the park in the middle of town. Funkadelic, Nugent and the Amboy Dukes. Everybody played there except the MC5—that was where they drew the line. One afternoon they bring in Alice Cooper, just before the band got really big. I was just out of eleventh grade, you know, and I'd heard how cool they were. Me and my buddies get over to the park early to see them set up. They had this van and it's pulling a U-Haul trailer, we think with the equipment in it. But it wasn't. The road crew was in the van. The trailer gate opens up, and out come the guys in Alice Cooper, all in their stage clothes, hair all over the place. It was surreal, seeing them standing in broad daylight like that.

David Teegarden (*Teegarden & Van Winkle, Bob Seger and the Silver Bullet Band, drummer, vocalist*): Detroit was a giant city to Skip and I when we moved there in 1967. I mean, we had lived in LA, and we were from Tulsa. In Oklahoma, musicians and players I learned from were all very much into southern blues, and Motown was part of the upbringing in Tulsa. I was like, "Let's go to Detroit, that's where Motown is," not realizing that we were segregated from that whole scene. The whites were adamantly distressed about the rioting; it drew some lines there. We didn't discuss Motown for a while.

Playground of Noise

Russ Gibb: The Grande started in 1966, and within ten weeks it became a positive cash flow.

John Sinclair (*MC5 manager, poet, the Blues Scholars*): The most we ever got there was $1,800, but Gibb paid us $125 a night usually. We were just so fucking offended at this $125, and they were making money hand over fist. They were bringing these bands from England, and they were giving them thousands of dollars. And we're getting $125.

Iggy Pop (*The Stooges, Iggy and the Stooges, solo, vocalist*): When we played for Russ we'd make $50—that was for the whole group you know. And then we worked our way up. Over time we were headlining and we were paid pretty well. But with John Sinclair, on bills with the MC5, we played for free.

Jaan Uhelszki: I got a job where I was working as a Coca-Cola girl at the Grande. As a Coca-Cola girl, you did two things: You sell Coca Cola, Sprite, and orange pop, and what you really do is make sure no one doses those said drinks. That was the bigger part of my job. They didn't sell alcohol at the Grande Ballroom. While it wasn't all ages, I think it was seventeen and above; all they sold was soft drinks. Nobody drank; everybody did drugs. It was a psychedelic ballroom.

Gary Rasmussen (*The Up, Sonic's Rendezvous Band, bassist*): The Grande was not a bar. It wasn't really a big drinking culture at that time.

S. Kay Young (*photographer*): You could get every drug you wanted—Sandoz right from the source—but nobody really drank.

John Sinclair: There was a guy named Neal. About ten o'clock on Friday night at the Grande, Neal went up a staircase that extended from the floor of the Grande Ballroom. And he would appear at the top of the staircase and just hang out with a big smile. Everybody would go to Neal, and he'd give them samples of this week's acid, and all the acidheads would drop. The first band had played at nine. The second band played at 10:15. And at 11 o'clock it was time for the MC5, when everybody was peaking on acid—the audience and, often, the band.

K. J. Knight (*Ted Nugent and the Amboy Dukes, drummer*): Neal was this guy who would hand out hits of acid at the Grande Ballroom. He had a house downtown, and he hung with a girl name Dirty Debbie. We used to go down to his house in Detroit and he would always turn us onto drugs. John Finley was a huge drug dealer back then. Finley and Rusty Day had the Day and Night Dealers Blues Band. One time I was backstage waiting to go on, and Alice was backstage, and I offered Alice Cooper a stick of gum, and he said, "KJ, you gotta promise me that this isn't coated with acid," you know.

Ted Nugent (*Ted Nugent and the Amboy Dukes, solo, guitarist, vocalist*): *Creem* magazine printed a story about how I shot two guys at the Grande Ballroom after they tried to steal my briefcase. I never shot anybody. But they printed it.

Dennis Thompson (*MC5, New Order, drummer*): We practiced at the Grande as well as being the house band for a while. Everybody used to come to the Grande to rehearse, from Janis Joplin to Procol Harum to whomever. And we used to take LSD, turn all the lights out, middle of the night, and go downstairs and just listen to the music. Couldn't see anybody. All you saw was those little lights on the amplifiers, right?

Gary Rasmussen: They were better drugs at that time, cleaner. One time we all took a lot of LSD and went and played at the Grande Ballroom; we thought that would be a good idea. Frank Bach, our singer, didn't because he was macrobiotic and not into drugs, but the rest of the band did. So we go on, and we'd start a song, and we'd be fine. Then we'd get to the guitar solo, and as soon as it would start, we're looking at each other going, "What song are we doing?" None of us knew how to get out of the solo. So we'd play the solo for ten minutes and just sort of end the song. We'd look at each other and sort of go, "Wow, that was weird." We'd start the next tune and play the song fine until the solo, and as soon as the solo, we're gone again. We don't know where the fuck we were or what we were doing.

Bob Sheff (*Iggy and the Stooges, Charging Rhinoceros of Soul, piano*): The Charging Rhinoceros of Soul were the warm-up band for the Mothers of Invention at the Grande one time. Oh God, I refer to it as cookie Sunday. I was late getting to the van, and I jumped in the van, and I hadn't had breakfast and there was this jar full of cookies and I was really hungry. I ate about half the jar of cookies. Our bass player noticed a lot of those cookies were gone, so she asked, you know, "Who ate those cookies?" I said, "I did, I'm sorry, I'm really hungry." Well, they were marijuana cookies, and by the time I got there I was so stoned I couldn't get out of the car. I couldn't put one foot in front of the other. One second I was in the car, and a second later I was up the stairs, and then a second later I was on the stage. The only thing I could hear was the bass drum, which sounded like it was in a huge cave. I knew everyone else was playing, and when I played the keyboard it was like the keys were undulating and it was like a river. I got scared after the set and went outside to the parking lot. I wanted to hide until I felt better. So I got underneath the van.

Russ Gibb: Cream played at the Grande a couple of times. The first time they came through, Eric Clapton wanted to go shopping, and I took them to Dearborn around Michigan and Schaefer. There was a Montgomery Ward there and in the window store display was a corduroy jacket that was all faded from the sun. He really liked that, so we went in and they couldn't understand why this English guy would want to buy that. But he got it, and then we walked out onto Michigan Avenue and some car went by with some guys in it, and they called out to him, "Are you a girl?" You know on the inside of *Disraeli Gears*, in that picture he's wearing these chaps? He got those in Detroit too. Cream loved Detroit. They wanted to go swimming one night, and so we took them out to one of our lakes. At the time I had a portable phone, one of the first. It weighed twenty-one pounds, and only eleven people in the state of Michigan could be on that phone system at any given time. It cost $4,000—a lot of money. We're in a boat, and Jack Bruce wanted to make a call and he dropped the fucking phone in the water. That's $4,000 going down. We brought it home and took hairdryers to dry it out. And it worked.

Rick Kraniak, aka Rick K (*booking agent*): When I was in high school, I had a part-time job in the Dearborn post office, and I would see all these Grande Post Cards that Russ would send to Blue Cheer, Jefferson Airplane, whoever. It was cool being able to read what he was saying to them.

Leni Sinclair (*photographer, wife of John Sinclair*): Russ Gibb paid us $25 a night to do the light show every week at the Grande. There was Gary Grimshaw, Robin

Sommers, and me and two or three other people. The light stand was way up at the top of the room, so you could project it on all the walls on the stage. There was no air conditioning, so when the light show was on and all these lights going and all these machines going, the temperatures up there used to go to 120 degrees. We would always be sweating.

Robin Sommers: It was Grimshaw, Leni, and Sigrid—who would later marry Fred Smith—with me. We made $25 a night at the Grande, and I never saw a penny because it went to Trans Love. We had four overhead projectors and four slide projectors, and there was a light stand built in there, twelve feet off the floor. The ballroom had a wooden dance floor, and all the way around was a fifteen-foot-wide ledge where you could sit or stand. There were also booths that were three steps up from the dance floor. The light stand was at one end; the place was a rectangle shape with corners cut off. We projected on walls and the stage behind the band, which played like in a bay. I had these slides with thin glass on them and special inks and colors, and I used this 1,500-watt overhead projector and put these slides in there. I put vegetable or baby oil in there and then water and then food coloring.

Russ Gibb: The weirdest guy I ever booked was Sun Ra. But I loved him for a good reason. Whenever I'd have a big band, I wanted to do two shows a night. Now, we had a ticket policy where if you came to the Grande and you got a ticket, you were there until 2:30 a.m. We were already violating the law with the number of people we were jamming in to the Grande. I think there was a legal thing of twelve to fifteen hundred, and we were packing two to three thousand in there a night. So I could have a big band and book them two shows, an early and a late. After the first show I put Sun Ra up. With Sun Ra, you can take the first five minutes and you're wondering what's going on. After about a half an hour you're going, "This is shit! I can't stand this!" People would leave. We'd practically empty out the place, and that allowed me to bring in more people. That was my strategy with Sun Ra. I never told him. We paid him. He was happy and he was getting the gig and people were hearing him. John Sinclair was happy because he loved Sun Ra.

John Sinclair: In the spring of '69 I brought in Sun Ra. We rented the house next door and they lived next to us. They were about the weirdest Negroes in America, there's no getting around that. Sun Ra just wanted to make music and stun the audiences with his great ideas. I was happy any time I could get them a show.

Russ Gibb: The Grande had such a great sound because there was horsehair in the plaster. We knew that they had done that at the Orchestra Hall and so we had them do it at the Grande. It absorbed the sound rather than having it bounce.

Dennis Dunaway (*Alice Cooper, bassist*): It's interesting how people called it the Grande, when I think it was really the Grand ballroom with just a European spelling. But they called it the Grande. The Grande was sort of our rival because we got a lot more gigs at the Eastown Theater. We related to the Eastown Theater a lot more. And the Stooges played the Eastown a lot more. We played with the Who there one time, and the place had this curtain, like a movie screen. So when we opened for the Who, they brought down the curtain so Keith's drums were behind the curtain and then we were set up in front of the curtain. When we did "Black Juju," I thought, "Wow, the drums sounded incredible tonight." When we got done with our set, one of our roadies came and told us that Keith Moon went out to his kit and was playing right along with Neal through the whole song. That gave me the idea to stand behind the screen when the Who played. If that screen wasn't there, I could have set my hand right on Keith Moon's head. I watched the Who do their whole set there. Nobody could see me. The Who would come together between songs, and you'd think they're discussing what they were going to do next. No. They were coming together going "Fuck you!" "No, fuck you!"

Norm Liberman (*Frut, vocalist*): When people got tired of the Grande, we had places in Macomb County, which is north of Detroit. There were two geodesic domes out in the middle of nowhere, that was the Frut Palace. Every band that played there got $400, and we had every band in Detroit play there. My mother would take the money so that no one would steal it. I was standing there one night and my mother's taking the money, and Alice Cooper says, "Mrs. Liberman, why don't you let the guy over there inside?" "No, Alice, he can panhandle a little more before he comes in."

John Kosloskey, aka Kozmo (*Frut, bassist*): One of the guys around the Frut, his dad was the pastor at a local church in Mt. Clemens. The pastor wanted to have a gathering for the youth that would, you know, put them in the right direction. They had a hall at his church, and we played and gave everyone a hit of THC as they went in. We were exposing people to a lot of the creative things of the mind.

Norm Liberman: We also had the Frut Cellar inside this old hotel in Mt. Clemens, the Colonial. We used to have 600 people inside and 250 on the steps waiting to get in. At that place we could pay the bands for six, seven hundred dollars. Alice Cooper would come in for $800, and we packed the joint. Everybody was drunk on their asses. Drinks were a buck apiece. We would take the cover and pay the bands that were playing. We were usually on the bill too, and we would take the rest of the money and party with it ourselves. The guy who owned the joint would take the bar money.

Neal Smith (*Alice Cooper, drummer*): We had the Eastown, the Grande, and the Sherwood Forest Rivera, with short drives to Ann Arbor and Lansing, so Detroit was a good spot for us to be.

Pete Woodman (*Popcorn Blizzard, Floating Circus, Bossmen, drummer*): There was a place in Bay City, way north of Detroit, that all the bands played. Ted Nugent came out on his motorcycle.

Susie Kaine (*Popcorn Blizzard, Floating Circus, keyboardist, vocalist*): Pete's mom would let the bands stay at the house. Ted would sleep in the woods out back.

Pete Woodman: He knocked on the door and my mom opened the door and he wanted a cup of coffee or something. She said she'd seen this beautiful guy.

Jack Bodnar (*scenester*): We lived at Lahser and Lois Lane not far from Southfield High School, and I was this geeky kid. I loved music, going to clubs, going to see anyone who played around town. You could see so much free or cheap music; going to the Grande was $2. When I graduated from high school, I wanted to have this little party in my parents' basement. It was a cinderblock thing, fairly small. I had invited these twin sisters that went to Edsel Ford High School, and they said, "Can we bring a band?" They were groupies; they hung out with bands. They were flat-out gorgeous girls—long straight blond hair. Mostly they hung with Wilson Mower Pursuit.

Bill White (*bassist, Ted Nugent and the Amboy Dukes*): Liz and Ilka, Swedish twins. They followed us around. We met them at the Grande.

Jack Bodnar: I said, "Sure, bring a band," because we were just gonna play 45s. This was a straight party, no alcohol—my friends didn't drink. All of a sudden a van pulls up and it's some of the guys from the Amboy Dukes and all this equipment.

They had a full drum kit that took up about a quarter of the room. They started playing, and it literally shattered some of my parent's crystal. Stuff came crashing down. It was wonderful. I was suddenly the coolest kid ever.

Bill White: We'd play a lot of weird places. That very well coulda have happened.

Rick Stevers (*Frijid Pink, drummer*): We played at some Catholic high school with the MC5, and the school told them not to play "Kick Out the Jams." Of course they did, and the place tried to shut them down, and in the process shit started getting tossed around, and Dennis Thompson threw his cymbal into the crowd and it hit this kid in the head. There was blood everywhere—can you imagine if that happened now? But Thompson went into the crowd. He was really sorry; he gave the kid the cymbal, and that was it.

John Kosloskey: We played in Sault Ste. Marie in the upper peninsula of Michigan with the Amboy Dukes at the armory. We were on our way to the show and we got harassed by some local rednecks, and Mosley threw a bottle at their car. These guys called the cops on us. By the time the show ended the National Guard was called and the troops were circling the block where the show was. We thought they were protecting us from our crazed fans.

Rick Kraniak: Frut were so stoned out. Leo Fenn booked them on a pop festival in Ohio, and they were so altered in their state of smoke that they not only missed the exit; they ended up in a different state.

Norm Liberman: I seem to think there was a train involved that also held us up.

John Sinclair: The most the MC5 ever made at the Grande was $1,800. We were on the bill with Ted Nugent and the Amboy Dukes, who were making a rare appearance at the Grande. The Amboy Dukes were great guys, but Ted Nugent—how could you trust a guy who didn't get high? Anyway, they had a place they played all the time in Northland Mall called the Mummp. It was like a dome, and they played there every weekend.

Don Was: The Mummp was formerly Northland Playhouse, which was like a regional theater. It was taken over by the Weinstein family of Oak Park, and the house band was the Amboy Dukes. I could lay in bed and listen to the Dukes on Friday and Saturday nights, it was that close to my house when I was a kid.

Bill White: I met Ted at the Mummp. They were playing, and they didn't have a bass player and he announced it on the PA. So I went back and met him, then went over to the house and played and I was in.

Ted Nugent: It didn't really matter where we played. As long as we didn't blow the power and the amps kept working, I was a happy man. I mean, early days you look at the Crow's Nest East, the Crow's Nest West, and the Crow's Nest South, you look at the Birmingham Palladium, you look at the Hideouts, you look at the Shindigs, and the Hullabaloos, and the Fifth Dimension, I mean, they were all just makeshift facilities that were, you know, just rooms with the dividers blown out so we could pack in a lot of people and play. I loved 'em all. I loved the intimacy.

Russ Gibb: John Finley was this young kid who worked for me, one of the original Grande kids. I always used these kids as a gauge for what was popular, who people would go see. John helped me develop the Grande actually. He went to Redford High School and would hand out handbills for the shows, so we'd always have all these Redford kids coming in. So he was a very early opinion maker. He introduced me to Ted.

Donny Hartman (*The Frost, guitarist*): When the Frost broke up, Ted called me up and goes, "Hey, man. Ted Nugent." I go, "How the hell you doin', Ted?" And I knew some of the guys in his band, and they were all bitchin' 'cause they had just done some stadium show, and he took, I think, almost a quarter million bucks outta there. Paid everybody in the band $850. Ted says, "Yeah, man. God, my guys are high. I'm having some problems with my guys." "I wonder why, Ted." He said, "Man, I'd really like you to sing in my band, man." I said, "Yeah?" He goes, "Well, I'd love to pay all your expenses and everything, and I'll pay you $250 a night." I said, "You shouldn't have made this phone call." He says, "Why?" I said, "'Cause if I never talk to you again, it'll be too soon."

Michael Lutz (*Brownsville Station, guitarist, vocalist, bassist*): I went for an audition to sing with Ted one time at the Fifth Dimension in Ann Arbor, where the Amboy Dukes were doing both rehearsal and auditions. I auditioned with "Sunshine of Your Love" and "Manic Depression." They were getting ready to do what would eventually become the album *Journey to the Center of the Mind*. They played the song "Journey to the Center of the Mind," and I thought, "Holy shit, man. This is cool." I got the call from Ted and he said, "You're it." But John Drake owned their

PA system, and they couldn't afford a new one. So they had to keep Drake. But for one week I was the new singer for the Amboy Dukes.

Shaun Murphy (*Bob Seger and the Silver Bullet Band, Stoney and Meatloaf, vocalist*): A lot of people kind of misunderstood Ted. They thought he was drunk, they thought he was high, but he never took any drugs, never took any alcohol— that was him.

Russ Gibb: He was around a lot of people who partook of the sacrament, but I don't know that I ever saw him indulge.

Ted Nugent: I was hopelessly inebriated by the music.

K. J. Knight: Back then Rusty Day and a lot of Ted Nugent's peers looked down at Ted because they felt as though he had a disingenuous onstage persona because he wouldn't take drugs. Ted was just a young guy trying to feel his way around, you know, and he wanted to put on a good show, so these guys felt as though even though he was so much against drugs, he acted like he was stoned when he was on stage. They always were trying to feed him drugs, persuade him and encourage him to take drugs.

Bill White: Ted never took drugs, but he should have been on Ritalin.

K. J. Knight: He was always down on that whole thing. I don't know if they just decided to come up with this bullshit way of looking at things because they were jealous of him. We'd always talk about a good rap onstage and being a good front man. He would try to come up with a cool rap, and he would maybe be a little bit jive.

Shaun Murphy: Ted was living with the band in a huge carriage house. The bottom was a bedroom, a place for a car, a big rehearsal area. Upstairs was another bedroom, a kitchen, living room. Everything was pretty sparse but neat. Ted was a perfectionist; he's very fastidious.

Ted Nugent: The band had a house out there on the west side, in Livonia on Middlebelt. We always rehearsed, and we were just obsessed with creating this new music and writing our own songs and discovering new musical adventure. Dave Palmer, Greg Arama, and I would do twenty-hour marathons in the basement at the house on Middlebelt. I didn't go hang out much.

Bill White: We got signed to Polydor there. The guy came to see us practice, and he went upstairs while we were playing, got the phone and called New York, put the phone to the floor. That's how we got that deal.

Ted Nugent: We played almost every night, and the nights we didn't play we'd go and see other bands. I would go the MC5's house over on Hill Street once in a while and then when they had the place in Hamburg. The SRC had a band house too, and I'd go over there. But again, it was all about smokin' dope, and I couldn't last more than a couple minutes because I thought we could play music and talk music, but the hippies couldn't talk. It was a heartbreaker, really.

Bill White: The lick from "Journey to the Center of the Mind" came from the TV show *Rawhide*. We were sitting there, hanging out, watching TV, and Ted had his guitar in his hands and we said, "Play the next thing that comes on."

Al Jacquez (*Savage Grace, bassist, vocalist*): I sat in the back row of the Grande Riviera with Ted watching the Who one time. Pete Townsend went over and hit Keith Moon in the head with a stick during the set. Nugent was like, "Did you see that?" I think he really liked that idea.

Bobby Rigg (*The Frost, drummer*): The first time we met Ted Nugent all he could talk about was himself and how he was the greatest guitar player in the world. We were in a hotel in New York City. We were staying there, Led Zeppelin was there, Nugent and the Amboy Dukes were there. And Nugent was on the same floor as Jimmy Page, and this hotel was built in a U-shape. Nugent's window was across from Jimmy Page's room; he put a Fender Twin Reverb in the window and started screaming at the top of his lungs, "I'm the greatest guitar player in the world! Jimmy Page sucks!" and started playing his guitar as loud as he could facing Jimmy Page's room. That's the way Ted Nugent was. What you see is what you get.

John Sinclair: Ted Nugent is an asshole. He always was.

Ted Nugent: The Amboy Dukes were invited to play Woodstock, but we had been burned by all these hippie promoters, where you didn't go on stage on time, sometimes you didn't go on at all. I'll never forget the Black Arts Festival at Olympia that Mike Quatro put together. He let the stage managers from the Grande Ballroom manage the thing, and they were all so stoned out of their minds that we never even got to go on stage, it was so inept. So I was so let down by the disrespect

towards the music—and the musicians—not just because it was us, but any musician. Look at Hendrix, going on at 6 a.m. at Woodstock. Are you shitting me?
Who would do that to Jimi Hendrix? I'll tell you who would do that: an uncaring,
an inconsiderate, soulless, piece-of-shit, stoned fuck, that's who would do that.
So I was invited to Woodstock, and I go, yeah, it'll cost you $2,500, just send the
check here, and if the check shows up, we'll show up, and if not, fuck you. So I
would refuse to do those things and get stiffed anymore. You know, we still had to
buy our speakers and buy our guitar strings, we still had to eat, we still had to get
gas and fucking tires and oil for the vehicles. What do think—it's a donation from
us to you? Fuck you.

Patti Quatro (*Pleasure Seekers, Cradle, guitarist*): My sister Nancy was dating
Ted for a long time. My dad had a car chase with him one time. Nancy snuck out
of the house to go out with Ted, and they're tooling around, and my dad gets in his
car and follows him, and they had a chase all over town. He never caught him. Ted
got real pissy when she dumped him. She just didn't want to date him anymore;
she was over him.

K. J. Knight: Everyone fell in love with Nancy. She was beautiful. I had a big crush
on Nancy, and we kinda dated for a couple of weeks.

Suzi Quatro (*Pleasure Seekers, solo, bassist, vocalist*): Nancy and I went to New
York at one point to find a girl drummer, and Jerry Nolan showed up. He looked
like a girl anyway, with the long hair and the makeup, so we said okay. He came to
Detroit and stayed at my folks' house. But he fell in love with Nancy, and we said,
"Well, okay, you gotta go."

Pete Cavanaugh: Ted Nugent and Mitch Ryder had the most fearsome road crews
of anyone. They were mostly bikers and ex-criminals who had a lot of experience
beating the fuck out of people, some of whom had spent some time away for beating the fuck out of people. I had Ted at one show, and it was getting late, and some
guy came up to the front—the stage at Sherwood Forest allowed people to get six
feet away from the band—and started giving Ted shit. And there was a big roadie
behind the amps, but this guy couldn't see him. Ted knew he was there, though,
and he starts to yell back at the guy and invites him up on stage to kick his ass.
The guy made the mistake of getting up there, and it was like watching the spider
and the fly. The roadie came out and threw this guy ten feet into the crowd. Brutal.

Ted Nugent: I got thrown in jail one time because I looked like a hippy. We were playing in Traverse City, what I think was the Cherry Festival, and we were getting ready to go on stage. At that time I wore a loin cloth, a belt knife, and moccasins, headband, and a fur vest—dressed up like an Indian. Because a lot of my songs were starting to reflect my hunting lifestyle and I started shooting a bow and arrow on stage back then, so I dressed like an Indian. Because I looked like the ultimate hippy, and there was a broken knife on my belt that was perfectly visible, this one hot-dog, corrupt cop, power-abusing, punk cop, arrested me for a concealed weapon, a felony. My stage outfit had the knife on a belt. If it was concealed, how could he see it? I was literally walking up the steps to get on stage, with my guitar on, and he stopped me on the steps and handcuffed me and put me in jail for two days, in a drunk tank with a bunch of migrant workers that I had to beat up to get toilet paper. I got my life savings—I think it was a couple grand—to bail out, and they finally dropped all the charges because the photos taken of me prove that nothing was concealed. All that, and the knife didn't even have a blade.

K. J. Knight: There was a point that I kinda thought that, you know, Ted's career was starting to go down the toilet. I know that he blames the fact that he went through a lot of musicians, but he canned a lot of musicians too. It's not as if they all quit on him. I think I might have been—me and Dave Palmer might have been the two guys, the only two guys that ever quit the Amboy Dukes. Everybody else he eventually fired. While I played with Ted, starting in about 1970, drugs never really even entered my mind. You know I did a lot of drugs, but there were times when my music was kinda like the main focus, and I kinda got away from that for a while, and I kinda got away from my criminal activities.

Ted Nugent: When KJ joined that band, that started a great run. He and I shared an apartment on 6th Street in Ann Arbor. I think it was 609 6th Street.

K. J. Knight: Ted handled everything on his own. He drove the limo he had bought, he drove it, he helped unload the truck. I had two stints with Ted. I started with the *Survival of the Fittest* album, and things were pretty good at that point. And I got to hear these stories. Ted told me about one when Rusty Day was in the band. The Amboy Dukes were on their way to a gig. Ted was driving, and Rusty was sitting in the back of the limo. During the drive Rusty whipped out a pipe and started smoking some hash. Rusty began passing the pipe around to the other guys in the band. When the pipe got to Ted, he turned and fired it at Rusty and hit him square in the head. I believe later, perhaps after the gig and back at the motel, Ted was ready to go up and kick Rusty's ass. He went charging up a flight of stairs to get to Rusty's room, but he tripped and fell down the stairway, hurt himself, and retreated to his room. I don't know if Ted could have kicked Rusty's ass, because Rusty was a badass too. Rusty and Ted really hated each other. Ted told me that one time Rusty called all of the guys in the band together to meditate and got them to sit in a tight circle and start chanting "Om." However, Ted thought it was a big joke and began chanting, "Om Om on the Range." Rusty was really pissed.

You know what was really weird, it was like afterward when Rusty got in the Cactus. Sometimes we would play on the same bill with them, and then I would have to struggle whether I wanted to go into the Cactus dressing room and hang with those guys because I felt such a tight connection to Rusty or stay in the Amboy Dukes dressing room and stay loyal to Ted, and so, you know. I was friends with Rusty right to the end, when he was murdered in Florida. Certain things about Rusty Day are not known. People don't realize because he shot his wife, Sharon, and paralyzed her, Rusty had to leave Detroit. Because he was dealing drugs and I guess he felt as though this shooting was going to bring a lot of heat on him. Those were his exact words to me: "I'm feeling the heat and I gotta get out of town." I think that because of the fact that he was dealing drugs in such a large volume and the fact that this had taken place, that made him believe that he had to get out of Detroit.

Johnny Badanjek (*Mitch Ryder and the Detroit Wheels, Detroit, the Rockets, drummer*): We tried to put the Wheels together with Rusty Day for a while. Playing a bunch of the same kind of like ballrooms out in Iowa and that kind of stuff. Rusty was fine at the time. He wasn't as nuts as he got later, you know. That all happened later with Cactus. He went down the wrong road.

Ron Cooke: Rusty's from Garden City, man. West side is tough guys. His was a horrible story. We went down and played the Orange Bowl or something in Miami or some fucking arrangement with the Cactus deal. Rusty got fucking arrested before we went on. He was probably telling some cop to fucking suck his dick. I don't know.

Ray Goodman (*SRC, Detroit, Cub Koda, guitarist*): Rusty was a good guy and I loved him, but he was very violent and very prone to addiction. He was as tough as they come. He wasn't a guy you would fuck with ever. Not that he was that big and strong; he just had the kind of mentality where there was no hesitation. None whatsoever.

K. J. Knight: Once he moved, I didn't have a number. I didn't know where he was. And then just miraculously it turns out he is living in a city just a few miles away from the city that my wife's parents lived in Florida. That's how we reconnected. When I quit playing music in '77, we were still in touch with one another. We would talk from time to time, and we'd see each other a couple times a year. I knew that he was into drugs, but here again, he kinda shielded me from all of that. When I came over there, he was never in the middle of a drug deal or he didn't sit there and say this is who I sell to or anything like that. But can you imagine going over to his house, and there everyone's got a gun in their hand, and he's got his son living there? He must've known someone was gunning for him, but just to let things go that far, you know. You would think that maybe he wouldn't have had his son living with him if he knew that he was in danger. They killed him and his son.

"You Can't Be a
Leader on LSD"

Gary Quackenbush (SRC, *guitarist*): Everybody lived in Ann Arbor at some point. Seger was there, and he was way behind the curve. We never thought Bob would make it. Goofy ideas. And he didn't have a good show. He used to come over to the house every week because he was living at home with his mom. Bob was the sole surviving male; they lived over on Pauline by the stadium. Bob would come over and play DJ. He was one of the first guys that ever sat me down in front of a stereo and said, "Listen to how the drums get louder at the end of this recording, listen to the reverb at the end, listen to how the bass gets . . ." You know, just all kinds of, like, production. He's a fiend.

Leni Sinclair: We moved to Ann Arbor, the MC5, after our place in Detroit got firebombed in 1968. We moved to Hill Street.

Scott Richardson: We had a nineteen-room Victorian farmhouse in Ann Arbor divided up into apartments on five acres of land bordering on five hundred acres, and we had a Quonset hut studio and a swimming pool and five-car garage, and we used to have parties with, like, three to five hundred people up there.

Dennis Dunaway: The SRC at the time had a record deal, and I was jealous of that.

Susie Kaine: When they had the opening of Morgan Sound studio—that was the SRC's place—they had big bowls of acid. It seemed like SRC camp had done a lot of acid.

Billy Goodson (*scenester*): I knew Scott Richardson by seeing him at performances and then his brother introduced me to him at the Palladium. So we went to that party, and at the time we were taking acid almost every day, like five times out of seven days. Mr. Natural stamps.

Scott Richardson: My first acid trip was fall of 1967, and it was also Bob Seger's and Glenn Frey's. We all went to the arboretum at the University of Michigan—this was before SRC got going. We got it from Ed Fritch, a kind of famous character around Ann Arbor, him and Steve McCann. They hung around the bands—they weren't musicians; they were heads. Fritch went out to California and came back with a boatload of Owsley—that Sandoz acid. It was the best.

Gary Quackenbush: One night the Five were over and we were all hanging out, and Wayne said to me, "You know I just hooked up with these hippies because we want to make it." I said to myself, "That's a bad idea." But there were plenty of hippies in Detroit for them.

John Sinclair: No, no, I doubt that. All of this social stuff was stuff that Rob Tyner and I cooked up together.

Scott Richardson: Some of the most famous rock-and-roll parties of that era took place at our farm. We recorded an entire jam album with Procol Harum, who stayed with us for a week. I don't know what happened to those tapes. Traffic came out and stayed with us, and we recorded with them too. I don't know if those things are ever going to surface or not.

Ray Goodman: I was traveling with the SRC toward the last album, learning the songs. And unbeknownst to me at the time, they were plotting to plug me into Gary's spot and let Gary go. The band didn't go over very well in California; they didn't know quite what to think of them. We drove straight from Ann Arbor to our first shows in the LA area. Trucks, two vehicles—the whole thing. We were one of the few companies in the world that had PAs; I think there was us and Showco out of Texas. So the SRC was very pioneering in that regard. And they made quite a bit of money renting out their PA. But it was tough. Things didn't go well, like at the Whiskey. Spencer Davis was on the bill, and he was an arrogant Brit, and he was insulting when he said, "Coming up next—SRC, who will no doubt entertain you." And the original T. Rex was on the bill too.

Scott Richardson: We were getting on good bills though. We played the Kinetic Playground in Chicago. Here's the bill: the Grateful Dead, Quicksilver Messenger Service, the Velvet Underground, SRC. Lou Reed and I are standing backstage drinking beer. It was the first time I saw that super backstage concert layout of food and shit. Some girls would always have stuff for you: brownies, and everything was laced. I turned around and saw someone spraying the food and the complete thing with Listerine bottles filled with liquid LSD. And Lou Reed, well, keep in mind that the Velvet Underground were not a psychedelic band. This was a band that got up in the morning and took Valium. His eyes are going counter-clockwise in his head, and he's going, "Scott, you've got to get me to the hospital." Everybody's on acid. Everybody. And he's freaking out. We went out and got in a cab and took him to a hospital. Sterling Morrison got him a Thorazine shot. They couldn't go back to the ballroom. They couldn't take it. They canceled it.

Ray Goodman: Most Michigan bands weren't well received at the time. Scott said to someone, "Well, if California bands and audiences don't like us, if the Five was out there, their name's mud." Not too much later the phone rings and Scott goes, "Hello." It was Wayne Kramer. "Mud here." They'd already been out there. The attitude out there was San Francisco was it and anything else was an invasion.

Scott Richardson: Gary had a motorcycle accident after we put out *Milestones*, and he didn't really recover from it personality wise. But we were all doing acid, and everybody had their own reaction. I'm talking about the stress of being there the first time through, and we were inventing PAs and inventing pop festivals, and you know all that stuff had never happened on that scale before. The stress of all that combined with all those drugs, making all that money—we were making $2,500 a night at that point, which was pretty good. Living together and the normal stuff that happens because when you go out on stage, you have a closer relationship to your bandmates than you do to any old lady that you'll ever have.

Shaun Murphy: When SRC broke up, I don't know whether it was just that Scott was not focused or so focused on himself that it just didn't happen.

Scott Richardson: I was this personality, see? I was the front man. I had all this charisma, all these great looks, and the girls were all coming and that was why. And the band and everybody recognized that. And so I still had that, for a very brief instant I had that cachet of leadership. LSD destroyed us. You can't be a leader or a personality on LSD.

"Mitch Ryder, Eat Shit"

Mitch Ryder: MC5 said about me, "Mitch Ryder, eat shit." The reason I know this is that my bodyguard had taken me to Detroit, dropped me off, and was flying back to New York. Guys in the MC5 were on the same flight with him. Everybody was sitting in first class, and they didn't know who he was. He just sat there and listened and heard them dissing me and dissing everybody else and talking about how great they were, you know. They were just insecure because they were groomed as the military arm of the fucking communist fucking organization. And there they are going to Popsville.

John Sinclair: That's what Ryder always would do. He'd have an opportunity to say something, and then he would say the most outrageous stupid shit to *Rolling Stone*. He's really been good at making enemies. But he's just such a great fucking artist, you know? You gotta work around this dude.

Dennis Thompson: Communism? No! No! Well, there was this communal paradigm happening across the country. You know, people, especially in 'Frisco, but it was happening in New York, and it was happening, ya know, eventually even in Texas. And people were banding together, living together—people of like minds. And that was fine. But what Sinclair gave was his philosophy. Because our rhetoric was "Screw the establishment. Tear it down. Start over again." This whole political thing, that was Sinclair's philosophy. That was not Dennis Thompson's philosophy. At all. I'm in college, man. I mean, I'm a regular guy. Ya know, I want to find a pretty girl. I want to play great music. And I want a fast car. We're nineteen years old. Come on. We're getting this Beatnik philosophy pushed onto us.

Wayne Kramer (*MC5, Gang War, solo, guitarist, vocalist*): Well, when we started, we were communists. And part of that purity was that sense of equality. There were no class distinctions, and that was pretty incorrect and idealistic. And that became clear as we became aware that some people worked more than others. It's hard to be honest without sounding egotistical, but the MC5 really was central to anything in Detroit that had to do with music in that time. All the other bands were satellites swirling around this thing with MC5 at the center. Even Seger and Ted Nugent were minor players in this era. We dominated completely because nobody played like us, no one was on me and Fred's level; we could solo simultaneously. No one was writing songs on the level of Rob Tyner; no lead singer was as dynamic and compelling as Rob.

Becky Tyner (*wife of MC5 vocalist Rob Tyner*): I was going to Wayne State University, living on Prentice and Second with my friend Donna. We wanted to move to New York, but we were too afraid. So we got an apartment in Detroit. I was working at Hudson's in the Northland Mall, and I got off the bus coming home. I was walking down the street and was approached by this tall person with a British accent asking where the party was. I said, "Oh, it's at Neil and Sandy's"—these were some friends who were actually having a party—"right down stairs in our building." And we chatted for a minute and I went out with my boyfriend. And later that night I came home and my roommate Donna said, "Well, you know that guy from England that you sent to the party? He's really not from England. But he seemed nice enough so I invited him to our party next week." It turned out it was Rob. He came by the next week and just kept coming around. I have no idea what was up with the accent. I mean it's a good line to pick up a girl, don't you think? The boyfriend went away. Rob and I were married in 1966.

Wayne Kramer: You know, youth has certainty. When you're nineteen years old you've got it all figured out. You know what's coming, how it's going to play out; you've got all the answers. And if you've got a few people who agree with you, you're really certain. And that's what MC5 and our community—we were all in total agreement about things like politics, the country was heading in the wrong direction. About art and culture. The music we liked was the most advanced and forward. That our band was the cutting-edge band of all bands; we were doing stuff that was more forward. And if you achieved some recognition, that reinforces it. There's very little self-criticism and looking inward. And very little criticism around us. We weren't good Marxists; we weren't that dogmatic. We smoked a lot of weed, dropped a lot of acid, and were having a ball doing what we were doing. Everything was hitting as it was supposed to hit. The politicization came as a result of just living in America in those years, the sixties. We just wanted to be a great rock band; I wanted to be a world-class guitar player, song writer, and performer. When I was younger my goal was just to be able to work in nightclubs. Just have this nighttime world, late-night musicians—that was living to me. In those days there were a lot of clubs to play in. The auto factories went 24/7, so there were clubs open seven days a week, five sets a night, forty-five minutes on fifteen off. We quickly came to the conclusion that we wanted to be the band on the radio rather than the bands playing those songs in the clubs. We wanted to write our own songs, and then we realized we could go on tour and play big venues. Once we saw the model—the British band model once they started touring—we realized it was doable.

John Sinclair: They were just kids. I mean, they were just unorganized. Well, they were fucked up. I loved the band, so I went to see them whenever they played. They had these two little hippie guys working for them; they carried around a box full of wires and stuff. The band showed up for the gigs right about the time when they were supposed to hit the stage. Instead of hitting, these two little guys were up there, wrestling around the spots, pulling all the wires and trying to figure out what went to what while everybody's there waiting for the show to start. Well, that's where I thought I could help with this. This is embarrassing.

Leni Sinclair: Slowly things started improving because John, being a writer, he started writing a column for the *Fifth Estate* every week. A lot of times he would be late with turning in his copy; the paper was supposed to go to the printer in the morning, and they'd get home from the gig at two or three in the morning. Everybody else would go to bed or have some girl over, something. John would type up what happened. Every week there was something happening with the band that was worth writing about. John, because of writing about them all the time—that helped create interest in the band. Then he got them to be the house band at the Grande Ballroom when the Grande Ballroom started.

Wayne Kramer: John proposed that he would take over. He was getting this commune concept together, which was still kind of ethereal. Tyner had tried to explain the idea to me. Through that kind of utopian, amorphous structure, John came to the conclusion that the five of us were completely out of control and couldn't even get to rehearsal. That really was the case—we missed gigs, we were a mess. I'd have to go find Fred, and he wouldn't be ready, and I'd sit in the car, and finally he'd be ready and we'd get there too late and our slot would be gone.

John Sinclair: I never had a contract with the MC5. Why would I?

Becky Tyner: We had to make money somehow, because all the money the band made went to Trans-Love Energies, our little collective.

Pete Cavanaugh: MC5 did not play without pay. They presented this revolution and music for the people, so on one hand, it was free this and steal this and take it, but this was a business.

Billy Goodson: We would use Gary Grimshaw's first-print posters to soak up water puddles in the basement of Trans-Love. And now they're worth thousands—what did we know? We were all so freakin' high, no one thought about any kind of future after the revolution.

Becky Tyner: We only had money for groceries and for laundry and cleaning. And we would sew. Wayne's girlfriend, Chris, Fred's wife, Sigrid, and I all got sewing machines. Making clothes for the bands and anyone else. I made a pair of pants for Iggy that was out of a vinyl material. I made those while we were living in Ann Arbor. And you know we would fit the pants to the person and to make them really, really tight. Gotta be tight. And Iggy was really insistent on them being very low. So at the end the top of the pants came right at his hair line. From what I understand, it was that he was playing in those pants and his little thing came out—I guess I shouldn't say "little thing." His organ kind of slipped out of the top of the pants.

John Sinclair: The band was always on; they looked good too. They come out an hour after they were supposed to and then they played a great set, you know. It was always just real straight ahead rock and roll, man. And they would end with playing "Black to Comm," where they just go totally out from the first time I saw them. That was how they ended their show—that was Tyner's concept. Different every night. It was just an incredible thing. Incredible.

Russ Gibb: MC5 played "Black to Comm" the first time at the Grande Ballroom. I had just had two strobe lights made for me by the guy who made them for Bill

Graham. And so this night the MC5 figured them out, and I walked into the ballroom and they were playing "Black to Comm" using them. It was like some far out, Middle Ages village, with people dancing without shoes in this horrifying stop-motion flicker, and it was almost like no one understood what was going on but just reacting. The room was vibrating and the feedback was screeching, and my audience was reacting.

Wayne Kramer: It took three seconds to write "Black to Comm." We were experimenting with this sound, and Fred found a way to play this chord in this big amp—it was just thunderous. This was before Michael and Dennis were in the band, and we had a great rhythm section. They were a package: they had worked together before, and they were terrific; they really powered the MC5. But they were conservative guys—no experimental anything. And we were all taking acid and listening to Sun Ra, and they just weren't down. Fred was a provocateur, and he knew they could really irritate the drummer by playing this riff, and one night on the job Fred played the riff, and eventually the drummer gave in and played along with it; it all came together, and that was the song. We all started improvising our parts; the bass player was just swinging.

John Sinclair: They'd set up "Black to Comm" with "I Believe to My Soul" by Ray Charles. And then that would end with a huge ending, and then they'd go on to doot doot doot (humming the beginning) and they'd start with that "Watch your world come down," and then it would just go, and Tyner would make up lyrics and they would make up parts—saxophones would come in, and they would all just get crazy.

Robin Sommers: The first album on Elektra everyone was really excited to get out there. You know, we had this LP that said, "Kick out the Jams, Motherfuckers." Gary Grimshaw had done the cover with a pot leaf. That's what we wanted. Elektra hated that as well as the dope smoke that looked like it was in front of the American Flag. But Elektra's cover sucked. I mean, there was a picture of Bruce Botnick in the corner, on the cover. Why? Because he was an executive at Elektra. Then there's another executive, Jac Holzman, with a suit on the front. The faces of all the kids in the audience are blurred because Elektra thought they would have to be paid. Look at that cover. Dennis Thompson has a drumstick up his nose. You can't see Fred's face because of his hair. Michael Davis is always hidden. But part of this thing was that Elektra didn't want the "motherfucker" to be there and had albums that said, "brothers and sisters" instead of "motherfuckers." They also left the "motherfucker" out of the liner notes John Sinclair had written.

John Sinclair: You know Jac Holzman convinced me that we should have "motherfucker" on it. It would be all right in the notes and everything. I said, "Man, you know they're not gonna like this." And also, "Man, if they do, are we going to be powerful." And he said, "We'll back it up. It will be good publicity for the album." I said, "Well, okay."

Robin Sommers: Then Hudson's, which was the big department store in Detroit, decided it didn't want to carry an album like this and threatened not to carry any of the Elektra catalog. They threatened all these things. And I was pissed. So John asked me to do an advertisement for the album for the *Fifth Estate* newspaper that he edited. And I did it and decided to put "Fuck Hudson's" at the bottom. And Elektra really hit the roof. I didn't do it to get in trouble. It wasn't like I ran this myself.

John Sinclair: Elektra's thing was blaming the legal department. You know, they said, "This is way beyond us. This is just gonna be blah blah blah," and then they are starting to threaten to pull the other Elektra products out of these big department stores like Hudson's. So they pulled the record off the market. They stripped off the liner notes. They changed . . . they put the single version on the album, without the word "motherfucker." They presented this to me and I presented it to the band and we all said, "No, we can't do this. We can't. We will eat these. If you have to take it off the market, we'll eat the album and we'll start the second one right away, and we'll do a different approach so we won't have this problem."

Dennis Thompson: Every hip-hop or rap artist now, they use all these nasty words in a nasty manner. We were the first band to use the word "fuck" in print and on our album. We weren't doing it to be bad-mouthed, bad-talking, tough-talking kind of people. We actually used the word like everybody did, but we were the first to put it on vinyl. Then you backpedal and take it off, and you insert "brothers and sisters" into it because the rack shoppers are getting lawsuits. Guys that put the records on the racks. Big chains were dropping it because of the language. And the reason why it didn't go to number one across the nation was because of the language. That was in the Top Ten of destroying that band. Listen to me: one simple word. You know? It stereotypes you. Immediately.

John Sinclair: We left and went to the West Coast at our expense. No support from the record company. I booked some gigs in San Francisco and Oakland and around LA. We got to San Francisco, and I went out to the distributor to pick up a couple of boxes of records to promote with and they said, "Well, we don't have any." I said, "What do you mean?" They said, "Well, they called them all back. They're in New York." And that's when I had to fly from there at my expense to New York and argue with them. I lost. We recorded three songs at Elektra in Los Angeles: "Human Being Lawmower," "American Ruse," and one more. The tapes are gone, they told me. Lost, lost in a fire, water. We got back to Michigan. I went to prison two months later, so I lost track.

Wayne Kramer: Practice, that's all we did. As many hours of the day as we could get ourselves together to get there and practice. Organization was the main problem. For me, as the band leader, that was always on me. I would set the rehearsal and then find everybody. Wasn't so much a matter of forgetting; there was a passive aggressiveness from Fred Smith. It's a controlling tactic.

Becky Tyner: Wayne will present himself as a leader of the band. There are not really a lot of people that would dispute it. In a sense he was, in terms of questioning John, questioning the money, questioning what's going on with this. The other guys were into other things.

John Sinclair: Fred Smith assaulted the police on my behalf; that's as good as it gets in my world. You know, a guy who'll do that is all right with you. They're risking their fucking life as well as jail time.

Becky Tyner: Fred was an individual. He would act in kind of an authoritative manner—you know, he had a really deep voice. His word was law kind of thing.

John Sinclair: We had a beef with the management at a club called the Loft in Macomb County. They owed for the last gig we played there and this one, and this guy was supposed to pay me for both that night. And then they pulled this flimflam and we got into it. We were packing up, putting the shit in the van. I was doing the idiot check, make sure we had everything. All of a sudden these coppers come in and the guy says, "That's him. He refuses to leave." I was just flabbergasted, you know? And then they assaulted me and I was just, fuck this. I was getting ready to leave and then all the sudden the coppage came in, and he said, "Well, that's the guy there. They refuse to leave." So these cops came to throw me out and said, "Put your hands up." And I smacked the guy in the face. They weren't really coppers.

He was like a rent-a-cop. So I smashed him in the face, and then these other guys started wailing on me. Fred Smith heard that I was under attack, and he came racing across the room and flew through the air and landed on their backs. That was so cool; it was like suicide, you know? Just beautiful.

Wayne Kramer: Fred was always defiant and grandiose. He had what you could call defiant individuality. He was kind of an outsider and was known as a delinquent. Had his run-ins with authority figures: teachers, principals, parents.

Becky Tyner: He loved baseball. He would organize these baseball games, and we'd all go and try to play.

Wayne Kramer: Fred was a gifted athlete and really good at baseball. When the MC5 was living in Ann Arbor, we would have regular Sunday baseball games at West Park with the other bands. It was so much fun. Seger. The Jagged Edge. The Sunday Funnies. Not the Stooges—they're not baseball types.

Dennis Thompson: The band went through various phases, and I don't think anybody's ever explained the drug-related connections. In the beginning of the band there was no hallucinogenics. There was beer . . . it was a beer band. Then, a pot band and then, beer, pot, and hallucinogenics. I mean everything from mescaline to LSD, and that was our hallucinogenic phase.

Leni Sinclair: As long as they were with the MC5, as long as they were with the White Panthers and John Sinclair, we preached and preached against all drugs. That was one of our main things—to keep kids from using drugs.

Dennis Thompson: Jon Landau produced our second album, and we quit everything. So our second album was sobriety. Our third album, we had sort of shifted into, not really heavily at all, just chipping heroin. Just chipping. Everybody wasn't a junkie or anything. But eventually the heroin influenced Michael Davis to the point where we asked, "Did he want to play in the band or did he want to use a substance?"

Becky Tyner: Dennis and Michael, they were really bad. Like come into your house, go in to the bathroom and pass out on the floor. There was a really bad night, and Rob was furious. And he called up the morgue and said, "Come get this asshole out of my bathroom," and they thought he was nuts and, you know, like a crank call. It was Michael on the floor in the bathroom. Just gross. Gross. And Dennis was, like, pathetic. Nonfunctioning.

Wayne Kramer: The decline of the MC5 and the parallel decline of Detroit is not a mystery to me—the things we were going through; we were not alone. A lot of other people were in desperate situations as well. And some of them had guns.

Dennis Thompson: The most prolific album in terms of creating new ideas was the LSD days, but the band coming together with all the ingredients that we were working on, finally gelling into a nice soup, was *High Time*.

Wayne Kramer: Clearly, the MC5 was on its last breath. If we didn't make a great record, it was all over. Our reputation was shot: we had confused so many people with *Back in the USA*, the record company was sick of us, we had no management, no one in our corners, grave internal problems. The purity of '68 was a distant memory, but challenges in the band itself—heroin, poverty, we had no money. If we didn't make money through the MC5, there was none. Fred had a baby and the baby died—terrible things to endure. The Detroit underworld was slipping into our sphere.

Becky Tyner: *High Time* is when they began to divvy up the songwriting credits. They were moving out of the communal situation, moving into their own houses, and establishing their own lives. Whether it's doing heroin or you're doing this or you're doing that. It's the individualism, and it's like, "Okay, enough of this, everything is everything."

Wayne Kramer: We had to dig down deep and do the best work we could. The producer we had, Geoff Haslam, was really a band guy—he let us lead and was a great collaborator. But we didn't get much support for *High Time*. We were managed for a time by Dee Anthony, but that was short lived. The guy is very cagey. He kept money in escrow from some of the gigs. I don't know who paid the hotels and everything, but I know he handled all the money, and he was tough. So then he went to the union said, "They didn't pay my commissions" and got a lien on us from a mediation decision, and we didn't even know. So finally he's not returning our calls; Fred and I flew to New York to see him. We had no money. We were going to beg Atlantic records for some money. We went to Dee's office and sat in the waiting room. He went out a back door so he wouldn't see us. We went back to the airport and slept there, then took a bus back into the city to Atlantic records.

Jerry Wexler had signed us and then retired, so we were kind of inherited to this guy Ahmet Ertegün. I told him what kind of shape we were in, and he explained to us the concept of "sending good money after bad." He said they weren't going to do that. And he just picked up a phone call during our meeting and started talking French. He actually turned around his chair, turned his back on us, so all you could see was the back of his bald head.

Dennis Thompson: The thing is, we didn't have a record company. Pretty soon Atlantic dropped us, and we were searching for a record company and playing in Europe. You know, we lived in England, and we would take the ferry across to the Continent, and then we would play shows in France and Germany and Belgium, whatever. And we were making a living, but it just wasn't enough. What we needed was a label that would stand behind us and spend money in the PR department.

Becky Tyner: When the MC5 broke up, it broke Rob's heart. He had a tough time. Alright, now it's done. Shattered dreams in the Motor City and all that. I don't even know. So it stopped. Rob was born in '44, and MC5 stopped in the fall of '72. That's a big part. Okay for four years of your life you played in a band. Okay, and it attained a small degree of success.

Leni Sinclair: Everybody thought the MC5 should have been big, and they didn't do it. Then here comes Grand Funk getting all the big accolades, you know.

Dennis Thompson: Grand Funk took our spot. Had the MC5 not made some of the tactical mistakes we had made in the business community and in philosophy, we would have been bigger than Grand Funk. As big as or bigger than Grand Funk Railroad. That's cruel.

"I'm No Statesman,
I'm No General"

_____

Gary Quackenbush: The draft came in hard on me. On my eighteenth birthday I got a 1-A. Inductable at any time. And I was one of the first ones where—they didn't publicize it enough for my taste—but we were classified all high school seniors until you get your deferment. In '66. Most terrifying thing that ever happened to me. I'm in high school, I'm a musician, rocking to the band scene, and I get a 1-A? If I was my dad, I would have gone insane. I would have called the draft board, I would have called the governor, I would have called my congressmen. They were killing us. And so later on it came out that we are classifying all high school seniors as 1-A. So I knew I was going to college just to beat the draft.

Wayne Kramer: All young men in that time period faced conscription. It was inevitable, and you had to go, unless you had a helluva plan. And everybody in our world, it was a constant subject of conversation. What'd they do to him? What'd he say to them? What was the result? What I discovered was that if I showed them who I really was, they wouldn't want me. Went down there stoned, told them my ideas about how the world should work, and they said I wouldn't make good soldier material. I had been up for ten days; I was out of my mind. Just let our freak flags fly—it wasn't easy, and it was high stakes. But it worked for me. A couple of our guys were in school, or were married so they had those outs.

Scott Richardson: I was right there in the middle of it, and my dad didn't think we were going to win in Vietnam, so anything short of declaring myself gay, he was okay. I 4-f'ed along with Ronnie Asheton and Iggy Pop, and under the direction—under the brilliant direction I might add, of Jeep Holland. It took a week of speed and not changing clothes. When I went down for my interview, I went with this black shrink—pretty much like Bill Cosby—and he said, "Well, it's obvious you're not military material. But I would like to ask you, what is the main issue?" At which point I told him I was not going to be confined to this planet. He took his glasses off and said, "You mean astroprojection?"

Gary Quackenbush: Jeep Holland coached ten of us on how to get out, including me and some of the Five. All ten of us got out. There was a written questionnaire, and Jeep was so wise that he said these are the questions you don't answer. Have you ever had any drug experiences? You don't put yes. It's too fucking obvious. If you were a drug addict, you wouldn't want people knowing. This is 1967, okay? Plus he knew what happens when you go down there. You ride on a bus from your draft board with people you went to school with. He says, "Don't talk to them, make sure you smell bad, stay away and see a shrink if you can." I had to go to two draft physicals. I had so much speed in me for the first one that my blood pressure was off the chart. They wanted me to calm down and come back. The second time I went down there I got to see the shrink so fast I broke the house record for getting out. I dressed in wild clothes, I smelled bad, I did everything Jeep said times ten. I had little speed pills in the panel of my shirt in case they kept me overnight. That was my golden parachute. The shrink realized I was completely unfit, and I was outta there like that. Broke the house record. It was a good thing, too, because that was the day Jimi Hendrix played at the Fifth Dimension in Ann Arbor. I missed the afternoon show because I had to be at the draft board. Caught the evening show.

Steve Mackay (*Iggy and the Stooges, Charging Rhinoceros of Soul, saxophonist***):** A friend of mine told me about a psychologist who he said would write me some letters to the draft board. In the letters he kept making up this wife for me that didn't exist. I got to the draft physical, and they said this guy has written so many fucking letters, we could keep you all night you know? I said, "Keep me as long as you want, just don't send me to Nam." I had to talk to a psych every morning, and as long as I still knew what a jones was, I was fine. That's what I told them I had. They didn't want that kind of thing in there. They gave me a six-month deferment for drug addiction, and then they were hounding me again, but my draft number didn't get called. I wasn't gonna go, but I wasn't gonna go to fucking Canada either.

Hiawatha Bailey: You could get arrested more readily for not having a draft card than for not having a driver's license or a birth certificate. You could get held for seventy-two hours.

Mitch Ryder: I got my draft notice and Jimmy McCarty got his in 1965. Both of us were able to get out because we were classified 3-A. He got out because his mother was disabled, and he had to care for her and the kids. My management had the best lawyers that money could buy and some connections as well, so I avoided being drafted.

VC Lamont Veasey: I only went to high school for a month or so in the tenth grade, and I got drafted and went in 1965. I was kind of going through some emotional changes at that time, so I just kinda figured I would get away from that area and kind of, I don't know, get into a whole different scene. I didn't really think about it too much back then. I went to basic in Washington State, then I went AWOL in 1966 before I could be deployed. I was AWOL for eight years before they caught up to me. I was in Detroit. My former wife, she was living on the east side near Gratiot and 6 Mile area. One night she was saying, "Hey, why don't you go with me to the store." I had heard on the radio that President Nixon had issued an amnesty for all the people who had gone to Canada to get out of Vietnam. It was the last day of amnesty, and they were saying just come in, no questions asked. You just get processed. So I get in the car with her, and we were riding down Gratiot. We see these white cops pass us down this side of the street. I said, "You know what, they're going to turn around and follow us 'cause they see me and you." She said, "Oh, no they're not." They turned around and came up behind the car. They got our IDs, and I stayed in the car and she got out. I see this flashlight flashing in the window. I opened the door and they said, "Come back here, sir! Come back here!" I get out, cop has his gun out, and I think he's going to shoot me. I put my hands up, walk up there, put his handcuffs on me and her, and put us in their car. They asked, "Do you know a Roosevelt Veasey?" because my birth name is Roosevelt. She was like, "No, that's not his name. His name is blah, blah, blah." I said, "Just be quiet." I said, "Yeah, I know who he is." They go, "Were you in the Army?" "Yeah." "There's a warrant out for your arrest." They took us to this precinct on Gratiot. Finally the cop comes up and he goes, "We called the military. They said let you go." The military gave me a bus ticket to Indianapolis and I got processed out. That's how I got out. It wasn't as easy as acting crazy to begin with.

Hiawatha Bailey: The draft letter would be, "Greetings, this is Uncle Sam, you are notified to appear at . . ." wherever. I knew there were ways out. One way out was to be an only son, the other way out was to have psychological problems, another one was to be a CO—conscientious objector—which is supposedly like a scarlet letter. But I stole my younger brother's social security number, and when

I showed up and gave that to them and they checked me out. They thought I was too young.

Bill White: I served. I felt it was my responsibility. And I probably didn't have the balls to do all that was required to get out. I got my notice at the Amboy Duke house on Middlebelt.

Ted Nugent: I would do interviews with Lester Bangs for *Creem,* and all these stoned, drooling, unprofessional, idiot antijournalists. He printed that I played "Johnny B. Goode" on my umbilical cord, and then they printed that I shit my pants to get out of the draft. I went down to my draft physical, and I got a deferment because I was enrolled in the Oakland Community College. I've never shit my pants since I was eleven. And that I did because I couldn't get back from deer camp fast enough. I did not—I made that up too, by the way: I didn't shit my pants when I was eleven—I haven't shit my pants since I was one. I never shit my pants; I never pissed my pants; I never did anything to get out of the draft. And by the way, it's important to note, had I shit my pants to get out of the draft, you think I would deny it? That would be a funny fucking story.

Bill White: What's he talking about? He never went to college. I got a lot of respect from the other soldiers because I was in a band. I was coming into Vietnam on a chopper, and we had just landed in camp. I was walking off and someone had a radio, and it was playing "Journey to the Center of the Mind."

"They Didn't Call Them the Stooges for Nothing"

Scott Richardson: I met James Williamson in a record store in Birmingham Michigan, called Marty's Records. I had the same impression I have of him now. An intellectual delinquent. He had other problems. His stepfather, the Colonel. You've seen the movie *American Beauty*, right? That's the Colonel. James was in the Chosen Few with me for a time. But James had to go to an institution. He was institutionalized. Not for delinquency, more like a perceived mental problem. He just didn't want to do what he was told to do, that's all.

James Williamson (*Iggy and the Stooges, guitarist*): I started out in a juvenile home after the ninth grade, as I was truant and I wouldn't cut my hair. The principal and I were at odds, so no hair cut, no school. Once out of there, I went to high school at a place called the Anderson School in Poughkeepsie, New York, which was a kind of clearing house for fuck-ups. From there I went to Bloomfield Hills High School outside Detroit for the better part of a year. I finally cut a deal with the principal that if I finished my high school course work at night school, he would give me a diploma.

Gary Quackenbush: James Williamson used to take guitar lessons from me. He later said, "Yeah, you taught me how to play 'Ticket to Ride' in 1965."

James Williamson: He taught me to play "Help" by the Beatles. That's all I really wanted to know.

Scott Richardson: I had the Chosen Few, and I get a call from Jeep and Ron Richardson separately, each saying, "Look, we wanna manage you." And they're both located in Ann Arbor. They both said, "I can guarantee you this gig and this, that, and the other thing." Now I have a decision to make. So I hitchhike to Ann Arbor to have a meeting with Jeep, who's also the manager of Discount Records down there. I walk in the store, and there's nobody there except this weird-looking guy stocking records on the shelf. I go, "Is Jeep here?" He goes, "No. Who are you?" I said, "I'm Scott Richardson." He says, "Oh yeah. He wants you to hang around." I go, "Who are you?" He says, "I'm Jim Osterberg." And I shook his hand. So he goes, "I'm a drummer." I go, "Oh cool. Which band?" "The Prime Movers." So Jeep doesn't show and Jeep doesn't show. Iggy picks up the phone and calls Ron Asheton and says, "Hey man, you better get down here. There's this really cool guy here." So twenty minutes later in walks Ron Asheton, Scott Asheton, and Dave Alexander. The three homeboys. They were never without each other. Iggy introduced us. Jeep never showed up and Ron Richardson calls Discount Records and says, "Is Scott there?" and Iggy says, "Yeah," and he says, "Well, tell him to come over to my place." So me and Ron Asheton and Scotty and Dave Alexander—Iggy was going to come over later—we all left and walked across the plaza to University Towers. A week later Iggy and I became roommates. Then he decided he wanted to become a lead singer. I got in a whole bunch of trouble because Iggy was a really good drummer. He was a fine percussionist, okay? The guys in his band, the Erlewine brothers, had big plans for him. They sent him over to Chicago to study drumming with Sam Lay of the Butterfield Blues band. I got held up in an alley and had a knife put up against my throat in Ann Arbor and was told to stop inviting Iggy to my gigs because he was going to quit playing drums and he wanted to become a front man after hanging around with the Chosen Few. I said, "It's not my fault." They said, "Ever since he met you he doesn't want to play anymore. He wants to dance around on stage."

Ron Asheton (*Iggy and the Stooges, Chosen Few, guitarist, bassist*)**:** I ended up playing in the Chosen Few with Scott Richardson, and that was our high school band. Those guys were in Birmingham, Michigan, and I was in Ann Arbor, and they'd come here and we'd do all the TGIF parties, frat parties on Friday night, then on Saturday we'd either do a frat or go do a teen set at a club. The Chosen Few played the very first night of the Grande Ballroom opening for the MC5. That was Scott Richardson on vocals, Richard Simpson on guitar, Al Clark on guitar, Stan Sulewski on drums, and I was playing the bass. We did that Stones EP where they ran together "Everybody Needs Somebody," "Pain in My Heart," and "Route

66." That was a nice little EP that came out in England, and they had Bill Wyman playing that do-do-do doot-do doot-doot doot doot; they had the bass starting out "Everybody Needs Somebody" rather than guitar, so I am proud to say that I played the first notes at the Grande Ballroom.

Iggy Pop: Finally we had the Stooges and needed a manager. At one point it was going to be Russ Gibb. There were two people that needed to help us for us to get on stage where the right audience could see us. One was Russ Gibb and the other was John Sinclair. I remember going out of my way to communicate with each of those guys personally. I went to Russ's home one day, sorta being kind of summoned, "Well we're kinda interested in you guys." I think we already played once at the Grande. "Why don't you come over and talk about where it's going?"

Jimmy Recca (*Iggy and the Stooges, New Order, bassist*): Russ Gibb had every intention of becoming the band's manager. Russ was wanting to take the band to England and play.

Russ Gibb: At that time John Sinclair was hyping that band too. He was hyping Iggy because that was an Ann Arbor thing that he had going with the White Panthers, or whatever he had going along with the MC5.

John Sinclair: The Stooges had no social aspect or facet whatsoever. Iggy was a genius, and the other guys were his stooges. They weren't called the Stooges for nothing. Literally, he gave each one of them a part.

Iggy Pop: Russ certainly put us on with fucking everybody, all the time. We basically opened for half of the great young bands and musicians in the world at his place, and I am forever in his debt because of that. We'd be second or third on the bill with these terrific people. It would be Van Morrison or Love or the Who.

Russ Gibb: Iggy's father taught with me at Fordson High School. I had subbed there when I first came back to teach, and that's where his dad taught. When I first hired him, Iggy's daytime job was working as a counselor at the YMCA summer camp around Ann Arbor.

Iggy Pop: I was a junior counselor. I went to a day camp in Michigan called Varsity Day Camp, which was run by a fellow who was a basketball star at the U of M, Irv Wisniewski, called Wrong Way Wisniewski because he scored a basket against his own team. And when I got a little older they gave me a job. I think I started at a buck a day when I was fourteen, teaching little kids how to swim and catching frogs. Russ sort of kept an interest in us. When I got married, I had a marriage ceremony on the lawn of our house in Ann Arbor. Russ called in from the radio station where he was hosting a show, and the gag was—everyone thought it was a Kardashian thing—you know who would marry Iggy Pop? That was a contradiction in terms, so he had a certain outlook on us.

Patti Quatro: Iggy was like a frat kid, and he was wild. But he was still a frat kid.

Jimmy Recca: Guys would bring their girlfriends to shows, and the girls would sit and be enamored with Iggy. And he was just like this fucking guy that—this skinny guy. These guys working at Ford Motor Company, they want to do something nice for their girlfriends on their birthdays or their anniversary, and what do they want to do: "Let's go see the Stooges." The Grande was festival seating. Everybody's crowded up and they're all sitting, and the girls, and Iggy out there working the crowd. And it's like he's got his shirt off, you know, and these guys just stand by, and it would be the biggest thrill to see the Stooges, and they would put the lights right down there on the fucking crowd, man. I'd move in closer to see the whole fucking psychodrama unfold. The girls just want to touch Iggy's chest, and Iggy's, like, looking right at her, and all of a sudden he just hacked out and spit right in this girl's fucking mouth, and next thing you know the guy is looking like, "Wh-hhatttt? What'd you just do to my fucking girlfriend?" He'd just be set to throw a swing, and the next thing you know these cats would come out of nowhere. I mean these fucking guys, these storm troopers fucking commando. And Iggy was saved.

DJ Dianna (*Club DJ*): I was just a little girl and I loved the Stooges. They played them on WABX, and I was really into what was going on. But I was fourteen or so. But my mom finally let me go to a Stooges show at the Eastown; my friend's parent took us and dropped us off. It was really cold out—this was 1971. We're sitting, and finally the Stooges come out, Ron comes out, then Scott, and they start the intro, and Iggy comes dancing out and he has no shirt, the jeans—the whole thing—and looks like a complete madman. I was twenty-five feet from the stage, and I think, I have to get closer. The Eastown had a low stage, and you could walk up, and I was tall for my age, five-seven, and the edge hit me in the middle of the chest. So I'm up there watching, and I am literally on the stage, hands resting on the stage, and Iggy comes dancing over to me, and he has this big smile, and he's wriggling away, and he reaches down and runs his hand over my cheek, and I'm frozen. I can't move; I'm like "Oooooo." I had very long hair, wavy, down past the middle of my back, and he runs his hand into the back of my hair, and—wham!—he smashed my head into the stage. My cheekbone hit the stage, and he laughed and danced away.

Dennis Dunaway: The shows with the Stooges at the Eastown Theater always had a lot of violence. Iggy would jump off stage and pick a fight with somebody, and if he picked a fight with you, then you were the hero for the next week or two.

Stirling Silver: The Stooges opened for everybody, and no one gave a shit.

Niagara (*Destroy All Monsters, Dark Carnival, vocalist, artist*): Iggy always says, "Everyone says, 'I was there and I loved you.'" He says we'd have shows where no one was there all the time.

John Kordosh (*Mutants, bassist, journalist,* Creem *magazine*): At one point I was seeing the Stooges, like, every weekend.

Cathy Gisi (*journalist,* Creem *magazine*): There were people who didn't bathe for days afterward because there was sweat on them from Iggy.

Russ Gibb: Iggy did invent the stage dive. The Grande was the only venue in the world where the audience could go right up to the stage. On each side were the dressing rooms, and the girls were crawling all over the place to get with the musicians. And Iggy would do that thing where he would bend over almost all the way backwards. And he fell over backwards, and people thought it was an accident. I don't think so. He would be in the crowd, and next think you knew, he was floating on the audience. All these things were transpiring while I was trying to figure out if I made any money.

Mitch Ryder: We learned how to jump into the audience. Iggy started it and got caught. That was good. That was a new one. Of course, nobody would catch you in those days. We would leap into the audience and they would make way for you and you would hit the floor. I didn't get that memo. And I didn't get another one. I was talking to James Brown one day way back and I said, "James, you know when you do your knee drop? I do the knee drop in my show too. Man, when I hit those wooden floors, my knees, I feel like they're gonna break." He just looked at me for a second, and he said, "Huh, you don't wear knee pads?" I said, "knee pads?"

Leni Sinclair: The Stooges had a house out in the country at one point, and I went over there one time. The Stooges were in their garage, and the garage was sound proofed with egg cartons. They were sitting there in the dark listening to Dr. John doing "I Walk on Gilded Splinters."

Billy Goodson: They lived in this white house that had this light bulb glowin' over the back door. All dirt all over the place and cars and stuff. You couldn't find a neighbor or nothin'. You had to drive there. But it was a very, very bizarre place. Really cold.

Steve Forgey: I had a friend who was going to trade a Marshall bass amp to Dave Alexander, so he gets in his car and drives over to the Funhouse in Ann Arbor. Everyone is stoned to the bone, sitting around looking at the walls. This is in the middle of the day. So he says he's got the amp, where is Dave? Pretty soon Alexander comes stumbling down the stairs, one step at a time, dragging his bass behind him, thump thump, thump. And he says, and I quote my friend, "Mph duh ga dewgathao."

Iggy Pop: I used to hang out with Glenn Frey at the Birmingham Hideout a lot. At one point after the Stooges had formed, we used to break up every few years. He was trying to start a band with Bob Seger, you know, he said, "I'm sick of work-ing for Bob Seger. Come on, we could start a great band," you know.

Rick Kraniak: The Stooges didn't like me. The band owed Diversified Manage-ment money, we were booking them, and I was a junior partner. Dave Leone was booking them. I had to go to the Stooges farm, trail them to the job, and make sure they got there so we could get some of the money they owed us. So I don't think the band—I don't think Iggy—saw me as one of them.

Iggy Pop: We had no idea about a career at all. What was very important was how we wanted to look and how we wanted to sound and what we wanted to do. Although we didn't use the term then, today it would be "as artists." That term would have been a little bit too pretentious for us to use then, but that was where we were coming from. I always believed that if you do that superbly, the career would take care of itself.

Hiawatha Bailey: The Stooges were gods in both Ann Arbor and Detroit. Ron saw me on the Diag at U of M one day when I first came to town, and he said,

"You know what, you're the most suspicious black person I ever saw in my life. Hi." Then I saw Scott, and I couldn't believe it was the drummer in the Stooges and I was like, [sound effects] . . . Scott goes, "Hey, I know you . . . you know where to get some good drugs? Go get me some drugs." No, I didn't. I made sure he got them, but I didn't give them to him. I was working for the White Panther party at the time.

Iggy Pop: Between the first album and *Fun House*, I'd say we had the sound, but what I'd say changed was the drummer. We wanted the more aggressive approach, and the sonics of the band had been sort of a thick-layered guitar sound, guitar-based sonic approach on the first album. I was really, really influenced by what James Brown was doing at the time and also people like Coltrane and Miles Davis to a lesser extent. But especially James Brown. He was in the period of "Can't Stand It," "Funky Drummer," that sort of thing. Ron had a riff for something that became "T.V. Eye," and the original way he was playing it sounded a lot like "No Fun," and I thought we needed to push a little farther, so I said, "Will you start out, play that single note like you were Hooker?"—John Lee Hooker, who was pretty much a Detroit musician. From a lot of other things on that whole record we used a contrast between parts of each song where the guitar is very spare and you can hear holes. Really, you can hear every, every note the rhythm section is playing, and you can hear big holes in the music and then each song, when it's time, blows to a climax. There's more dynamics, but it's less like usual rock, then we added the saxophone. I was taking a lot of LSD at the time, and that may have had something to do with it too.

Steve Mackay: When we did "LA Blues" in the studio in Los Angeles, it was originally a hippie vibe. But the producer said, "Let's make a completely different song out of this." So when we did that, that was when I took some acid. Iggy scared the shit out of me. I was tripping, and just the whole thing was like, "Whoaaaaa, this guy is being really scary now. I better play really scary." That's exactly how it came out. As the years have gone by, people have said to Jim, "Well, Steve Mackay says he was high on acid for that session," and he says "Oh well, that's great, Steve. I was on acid every single day."

Iggy Pop: All I'd ever had before *Fun House* was recorded was marijuana and LSD. I would call it occasional LSD, but that's a relative term. To me occasional meant about twice a week. Marijuana for me was like when I became conscious in the morning then right through the day, right into the evening. Any time I woke up in the middle of the night either I was . . . I was smoking it or trying to get it. Acid about twice a week was probably my average. We recorded the album in that way, but towards the end—towards the end of the vocal overdubs and the mixes—two people turned me on to cocaine for the first time, and I was one of those people that takes it and goes, "That's great!" There were some points in some of the songs, the outtro and the verses to "T.V. Eye," the outtro and maybe the second part of "Loose"—those were done with some coke up my nose. But the rest of them was strictly LSD and marijuana.

Jimmy Recca: They played the Goose Lake pop festival that summer, 1970. It was, like, a miserable fucking time. It was like 115 degrees all day long, and the Stooges go on at, like, five o'clock in the afternoon and it's fucking like a hundred percent humidity and, you know, it storms on and off all day long. Nothing's in tune, and Traffic was ready to pull out themselves. That's the gig that Dave Alexander quit. They said he was fired. Iggy fired him, but he forgets. Dave just said, "Fuck it." He was resigned to the fact that they were going to cancel the show and that no one was going to go on, so he just started drinking and took some acid. So he got up on stage, and they put him up there and Iggy may have made a point to embellish on it, and Dave gave him the finger and that was history. After that Iggy, having the power to fire people, did so.

Iggy Pop: To the best of my recollection, I would say I fired him.

Scott Richardson: I lived with Dave Alexander. He was an only child, and his parents really doted on him.

Iggy Pop: But at that point he had been leaving on a regular basis as far as not staying at the group's house for weeks on end, not being in town for weeks on end. He had a girlfriend he was kind of obsessed with. And just not making rehearsals sort of thing. On this particular show he could not play one note on his bass; he just froze. It was, I'm told, a case of being extremely drunk. It could have been. He was a less experienced musician than most of us; he was the guy down the street. He was a really witty kid who never opened up to anybody in the world outside of our group. He got into the group because he was the buddy down the street of Scott, and we needed an extra guy at one time. Also, he had the only car in the group and he did a great job, he really did. When it got to the point where, you know, I was trying to run the group at a really large venue and, you know, there's no bass. That was it. There's a lot of our live recordings on YouTube, and you can hear it. So we finally fired him. I'm not a formal leader of the group but was like, "I'm not going to do it anymore. I'm not going to play with that guy."

Ron Asheton: We went on later in the day on Saturday. The band was hot, and when we were hot, kids would get worked up. But the time we got to "Down in the Street" in our set, Iggy had those kids pretty damned worked up. There was a trench in front of the stage, four feet deep and four feet wide and running the length of the stage. It was secured by two police officers on horseback on the stage side and a wooden fence and Cyclone fence six feet high extended on the audience side of the trench. It was a wall of security to diffuse the crowd. As the song hit its groove, where the band holds the groove, Iggy raised his arm and beckoned to the crowd that was now smashing against the fence. When we got to the chorus where Iggy wails, "the wall," those kids must have thought we were talking to them because they pushed the fence down and rushed the stage, which pretty much ended the festival.

Iggy Pop: The other three guys grew up within. Ron and Scott were brothers, for Christ's sake, and even spent more time together than most brothers because they didn't go to school. Dave was their buddy from one block down in the subdivision who also didn't go to school, so they had a bond forged many years before I met them. I tried to join as much as I could, and I could only get so far. Once the group got going I started getting a lot of attention. It never bothered Scott, but Ron and Dave would scribble on the walls, "See Iggy. See Iggy puke." It was funny, but on the other hand, there was something going on, and I was the guy who was forced to be the nag to get it. There wasn't going to be a rehearsal unless I asked eighteen times. So as the group went on, there were a couple of camps. More like three or four camps. You know, like Scotty was pretty much his own guy. Ron and Dave liked to hang out all night and watch TV together and smoke marijuana, and then there was me. So it was kinda like that, but at times there was the illusion and convenience of being part of a pack of guys that could help you go somewhere and do something cool that involves some intoxicating art and getting enough money in your pocket to score a little weed and meeting some cool chicks, and some things you do in America that you do when you're young and don't know any better. We had all that in common.

Ron Asheton: At Olympic Studio in London, it was rehearsals for *Raw Power* in July 1972. That was pretty much the beginning. Iggy and James had gotten some material worked up, and this was the kickoff so they could hear and we could hear, and things developed while we were there. Some great tunes came out of that: "I Got a Right," and, of course, the classic "Good Bye Betsy." Those guys were all clean, no one was taking any drugs—that was the deal. It was a good chance for him; he was working with Tony DeFries and he's got a record deal with CBS, so you don't want to screw up—he'd already screwed his life up and he pulled himself out of that hole, and it was a totally work-oriented situation. There was no fooling around; we had schedules for rehearsals—all we did was rehearse every day up until the recording of the record, and then even when we were done and Jim took off with Bowie for the states to mix and stuff, we still had to rehearse. It was like "Ehhh? Oh, you're kidding right?" So Jim was quite the taskmaster.

Bob Sheff: Iggy called me up—it was 1973, I was in California to work at the Center for Contemporary Music at Mills College—and he said, "Would you come and do a tour with us?" I had played with Iggy in the Prime Movers; he was a good drummer. He'd just gotten out of high school, whatever that age is. He was the first guy to dye his hair silver at that age. That was the midsixties. So I said, "Yeah, that'd be great to see you" and all that. I got to Los Angeles and we were staying on Mulholland Drive, and he had this house—he was right in front of this mansion and it was very strange. Then we went to Detroit to do a show at Ford Auditorium.

Ron Asheton: My only disappointment was with how MainMan ran their operation. They had a really nice spread when we got done playing Ford. It was "Oh wow, look down in the dressing room." They had luncheon tables full of food and champagne and a bar with all this food and stuff, and we just got finished playing and we were told we can't be at this party—it was for press. It's not really a party; Tony DeFries is holding his press conference, so we came off the stage, and I remember my brother going "What?" and my brother and I making a sandwich and stuffing it in our pocket and grabbing a couple of beers like some hobos on the run and then shuttled right out to the Book Cadillac, which was kind of funky at that time. It was Tony DeFries doing his big manager showcase dealio with the big cigar and his bravado, so it was the little guys gotta go along with it. He was only Jim's manager; we were just hirelings. We weren't considered—James, Scottie, and I.

Bob Sheff: One of the MainMan people backstage was this arrogant, obviously Mafioso guy, very insulting like the guy who shakes your hand but he's staring the wrong way. Just before the show in Detroit and Iggy sent me on stage by myself.

He said, "Just go on out there and play." I started playing off some of the simple rock licks of primitive, rock licks and a couple of little gospel things before they came out, and then they gradually came onstage, and people were getting more and more excited and screaming and hollering.

Robert Matheu (*photographer*): I had tickets for the Stooges at Ford Auditorium, but I had been playing hockey without a cup on, and I got nailed in my right nut. I was living with my older brother, who's ten years older, and my sister-in-law, who's six years older. That was excruciating trying to tell her why she needed to take me to the hospital. I was due to get out of the hospital the next day, but I could not convince them to let me out. So I kind of snuck out the back door and went to the show at Ford Auditorium, shot photos, and then I went back to my hospital bed.

Nikki Corvette (*Nikki and the Corvettes, vocalist*): It was a Detroit thing to do. I saw the Stooges so much that the guys in the band used me to get rid of the girls they didn't like. They'd call me over and, like, "Nikki, come here." They'd put their arm around me and introduce me as their girlfriend. Then when the girl would leave they'd be like, "Thanks."

Bob Sheff: After Ford we did the Whiskey-a-Go-Go in LA. I was doing some clothing things—I was dressing like a punk before it was punk. I had these clothing pieces and I put LEDs in my hair, and nobody knew what they were, and basically my hair was . . . I had little spots of light, electric light, and everybody thought it was cigarette ash and trying to put out my hair, and I was yelling, "Stop, stop," and as I was playing I was sweating also, and so that started making contact with the batteries for the thing, and I was getting these little shocks, sort of like Frankenstein. Before the show, that week, Iggy took me, we went to the driveway basically in the back of the house in LA and talked for several hours about, you know, things he'd been through and he wanted to talk to somebody he'd known before and felt more down to earth, because it had been a really wild number of years for him, and he felt he really wanted to get back in touch with friends.

Ron Asheton: We just did that one show in Detroit, and I think DeFries dumped us after that, so we were just on to another manager, Jeff Wald, and he just put us on the road, and literally we were on the road for three or four months nonstop.

Bob Sheff: The money situation was very weird, and I wasn't getting paid. Iggy was getting paid because they had to keep him happy, but no, the rest of us weren't getting paid. The young manager that we had—I don't remember his name—he went to get money out of the bank, and he had a gun in his pocket, and we walked into the bank and he said, "This is for protection." And we said, "Oh man, you brought a gun into the bank," and he hid it of course, and he got out, $10,000 or something like that, and we walked out. It wasn't Iggy's fault. The manager was MainMan, and I told Iggy, "Look, Iggy, I'm running out of money, I don't have any money, I have to catch a plane back to Berkeley" and he said, "Well," and I just packed up and I left.

Ron Asheton: Max's was great fun times. We loved Max's Kansas City, the original studio's pre-James times, which I call the real Stooges—used to go to Max's all the time when we were in town, so we were quite comfortable. "Alright you boys, you've got a credit line at the restaurant, and at the end of your week of playing, we'll tally up your sums, pay your bill downstairs." So every night after we played, we'd go downstairs and hang out and have our dinner and our drinks. We'd see a lot of our friends; a lot of people from Michigan came to the shows. One time Iggy came in pretty stoned. He was getting back into getting stoned in New York—people want to give him stuff; they want to make him a little monster, people were always shoving things into his face, into his hand. I'm sitting in the restaurant, and here comes Jim—Iggy—walking into the restaurant, and he's wearing like a turn-of-the-century nightgown—you know the big flowing, white thing that goes from the neck to the floor, has no shape, you look like a ghost—so I'm going, "Oh Jesus Christ," and we're all kind of like, "Oh don't look at him." It's not terribly embarrassing, but I know something's gonna happen. So there were these yuppie types who were not your normal Max's Kansas City musician-type people—high-end younger couples, two couples. So Jim's just walking around the restaurant, seeing who's there. So when he gets to their table, they had just gotten their wine and salads and stuff, and he falls and he grabs on to their table cloth, and the stuff comes pouring down on him; a couple of us just got up and split. I remember the guy swearing at him. Now it's funny, but then it was "Oh no."

He'd see somebody or maybe people, or they would say, "Hey Iggy" and he would just sit down at people's tables and start eating their food, and no one was pissed or anything, but he would sit down and partake a bit of that, then he'd talk and then get up and just move on to another table. So at the end of the week, when it was time to pay up the bill—I think only I perhaps got paid for the week—I know Scottie, James, and Iggy had spent all of their paychecks downstairs in the restaurant, which I think was their [Max's] secret plan anyway. They're going, "They're playing upstairs and all the money will be spent downstairs."

I remember Jim being very generous. He was signing his name; he would sit down at a table and have a couple bites and sign their check, so I think he actually ended up owing money. And that was the classic time he got cut, he had those bad slices—you see those pictures—and after one of the shows we went to Alice Cooper's penthouse to hang out after the show, and when I looked at his chest, I'm going "stitches." So Alice actually got on the phone and woke up his personal physician and had a cab take Iggy to the doctor's to get stitched up, you know, like, at what, two or three in the morning?

Stirling Silver: I was in New York that summer and went to Max's Kansas City every single night. I would go to Arthur Kane's apartment, pick him up in my car—of course everybody took taxis or subways, nobody had a car in New York—and park it by South Park Avenue. Max's was right there, and there was this little playground in Gramercy Park with, like, a tree fort made of metal. No one could see you in there, and we could sit in there and drink a couple of 40s of Old English 800—we didn't have that in Detroit and I loved that stuff. Iggy was there for that week, but it was sold out. Everyone was there—Alice Cooper, Todd Rundgren, Wayne County.

Art Lyzak (*Mutants, vocalist, manager Lili's bar*): In 1972 the Mutants were fourth on the bill in St. Clair Shores Civic Arena with Iggy and the Stooges. This was like when they were just on their last legs; it was the Stooges, Bob Seger, Catfish Hodge, Mutants. They were just so junked out; they were fucking horrible. The band came out and started playing "*Raw Power*," and it was about ten or fifteen minutes before Iggy even came out. And right before he came out to the front of the stage he took a dump behind the Marshall amp. I guess that's a junk thing or something. Then he kind of came out with a little skimpy thing on; it was just like fucking horrible. I mean I stood there for like ten or fifteen minutes after he started and thinking, like, just how bad they'd gotten.

Mike Rushlow (*Pigs, Rushlow-King Combo, guitarist*): It was Catfish Hodge, Bob Seger, and the Stooges. Bob Seger wore this giant hat, and he came out, and the first thing he said was, "Well, I'm not going to play any of my old stuff." Everyone was like, "Get off the stage! Where's the Stooges?"

Bob Mulrooney, aka Bootsey X (*Ramrods, Coldcock, Bootsey X and the Lovemasters, drummer, vocalist*): I saw 'em at St. Claire Shores Civic Arena, with Seger opening for the Stooges. The Stooges only played five songs, and Iggy was in the

54

crowd the whole five songs. It was fucking great. This girl I went to high school with liked me, and Iggy liked her, so we got to go to the party afterwards. It was at a motor inn or something, and there was this hippie-ish guy—he probably had one of the first video cameras ever—and he probably, once he got it, he shot every band, because he didn't look like a Stooges fan. But he was showing the concert, and Iggy was there, and this guy's going over all the technical stuff, and Iggy's going, "Shut up man, I'm trying to watch this.'"

Nikki Corvette: I went to the show in Toledo when they played with Slade. James and Scott were sharing a hotel room, and me and my boyfriend were sleeping on the floor, and because we just went down there—we didn't have a place to stay or whatever. Scott was a little mad that I wouldn't sleep with him, and he was getting a little out of hand, and me and my boyfriend went out and sat in the hall. Slade was out there and everybody was arguing. Iggy walked out of his room totally naked and said, "Hey, want to fuck?" And I went "Me? No." So he came out a couple of minutes later and said, "Will you wash my hair?" I said, "No." I left that night because Slade was kind of scary and there was a fight I didn't want to be around. People were out in the halls yelling at each other, and the whole night was crazy. James got a call from cops in the coffee shop saying that he had to come get Iggy because he was trying to get drugs from the cops. But when Iggy went back to LA he sent me this really nice poster with a black-and-white kind of etching of Bowie, and he wrote on the back, "Nikki, we never did fuck, did we? Love Pop." My boyfriend got mad and tore it up.

Bob Mulrooney: I saw the last show at the Michigan Palace, the second *Metallic KO* show. I hated it. All you could hear—it's just like the album, all piano, all those high notes. It was horrible, and they kept stopping and starting, and I just wanted to see some rock 'n' roll; I wasn't into how unusual it was. I thought, Iggy's just—he's like my hero—he's just embarrassing himself. He was just really belligerent, and it just wasn't a good show. Scott Asheton, by that time, the band was not playing well. Scott Asheton was no longer hot. James, at the civic arena in Saint Clair Shores, James looked great—he had that spider outfit. They just got progressively worse 'cause of the dope and the traveling and shit. Everything was going wrong for them.

Skid Marx (*Flirt, bassist*): Nikki Corvette would say, "Fuck you" and "Play 'Louie, Louie'" between songs. You can hear her on the tape.

Dave Hanna (*Ramrods, Space Heaters, guitarist*): There was an ad in the paper for the Stooges' last show. It was tiny, but it said, "Iggy and the Stooges at the Michigan Palace," and you could buy tickets at Hudson's, $5. So my dad drove us down there and waited in the car. I was so impressed; it changed my life. Iggy was down in the crowd, and some guy jumped on his head—like on top of him—and in a split-second that guy was on the floor, and Iggy just kept moving. That was my first concert.

Robert Matheu: For years we had gotten together as kids and sang, "Cock in My Pocket," and when *Metallic KO* came out we were so happy. It was like we had a recorded version to sing along with.

Scott Asheton (*Iggy and the Stooges, Sonic's Rendezvous Band, drummer*): If you think about what was going on at that time, in the early seventies, we were so far harder rock out there than anyone else—that's why we didn't fit in. When you think what was going on was kinda glittery, kinda gayish, kind of going taking the edge off of it, other bands of that era were not even close to rockin' like we were. I'd say the biggest reason that stuff didn't do well is because we were rocking too hard.

Iggy Pop: What we were, we were just so special, we were just so out there, that at some point you could see jaws drop and you could see the thought go, "Oh my god," and people would just walk away. The band was never dropped by CBS, despite what people say. I'm not at liberty to tell you what is correct. I just don't want to get into it except to say that we were never formally dropped, and I have copies of all the paperwork. And there was an overture made to me to do a kind of, they described it to me, I could do a David Cassidy or sort of solo trip.

Dennis Thompson: Don't forget, Iggy was a valedictorian in high school. Smart. Fucking. Guy. The reason he's rich today is because he's a very smart man and got himself some very smart business people all the way down the line. He had his rough times. Michael Davis and I saved his life after he shot some heroin up in Michael's house and we threw him in the bathtub with the ice cubes and shot him up with salt water.

He met his maker a few more times than that.

Iggy Pop: I don't want to put a number on it, but a few times, yeah.

Riots in the Motor City

Ted Nugent: When the riots of 1967 hit Detroit, I was behind the counter of the Capital School of Music, on Grand River, with a shotgun. It was a heartbreaker 'cause I saw my beloved birth city of Detroit goin' up in flames at the hands of idiots.

K. J. Knight: I went down to Grand River, where it was happening. They had the area blocked off, and we wanted to see the action. And it would be a chance for me to steal something. I was into snatch and grabs. But they blocked off the downtown area. You couldn't get all the way down there. I tried. That kind of shit was right up my alley.

Leni Sinclair: We had flown a flag about a week before the riots—around the middle of July—that had a black panther on it and the slogan "Burn Baby Burn." It was hanging on our building at Trans-Love Energies on the John Lodge. We had no idea really what it meant. When the riots started and everything started burning, the cops came and knocked on the door. They thought we were conspirators or something, and we told them it was just a design. Then we sat on the roof of our apartment, watching the riots on TV.

John Sinclair: It was just exhilarating. I thought, this was the greatest. We were at our Trans-Love Energies building at John Lodge and Warren. Right in the eye of the storm. We helped people loot stores. We got some bolts of cloth that the MC5 made into clothes and wore 'em for months. I like to point out different ones that we got from a store on Trumbull. If I saw 'em, I could point it out to you.

Robin Sommers: I lived at East Grand Boulevard and John R in a commune called Broken Claw. The riots started on July 23, which was my birthday, and I lived in the front room, and there was a wooden porch along the front of the house, and they had filled the room with balloons, and by the end of the evening they had started to pop in the heat. And there were fire trucks with soldiers going by, and we had to pop all of them in a hurry to make sure they didn't alarm the soldiers and get us shot.

Barry Kramer came by in his Firebird, and about five of us got in the car and drove over to the burning part of town. We drove down 20th or 18th or something, and this crowd of black guys started throwing bottles at us.

Wayne Kramer: I was arrested and they were going to throw me in jail. It was the last day of the burning, and I had a telescope in my house; I liked to check things out. But there I was that day, looking around through the telescope, and the next thing I know, the National Guard are at my door. They thought I was working for snipers. The only snipers I saw were the National Guard troops on the rooftops, but they took me in, beat me up a little, and then realized that they had no room in the jail for me. So they let me go.

Dennis Thompson: I was at my parent's house. It looked pretty scary on TV, what with the tanks and whatnot, and I was in touch with Wayne, and he said, "There's a tank parked in the corner of our house of the Artist's Workshop"—where they lived and we practiced. We lived above the Artist's Workshop in an old dentist's office. The whole band was there, and they said, "Yeah, there's a tank right across the corner from us, and there's guys floatin' around here with guns, and if you want to come down here, it's cool. If you don't, that's cool too." I chose to stay away from it because, you know, with my hair and everything, I was obviously a prime target. Anybody that had long hair and colorful clothes was lumped in with the black people automatically. There was National Guard around—not on every street— but their presence was strongly felt. There really wasn't that much damage, and what there was was limited to a few areas, with the looting and the broken glass. That riot didn't last that long.

Dan Carlisle: I was downtown and parked my car and the police pulled up. The riots must have been just starting up. Police were different then than they are today. They harassed me and ran my plate, and I had some outstanding parking tickets. So they took me to this jail over by Cass, and once I was in, they started filling the cell with angry black men. There I am. And the cop came and said, "You, come out." Out I came, and he said, "You better sit out there because it's getting bad out there." Hal Youngblood was producer of JP McCarthy, and I called him to come down and bail me out. That was no place to be.

Russ Gibb: The rioters came right down Grand River and never fucked with the Grande Ballroom because we were all cool with the neighborhood people. I think the neighborhood was a little scared of us. We had our regular schedule that week, even as the neighborhood burned.

Rick Stevers: The Grande didn't get hurt at all. They canceled Tom Rush, but we came by after it was over and saw Russ. We're out looking around, and we were all shocked the place didn't get hurt. Russ said to this young black kid, "Why didn't this get touched?" and the kid told him, "Because you got music in there."

Shaun Murphy: The night before it all happened we went and saw Tim Buckley at the Grande with the Up. No one had any idea what was coming.

Gary Rasmussen: From our house you could almost see the Lodge Expressway, and you could see the tanks and the National Guard going down there.

Robin Sommers: The Boulevard had become the main street to run the fire trucks down, and by 2 a.m. it was a parade, and by 3:30 there was National Guard on the trucks with their weapons out. I had this big front window in my room, so we put two layers of blankets over the windows in hopes of stopping a stray bullet if that happened. There was this telephone building five blocks north, and I watched tracer bullets bouncing off all the way to the top. This lady got shot and killed in a motel after she opened a window and stuck her head out. The National Guard opened up on her. I was working at Mixed Media, a head shop where we sold records, books, candles, papers, pipes. The Wayne State Police opened up with a couple of rounds of shotgun into our front windows at Mixed Media. So we boarded it up and wrote, "soul brother" over it. There was a drug store that was burned down near my house, and there was a safe they had found. They broke it open, the safe, and there was $200 to $300 worth of change in there. Everyone was happy.

VC Lamont Veasey: The Soul Agents had had a show in Lima, Ohio, and afterward we got a bus back to Detroit, and then a cab back to my house on Wisconsin near 6 Mile. At the foot of my street was a tank, with the turret pointed down my street. I walked in, and we watched it all on TV. It was wild to see this all happening, and it's right down the street. We went out during the day, but at night it was martial law. Our neighbors were coming home with new TVs and appliances, but we sure didn't. My mom set that straight right away.

Greg Errico (*Sly and the Family Stone, drummer*): We were on the road, taking turns driving, and it was the middle of the night and we needed gas. We happened to be passing through Detroit on the highway, and so we innocently pulled off, you know, and we happened to be downtown at two or three in the morning, and it looked like a ghost town—we were in a warehouse area. All of a sudden, we're surrounded by Army jeeps, which pulled us over, and within moments we were up against a brick building with our hands up and our legs spread. These were guys with machine guns. They saw us—black, white, male, female, dressed funny. We said, you know, "What is this?" and they said the city was under martial law and there was a curfew. They couldn't figure out what we were up to. Sly responded with a knee-jerk reaction—you know, at first you gotta react—and that didn't go down well. But when they realized who we were and that we weren't aware of the situation and we eventually walked. We got out of there.

Peter Rivera (*Rare Earth, drummer*): Gil Bridges, our saxophonist, had a pilot's license, so we went up and flew over the city. We saw the smoke pouring out of the burning buildings, where they were burning down. And I was thinking to myself, "You know, a high-powered rifle could reach this high easily. Maybe this isn't a good idea." . . . Yeah, we did that once, saw the riots from up above.

Jimmy Recca: I lived on the west side at a drug house. We hunkered down and watched the armored personnel carrier go between Greenfield and 7 Mile. I had friends who worked at the Chrysler plant near there, including this guy T Bone. He was a drug dealer, and he had a house in Redford Township. He was a gypsy biker, and during the height of it all they were torching an area by Livernois, and we were watching it on this little TV. They showed all these people looting, and T Bone said, "Look at that, I don't want them to get all the shit," and next thing we hear him firing up his chopper and off he goes—it's curfew, after dark, and you could see the half tracks going down 7 Mile, but you hear that bike sound out all the way down Livernois and 7 Mile. He comes back the same way, and we hear the guys on bullhorns shouting at him, "Pull over." Then we hear the bike coming around the corner. He's got his lights off and he's got forty to fifty really nice suits—Gaslight-era suits, these old, cool, pimp-styled things—thrown over the gas tank, which is completely covered, and you can hardly see him.

Johnny Badanjek: We lived in the same area, some of us. I was on Hall Street, and we all piled into a car and went down to see the bullet holes in the Howard Johnson. That was down by the GM and Fisher Building.

Robin Seymour: We were doing a show, *Swinging Time*, at the Fox Theater with Martha Reeves and the Vandellas, and it was packed when things started. This was about 1:30 in the afternoon. The theater owners came in and told us we'd have to stop. Martha got up and explained to the kids, told them be quiet, to relax, that there was a problem and not to go running around.

Then we walked onto Woodward Avenue and looked up in the air, and you could see the smoke from the fires; it was like a war zone. Art [Cervi, coproducer] and I came back the next day and realized that the city was shut down. So we got on and described what was going on to our viewers, and since we couldn't have any guests, we played videotapes. That day going home to where I was living in Dearborn, I drove down the highway, and it was empty. All I could see all around was smoke.

John Sinclair: At one point I was really inspired by watching the news, until we were watching it on television, and at one point they said, "The Tenth Precinct, over on Livernois, was pinned down by sniper fire." And I just thought, "Yes. Yes. This is it. We're gonna win now." And I went next door to the Artist's Workshop, downstairs, where our mimeograph machine was, and I made up a stencil. It said, "Bastille Day. Tear down the Wayne County jail, let the prisoners out." I made this into a mimeographed flyer, and I made a stencil, and then I put it on the machine, and I said, "Wait a minute. If we don't win, this is going to be seen as an act of sedition. I'm going to get into a lot of trouble." And I just put it off—one of the smarter things I ever did. I would have been in prison even earlier than I was. Very few legs to stand on as far as a defense of your position. We were on the side of the black people, man. We were in business, one hundred percent. The only white people we had any use for were hippies.

Iggy Pop: During that time I was getting it together with the Stooges, and there was a nice atmosphere around downtown Detroit. If you didn't have any money and you wanted to do something, it wasn't difficult to get control of a structure. Yeah, it was pretty much emptied out.

Ted Nugent: It just broke my heart. But I was there; I watched it burn. That was our Detroit, our city.

Here's New Pretties for You

John Sinclair: We played a gig with Alice Cooper in Philadelphia—MC5, Alice Cooper—spring of '69. We'd both come a long way to play this night in Philadelphia, and there was nobody there. But we were wild about them; we just thought they were the fuckin' greatest. They loved the Five. We said, "Man, you guys ought to come to Detroit, man. They'll love this shit in Detroit, man." And they came.

Alice Cooper (*Alice Cooper, solo, vocalist*): It was a hard-drug city, but it was the best rock-and-roll city ever. We probably had the best years there. We were used to staying in little tiny places and we were always traveling.

Ray Goodman: They crashed on our band house floor for a week until they found a place. There were literally sleeping bags in the living room. Shep Gordon got a hold of Pete Andrews somehow, but it was also pretty common for WABX to put out calls on the radio: there's a band moving to town and they need a place to crash.

Alice Cooper: We never lived anywhere, let alone a house, so this house we got on Brown Road north of Detroit was quite a treat. At that time—1970, 1971—you'd play the Eastown. It would be Alice Cooper, Ted Nugent, the Stooges, and the Who, for $4. The next weekend at the Grande it was MC5, Brownsville Station, and Fleetwood Mac, or Savoy Brown or the Small Faces. You couldn't be a soft-rock band or you'd get your ass kicked. We knew how good the Stooges and MC5 were, and if we had all just stayed in Detroit, that would have been fine with everybody, I think. When we started breaking nationally, you almost hated to leave Detroit. I loved that house. I think we had ten acres.

Dennis Dunaway: Before we got our house in Detroit, we were staying at this dive motel on Gratiot Avenue, and all I remember is there was this Big Boy across the street and I was always wishing I could afford to eat something there. But instead of us hearing about Detroit and migrating there, it was more like we were going anywhere we could get a gig, and the Detroit area and the Midwest liked us a lot better than the rest of the country did.

Bob Ezrin (*producer, Alice Cooper, Detroit*): I had to go to meet the band there when we started getting ready to do *Love It to Death*. First of all, I drove past it about four times because it was boarded up from the outside. It looked like a derelict farmhouse that no one had been in for fifty years. After traveling this road four or five times and realizing there was no other house, I finally pulled around the back, and then I saw that there were vehicles and there was a three-legged dog and the screen door was open to the house, so I let myself in.

The practice hall was a big barn on the property—this was a big farm. It could have been hundreds of acres for all I know. In the practice barn they had some of their props; they had a whole stage backline set up and there was also a shooting gallery where they used to put up bottles and cans and shoot them with BB guns to let off steam. No one was awake when I first walked into the house, and I came in through the kitchen, which looked like a science experiment. There were filthy dishes that had been piled there forever. There were dishes of casserole that had been there for so long that things were growing in it. I wandered through the kitchen into the next room, which was totally dark, through a beaded curtain into the room, and I reached around to try to find a light switch, and instead I had my hand on a ceramic cock and balls which had a cigarette sticking out of it—it was stuck to the wall. As my eyes adjusted, I saw that and kind of leapt back, and then there was clothes rack with falsies on the other wall—you know I backed into that. I realized there was a bed in the middle of the room, and on that bed were two creatures of indeterminate sex, both wearing Dr. Denton's, with the button back. The only way I could tell that one was a guy was because one of them had mutton chops. Everything else was identical. They both had long blonde hair, they both had nail polish, they both had Dr. Denton's on, lots of jewelry, and they were dead to the world—they did not notice me.

Neal Smith: That was Glen's room, which was the living room. It was Glen and his girlfriend. Alice and I had the two bedrooms upstairs, and Glen and Mike and Dennis were downstairs.

Bob Ezrin: So then I tried to leave the room by the other door. There was another beaded curtain, which I thought might lead out to civilization. As I parted the curtain, standing in the doorway was a six-and-a-half-foot frog. There was a guy with a frog's head on, which later I learned was Dennis Dunaway, but he was just standing there with a frog's head on and I parted the curtain and bumped into him, and he looked at me and said, "Ribbit" and then turned and walked away.

Dennis Dunaway: I didn't know Bob Ezrin was coming over. It was kind of dark in the living room. He comes in, you know, and I said, "Ribbit" and he's like, "Oh hello, Mr. Frog," and you can tell he was really nervous. Because he just didn't know what to do. He was already apprehensive. He was just a kid. We called him the Boy Wonder because he really was just a boy.

Bob Ezrin: Then I heard this kind of—what would be a good word to describe it?—chattering sound beside me to the left of me, and I turned around and there was a green monkey looking at me and masturbating.

Alice Cooper: We had a bunch of pets. We had a raccoon that was the most horrible thing ever, and it would wad up its crap and fling it at people. It was a horrible little animal. And the monkey, if a girl walked in, the monkey would immediately start masturbating. It was so embarrassing. My mom or my sister would come in, and the monkey would start.

Bob Ezrin: As I backed away from that I bumped into my first real human being, who was Mike Roswell, the road manager with the band. He was sleepy eyed, had just come out of his bedroom, which was just off of this main room that I was in, and he said, "Oh yeah, the guys are just getting up. We played last night. Yeah, sorry, you know. Sit down here and we'll all be there in a minute." Finally everybody finally assembled; we went back into the room with the thing with falsies that turned out to have been the living room. So then we all sat in there and had a meeting, and we started playing material off of cassettes. We picked "I'm Eighteen" as the first thing; I think actually it might have been "Is It My Body?" was the first thing that we worked on, then "I'm Eighteen."

Alice Cooper: He said, "I'll produce the album, but we have to relearn everything." And it was like what? He said, "Everyone likes you guys, but you don't have a signature," and we didn't know what that meant. He said, "When you hear the

Doors, you know it's the Doors, and when you hear the Beatles, you know it's the Beatles. When you hear Alice Cooper, you could be any psychedelic band. There's no signature to anything."

So Bob came in and we went out to the barn every day, rehearsed for ten hours a day.

Dennis Dunaway: There was a hospital for the criminally insane across the road from us. You could throw a rock and hit it practically. On a decent day we'd open up these big gigantic doors to the barn we practiced in, which was part of the deal we got for the house. They didn't clap at everything. But when we played something that we really nailed, you'd hear them at the prison farm cheering. The song "Dead Babies" never would have happened if that prison farm hadn't cheered for it. The verse was from a song that had kind of a crappy chorus. And so even though it was a good verse, the song fell by the wayside. I was trying to talk the guys into putting the good verse with the good chorus, and they weren't going for it at all. I wrote a bass part to tie it all together, and I finally got it. We had a rule that you couldn't throw out anything until you actually tried to play it, so the doors were open and I got them to play it, and the prison farm cheered like crazy, so that was it. That was the stamp of approval.

Alice Cooper: We pretty much were the pretty entertainment for this hospital for the criminally insane. Perfect for us. We would rehearse ten hours a day, and they would sit and listen to us rehearse all day.

Mark Parenteau (*WABX, DJ***):** We went to the house on Brown Road in Pontiac, which was farm country. Gail, my wife at the time, knew Alice Cooper and all the guys that were in the original band as well as their pet snake, Katrina. I'm sure now it's all suburbs, but then it was pretty far out there. The place was like a scene out of a horror movie. It was this house, which was a crash pad. It had no real furniture in the living room or anything. And they would go out and Michael Bruce would shoot chipmunks and squirrels so they could feed the snake, which was fun. Alice would sit, and there was a black-and-white console TV in the living room of this house with a couple of folding chairs. Alice sat in one chair surrounded by a huge amount of Budweiser empties. Alice had a gun that had those suction cups on it, like the little bullet would fly out and had the suction cup. Every time he would see someone on TV that he didn't like, he would shoot one of those suction cups, so the front screen of that TV was covered with like fifty or sixty of those little suction cups that were stuck to the glass.

Bob Ezrin: I froze my ass off in that house when it got to be winter. During that time I actually spent a couple of those nights in—you know those Christmas tree lots that have the trailers that always have a trailer outside? That's where I spent a few nights because it was warm in there; there was actually heat. Alice's girlfriend's girlfriend had this Christmas tree lot.

Neal Smith: First time I heard "Fields of Regret" on the radio, it was the first night we played in Detroit. I was stoned out of my head on acid and I just heard "I Wanna Be Your Dog" by the Stooges. At that time I had never heard the Stooges. I put the radio up to my head, and I'm listening to it like it's the fuckin' nastiest song I've ever heard in my life, and it's drivin' like a mother fucker and I loved this song. It's as loud as it can be on the radio, pushed right up next to my ear, and then all of a sudden it stops and it goes [imitates chords], two big power chords and then my head just suuucked into the radio. Then [imitates the music] it starts firing up again and then it goes [imitates music again], and my head gets sucked back in there again, and then I go "Who the fuck is this band?" I'm sitting there and the next song comes on, "Holy shit, that's us!" It was "Fields of Regret."

Dennis Dunaway: We got played on the radio before, but not on pop radio. The first time I heard "I'm Eighteen" on the radio we were all in the living room at the Pontiac farm, and it came on a crappy little transistor radio. It about knocked me over. We were yelling, and Neal came running down the stairs. Glen was there. By the time the song was halfway over, we were all in there, just ecstatic.

Russ Gibb: I made a mistake one day booking a show at the Grande, and instead of putting B. B. King on as the last act, as the headlining act I put Alice Cooper there and B. B. was the second billed band. Usually we had three bands. When I realized I said, "Oh, shit." So I call up Alice, and I say, "Vince, I'm sorry. I made a mistake. You're going to have to play second. It's B. B." He said, "No, no, we're the top of that bill, Russ. I got the contract." I said, "Vince, I made a mistake." He says, "Well, I gotta hold you to it." He was polite about it, but he was saying no, you're not gonna move me, and that's a union contract, Russ. And I knew the union would back him. Now I gotta let B. B. know. So I call him. He was staying somewhere in Detroit, and I call him up. I said, "B. B., I got a mistake here. You're supposed to be the top of the bill, but I made a mistake in a union contract," and I told him. He said, "Well, I'll be over before rehearsal and we'll talk about it then." So around 2:00 in the afternoon in comes B. B with his guys. I bring them in the office and said, "Look here's the problem I have." He said, "What are you saying to me?" I said, "Well, instead of coming in at 11:00 to play at around 11:30, you're gonna have to come in around 8:30 and be the middle band." He said, "You mean I'm not gonna be top of the bill?" I said, "That's right, and there's nothing I can do about it. If you want out of the contract, then fine, I will let you out." He said, "Who's going to be the top of the bill?" I said, "Alice Cooper." And he said, "Who is she?" Yeah, yeah. He said, "Who is she?" Well, I said, "That's some guy in a band who thinks he's a girl," or something, I forget. We talk and talk, and he says, "Now what time will I be going home then?" I said, "Well, you'll probably be out of here by 11:00." He says, "You mean I'd get back to the hotel by 11:00?" He said, "That's great with me, Russ." And as he left he picks up Lucille. He'd done his rehearsal and we were in talking again, and he says, "By the way, who was that girl?" I said, "No, no. Guy, Alice Cooper." He said, "What kind of music does he play?" I said, "Well, mixture of rock 'n' roll blah, blah." He said, "Well, Russ, I will blow him off the stage. I'll see you at the show." And he did, of course.

Rick Stevers: We were playing with Alice Cooper on some bill, and we pulled up and our crew was loading in. So the bass player and I went backstage to check things out, and we walk into the dressing room, and there was a girl with her back facing us. She had really long hair and a bra on, and we were like, "Cool." But it was one of the guys in Cooper. We were like, "Oops, sorry ma'am, never mind."

Jim Kosloskey (*Frut, guitarist*): Alice's girlfriend in Detroit was Cindy Lang. She got around a bit.

Stirling Silver: Cindy and I were backstage someplace where there was hors d'oeuvres and crap like that. Alice wasn't there at that moment, and I made out with her, that was it. I had her phone number, and I was living in the basement at my parents' house. She gave me her number to the house on Brown Road. You know, I'd call and say, "Is Cindy there?" No matter who'd answer, I'd always go, "Is Cindy there?" Maybe Alice even answered, I don't know. And I'd talk to her. She was kind of flirty on the phone. I drove out there. Cindy was kind of the hostess of the house. That monkey must have masturbated a lot over Cindy Lang. That girl was so sexy.

Neal Smith: We had played at the Eastown or the Grande, and there was a party afterwards, and this was, again, one of the first times we had been to Detroit, early on. And we walked into the party, and I remember Cindy coming up and meeting everybody. Pretty much after that first night that they met Alice and Cindy were an item.

Jim Kosloskey: Cindy was very attractive, very nice. She had a reputation for liking guys in bands. One night I went out to the farm, typical party stuff. But I had been with her before and she was worried. She looked at me and said, "Don't say anything to me." She didn't want to make Alice jealous or something, you know. She was later trying to sue Alice for palimony because he never married her.

Patti Quatro: Cindy was just a piece of work. Is she still alive? She wanted to marry Alice—that girl was so after him. She was what I would call the old word, a gold digger. She wanted to do that with a rock star; she started hanging on to him.

Neal Smith: Yeah, Alice had Cindy, so we had somebody who lived at the house when we were gone. Then Glen had his girlfriend, this Canadian girl that was living with him, but it was off and on. I had a girlfriend there in Detroit for a period of time, but most of the time I was in Pontiac I was by myself. There were a lot of girls, and unfortunately, I had to go to the free clinic a lot of times. But back in those days you get a shot of penicillin and it would cure whatever was ailing you.

America's Only
Rock 'n' Roll Magazine

Dan Carlisle: I lived for a year in the *Creem* commune, this big house on Cass. After a year there I kept an apartment out and kept renting a place at the *Creem* house since it was convenient when I was working downtown. One of our roommates was the son of the governor, William Milliken. He was a heroin addict, and one day I woke up with a horrible hangover and my bedroom was right off the kitchen, and I walked in and sitting at the kitchen table was the governor, reading the riot act to his son. I thought, "How could this be?" I suppose to the governor we all looked like Satan.

Dave Marsh (*journalist, author,* Creem *magazine,* Rolling Stone): *Creem* evolved pretty quickly. A British guy named Tony Reay had a vision and Barry Kramer had a vision, and they started it.

Tony Reay (*cofounder,* Creem *magazine*): Jeep Holland had suggested to me that Russ [Gibb] might want someone to do PR for the Grande and that I might be able to parlay my current writing outlets with the *Fifth Estate* and the *Detroit News* into a viable PR company for Russ and the Hideout/Palladium axis of teen clubs as well as the other bookers of teen clubs and dances. So after some late night brainstorming, Jeep and I decided that what the area needed most was a calendar with comments, editorials, and maybe even a few ads to offset the costs. So we would mimeograph a small flyer with a calendar of local events for the upcoming week, maybe a few words about a particular club or band, maybe a small ad on the back to cover costs, and put a coupla hundred at each venue. And that was the beginning of *Creem*. I told Barry about it, and he laughed at me and said he had zero interest in such a thing.

Dave Marsh: I came along fairly early. I went to Kettering High School in Waterford. I wrote a little bit in high school about various things. I think I wrote about *Blonde on Blonde*. I had bad experiences in high school, and I had a bad home experience.

Tony Reay: Russ, always with his ear to the ground, heard of my idea and started to talk first to Jeep and then me about maybe getting financially involved and expanding the scope of the flyer/calendar. When I mentioned that to Barry, he suddenly got quite interested.

Robin Sommers: I used to drink at the Decantur Bar at Palmer and Cass, and next door was Mixed Media, this head shop. Barry Kramer had worked at a place down the block called Cambridge Book Stall, and Barry knew about head shops because he would travel around a lot. He'd been to England and Carnaby Street, and he had some friends with money and talked about opening a shop. So here it was—he opened Mixed Media. It was going to be called Live Poultry, but then they changed it to Mixed Media. They sold records, books, candles, papers, pipes. No bongs back then; it was a bongless period in our lives. Eventually someone brought in this incredible machine—it was a motorized pipe with two chambers and a pump that circulated the smoke; it was like $200. I worked at Ford for a while and I also worked at Mixed Media there when I had some spare time, and I was just hanging out. One afternoon I went in there and Barry had to go somewhere, and he asked me to sit at the register and sell stuff and talk to people. There were some people who were friends of Barry and this girl Edie Walker— her dad owned a jewelry store; they were rich folks. Her best friend was Gilda Radner, and she started to hang out with us a lot. We used to all hang out and smoke dope together. She was in her early twenties, and we had this chair with a ladder back with a rattan seat, and Barry would make her sit in it if she got too wound up.

Dave Marsh: I went to Wayne State for a few months, and in the middle of one of John Sinclair's trials they were needing some help in putting out *Fifth Estate*, the first nationally distributed issue, which also included a program to the Ann Arbor Blues and Jazz Festival. I agreed to help them out on that. By then I was living at the *Creem* house on Cass. Barry lived there; Charlie Auringer, John Angelos at some point. Danny Carlisle lived in the separate apartment downstairs.

Robin Sommers: Barry was the rich Jewish kid I would never had known unless I walked into a situation like that. Then Barry asked me, because I had done all the artwork for the Five, if I wanted to work for *Creem*. So I started working there, and we moved to this huge house on Cass. It was a business, with big open spaces to have writers come in with desks and big layout tables. And a practice room on the third floor, where Mitch's band, Detroit, practiced.

Dan Carlisle: Barry Kramer owned the *Creem* commune and Mixed Media, which was a hippie shop. Barry gave Tony Reay the money to do the magazine. You could see right away that Tony wanted to do a fanzine and Barry wanted something like *Rolling Stone*.

Robin Sommers: *Creem* was to be the alternative to this hokey magazine from California called *Rolling Stone*. It was about hard-core rock and roll rather than what was going down in California. It was the real deal about the music—that's what got Lester Bangs and these guys. It was no bullshit.

Dave Marsh: Tony wanted *Creem* to be more local than Barry did. I had a vision, but it was transplanted onto someone else's root stock.

Tony Reay: Something that gets lost in all the retelling is that Barry and I were good friends from the very first day we met. We had a lot in common, attitudinally. He was best man at my wedding, and we fought like an old married couple about damn near anything, but there was never, until the last few days, any real animosity between us. And after the smoke cleared we remained easy friends. He continued to steal my ideas even years later and admitted it readily to me. The only time we really battled during my *Creem* days were when he wouldn't pay R. Crumb the $50 he asked for the "Mr Dreemwhip" cover and only authorized $35. I paid Crumb the $50 anyway out of store petty cash, and Barry took the difference out of my pay.

Dan Carlisle: So Barry got rid of Tony because he owned it. I would write for *Creem* occasionally the first year. Then there was no need for me to be scribbling away; they got some real writers. Living there, I was a rock-and-roll DJ, and I could come home at night and there would be a party. Lester Bangs came along; he was different. You could sit down with Dave Marsh, who also lived at the *Creem* house, and while I didn't like all his ideas on music, we could have a genial conversation, something intellectual. With Lester, if I told Lester, "You are full of fucking shit," Lester would see that as a declaration of war. He was on a crusade twenty-four hours a day.

Dave Marsh: I was so ambitious. I could do what I said I could do. There was not lot of demand for credentials back then—it was so different from now. We got amazing access right away.

Mark Parenteau: I met Dave Marsh and thought, "This is the most cocky arrogant kid I've ever met."

Jaan Uhelszki: I knew *Creem* right from the first issue because they used to sell it right next to the bar at the Grande. So I would get them free. Tony Reay and I were friends, and I said to myself, "Well, I wanna write there," and he said, "Come on, just come on down." It took me some time before I was a writer. First I was the subscription girl.

Leni Sinclair: I never liked *Creem*—Lester Bangs and all those cynical people. I had a bad run in with Barry Kramer one time that really disappointed me. The Blues and Jazz Festival owed him some money for an ad they ran. And we didn't pay it, and when it came time for the next festival I was sent to the *Creem* office with the check for what we owed and a request for a picture of Ray Charles. I handed him the check and he said, "Just so you know what it feels like to be an asshole"—something like that—"I'm not going to give you the picture." I thought he was joking. When I realized he was serious, I just dashed out of there crying. Maybe he was crazy in the head at that moment from doing something or just vindictive, but later on he gave the picture to somebody, but not me. I don't know if he had anything against me personally. I mean, we used to hang out together and smoke DMT together at the house on Cass.

Dan Carlisle: I would sit in that office at *Creem*, and there would be ten hippies trying to do business with Barry. He would light up a joint and pass it around, and I would notice that he would never take a hit off it. So by the time they got to business everyone was blasted except Barry. He knew he was in a business of people who liked to be high and weren't really business oriented.

Dave Marsh: Barry wanted to be Jann Wenner, the publisher of every successful publication, an economic and mass-cultural success. I wasn't against any of that—in fact I was for it. But my way of executing it precluded it from happening. Barry wanted to be a marker, and there was a thing between *Creem* and *Rolling Stone*; we wanted to be as good as they were and they didn't know we existed. In our recreational time we made fun of *Rolling Stone*. I'm sure Lester and I sat around and made fun of *Rolling Stone* with James Taylor on the cover, but as far as we were concerned, that's what James Taylor had been born for. Even when I went to *Rolling Stone*, I felt like a fish out of water the whole time. I was a rock-and-roll guy from Detroit. I wanted to be respected, but didn't know how to be respectable.

Kim Fowley (*musical raconteur from Los Angeles*): Barry Kramer called me on the phone and declared me God. I said, "Do you have an album out called *Love Is Alive and Well* on Tower Records?" He said, "Yeah. I like some of it, but I hate some of it. But you seem interesting. When you show up on your promo tour, I will drive you around." So he meets me at the airport. And he said, "You have normal boring clothes. We gotta put you in some love-in stuff because you're doing Robin Seymour tonight." It was at CKLW Television. So I said, "Well, let's go somewhere." Dearborn, of all places, he took me to. And both of us were looking for what we thought would be love-in, hippie garb. So there was this bright thing, and I put it on. I didn't know that it was an Arab woman's outfit. So when I went on CKLW, there was a bunch of people from the Mideast who live in Detroit, suddenly they're watching TV, and here comes some white guy, who's like Ichabod Crane, bouncing around to a song called, "Funky Flower Flower Drum." So many people called up to complain that they blew out the switchboard. Linda Ronstadt was on the show that night with the Stone Poneys, and she fell in love with me that night. That was Barry Kramer. He helped me out.

Robin Sommers: Deday LaRene was this law instructor who had taught law in Detroit, and he came down and started writing for *Creem*. So we did an article on this new band called Black Sabbath. When they first came out they really were thought to be Devil worshippers. Between articles that were written in other magazines and doing some research, Deday wrote this article. Deday had written something like, "Fuck God in the ass." This whole devil thing was bugging him. But we couldn't get the magazine printed because the printer at that time was a kind of religious guy. He usually printed Catholic newsletters. So the printer wouldn't print it. They took the whole paragraph out and left it white space. It was too late when we saw it; we had to get this thing out and didn't have time to fix anything.

Jaan Uhelszki: I went to New York when I was fifteen because I wanted to be a writer. I didn't tell my parents; I just stuffed the pillows and took off. It was a bolt. I didn't go away to New York to get away from Detroit. I didn't go really at fifteen to think I was going to stay there. It was like, "Wow, let's go see New York. Let's go stay in the Village." This is *Eye* magazine come to life. I wanted to see what I was reading about, so it really was more like an unfettered vacation where I should have never, never been out on my own at that age, you know.

Dave Marsh: *Creem* moved to the country, this place called Walled Lake, out west of Detroit. It wasn't a great idea, this fuckin' farm. That's what was wrong with it.

Jaan Uhelszki: In Walled Lake we were in essence a commune. We all made $22.75 a week. They paid for our rent, they paid for our food, and we got our little stipend. We were not, you know, we were not living high on the hog. Barry Kramer lived with us, and I'm sure somehow he had a scheme. You can't forget that he was a rich kid. Everybody had stereos in their room, and then we had a common room. Barry's wife, Connie, usually cooked, so it really was hippyesque. It was a twenty-hour day often. We would all unwind by playing pinochle, you know. We functioned as a group; we would go to these shows together en masse. We'd go to wrestling matches.

Dave Marsh: We went to Olympia to see wrestling; sometimes we went to dinner. If there was the right local band playing, we'd go to that. Like, "I'm going to write about Alice Cooper. Who wants to come with me?"

Jaan Uhelszki: Lester Bangs and I started the same day. I think that always forged our friendship. I was going out with the art director, and Barry told me that he wanted me to work as the circulation manager, and that was the day that Lester came from California. You know I just remember that because I was so on cloud nine that Barry had hired me.

Lester wasn't anybody then. Nobody was anybody. The thing is we all started together, none of us had anything going. We all were like people inventing ourselves, inventing the art form.

Dave Marsh: Lester and I had fist fights. His dog shit all over, and I was tired of picking up after it. So the shit went in his typewriter, but it wasn't about the typewriter—it was more complicated than that. It was what precipitated one fist fight, but we had other encounters. We liked each other, but why would that stop us from fighting?

Mark Parenteau: We would go up into Lester's room, and he would bring a hand can opener, a bunch of Campbell's soup. He would bring a coil that you plugged into the wall and stuck into the can of soup so it would heat it up like you were in prison. He would bring a typewriter, a pound of paper, and he would wait until the very last two days before the issue had to go to bed, and then he would just pound it out. He would take a bunch of speed, he would stay up for two or three days, lock himself in that room, heat up a bunch of soup, and then come out and hand Ben Edmonds forty or fifty pages of typed stuff.

Jaan Uhelszki: Lester ghost wrote a piece for me for my journalism class because I had to write something and I didn't have time; I had something else to write. I decided to write that, and Lester did it for me 'cause I had no idea what I was doing. He wrote a piece about the wrestling matches that we had seen, and he got a B on it. He was a fast writer—much quicker than the rest of us.

Mark Parenteau: I'd go to parties with Lester because back then it was all limos, and the record companies couldn't kiss our ass enough. The *Creem* people and the WABX people lived and hung out together; it was kind of like a two-for-one for the likes of Larry Harris and all the national rep guys who would come into Detroit. They'd get not only the big rock station but the magazine and my wife, Gail, the promoter. So it was a very powerful situation. Lester was a part of that; he was unbelievable. They would have these great big dinners, you know. And everybody wanted to go to dinner. We'd go to Charlie's Crab or the Greektown, and Lester would start getting drunk and start throwing food. We're backstage at Ford Auditorium and Todd Rundgren was there and he had sold out the place, and you know he had all that exotic makeup on, skin-tight, air-brushed suits on and stuff. Backstage it was Lester's birthday, and they brought him this big huge birthday cake and everybody sang "Happy Birthday" to Lester, and immediately he just started grabbing fistfuls of the cake and started throwing it at everybody, including Todd Rundgren. It turned in to a free for all because Lester's stop-gap thing was broke. He didn't know when enough was enough. But he wasn't evil or anything; it was just like, "Wow, this guy is crazy, over the top." Lester was brilliant in perceiving rock and roll. We'd be listening to new albums, and he'd go, "You're not going to play that shit are you?" and he was very opinionated about what we should play and what we shouldn't play. Once in a while he was wrong, but not very often.

Ted Nugent: *Creem* became a showcase for Lester Bangs's stupidity. What he thought was hip and clever—you know, stream of consciousness—was basically stream of nonsense. That started off right away and from then on, I went, "Fuck these guys, man. They don't write anything down." It said in *Creem* magazine how I smoked hash with the MC5. I've never smoked hash. I was at the MC5's Hill Street house many times, and I knew they would put stuff like that in food, so I never ate the food. And I never smoked dope with them. But they wrote that I did. You think if I smoked dope with the MC5, I would try to hide it? I mean, what's there to hide? I was eighteen. I think one time I told them, I made up a story about how we'd go to a convent to ask directions to someplace, and put a slice in the map where we claimed we were headed to. And when the nun would point at it and give us directions, we'd stick our dicks through the slice in the map: never happened.

Dave Marsh: The classic moment a week before I left was when Nick Kent showed up. That nitwit. He and Lester were listening to *Metal Machine Music* at one end of the hall and I was listening to Al Green at the other end, and that was it. When you look at when I left, black music coverage was entirely eliminated. It became all white rock and roll.

"What Happens in Detroit Stays in Detroit"

Al Jacquez: There were bands playing around the city—Detroit bands—that you would see and say, "I can't see these guys again." Then again, when you are involved in a scene like that, you go see a band and you say, "Man, these guys are really good. I have to get my stuff together."

The whole scene in Michigan was ignored on purpose. I mean some in New York picked up on the Stooges and MC5 and that led to glam rock. I'm just thinking, "Okay, regardless of what you think of our music, you have this East Coast major publishing center with a history of great journalism. And on the West Coast you have *Rolling Stone*, and even if you think every band that's playing in Michigan is terrible, the fact of the matter is people are coming out by the tens of thousands to see these bands. How can you ignore this music?" Sometimes I felt people were wrapped up in the Five or the Stooges, which is cool, but there were other amazing things going on at the same time. When you look at what was going on at the time, the Five was part of a group of bands getting standing ovations and just this wild adulation. Detroit, the Detroit area, from Flint to Ann Arbor, was this machine.

Niagara: Detroit has a deadly desert around it. Jerry Vile told me, "What happens in Detroit stays in Detroit."

Wayne Kramer: One of the reasons that Detroit failed was because we didn't have a Bill Graham, somebody with that business acumen who could kind of market the movement.

Bobby Rigg: It was not just the music scene they were ignoring. They ignored Detroit. Which is the strangest thing because, all of these acts that were coming from Europe and wherever they were coming from, Detroit was their favorite place to play.

Bob Seger (*Bob Seger and the Silver Bullet Band, Bob Seger and the Last Heard, solo, vocalist*): I think those bands came and went because they just didn't have the stamina to go all the way. Either that or, in some cases, it was drugs. There's only three acts I can think of that really kept at it, kept pounding away. That was Glenn Frey, Ted Nugent, and myself. The others just burned themselves out. They had attitudes too. You just can't go out and piss people off and expect to be superstars. It just grinds people, and sooner or later it's gonna catch up with you. Like when I'd talk to the MC5, they were fine, real level headed and everything. But then when they went to a concert, they would just give a promoter a whole bunch of shit, and at times they'd even give the audience a whole bunch of shit. So you could just sorta see that it wouldn't last. Whereas Nugent would go out there and sweat, and so would I.

Toby Mamis (*manager, Alice Cooper, journalist,* Creem *magazine*): I don't think being from Detroit was a handicap at all. The scene there was great, and it was healthy circuit of places to play. I think the bands all got their fair shot, just with varying degree of success.

Rick Kraniak: The problem was that no one respected Detroit. You had five national ballrooms, four national promoters. Bill Graham on both coasts with the Fillmore. You had Electric Factory Concerts with Larry Magid in Philadelphia. You had Don Law in Boston; Howard Stein doing New York, Atlanta, Miami; and no one had any respect for these Detroit bands.

Donny Hartman: The Frost opened for B. B. King for three nights at the Fillmore in San Francisco. We got three standing ovations. We're all excited, and we go into Bill Graham's big office at the end of the night. Graham looks at us and he goes, "Well, boys. You know I hate Michigan bands. I hate 'em. I don't like you guys, either. I don't like the music you play."

Rick Kraniak: It was like an attitude: "They didn't come from England, they weren't represented by Premier Talent," who had Ten Years After, Jethro Tull, and so on. So it was really hard to get Michigan bands booked. The MC5 did a gig in

New York—it didn't go well for Graham, as I recall—and so it was really, really difficult.

Dennis Dunaway: We followed the Stooges a couple of times at the Fillmore West. We took Detroit to the land of the hippies, and Bill Graham hated us. He thought we had ruined everything. We finally got big enough that he had to hire us.

Tom Weschler (*photographer, Bob Seger road manager*): If you think about how many records are sold by artists out of Detroit, it isn't even close. You can tie New York, LA, every place else together, and it ain't even close. Everyone is hard tilt.

Dan Carlisle: One of the things about the MC5 that people didn't understand is that MC5 was laughed at out there by the radio community outside Detroit. That group of people was very elitist, and I worked at some of these places; KLOS, places in San Francisco, and I would play MC5 and receive hell for it. They didn't understand that if you couldn't play the MC5, the Stooges, and Elvis at the same time, then you weren't a rock-and-roll radio station. When MC5 came out they wore sequins and big flashy clothes; they didn't wear jeans and T-shirts. They would tell me they weren't a hippy band; CCR was a hippy band. Every band out of Detroit had a shot. SRC, for example, made it as far as they could. I think that their manager, Pete Andrews, was very hard working and did what he could for them. He got them on Capitol, and they toured and didn't make it, simple as that. I understand why Iggy and the Stooges made it and others didn't: they never sat down and said, "We're going to be forerunners of a new sound." They were something else; they were world beaters.

Iggy Pop: What we were, we were just so special, we were just so out there that at some point you could see jaws drop, and you could see the thought bubble go, "Oh my God," and people would just walk away.

Dick Wagner (*The Frost, Lou Reed, Alice Cooper, guitarist*): The Frost never made it really big and we should have. We got to tour quite a bit, but our label was just trying to put records in the Detroit stores, and we sold fifty thousand in the first month the first album came out. We could have sold it all over the US. We were making it happen, but never got the right support. Even the covers to our albums were terrible.

Bobby Rigg: The reason the Frost never became huge was because we signed with the wrong record company. Vanguard had no idea what to do with a rock-and-roll band.

Donny Hartman: We were touring out west, and we found our first album in a wastebasket at one radio station in California. The DJ said, "I didn't think you guys were coming in. Nobody ever called and told us."

Michael Lutz: We always said we were an Ann Arbor band. You know, Ann Arbor rings a bell for a lot of people because of the University of Michigan.

Mark Farner (*Grand Funk Railroad, guitarist, vocalist*): People in Michigan hardly knew about us. We were more apt to be recognized in St. Louis or Atlanta, Georgia, or, you know, Miami or Dallas. That was all definitely directed by Terry Knight. We loved playing Detroit. We played the Eastown, you know. Are you shitting me? That was dreams come true.

Don Brewer (*Grand Funk Railroad, Bob Seger and the Silver Bullet Band, drummer*): Well, we'd been kinda outside the Detroit loop. It was kinda like . . . they were rock snobs. Oh, they're just that band from Flint. We were being written off. It hurt. We definitely felt like we were on the outside, and we really didn't play in Detroit that much.

Peter Cavanaugh: Thing was, Grand Funk would play around here, and it was not such a big deal because everybody knew them. Terry Knight was one of the best bullshitters I ever ran into. He had been a DJ at WTAC, then went to Detroit for a bit, then went to New York to work for Ed McMahon of *Tonight Show* fame, then came back here. Grand Funk was rehearsing at the IMA Auditorium in Flint, which I'm sure Terry arranged—it was a big stage. He lined those guys up and said, "I want all of you to play like your assholes are on fire." He wanted motion on that stage.

Dave Marsh: Terry did not bother us at *Creem*; we weren't on Terry Knight's radar. He was seeking bigger game than that. He cared what CKLW thought, not what *Creem* thought.

Ray Goodman: Actually we, SRC, were signed to Capitol before Grand Funk. I was at those meetings in LA. We walked out of there thinking we had got a deal with a billboard in every major college market in America, when in fact we got one in Ann Arbor. And Grand Funk got the deal. Terry Knight went in there, and he was a little more gung ho, and he could negotiate a little bit better I guess.

Mark Parenteau: Terry Knight had pretty much conceived Grand Funk, sort of like Kiss was later conceived. Like, it was like an image first, and let's go ahead and put together a band that conforms to this. And Grand Funk was huge, huger than huge.

Don Brewer: Terry really knew how to stretch the truth and make everything bigger and louder than real, and so forth and so on. He really was a Barnum & Bailey kinda guy. But we had starved with Terry too in the Pack. We were so broke Mark and I made a Butterfinger commercial. Farner and I were playing at a club in Cleveland, and some guy from Chicago that knew our manager called and said, "I need a couple of singers," so they flew us down there at six in the morning. We go into the studio at nine o'clock, and they said, "Here, sing this," and it turned into a Butterfinger candy bar commercial that ran for years.

Mark Farner: As soon as we signed with our management team, they were able to get us an opening slot at the Atlanta Pop Festival in 1969. We borrowed a van from Jeep Holland and you know, in Ann Arbor, and he got us a guy to drive. We rented a U-Haul, and off to Atlanta we went. About half way down there—this was long before I-75 was finished and so we were taking a back road to connect to it and I was riding shotgun. I was napping and I woke up and I see this sign, I-75 to the right. I said, "Dude, I-75's that way." He turns this van with the U-Haul on the back and rolls the U-Haul trailer down through the ditch. After we turned the trailer back up on its two wheels, we were kind of limping it on the side of the expressway to the next exit that had U-Haul trailers, and we were going to turn it in there. Then a tire came off the trailer—it actually went flying by, the tire, and passed us and bounced over in the median and over the top of this semitruck— and we thought it was going to go right through the wind shield but it didn't. We're going, "Oh shit! Oh shit!" and sparks are flying off our trailer.

Don Brewer: But we made it and got on to the festival, this unknown band. The audience just went batshit for this band that nobody'd ever heard of, and that was really the starting point for Grand Funk. We didn't have a record deal, we didn't have gigs, we didn't have anything. They invited us back the next day; they put us at a later time slot. And again the audience went nuts, again. They brought us back the third day, put us on—again, a better time slot—and so from there the word of mouth went all through the south.

Mark Farner: They introduced us as "Grand Frank Railway." The guy never did get it right that weekend. But we got on the Led Zeppelin tour in the fall. But it didn't go very good after the . . . at Olympia in Detroit.

Dave West (*West Laboratories, amplifier developer*): I saw Grand Funk open for Led Zeppelin in October 1969, and they tore the place apart. I mean the fans were going crazy, standing the whole time, every song into the next. About halfway through, the manager for Led Zeppelin, Richard Cole, and a couple of Zeppelin roadies came around to Terry Knight and told him they had to come off now. And Knight refused. So they went over to where all the sound equipment was plugged in—this was pretty small PAs and stuff back then—and unplugged the whole thing. All of a sudden Grand Funk was standing there just holding their instruments.

Mark Farner: Their manager, Peter Grant, came out and grabbed Terry Knight, and Terry thought he was going to kill him. So he told him to shut the band down or he was going to. Terry was just going, "A-a-a-baha . . . ," and their manager shut down all the PA systems. They didn't go on for an hour and a half after we got off. Half the people left. They didn't want us on the tour anymore because we stole the show from them.

Rick Kraniak: The only Grand Funk track that even got played early on in Detroit was "Time Machine"—kind of a I-IV-V progression, you know, blues rock, and other than that, they didn't even get played in Detroit. They were getting really big nationally, though. Detroit ignored them.

Jim Atherton (*manager, Terry Knight and the Pack*): I was working with Mountain about a year after Grand Funk began to take off in 1969. I sold amps, and you know we were out there doing the thing with the Mountain, and at the time they were having this big hit with "Mississippi Queen," first half of 1970. We were in their offices in New York, and they were telling about how they were going to Memphis and they were gonna be opening for Grand Funk and they were just gonna kick Grand Funk's ass—ya ta da ta da. They were going on and on with me about that and I was like, "Well, guys, let me know how that works out, will ya?" Just on volume alone, Grand Funk would prevail.

Mark Farner: I always wanted to create this atmosphere where the only thing going was the music. That's why it was important to play really loud. I don't want people talking while we're playing.

Dave West: I sold Mark his amps, amps that I made, West Amps. Mel used them too for a while. Mark did endorsements for me. And when they got really huge, they were flying all over, and they would come into the little airport near where I lived, in Lansing, Michigan. Send a couple guys on a private plane just to pick up sixteen JBL speakers, amps and some parts.

Don Brewer: Once we got a record deal with Capitol Records, and once the first record, *On Time*, broke, we were immediately in limousines, and actually we got into chartering airplanes, and all that kind of stuff.

Dave West: Money was no object—they had really made it. Farner used to have this set up, these amp heads were placed fairly close together, and he'd have a couple guys in the crew sit on a stool next to the amps during the live shows. Mark really cranked it up, and he would overload the tubes to get the sound he wanted. These were British made, $12 apiece. So the road crew guys are up there with asbestos gloves and, in a rack beside them, had these tubes. And when a tube would flame, they would quick grab it and put another in, just like that. They'd be almost on fire. They also changed all sixteen output tubes before each gig. $12 apiece, $200 overall—no big deal to them.

Mark Farner: Terry would tell them to throw the tubes out after every show and put matched pairs, brand-new matched pairs in. And they're, you know, for a matched pair it was a couple hundred dollars. These guys are going, "Are you crazy? We can't throw these things away." And it was our money.

Don Brewer: We eventually found out we had been completely ripped off by Terry Knight. He brought us into New York, and he got a couple of his attorneys, and they had us sign these agreements that were totally in their favor—and this was back in the day[s] of hippies and brothers and everybody loving each other, and nobody's gonna rip anybody off, and so forth and so on.

Dave Knapp (*Terry Knight's brother*): Remember that these guys were treated like kings everywhere and they went everywhere, and they were just kids—twenty, twenty-one years old. They didn't know how to handle money.

Don Brewer: This deal was where Terry was getting all of the money, and we were basically making a paycheck. That's what ended our relationship with Terry.

Mark Farner: We were paid $350 a week, man, and we thought we were big time, dude. You know from what we were making, we were big time. That was a lot of money. But we had no clue as to the amount of money we were actually making. That was all kept from us. We eventually got past it, but it was nasty.

Don Brewer: When we recorded *We're an American Band* Todd Rundgren produced it and he stayed at my apartment, the Knollwood Apartments in Grand Blanc. We'd pull into a 7-Eleven to get some milk or something, and he'd come in with me. I had the big afro and he had the multicolored hair, and we'd walk into these places, and jaws would just drop to the floor—"What the fuck is this?" C'mon, this was in Flint, Michigan. But I don't know if that would have made it in Detroit, either.

Mark Farner: Frank Zappa came to Michigan to produce us, but he stayed in Hartland, closer to Ann Arbor, not with us. When he got there—you know he came from Los Angeles of course—and he wanted to come and visit the area and see how we worked. But not Flint. He said the thing that he liked the most about us right off was when Craig Frost backed up against Brewer's leg and farted on it. He said, "Any band that farts on each other is alright by me."

Don Brewer: Frank Zappa never really made it all the way to Flint, just to our studio in Parshallville. He stayed in Ann Arbor. He'd go out to the club in Ann Arbor every night, try to pick up chicks. He'd walk in, and obviously everybody knew who he was. He'd always carry coffee with him and smoke cigarettes like crazy. Always. Always had coffee with him. In a thermos.

In Detroit, Woodstock Was the Weak Shit

Tom Wright (*photographer, manager, Grande Ballroom*): We were having this festival at the Michigan Fairgrounds in May 1969. There was the MC5, the Stooges, the James Gang, and the Frost, among others. Some kids brought flyers for Woodstock and were passing them out. This was Detroit. Everyone was laughing at them. Joan Baez? It certainly wasn't up to Detroit standards for rock and roll.

Michael Quatro (*promoter, keyboardist, Michael Quatro Jam Band*): In July 1969 Michael Lang and one of his partners were preparing to get Woodstock together the next month. I told them how to do it, and they didn't pay attention. I had this great bill over in Saugatuck—Procol Harum, MC5, Muddy Waters, Amboy Dukes, Brownsville Station, the Stooges—and it was the Fourth of July weekend. I told Lang and his partner to get their advance ticket sales together because they told me they wouldn't be able to keep up the barriers at night—anyone would just walk in free. I had sixty thousand paid admissions from eight cities at my show from as far east as Pittsburgh. And my cost to get the whole thing going was $5,000. And come Friday, all the gates fell down, and everyone could walk in free. But it was okay; I already had made my money. Lang didn't get that. I told him to get advance ticket sales up. He could have saved himself a lot of money if he had listened to me.

Mitch Ryder: When you look at Woodstock, you gotta look at the whole picture: the way that the cultural fucking fascist leaders tried to turn that into something bigger than what it was for their own selfish purposes. They wanted to be able to define what was hip, and Woodstock was going to be the vehicle that would tell them that was hip.

Michael Quatro: The next year I did the Cincinnati Pop Festival. That was the first nationally televised rock concert, and I had a great bill—a bunch of Detroit bands. And we paid. Terry Knight called me in January 1970 and wanted to get Grand Funk on a Joe Cocker bill. At Cincinnati Gardens, as it were; I called up Cocker and Dee Anthony and they just couldn't make it happen. So I called Terry back, and he knew I had a lot of pull, so when I said I can't book Grand Funk, you know, I used every favor and couldn't get them on the Joe Cocker show, Terry thought that I had just let it go. So Terry was pissed. Now it gets to be May 1970, and Grand Funk is number one in the country, and I need Grand Funk for Midsummer Rock, the Cincinnati Pop Festival. I called Terry and he said, "Well, we're up to $10,000 a night and were number one." I said, "I'll take them," and he said, "No, for you, it's $20,000." He doubled the price. Hell, yes I took them.

Bob Heath (*producer, WLW Cincinnati*): Michael Quatro brought this idea to me; I had been part of that Joe Cocker show—which Cocker didn't show up for, by the way—and he wanted to have it taped for TV on WLW and also broadcast in stereo on the radio when it was played. So the idea was we would tape the concert, then edit it, then distribute it through syndication later in the year. Which is what happened.

Bill Spiegel (*producer, WLW Cincinnati*): The day before the show and I was asking around for the contracts, this guy from New York had come in and told us he would handle all that. He didn't. So we had to move around quick to get these contracts signed. Some of the bands didn't want to be taped.

Bob Heath: Back then they had guys who were your consultants. This guy Mike Goldstein from New York, he would tell Marriott Hotels how to reach the youth market because that was a really foreign thing to most companies. He came to Avco, which owned WLW. The big fear was that because Cincinnati is this conservative town people would fall apart. So the protection is they put Jack Lescoulie, who used to host the *Today Show* on NBC in the fifties and sixties, in the broadcast booth. It was like bringing out Walter Cronkite to narrate a rock show with people smoking dope and having fun.

Tom Copi (*photographer*): I came down to Cincinnati from Ann Arbor with my brother-in-law, who had a canteen with acid water. It rained like hell the night before the show, a really soaking rain, and they didn't want to let anyone on the field. It was held at Crosley Field, a baseball stadium. The stage was at second base, but of course, as soon as it started, everyone ran onto the field.

Tom Weschler: The crowd was cool except for when they wouldn't let them on the grass.

Tom Copi: I took that shot of Iggy walking on hands from the apron of the stage. We had great access.

Iggy Pop: In Cincinnati we just sounded fucking bad. Imagine if someone got a hold of a copy of *Fun House* and turned the bass off—it just doesn't make it.

Tom Copi: I got that shot, then someone handed Iggy the peanut butter that he smeared all over himself and on the crowd. When Iggy came offstage, he had the peanut butter all over his hands, and there was a local DJ standing onstage near the edge, wearing a powder-blue silk shirt. Iggy just wiped the rest of the peanut butter on his shirt. The guy was laughing, but you know he wasn't happy.

Neal Smith: I was under the blanket on "Black Juju," and the TV camera's right on my face—I'm blowing kisses to it. Stations in the Midwest turned the station off. They went to black because they said, "This is too outrageous." It was immediately censored once they saw me winking and blowing kisses for the camera with my makeup on and everything. They freaked out. There were a bunch of stations in the Bible Belt that just, boom, pulled the plug on it.

Bill Spiegel: I think WNEW and WOR picked up the show, but very few stations carried it. There was nothing really outrageous about it, but people hadn't seen rock and roll on television in prime time before. For a reason.

Tom Weschler: Seger was on that bill in Cincinnati; he was still living in Ann Arbor. Mike and Russ Gibb put it on. We got to the airport; we were gonna fly the band down there. The roadies were already there with the equipment. And we got to the airport, and no Bob. Punch goes, "Gimme the keys to your car." I went [sighs], "Oh gosh." That's all I needed was a mad Punch Andrews driving my gorgeous Ford. I had this big, fat LTD. My dad worked for Ford, so he gives me this

LTD to use. Punch was a crazy driver. He takes the car, drives up to Ann Arbor, takes a later plane, you know he had to pound on the door to wake Bob up. He sleeps like a baby. So Punch woke him up, got him down there. My car survived, left at the airport with no gas.

Bob Heath: There are video tapes of many of the bands. We taped Bob Seger that day. We had to take breaks, and it was fifteen hours of music, so some bands we didn't get. But we got a lot of them. We also got some shots of the police going after kids when the show let out. The cops called us and wanted to see the tapes of after the show in case there were officers who got too aggressive. We got a subpoena to deliver those tapes. There was one that I saw where a cop hit kids with a billy club when he thought they weren't moving fast enough.

Tom Wright: A couple months later we did Goose Lake. A guy named Richard Songer wanted to do a festival in Michigan that same summer. He got hold of Russ [Gibb] to get the acts. Songer had no clue and no experience in that and Russ was booking not only the Grande but he was getting bands into Cobo and other places—the Doors, Hendrix, and national acts like that.

Russ Gibb: Goose Lake was the biggest deal. Before we even did, it we go up to the capitol in Lansing and meet with Governor Milliken and his chief of police, and we told them what we were going to do. We said, "We suspect there will be dope there. How do you want us to handle that?" So they mulled it around, and we sat there for four or five hours in that meeting. They said, "Well, tell you what: we won't arrest anybody in the park because that might cause a riot, but we want seventy undercover cops there."

We were giving the ticket holders chips we bought from Las Vegas. Yeah, you got a chip with a special emblem on it. That's how you could get in. We gave seventy of them to the state and that was it. And they said, "Don't do anything, let it go. We'll take pictures, and we'll get them on the way out." That was their theory. So we did that.

Don Was: The curious thing about that was Goose Lake had happened, and really people now think it was Detroit's Woodstock.

Letter to Editor, *Detroit Free Press,* **August 7, 1970:** I am a concerned citizen interested in the welfare of our younger generation and highly alarmed about the effects of the recent wave of so-called pop concerts. . . . [Goose Lake] will provide an opportunity to be free of social restraints for three days and will set the stage for orgiastic revelries, including the use of dope. No thinking person can question the adverse effect this has on the moral fiber of young people.

Mitch Ryder: I was supposed to be there for one day, but I dropped some acid, and I ended up being there for three days, and I slept in Teegarden & Van Winkle's trailer. I performed with two different groups and I was just trippin'.

Tom Wright: So it gets going, and Songer had an army of guys working for him and all the equipment needed to build a city. That was Goose Lake. We had asphalt parking for thirty-five thousand cars with yellow stripes. There was no chaos on the roads. The sound and light towers were built of bridge steel. You could have hit them with a missile and not taken them down.

Russ Gibb: Songer and his brother were starting to build expressways. They would tear away an old highway and they would haul it away. Before long they had two trucks, then they had five trucks, then they had twenty trucks, then he started to build. They used those trucks to build this whole village at Goose Lake.

Tom Wright: We went to the rotating stage after I learned at the Grande that if you want problems, just screw up the music. That's when they break urinals and windows, and so we just couldn't allow the music not to go on. Everybody got forty-five minutes to play, even if it was Mountain—they had forty-five minutes and that was it. It meant that was the best music they had. You couldn't even take a leak; you would go to the john and miss something.

Russ Gibb: The stage was the sole genius of Tom Wright. They were gonna put up a regular stage, and Tom said, "No, no. I want it to turn because I want to keep music playing. You'll have one band set up and as soon as they're over, spin that fucker." Before the first day was over the newspapers were loaded with "dope festival" because there they were smoking and selling and you name it.

Jackson Patriot, **August 9, 1970:** Youth, their spirits drug-broken, lie in the billowing hospital tents, some surrounded by friends talking them back to reality. One group, led by a guitar, sings softly to their fallen comrade.

Pete Trappen (*fan*): It was like Woodstock; there were booths selling hashish, mescaline, peyote, LSD. I was high on some mescaline and met a girl, and we wormed way up to the stage when Mountain was playing. I was twenty feet away from the stage. Security was a joke, and someone jumped up on stage with what looked to me like a knife. Felix Pappalardi saw this, took his bass, hit the guy. Everyone saw this, but the band kept playing. I'm not sure to this day if it was part of the show, but another split-second, and Leslie West would have been bleeding.

Michael Lutz: During our set a guy fell off the light tower. He was so stoned, nothing happened to him. We played on Friday afternoon and had to leave right after to drive to Kansas City for a show the next night.

Dan Carlisle: We covered Goose Lake from top to bottom. I went out to Goose Lake, and it was dirty and crowded and full of speed freaks. It is in the eye of the beholder, those things. Maybe someone who went out and got laid and got some good food had a good time—it all depends on who you ask. I was backstage and I looked at it for a brief time and thought, "If this is what it was coming to, then we have to stop it." But it was very successful, and everyone went.

Al Jacquez: *Rolling Stone* gave Goose Lake two paragraphs. There were all of these great bands. I mean this goes down and no one pays attention. People were not that far away from the stage as most festivals. They had a manually operated circular stage set up on the back half, and then guys pushed it and you would come around, then there was no time between acts. We went out there in the dark and then, wham, lights.

Don Was: *Rolling Stone*, because they couldn't get in to Goose Lake because they wouldn't give comp passes to them, they went to Newport Jazz Festival. You can go back in the archives and you can see the extensive wonderful coverage of the Newport Jazz Festival, but nothing about Goose Lake.

Tom Wright: *Rolling Stone* magazine had a lot of people there, like a gaggle of people who claimed they were from *Rolling Stone*. We didn't care if they were from *Time* magazine; they showed up at the last minute and were ready to camp out and be underfoot of all things going on backstage. That wasn't going to happen.

Russ Gibb: The cops came in and jammed up traffic. After the first day the newspapers were calling it a drug festival. And guess who started to act like they didn't know anything about it? Yeah, the state police and the governor. I said, "Wait a minute!" And I called our liaison to the governor and I go, "What the fuck is going on!?" The cops had planned this, to bust people, all along.

Dick Wagner: I met Steve Hunter for the first time at Goose Lake. He was playing with Mitch Ryder.

Ray Goodman: He may have met Steve there, but I played with Mitch Ryder and Detroit that day. Great show, and we left early for some reason, just as James Gang were going on, which pissed me off.

Dick Wagner: Steve and I met later on in Florida, when I was in Ursa Major and he was on the bill playing with a later version of the Chambers Brothers. So we had both of us there with that heavy Detroit guitar attitude, and we jammed for two hours together. It was incredible. Through Ursa, I worked with Bob Ezrin.

Bob Ezrin: Lou Reed knew who Steve was because of Detroit's cover of "Rock 'n' Roll." When I did that album, we got both Dick and Steve in there, and I kept using them.

Dick Wagner: We did the *Rock 'n' Roll Animal* tour with Lou Reed. He was sullen and unhappy, but he liked the way I played. I think he thought I was a quaint Midwesterner and wasn't hip, but it didn't matter to me. He was a mess at the time, but he wasn't difficult to work with at all.

He eventually got jealous of the attention Steve and I were getting. We played Detroit, and people were shouting out our names more than they were his. Detroit supports its own, you know.

"We Weren't Musicians, We Were Like an Outlaw Bike Club"

Mitch Ryder: To start the band Detroit, I think somebody just fucking opened the prison doors. It was scarier than true. It kinda put a lot of people, you know, on edge because that was the peace and love generation. It's who we were trying to target. You can tell the energy was there on the music, but that group frightened people. And we had so many different people in and out of that band.

Ray Goodman: I joined up what became Detroit in early 1970. Johnny Badanjek had brought me back into it, and he was good to be with. They were supposed to be the Detroit Wheels, but pretty soon Barry Kramer, who was managing, started calling it Detroit with Mitch Ryder. There were major issues, most of which revolved around money. There was quite a bit being generated and very little going towards Mitch. I don't know if he was suing Bob Crewe or not. I know that Mitch was having trouble paying bills, therefore he couldn't keep the band together and stay on the road. It ended very badly, with Barry Kramer actually keeping my equipment because of advances I'd gotten. They were making money hand over fist. It was criminal. I think I was getting $25 a show. Maybe it was $50. You know, at the time, the music was more important than the business end. You kinda took what you could get.

Johnny Badanjek: Mitch was in bad shape, really bad shape by that time. He had that big band, and guys were booking rooms and skipping out of the rooms and they left him with a huge amount of debt. He owed the musicians union $3,000 for not paying dues. So Barry Kramer had to straighten his whole life out. Barry went to the tax people and said, "Listen, he's not going to pay. You're going to get this much and be happy." And they said yes. To the musicians union, Barry said, "I'm going to pay you this much." He settled a lot of accounts and got Mitch out of the doldrums.

Robert Matheu: Barry was a badass at times. I heard stories from Ric Siegel about him jumping on record companies' presidents desks in New York with his cowboy boots to get Mitch Ryder out of those contracts.

Ray Goodman: We practiced at the *Creem* house on Cass. Third floor, open space. Then we began touring all over the place in a 1967 Cadillac limo.

Johnny Badanjek: After our first gig, Barry said, "I'm going to rename this band Detroit and we'll say featuring Mitch Ryder." We didn't really want to go back to the Mitch Ryder, Detroit Wheels whole thing.

Ray Goodman: We drove out to the Northwest and toured Oregon, Washington State, Vancouver. We followed the Mad Dogs and Englishmen tour all the way from Milwaukee; they played the night before us everywhere it seemed. It was a Holiday Inn Tour.

Mitch Ryder: You know how you have these balconies on the outside of the Holiday Inns and other hotels, like three feet in between them, where you could drop fourteen, forty floors to the ground? Well, yeah, but this one in Vancouver had no wall in between. It was just balconies outside. So there was this underage girl—I think she was fourteen—and she was in one room, and her father tracked her down and came with the cops, the Vancouver police. And so they knew the girl was in that room. So while they're banging on the door, trying to get in, she takes this leap from one balcony, over three feet of clear air, onto the next balcony, to be in the next guy's room so he could get her out of there and he wouldn't get caught with her.

Ray Goodman: Times were so innocent they put it on the marquee, "Welcome Mitch Ryder." They didn't realize the craziness that could attract.

Mitch Ryder: One night I was hungry, and one of the guys goes down and fucking breaks into the kitchen of the Holiday Inn and cooks me breakfast at 3:00 in the morning. There was so much shit on these tours with the Detroit band. We were playing this park somewhere; they were trying to make it available to homeless people. We played a concert to support the effort. A three-year-old kid comes up to me and says, "My dad said to give you this." It was a little tab of acid. So I dropped that, and his dad introduced himself to me as a guru. Okay. And I ended up in the woods for three days with this guy and his wife. I think I was in the woods, and I think it was three days. I came back down finally and I'm in the hotel, and they're still with me and they crash on the bed. I'm sleeping on the floor, and one of my band members comes in, one of the more aggressive ones, and he says, "Willie,"— he used to call me Willie—"what the fuck are you doing down there? What's this fucking mother fucker doing on your bed?" And I said, "That's the guru." He says, "Your guru?" and he pulls out his hunting knife, and the guy's naked on the top of my bed. He puts his hunting knife and stabs it into the fucking mattress, right below the guy's balls, and rips a fucking line down the mattress. He picks up the knife again and holds it up and says, "Get the fuck out of here." And so these two naked, fucking, hippie guru, spiritual people flee the room. He looked at me and said, "Get on your bed. You're embarrassing me."

Ray Goodman: We got back after that tour and played Goose Lake, and I quit. I was so burned out. Some others left as well. It had been a really rough time.

Ron Cooke: At one point just before I joined Mitch, me and Dallas Hodge were playing in a three-piece band, getting gigs around town. We were staying at the Hotel Le Buick up on 8-Mile Road. It was a '48 Buick behind Lefty's bar. That's how broke we were. We'd go to a gig, and these cats would go, "Where you guys staying?" We'd go, "Oh, we're at the Hotel Le Buick." Then after that the Catfish band started, and I got a call from Barry Kramer. He asked me if I wanted a gig. I said, "I don't know. Maybe, maybe not." So Ryder got on the phone: "What the hell you mean you don't want to play in my band?" I said, "Maybe I don't want to." I took the gig.

Johnny Badanjek: We got Steve Hunter in, and we got rid of some of the bad elements. Ray was cool. But there were some bad elements we had problems with. Some of them were doing bad drugs and stuff, and people were coming after them.

Mitch Ryder: We found Steve Hunter, actually down living on the farm with his fucking family in Decatur, Illinois. Somebody had told us about him, and basically he was just doing gigs playing to corn. We said, "Hey, we can up that. We can have you play to popcorn!" So he said, "Wow, I'm really excited."

Dave Marsh: Everybody had been on the telephone when they found Hunter in Illinois. They were like, "We found the next Hendrix, the next Duane Allman." They were calling from there, saying, "Wait till you hear this guy we found. We're bringing him home."

Mitch Ryder: He was so innocent. If you wanted to terrify yourself, you had to try to put yourself in the frame of mind of a country boy, witnessing what he witnessed, for the first time. I'm surprised his hair didn't turn gray immediately. It was just a culture shock for him. But, you know, what he did, which I really admire about him, he had done so much wood shedding that, in times of trial and stress, he would go to his guitar for safety, security, and comfort.

Bob Ezrin: The Mitch Ryder band played in Decatur, Illinois, and Steve Hunter was part of the opening act. They invited him up on stage to jam, fell in love with him, and as those guys would do, they would just collect people along the way, throw them into the hearse along with the rest of the band. So they threw him into the hearse with the rest of the band, and he just kept going until they got back to Detroit. One day I showed up for rehearsal and there was a new guy. He looked a little like a drowned rat—was just standing in the corner with stringy hair and coke-bottle glasses and a nice-looking little SG and a small Crate amp, quietly playing away, but doing some really quite remarkable stuff. But it was so quiet and polite. He was just trying not to get in anybody's way; he didn't want to be too loud. He was very, very shy—painfully shy. So we took a break on the first day. I took every amplifier in the room and strapped them all together, and I plugged it into that and told him to play Hendrix. It was louder than most of the music we had been hearing for the morning rehearsal. It was so loud—oh my God, it was so loud. So he strapped into this thing and started playing. He felt like God. He felt like Thor—you know, the God of Thunder—and just started to wail, showing off. Everybody in the building, from all three floors, came running upstairs to the rehearsal area to see who this was, and he was just amazingly good. I think that was a pivotal moment for him. Something exploded in his brain; then he went from being apologetic to believing that he could be a rock star. That really brought him out of his shell and into the place he belonged, which was on a stage, showing off, playing amazing guitar.

Mitch Ryder: He practiced and practiced and practiced, and avoided the gun fights, avoided the fist fights, avoided everything that the band was involved in—the drugs and everything else—and just play and play and play and play. He made it through.

Ron Cooke: Steve wasn't a party animal. The rest of us were just wild dogs. You had to be tough to be in that band. That band was a rolling circus, man.

Dave Marsh: Bob Ezrin had made hit records at the time; he was a real professional, and he was a guy who knew how to make records and clearly how to make hit records because he had made one with Alice Cooper, "I'm Eighteen." It was an important record. That's why he was there and he was also not coming from the street; he was not very blue collar. He was the first professional record producer I ever knew. Mitch and I were playing games, Barry and Mitch were playing games, and everyone was gaming everyone. It was a boisterous boys club, and then Bob walks in as a professional.

Mitch Ryder: *Creem* had some sway, and Barry was a good businessman and was able to sell it to Ezrin. He hadn't had any deep belief in the group Detroit, because Ezrin had been doing Alice Cooper. He was used to that kind of thing, but he wasn't used to the power that we had. He was not hands on because he was too intimidated. He was still a kid.

Bob Ezrin: To do the Berlin album with Lou Reed, Lou's manager called me and asked if I would be interested in working with Lou. The reason was because they'd heard the Detroit version of "Rock 'n' Roll," which they thought was the best cover of that song ever. He surely knew who Steve Hunter was because he knew the cover of Detroit doing "Rock 'n' Roll," and he loved it.

Dan Carlisle: It was a good time for Mitch; it was a time he really could have caught on again.

Dave Marsh: Mitch, like any great singer, needed great material, and he wrote something he was doing, "I Found a Love" and the Lou Reed song "Rock 'n' Roll," so he had the material.

Mitch Ryder: There are two different bass players on the Detroit album: John Sauter and Ron Cooke. That reflects the changes that occurred in the band while we were trying to record it. People were hurting people—physically, emotionally, financially. It was a high-turnover situation. The only constant there was the singer and the drummer, Johnny Badanjek.

Ron Cooke: I like to call Johnny the union steward on that job. He ran the band, you know. He drove most of the time—that limo was badass. Yeah, we used to have to damn near threaten to kill him to pull him over to take a leak. We'd go six hundred fucking miles like that.

Mitch Ryder: And the air conditioner didn't work. But I didn't want to lose my style. We would sit there, fucking dressed up with shades and fucking hats on and leather jackets, and it would be like 110 inside it. There would be puddles of water on our seats, but we were in the limousine.

Johnny Badanjek: The problem with those guys was they were always drinking. These guys are out of their minds. And of course after the gig they're drinking beer, and you would never get anywhere. They wanted to stop. They would beg me. They would beg me, "Please, please. I gotta pee. I gotta pee." And I'd pass the rest area up.

Ron Cooke: We were working two hundred nights a year. We came home to Detroit to have fun and relax. Stay a couple days and ship out. We didn't go hungry, but there wasn't that much money being made long term. There were probably times we were playing for damn near nothing, except towards the end when we were getting good dough. We were playing at Montreal Forum and places. But that was short lived.

Johnny Badanjek: What finally happened with Detroit is that the band became bikers. It was like we weren't musicians; we were like an outlaw bike club. We were playing clubs, and the club owners were starting to shoot at us, and it was just getting out of hand. The drinking especially. We pulled up at a Holiday Inn in Indiana, and a hairspray can fell out of the car and it's rolling, because there was just, like, this little hill in this parking lot. One of the guys is drunk, trying to walk a few steps, and he leans down to pick it up and it's still rolling. I'm watching him, and he's going through the whole parking lot, staggering around trying to pick this can up. It's like eleven in the morning on a Saturday in some college town, and we're going to play there tonight. Just what everyone needs to see: staggering around after a hairspray can. We had real bikers hanging around us—we're playing

Hell's Angel's parties. All the outlaw clubs, and then all of a sudden they'd all be fighting. It was time to stop.

John Sinclair: I took over managing them, and it was one of the most bizarre experiences I've ever had in business. Over a period of six months the entire band changed, position by position, and finally Ryder quit singing. He had developed polyps in his throat, and he had to have this surgery. He was gonna stop singing, and he just walked away. And I was really enjoying working with his band. It was a great band: Steve Hunter, crazy organ player and bass player for the biker contingent, you know, Ron Cooke, Johnny Badanjek, the hippest drummer in the world.

Mitch Ryder: We stopped, but not before Lou Reed showed up, backstage at the Lone Star Cafe in New York. It was a very blurred, slurred, druggie high, fucking thing he said. "You know, that's the way that song really, really was meant to sound." He was talking about "Rock 'n' Roll." I said, "Okay, can I have some of your drugs?" Yeah, that was kind of like his little payment. I want to congratulate you, because I'm about to fucking rip away your fucking guitar player. He took Steve Hunter.

Drugs Hate You

Gary Quackenbush: Heroin came in, and Osterberg and them got into it, and the Five got into it later. It didn't poison the scene. It was management that ruined the scene. No one could handle anything outside of Detroit. Dick Wagner and Steve Hunter didn't take it. Bob Seger never did; neither did Nugent. Alice Cooper didn't take it. People keep saying it was heroin that ruined the scene, but hell, no.

Leni Sinclair: What was left of the MC5 legacy then? Trying to get rich and shooting heroin.

Dennis Thompson: There were dope houses everywhere by the early seventies. Heroin was what killed it all. As the police clamped down, the birth of the war on drugs was beginning then. The drugs that people were taking became less and less available, and Quaaludes became available, cocaine became available, heroin was easy to get. People moved in that direction.

K. J. Knight: I knew two guys who were strung out on heroin: Greg Arama and Terry Kelly. I loved Terry. I had bromance with the guy, you know what I mean? I liked him so much that to try to be able to relate to him, I would go to his house and I'd shoot up heroin so that we'd both be high on heroin. One night we were high, and he told his wife to sleep with me. I said no, you know, let's not do that. Not a good idea. But he would be nodding out and he would play, and his playing was still phenomenal.

Jimmy Recca: All of a sudden the heroin come to town, and that winter of 1971, it was just fucking blight.

Leni Sinclair: At the end of 1971 we had the concert for John, to get him out of prison. John Lennon came to Ann Arbor. Getting John Lennon was Jerry Rubin's doing. Jerry told him about John. Then he sat down and wrote that song, "John Sinclair." Man, it would have been a total disaster if John Lennon hadn't shown up because we didn't sell too many tickets. Chrysler Arena holds fifteen thousand people, right, and by the time John Lennon came on the scene we'd only sold about four hundred tickets. It would have been a total disaster. What's weird to me is Yoko Ono, who's such a feminist and so into female causes and all that stuff. She never asked to meet me. She never talked to me. I was the wife of the political prisoner. Everything that comes out of her mouth is all metaphysical, do-goody stuff. John Lennon was down to earth. The difference was John Lennon had an education in England. Europeans have an education so they all kind of know a little bit about the class struggle and Marxism and capitalism. Yoko Ono doesn't know any of that shit. No, to her it's all about peace and changing yourself. Right, but she was living in America.

Hiawatha Bailey: We were putting the Free John Sinclair show together at the White Panther headquarters, and I'd get these calls from people trying to be guest listed and bands trying to get on the bill. Someone called and said, "It's Yoko Ono," so I just hung up the phone. Someone called back and said, "Hello. This is John Lennon. Can I speak to the chief of staff of the White Panther party or Dave Sinclair?" So I clicked off, put him on hold for second, and came back and said, "Hello. This is David Bowie and Dave and I are busy right now." Then it rang back and I listened to the message being left and I ran into Dave's office and said, "Shit, Dave, I think John Lennon is on line one."

Don Was: I lived in Ann Arbor in 1971, when I was going to school there, when Sinclair was in prison, and they had that concert with John Lennon, which I attended. David and I heckled John Lennon. We requested "Mr. Moonlight." Just a couple of smart asses, that's all we are, man.

Hiawatha Bailey: I'm at the arena, and John and Yoko are pulling up in their limo there, mobbed—I mean these fans are ravenous and I was trying to keep these people off him. So they get in and go backstage, and Lennon starts trying to teach these guys with him—David Peel and those Eastside New York guys—a song he wants to play. I was standing around, making sure no one bothered them. And he looks at me as he got up and said, "You look like someone I can trust," and hands me this little glass bottle of blow, and I went yayayayaya—I watched them play from the stage.

Then, three days later John Sinclair was let out of prison and he dissolved the party. I had nothing to do except for return from whence I came. I lived over on Fountain Street, and I turned into the most affluent distributor of the catalyst of enlightenment that this town has ever seen.

Dave DiMartino (*journalist, editor,* Creem *magazine*): I had come to Michigan from Miami and was going to Michigan State University. I was working on campus radio—this was late 1971 and it's a dead Sunday afternoon in December. There's a knock on the door, and it's two guys from WABX and John and Leni Sinclair. They came by specifically because he had just gotten out of prison and wanted to know if I wanted to interview him. Sinclair was talking about the benefit, the John Lennon benefit for him in Ann Arbor that had been held maybe a week or so before, and he was nice and friendly. But the thing that was great was that—and this just displays my ignorance about chronology, about the legal system, about his particular situation. All I knew about him was he was in jail for a couple of joints. So I asked him—and this is in front of his wife and the big, impressive WABX DJs, which I didn't grow up with so I could give a shit—"Did you enjoy the show?" Of course it was a benefit for him when he was in prison. I didn't know what the fuck. They looked at me like I was a pinhead moron. And it's like, "Oh, oh, you wouldn't have seen the show." But it was like the essence of Detroit uncool beyond belief.

Leni Sinclair: After John got out of prison at the end of 1971—that's when the real struggle started.

Billy Goodson: I came back to Ann Arbor and John had gotten out of jail, the house on Hill Street closed down, and everyone had moved out. The SRC had fallen apart. The Stooges had moved. MC5, no more. By then it was Detroit people stayed in Detroit—came to Ann Arbor for some fun and monkey business and all that, but always went back to Detroit. But the two twains never met. It was like, you don't bring Detroit people into Ann Arbor. One of the MC5 stompers and I rented out this apartment. She was like a groupie, but the Stompers were chicks you saw in Crumb books; they would beat the living crap out of you—thus the Stompers. They were groupies and bodyguards. They all had their legs spread and whatever and everybody got in there. They lived in the house, and when the Five moved out, a lot of the gals—well this one, she looked just like Janis Joplin, her name was Marcia Rabideau—they moved on. So we got a place. It was like a trilevel place, and Marcia and I lived on a middle floor that went up to the top floor, and my bedroom was in the middle and along with that middle was another apartment where Scott Richardson and Shemp [Richard Haddad] lived. I was selling coke. The guy that I got my supplies from got busted, and the gal that was his main dealer in Ann Arbor got busted too. I got a phone call telling me to get out of town. So I went to Scotty's apartment to tell him about it, and in walks this naked chick who looked just like David Bowie. I looked down and she had a snatch and I was like what the?—it was Angie Bowie. She was supposed to be there to sign Iggy up to MainMan, but Scotty got hold of her, and he always gets what he wants.

John Sinclair: When I came back from prison, the White Panthers had both houses on Hill Street. They were renting out 1510 Hill to a bunch of small-level ounce dealers from Dearborn and other suburban places who wanted to go to school. The Up was living there too. I observed what they had going there, and it was mind-boggling to me because it was like this anarchy of small-level marijuana dealing. One guy lived in this room and another guy lived in this room and this other guy would drive his little pickup truck with the weird cabin on it to California and he'd come back with a load of weed. The guy next door would do the same thing. They didn't know about efficiency, you know?

Becky Tyner: Rob worked freelance at an advertising agency. You know, it was looking to the future. I got a real job at the Federal Reserve Bank, the Detroit branch of the Federal Reserve Bank of Chicago in 1972.

Rick Kraniak: After about 1972 you didn't have that many Michigan bands headlining these bigger shows, as the venues got larger and some of the bands did too. There's a gap for people like Nugent.

Russ Gibb: The venues went down, and Detroit was going through what I call a movement, where the bottom line was shifting and the center of whatever was going on was being spread out. Television was making inroads. The giant concerts were being done, you know. The people were showing up just to show up. The wrong people were going to the concerts. When I say the wrong people, the people that were followers and not innovators. In the early days we were doing our things; they were the innovators. They were the opinion makers who were coming and doing things. Later on it became the ones that said, "Well, you're supposed to have bellbottoms. If you don't have bellbottoms, you are supposed to go and see Seger." And bands were starting to get into these catering things, and the whole thing was going the wrong way by the early seventies. At first they were just little additions written on the bottom. Then they became twenty-four pages long. Oh, yeah, that was one of the things that got me out. The riders got so great. At first they were just little additions written on the bottom. Then they became twenty-four pages long. They had certain beers and certain kinds of food, and it just got worse over a period of time. Then you'd get two or three bands having different riders that they want certain kind of instruments and organs. It became more and more, and I hated it. You know, "Go play! What the fuck—I'm giving you money, go play. Don't give me your shit! If you need beer, go buy it."

Dave DiMartino: All the Stooges and MC5 records went to cutout; so did Love. I was the guy who bought cutouts at Schoolkids in Ann Arbor.

Dave Marsh: Detroit was just quitting around the end of 1971. Mark Manko and Johnny Angelos and I were in my office at the *Creem* house on Cass sitting around. It was five or six in the evening, about February, and I knew Mark as one of the guys in the Detroit band. So we look up and there are these three guys standing in the doorway of the office carrying sawed offs. One of them said, "Which of you guys is Mark Manko?" And Johnny and I looked at each other and didn't say nothing, and to his credit, Mark did step up and said, "That's me," so they tell him, "Come on, let's go," and they marched him out. They had come in through the back door, which was locked, and up through the house, heard voices in the *Creem* office, and there we were. So Mark was found the next day in a car, all beat up in a parking lot. I guess that the problem was that he and his brother had been involved in a smack deal, then used too much product and burned the guy out of money. Apparently, it was time to catch up. Later on Mark's brother got taken out. That's kind of where the scene had been going, and it ends up with Wayne in prison and Michael did time and Hiawatha Bailey—they all ended up doing time and others got sick in various ways. That was really the pathetic, terrible, regrettable end of the Detroit rock scene that had inspired and moved us all and no one was exempt. The Five, the Stooges—they went down. Not Mitch, but it touched Mitch's band. It's one thing to be strung out or burned from too much LSD. But that was the end of the scene as a collegial community–inspired rock-and-roll scene; it became something else. To give you an idea how bad it was: one of the straight people was Ted Nugent—think about that—the idea that Ted, who doesn't have much to be proud of, should be the one emerging. It was inevitable that people would leave Detroit. It was not a show-biz center. Beyond any post-insurrection hippie or post-oil crises or whatever, it was simply show business.

Mitch Ryder: Detroit had become like *One Flew Over the Cuckoo's Nest.*

Gimme Some Action
(1973–1981)

New York:
"None of These People Have Seen Shit"

Chris Panackia, aka Cool Chris (*sound man at every locale in Detroit*): There was a big lull between the clubs and the shit that was going down with the MC5 and all that and anything else. There was nothing through the midseventies. No scene. All the bands that were playing were cover bands in bars. Bands like Strut and Salem Witchcraft. Those were the bands everybody would go see. Either you played something that somebody wanted to hear or you didn't play.

Tom Gelardi (*Capitol Records promotions*): We weren't developing anything for a long time. The industry was getting into an era where no one knew what to sign.

Cary Loren (*Destroy All Monsters, guitarist*): All of a sudden the cult rock ended. Arena rock started to happen in Detroit, and it wasn't focused exclusively on Detroit bands. Acts like Alice Cooper had broken, and there were these big concerts with bands like T. Rex and a lot of things from England.

Mike Skill (*Romantics, guitarist*): After the thing with the MC5 and all those other bands in Detroit, the music scene got into show bar stuff. You had actual bars, like the Red Carpet, where bands were playing. We had a band in the early to midseventies, the Bullets, that played a lot at the Zodiac on the east side on Mack. We'd do a set of originals, and then we'd do a set of Led Zeppelin, Rolling Stones, and David Bowie.

Skid Marx (*Flirt, bassist*): Because of the Grande and the Eastown and those other places shutting down, there was no place for bands to play. It was like a whole different atmosphere. That was when Seger started to get some national attention. We had a band called Medusa, and we used to play around and do the same damn thing. We'd play our first set: "Okay, this is a Bob Seger song."

Art Lyzak (*The Mutants, vocalist*): It took two years for the mayor of Detroit to close down the Eastown. He had to fucking close it the day the Mutants were supposed to open for Vince Vance and the Valiants.

Tom Morwatts (*The Mutants, guitarist*): We had our first show in Ann Arbor in 1971, in one of the dorms at U of M. Jerome Youngman, our other guitar player, had some friends from Kalamazoo, where there was the big state mental hospital. Jerome hadn't been through there, but three or four of his close friends had spent a certain amount of time in the hospital, and they weren't gonna miss this first show. I don't know what their mental health status was at the time—if they were properly medicated—but on the way from Kalamazoo to Ann Arbor they picked up as much roadkill as they could. About the second or third song in the show they came flying in the room with this bag of roadkill, and they would grab the tail of a squirrel or raccoon and smash it against the floor. That would be part of the dissection element in the show, because the guts were all over the place. We just kept on playing, of course. I thought that was a really cool way to start a musical career, myself.

John Kordosh (*The Mutants, bassist, journalist,* Creem *magazine*): I met Art Lyzak in the Mutants when he came down to become first our guitarist and then our white lead singer. We had a black lead singer, a guy named James Graves. This was 1973. James was older than us, and he was a pretty good singer, but he was only in it for the money. God knows how many women James was supporting, and he was not into the ramalama aspects of it all, you know, like Jerome was. We were doing something original at a time that wasn't being done in Detroit.

Art Lyzak: James was giving up on the band when I joined as a second guitarist. His thing was, "Man I got to make fifty bucks, I always got to make my fifty bucks." So that's what we got paid—enough money to give him fifty bucks. Then it got to the point where there wasn't enough money to hold on to him and he left. I said, "Well hell, I'll be the singer." The Mutants were writing songs, but we had to learn a ton of covers. We did that whole *Ziggy Stardust* album, Mott the Hoople, Robin Trower, Deep Purple. For some reason we just hated all that stuff at the time. But you had to mix that in there.

Don Was (*Traitors vocalist, Was (Not Was) bassist, vocalist; producer*): I ended up playing some gigs with a guy named Ted Lucas. He was from the Spike Drivers, a band that was alternative before there was alternative. The worst booking we ever had was opening for Black Sabbath, when Ozzy was still in the band, at the Toledo Sports Arena, '73/'74 era. We were a folk band, man. Ted came out with an acoustic guitar, I played bass, there was a black conga player, Dr. Don, and a drummer. And the crowd is a bunch of fourteen-year-old boys from Toledo high on reds. A song and half in someone was injured by missiles thrown; it was just like a hailstorm of bottles. The drummer was bleeding and we stopped.

Gerald Shohan (*Coldcock, guitarist*): I was in a band that played downtown in the early seventies, and I'm probably the only guy still alive from that band. Two of them were drug overdoses. There was a thing where there was a combination of things where you had heroin and coke that got swung back and forth in the seventies. There was no shortage of that stuff. Another of the guys, Abe Lewis, died in an accident on the Detroit River. There's the boat that delivers the mail to the freighters as they go by, and that boat capsized, and he and another person died in that accident.

Mark Parenteau (*WABX, DJ*): Detroit got to be all about cocaine. The first cocaine I ever did was from this church gospel singer from Atlanta, Georgia. This was maybe 1970, and he said, "Here, you wanna check this out?" I had interviewed him, and he was all decked out with his studded pants and everything. And boy, did I like it. My wife, Gail, and I started doing it and doing it. We would get some and go back to our house and just babble our faces off as if it was the coolest thing ever. Quaaludes were big at the time too. I never liked them. This guy owned this hip bootery in Birmingham, and he was heavily into Quaaludes. He had a lot of money and always hung out with us rock types, and everyone would take Quaaludes, and no one could walk because we were all wearing those high-heeled shoes. Here I am, six-five, trying to walk around on platform shoes making me six-eight. How ridiculous.

Bob Mulrooney, aka Bootsey X (*Ramrods, Coldcock, Bootsey X and the Lovemasters, drummer, vocalist*): The only people that played that I knew in the early seventies was one guy from my high school who played just like James Williamson, but he was a junkie. He had the best tone, man. They were getting heroin at that time, 1973. I tried it—a friend of mine was working at a factory. It's not something to go to parties with, but the reason I liked it was that it helped me focus on music. Of course it fooled me later.

Nikki Corvette (*Nikki and the Corvettes, vocalist*): Nobody had really left town, which was cool. Bands that were getting really big or trying to were finding out Detroit had the best audiences in the world, which is why all these people did live albums here. Detroit in the seventies was the place to grow up because everybody played there. You know, they'd do Detroit, New York, and LA. It was a must-have place.

Stirling Silver (*scenester*): I had been in New York to check out the New York Dolls after reading about them in *Rock Scene* and *Creem*. When I got back I was working at Harmony House in Hazel Park. The Dolls were on Mercury, and I knew the Polydor rep, and I put together an in-store for the New York Dolls when they came to play the Michigan Palace. They often call Hazel Park "Hazel Tucky." It's a hillbilly community. I told management: "This band is coming to Detroit. They're going on tour, and they got a signed deal with Mercury and they're really fucking good and they're funny to watch and all that. I know them, so let's bring 'em in." The store managers made this cheesy banner that said, "Welcome New York Dolls." So the Dolls show up, and we had this deal for in-stores for artists, where they can take whatever records they want. The deal is whatever they take, Mercury will pay us back in label material. So if someone takes whatever, they can be sure that their material will be among whatever goes back into the store. David Johansen went to the Elvis Presley, the biggest bin there. He went through every one of them pretty quickly. He was looking to see if the whole catalog was pretty much there, and it was. Johansen took every one of those records out of there, including the religious ones. He took them all out of there; they are completely empty, and of course we swapped out Mercury product. He knew this and was making sure we had a ton of Dolls material, even though they only had one album out at the time.

Bob Mulrooney: The New York Dolls at the Michigan Palace was one of the best shows I've ever seen. Better than the MC5. They blew out the PA, but I was in the orchestra pit, so I heard every note. Johnny Thunders—this was before he got into heroin—he was just jumping in the air, doing all these twirls, and his hair was just totally blown out.

Bobby Hackney (*Death, bassist, vocalist*): When we went to rock shows, we were black hippies. Michigan Palace was our hangout. We saw a lot of Wayne Kramer shows; Kiss were always there, Blue Oyster Cult. David Bowie played there, and we walked out—he was terrible, this soul revue.

S. Kay Young (*photographer*): We used to go to the bar at the St. Regis Hotel where all the bands stayed. After Bowie played at Michigan Palace in 1974, we were there and he was drunk; he was actually collapsing. I don't know why, but I remember that this was before he had his teeth fixed, because they really looked bad. Mark Norton and I had to take him up to his room.

Mark Norton (*Ramrods, 27, vocalist, journalist,* Creem *magazine*): We were riding up to his room in the elevator and he passed out again. The guy's this big. I could pick him up and put him over my shoulder. I was 150 pounds at the time, and he weighed about 98 pounds. I took his room key out; I opened the door; I took off his shirt; I took off his pants—he had orange underwear on—I tucked him into bed, made sure he was fine, sleeping on his side so he didn't barf and choke, and left his key there and walked out of the place.

S. Kay Young: First, though, Norton started going through his stuff, and he goes, "Oh my God, David Bowie's wallet!" I made him put it back. We were not about to steal David Bowie's wallet.

Mike Murphy (*The Denizens, the Rushlow-King Combo, the Boners, drummer, vocalist*): Our parents were dropping us off at these shows, and we were seeing these subversive bands. But they didn't know it. The New York Dolls, New Year's Eve 1973. There was a guy climbing on the light stand, and David Johansen kept trying to get this guy off the light stand. The crowds were Detroit crowds, and they were untamed.

Vince Bannon (*Bookie's, City Club promoter, Coldcock, Sillies, guitarist*): There were a lot of people going to the same shows, this seventies-glam stuff that was going over real big in Detroit. The New York Dolls, Bowie—you'd see the same people at the shows. Things were going on organically, because a lot of bands that were Detroit bands had broken up. You'd see Jimmy Marinos, Mike Skill and those guys in one corner. So you would start noticing familiar faces.

Mark Norton: We were trying to figure out what was next. I called CBGBs in '75 or early '76; there was a girl who tended bar there named Susan Palermo. She worked there for ages and she would tell Hilly Kristal: "Hey, there's this crazy guy from Detroit—he's calling again." I'd say, "Could you just put the phone down so I could listen to the groups?" I heard part of a set by the Talking Heads like that. It sounded like it was through a phone, but I was getting all excited, you know—this sounds like what I like. My phone bill was incredible, $200 bucks.

In the summer of 1976 I went to New York City. I saw the second Dead Boys show at CBGBs. I saw the Dictators. Handsome Dick and his girlfriend at the time, Jodi, said, "Who are you?" I said, "I'm from Detroit." They said, "Have you ever seen the Stooges?" "Yeah man, I saw them millions of times, the best shows, the ones in Detroit." I was thinking, "None of these people have seen shit."

Stranglehold

Don Davis (*producer, Stax, Motown musician*): Detroit was so full of talent at that point, the midseventies, that I didn't need a band telling me what the deal was. I was working with a lot of the people who were coming from Motown Records and a lot of the people who were at the front of the disco movement. And rock was still just as much a part of Detroit as anything else, but a lot of these guys were getting attitudes that were hurting them. I would work with Jim McCarty, and he was great. But then there were the stories about what Iggy Pop was up to in Los Angeles and how the MC5 had disintegrated.

Doug Banker (*manager, Ted Nugent*): In the midseventies I was promoting things like Bob Seger for $500, Kiss for $750. The first Kiss date I did was in '74 at the Thunder Chicken in Grand Rapids. They put on the full show with all the fireworks and the outfits and the makeup, and they acted like they were already superstars. Here's the rules: no pictures of the band without their makeup. They would do sound check without makeup, but nobody was allowed to see them. Nobody could have a camera. At the time I thought that was really silly because hardly anybody knew who they were. I was like, "Why would you do that? Nobody knows who you are—they're just going to try to take pictures. You want to promote yourself?" They said, "Strictly not!" It didn't take me too long to realize they were way ahead of the game. They knew they were going to make it big, and even back in '74 at that club, that was part of their plan. I figured all that out later and realized how genius the whole plan was.

Stirling Silver: There was huge promotion for Kiss's debut show in Detroit at the Michigan Palace. Aerosmith was also on that bill—spring '74. Harmony House organized a party with two hundred–plus people invited at the Hilton Hotel in

111

Grand Circus Park after the show for the record industry, retailers and people on the front lines that had to interact with the customers. I got good access as a guy working at Harmony House, so I had met the Kiss guys backstage briefly. We get over to the Hilton, and it's a huge bash with food and tons of alcohol and everything else you could want. It was a private party, and all of Kiss were there. Aerosmith were not because it was specifically a Kiss launch, industry party. Kiss kept their outfits on, and as the night wore on, they slowly shed items. The makeup got smeared, a lot people wanted to kiss them. I ended up staying until the very last person. There was a portable record player at one end of this room all night long, which I didn't really notice until later on in the evening. I sat down with Peter Criss. People are drifting off; there might have been twenty people left. We started talking, and he said that his hero was Gene Krupa, and he whipped out six records that he carried with him on the road. Of course he put a Gene Krupa record on the turntable that was sitting there. He stopped talking and sat there just listening, because he's a total freak nerd.

Mark Parenteau: I didn't like Kiss. I thought the music was lame. So Larry Harris at Casablanca made me a deal that if he paid for a whole concert and the crowd went crazy, I would play Kiss on the air. They really, really wanted Detroit; it was predetermined in their mind that they had to have Detroit and that if this band didn't go over in Detroit, it wasn't going to go over anywhere. It was true, actually, and they knew it. It was fire breathing, black leather, loud and over the top and just what Detroit was all about. Except the songs were really lame. Larry did this concert at Michigan Palace. Bob Seger opened, and then there was a long wait because Aerosmith was also on the bill, and here were big arguments between Aerosmith and Kiss. Kiss didn't want Aerosmith to use any pyrotechnics, and there was a fist fight backstage amongst the road crews. Then Kiss played, and I'm with Larry Harris, and he's trying to make sure his bet goes well. So far we had been playing the album, but it really hadn't caught on fire. But people hadn't seen Kiss. It wasn't like now where there is unlimited access to visual representation anywhere. It took a while for magazines to get pictures of a band, so the album hadn't done much. When Kiss went on stage, for the first song the audience just sat there and watched them. But the second song or third song was "Firehouse," and Gene Simmons breathed fire, and the place went out of their minds in full Detroit fashion. Suddenly they were deep into it and on their feet and it was all about Kiss for a long time. Kiss went on to do their live album there, and then did "Detroit Rock City," and it became the city they had needed.

Rick Kraniak, aka Rick K (*booking agent*): By then Seger was getting a pretty good ride outside of Michigan. Atlanta was a good pocket—there was a promoter down there, Alex Cooley, who would buy my bands from me—and Florida was a really good pocket. So we started to try and get like a little regional thing going for the bands—that was the strategy—and it worked with Seger a lot like that; it worked with Nugent.

Tom Gelardi: Bob hadn't broke through all the way by the early seventies. Then there was a fellow out of Orlando or Tampa, I'm not sure, a broadcaster by the name of Bill Vermillion. Vermillion had family in Traverse City, and every summer he would come to Michigan for a couple weeks' vacation up there. He kept hearing Seger records, and he picked them up, 'cause all he heard was Seger records all around the state. So he picked up the 45s and would go back and he played them. He got Seger so hot down there off those 45s that he called Punch Andrews and said, "I want to do two concerts down here." He did two concerts down there on two successive nights—a Friday night and Saturday night—and drew eleven thousand and thirteen thousand people. I said to myself, "They don't know Bob Seger from Adam except for the records." He's got to be a phenom for goodness' sake to draw that many people. That was the sign. The radio was really taking off, and it just said to me, "Wait a minute. Nobody can do that." I don't give a shit. As an unknown? Just off records? What they hear and what they like. So you gotta know that he had it.

Rick Kraniak: The bookings were really coming more and more out of New York by '73 or so. We were handling Seger still. He worked really hard as it led up the Silver Bullet Band. But he was still a warm-up band mostly, even in Michigan. We fed Bob Seger McDonald's one time when he opened for BTO at Northern Michigan University. I felt terrible about it.

Kim Fowley (*musical raconteur from Los Angeles*): Diversified Management at that time began to run this "L" touring scheme, where the Detroit bands would play from Detroit down to Atlanta and into the armpit of Florida. It was really effective, and they kept bands on that circuit. Seger and Nugent broke that way even if they weren't booked by Diversified.

Ted Nugent (*Ted Nugent and the Amboy Dukes, solo, guitarist, vocalist*): We started doing these guitar face-offs. That was a concept created by Dave Leone and Nick Harris at Diversified Management. Because we didn't have real smash records, and we were kind of stuck in that Grande, Eastown Theatre, Silverbird, Palladium, two to three thousand–seat places. They wanted to generate more revenue and more ticket sales, so they got into the Dick the Bruiser wrestling kind of competitions, where I would challenge Mike Pinera of the Blues Image and Frank Marino of Mahogany Rush and Wayne Kramer of the MC5 to guitar battles.

Rick Kraniak: The most amazing band for us was Brownsville Station. We would see these makeshift pop festivals pop up on weekends, and their manager would take it. They would just jump on a plane with their Marshalls and drums kitted up and go. There was a New Orleans festival they had agreed to do, and they took off. Meantime the promoter who had originally booked them was arrested, so now we weren't on the bill. But they landed, got a van at the airport, and showed up anyway. They arrive, and the stage manager is, like, tremendously stoned, so they just talked their way in and ended up on stage at 3:30 in the morning. Paid. That's how we did it for a bit. We'd just fly bands to these hastily organized festivals and just show up.

Michael Lutz (*Brownsville Station, guitarist, vocalist, bassist*): We were playing everywhere. Warner Brothers had us do this show at Oberlin College with Parliament Funkadelic. Big mistake. There was a girl sitting down in front of me while I'm singing my ass off, and she's goin', "You're for the white folks. We want P-Funk." That was one of the worst gigs I've ever played in my life, man. You know, we come out there, and it's all basically a black crowd, and we open up with "I'm a Roadrunner, Baby." We did another show like that with Junior Wells. "We want Junior." In '74 we did 327 one-nighters and ten days in the studio for a follow-up record to "Smokin' in the Boys' Room." Think we had about fifteen days off. That song, "Smokin'"—that really did it. Cub and I talked about writing a song called, "Smokin' in the Boys' Room" at some point before I woke up one morning somewhere near Houston, and Henry and I were gonna walk to NASA. We were walking down the street, and I was reciting the chorus to Henry, our drummer. I mean, here's my Beatles influence: "Smokin' in the Boys' room, teacher don't you fill me up with your rules." That's totally English. Henry's objection was "fill me up." But I thought it was totally cool because it combined Americana with English. At that point I had the chorus. When we got back home Cub and I sat down and I showed him the chorus and he loved it. We wrote the verses together. It came out, and now you're talkin' about a band that is hardcore blues, and now we've got the biggest rock 'n' roll single in the country at a time when FM radio was the thing and nobody wanted to even talk about AM radio. If you got played heavily on AM radio, you'd sold out. It was really separated.

Ted Nugent: I had to fight to record "Stranglehold" because the guys that were in charge, the producers, Lew Futterman and Tom Werman and the band, didn't think it was anything but just an indulgent jam session. There was no chorus: "It's called 'Stranglehold,'—where do you sing 'Stranglehold?' Where does the song title appear?" They were kinda choked by the status quo of music. I said, "No, no, no, man, this song makes the girls grind, this song makes the audience grind every night. This is a cool song, and just shut the fuck up and record it." I had to fight for that, man, and I stood my ground. God knows I was right.

Gloria Bondy, aka Gloria Love (*Sillies, backing vocalist, scenester*): I was traveling with the Amboy Dukes at the end, just before Ted went solo. I was John Angelos's girlfriend, and he was singing with Ted at the time. He was frustrated because he was singing Ted's songs but didn't like the material. It seemed like Ted was going to make it big.

Tim Caldwell (*artist*): I met Angelos at Magina Books on Fort Street in Lincoln Park, a place Rob Tyner would frequent too. John was looking for some Philip K. Dick novels. He said Dick was one of his favorite authors, and I would venture Burroughs figured in there too. He had on big bug-eyed vintage shades, like Marcello Mastroianni in *10th Victim*. I came over to his house and gave or sold cheap to him a few P. K. Dick books, ones he hadn't been able to find. John was a nice enough dude, no rock-star pretentious bullshit. Seemed to me his promo pics tried too hard to copy the look of Thunders' Heartbreakers, down to blood-spattered white formal shirts.

Jerry Bazil (*Dark Carnival, drummer*): We played a show with Johnny Angelos and the Torpedoes, and when we were showing up they took Johnny away in an ambulance. Then he came back and did the show. I don't know what happened to him, but he came back pretty together.

Tex Newman (*RUR, Shock Therapy, Country Bob and the Bloodfarmers, guitarist*): We played with Angelos three weeks before he killed himself at the Roostertail. He was a real bad junkie and was having problems with his old lady. He was

always a very shy dude. Next thing I know Tim Caldwell had loaned him something by Philip K. Dick, and I guess he had a few drinks and went in the garage
and turned on the car.

Bill White (*bassist, Ted Nugent and the Amboy Dukes*): John was ahead of his
time as a character. But I saw him the night before he died at a party and he said
he wanted to go out with a drink and a sci-fi novel in his hand. And that's exactly
how he did it.

Chris Panackia: It was ridiculous. He was a great singer with Nugent. And the
Torpedoes were great. Asphyxiated himself in the garage. He was chasing that
needle after a while. And Tussionex. Drank it like a wild man, like fucking water.
I used to work for him: The Torpedoes. Warner Brothers was looking at them.

Gloria Bondy: I was with John Angelos for ten years. We weren't together when
he committed suicide. His mom, she said John's car wasn't in the driveway and she
thought Mitchell, John's son, was going to come home soon and no one would be
there. She went into the garage and saw John dead. She called and asked if I would
come over and help her call the police. She didn't want to be alone, so I went over
there and saw John dead in the car. I couldn't believe it. I never thought he would
kill himself. He was waiting for a contract to come from LA, and I think it came
the day after. I don't know if that was the only reason. He wanted to make it.

Gary Reichel (*Cinecyde, vocalist*): We all saw Bob Seger and Ted Nugent before
they were big, There were good then, and when they got famous in the seventies,
they weren't. That was the consensus. And they weren't even really local anymore,
either.

Rick Kraniak: The seventies is when you didn't have too many Michigan bands
headlining here. It evolved to where the ballrooms were bringing in these national
artists moreso than the Michigan ones. Nugent didn't really play some of those
really popular places like the Eastown very much. Then we started headlining
him at Cobo, and then he became a staple again. The big shows got really big. We
did the famous ELO playing-to-tape show at the Pontiac Silverdome. Our stage
manager for the show went to see ELO in Ohio before they came here. This was a
big show for us, our first at the Silverdome, and we didn't want to mess it up. He
came back and said, "You know, I think these guys are on tape." We said, "No, no
way." That was just a huge deal at the time; it was pre–Milli Vanilli getting busted

for not singing on their records. So we watched the soundcheck very carefully the day of the show, and we were able to affirm that they were playing from tape. The show was exactly the same length—the song order, the space in between songs. Odd things happen in between songs usually—you know, the guitarist turns up his guitar or there'll be some feedback. But these things were clinical. Detroit busted ELO.

Mongrel

Tom Morwatts: I owe Bob Seger an apology. We played with him on a big bill; he was the headliner. It was a nice facility, a hockey arena, and it had good-sized locker rooms separated by a chain-link fence so the teams couldn't get at each other. Bob Seger's band was in the one next to ours, I guess. We had finished and we played well, so I was happy about that. I was drinking Metaxa Ouzo—it's this Greek version of tequila—and it can make you insane. This girl comes into the dressing room and I was talking to her for a while, and I ended up chasing her around with a guitar chord, snapping it at her like a Three Stooges thing. We're running around in circles; I'm trying to get this guitar cord close to her ass. She would run out the door, and then five minutes later she'd come back in, and we'd repeat the whole process. As I got drunker, though, I started walking over to the fence separating us and messing with them. Finally I was hanging on the fence drunker than hell, going, "Bob, You're a homo, aren't you Bob? You guys are all homos. Tell me. You can tell me." I was just being a total jerk. They all just looked at me like, "You asshole."

David Teegarden (*Teegarden & Van Winkle, Bob Seger and the Silver Bullet Band, drummer, vocalist*): Bob Seger was doing this solo thing, that *Brand New Morning* stuff, when Skip and I started playing in his band. He was discouraged before we joined. He dumped the System and was doing that folk thing. Later Bob mentioned to me he had considered going back to college. Later on, when things got good, he told me, "I'm glad I didn't do that." Yes, that would have been a bad idea. When I first met him we had Teegarden & Van Winkle. We had recorded "God, Love and Rock and Roll" with Westbound, and we had a hit. Instead of us opening for everyone, we were headlining. Bob came backstage after one show ranting and raving about how he loved our deal, and we traded numbers and all became friends. He came over to our house and jammed. I have hours of tape of us jamming, with him playing guitar. He was pretty good on guitar, but he wasn't as serious about his playing because he was into writing and singing. But we hung out, and one day he went to Skip on the side and said, "My band the System is breaking up. Would you guys mind forming up?" We said, "No." But later on we played with him as a backing band sometimes.

Charlie Martin (*Bob Seger and the Silver Bullet Band, drummer*): Before I came along they were doing the albums in Oklahoma through Leon Russell's studio. They did *Back in '72* there. But Eric Clapton was coming out of this heroin thing and had Derek and the Dominos rolling, and so through Leon, he started falling into this Tulsa thing, since some of the Dominos were Okies. When Eric wanted to do *461 Ocean Boulevard*, Leon recommended the same group that he had recommended to Bob. So they all went with Eric, and Bob had no band to record with. He went through this six-month period where he had to slap a band together.

Tom Weschler (*photographer, Bob Seger road manager*): No, it wasn't like Eric came in and stole the band. That's not what happened. They were all ready to part.

Wayne Kramer (*MC5, Gang War, solo, guitarist, vocalist*): I called Bob when the MC5 was over and said, "Bob, let's start a new band. I play lead, you're the front man; this is a good idea." He said, "Yeah, Wayne, that is a good idea, but here's what'll happen: you'll be in a band with me, and at a certain point you're going to want to go out on your own, and that'll be too hard to me." It was pretty much a nice way of saying I'm not going to hire your ass. So all he hires is people who don't really matter if they're on the gig or off.

David Teegarden: Skip Knape and I had been playing with Bob, and we played on *Smokin' O.P.'s*. Skip sang one song on there, I sang one, and when we cut the tracks, Bob called me and said, "Your track sounds good. You mind if I sing it?" I said, "Hell, you're the singer. We're just filling in." So Bob sang all the tunes. The original idea was the album was going to be credited Bob Seger with Teegarden & Van Winkle. When the LP came out, I got a call from Skip and he said, "Hey, our names are not on there." So I called Punch Andrews and I said, "Hey Punch, is this a Bob Seger album?" He said, "Yes." I thought about it for a second and I said, "Well, you paid the bill." He said, "Yup," and I said, "Okay, I guess it's a Bob Seger album." Skip didn't like it, but Bob and I stayed friends. But that was the end of Teegarden & Van Winkle playing with Bob. For the next album he wanted me to play and I had commitments. I'll take credit for the Muscle Shoals deal, because in my talks with Bob, he was due to go in and record some of these songs we were doing in '72. I said, "Here's the number for Muscle Shoals. It's good." He talked Punch into funding it.

Drew Abbott (*Third Power, Bob Seger and the Silver Bullet Band, guitarist*): When I was in Third Power, we played one of Punch Andrews's clubs. He was really upset that we were playing so loud, and we just said, "Well, if it's that bad, don't pay us." He said, "No, no, keep the money." No one turned down money. Punch was so taken aback by that, we became friends. I knew Seger as well, and I was looking for some work—this was after he did *Back in '72*. I stopped by Bob's house and he said, "I'm playing tonight in Ypsilanti. Come on down and check it out." He had this great group he was calling the Borneo Band. After the show we went out to his Winnebago and he said, "How'd you like to play guitar with us?" I said yes right off, and that eventually became the Silver Bullet Band. We left three days later and did 260 one-nighters a year starting with that tour. We did a tour opening for Bachman Turner Overdrive, then did a Kiss tour. At first it was billed as Bob Seger. Pretty soon we added Charlie Martin on drums and changed some things around. We got Chris Campbell on bass. Alto, who is really Tom Cartmell, never toured with us until we got big. He had this regular job, and he didn't put in the hard road time with us.

Shaun Murphy (*Bob Seger and the Silver Bullet Band, Stoney & Meatloaf, vocalist*): I was looking for work and I called up Punch, you know: "What's going on back in Detroit?" I was living in LA; it was '73. And he said, "It just so happens one of our singers left. Do you want to sing background for Bob?" I said I'd never done that before, but it can't be that hard, so I got in my little '71 Honda and we drove back to Michigan. It was a horrible trip. I packed my daughter and a box of Cheerios and it was pouring rain getting out of LA. And my car could barely move—you know, thirty-five miles per hour on the freeway. This gig is looming, and I get to St. Louis and I'm in tears, and I'm at this gas station, my car is broken. This guy comes out of the gas station and he says, "You okay?" and I said, "I've got to go to this gig, and my car is messed up. I paid a bunch of money to fix it." So he looks at the car, and he says, "They rebuilt the carburetor wrong. It's upside down. Why don't you go to my house and my wife will cook you dinner and I'll rebuild your carburetor?" I'm thinking that he's either going to kill me or he's really going to do it. So I went to his house, his wife fixed me dinner, he rebuilt my carburetor, and I drove seventy-five miles an hour and I got to Detroit, and of course Punch was livid. He wouldn't believe me at all. The touring was mostly national stuff—Florida, Georgia, back to Detroit. We must have toured all of Florida that year. It was a call-and-response kind of thing. They kept getting dates booked in Florida, and they'd try and fill it in, but it didn't always work, so we ended up going to Florida a lot in a nine-passenger station wagon. I was driving because I figured, "If I'm driving the car, then I don't have to be squished in the rest of the people."

Charlie Martin: After losing his band and putting together that touring unit, Bob steps back from the road and licked his wounds. So I jumped in. Chris Campbell, who was playing bass, brought me into the band. Chris gave me a stack of things to play: learn this and that. Drew, Chris, Bob, and I met at Bob's place on White Lake so I could audition.

K. J. Knight (*Ted Nugent and the Amboy Dukes, drummer*): I auditioned for Seger when he was putting together the Silver Bullet Band. I didn't even own a set of drums when I got the audition, and I had to buy this crappy kit. I still thought I'd just go in and, because I knew Seger and Punch, get through it. I barely knew the songs. We played through some songs without Bob, and then when he showed up, it was obvious that it was terrible. I didn't get the job, of course.

Tom Weschler: K. J. flammed a lot. He didn't prepare. You'd think that because Bob's such a nice guy: "Oh, this is great. Seger wants me in his band, so I'm in the band." You don't think he's going to fucking audition you? This guy's a serious musician, born to it. Anybody that wasn't prepared got taken to the woodshed.

Charlie Martin: We got done with my audition and Bob said, "I'm sold." There are certain phrases you hear in your life, and that was one for me. When Bob said, "I'm sold," I went, "Wow." From then on we had a couple more in-depth rehearsals, focusing on specific things, then we started doing jam sessions, and Bob just wanted to hear me play as many pockets and grooves as I could.

Tom Weschler: Charlie's other attribute is he can sing almost as good as Bob. I wasn't there for the audition, but the next day Bob told me he had a drummer. He's like, "I got the drummer, and he's a motherfucker, man!"

Charlie Martin: One of the first things we did when the Silver Bullet Band was coming together was get Bob to drop the guitar, get out there, and work the audience. The band had the music end covered, and the only reason Bob was playing piano or guitar occasionally is because prior to that Bob had short-lived bands that kept changing members, and Bob found himself sometimes without these parts.

Drew Abbott: First thing we recorded with Charlie, Bob, and I together was the *Seven* album in the basement of a bowling alley, which is where Pampa Studios was. The core band only played on three songs on that album.

Charlie Martin: Then we just hit the road. Of all the guys in the band I was the one—probably because I was the youngest and all of this was really important—I was the one who kept calendars and every paycheck and all things about who was on the bill. We would open for Spooky Tooth one night with Montrose as the middle act, then open for Thin Lizzy, then Blue Oyster Cult.

Tom Weschler: We were really getting the touring thing together. Up until then we had rented U-Hauls we got from Gene's Hardware on 12 Mile and Farmington. It was a big box in the back on a cab. Then we had a station wagon that Punch got us in 1970. Pretty soon we got our own truck because we were explaining to Punch like, "Look if you pay $150 a week for a U-Haul why not just pay $250 a month for a truck?" His sister's husband was a Ford dealer, so we got a good deal on a wagon and a truck and it worked out great. Then I hired a great roadie; we called him Dansir. I hired a few more too. I never had to fire 'em because I picked 'em good. If anybody shoulda gone, though, it would have been Dansir. He stole the truck one day and drove to Alabama and beat the shit outta some guy who took off with his wife.

David McCullough, aka Dansir (Crew, Bob Seger): Actually, I took the truck to go to Alabama to pick up my wife, who had run off with this guy. I got there and told him if he didn't lay off of my old lady, I would be dancing on his head. I didn't actually have to do that.

Tom Weschler: He came back and goes, "Well, I fixed that motherfucker." I said, "If you tell Eddie—which is Punch's name—you'll get fired." He goes, "Yeah, yeah, you're right. I mean, I didn't mean to be gone that long." I said, "It's a good thing we didn't have a gig or I would have fired your ass myself." So anyways, this guy took off with his wife. He had to do it.

Drew Abbott: We'd tour, then come back and record. I didn't take this recording thing well, because he wouldn't use us for the whole thing.

Charlie Martin: It was that unique combo of us, minus Alto, that made the Silver Bullet Band. Drew, Chris, and myself defined that sound. Bob had cut eight LPs before *Live Bullet*, and none of them had made a dent in the national market. When people think of what is the definitive Seger LP, it's always *Live Bullet*. So we were often pretty bitter. Bob had cut the whole *Beautiful Loser* LP in Muscle Shoals. He loved to use session guys because they'll do whatever he asks and he loved that studio. Bob had more control with them too. We weren't that easily controlled. Which made us so good live.

Drew Abbott: At the same time, I was getting paid. We were the highest paid I knew; we did quite well and we also got a piece of the albums we were on. They were very generous to us. Then getting a stake in the live show was a big deal; it really inspired you. If Bob was having a bad night, that was too bad. He just had to get out of the way.

Tom Weschler: For a while Seger was the sole proprietor as it were. The Silver Bullet Band started in '74, the fall. Even though he had a touring band, it was always Bob Seger with, you know, whatever band, and there were different guys. Seger decided he wanted to step up and get a permanent band. So Alto, and Chris, and Bob are the nucleus of the Silver Bullet Band.

Shaun Murphy: Between '76 and '78 he didn't have background singers. Charlie Martin, Chris, Drew Abbott, and Alto were the band.

Drew Abbott: Our first rehearsal with the Silver Bullet Band, where we were going to tour like that, we all knew it was going to go somewhere. The first gig we did as Silver Bullet was opening for Black Oak Arkansas in Gary, Indiana, and we tore the place apart. Standing ovation, encore, and it never stopped, and that just hadn't happened in the Borneo band. Silver Bullet was really serious. We opened for Blue Oyster Cult in Eugene, Oregon, and Robin Robbins, who had replaced Rick on keyboards, got in a fistfight backstage coming off after the set because someone didn't like the organ sound he had. He just started swinging on the stage guy and the crowd was going nuts, and our roadies pulled the two guys apart and we went out and did the encore.

Charlie Martin: By the time we recorded that live album, there was pressure on Bob to come with an LP. He had to do one every ten months or so, and by the time he was close to submitting his next studio LP, he wasn't ready. You have

Frampton Comes Alive! and Kiss *Alive!* selling huge and they got it in their minds that a live album would be great and it would keep the record company at bay. But because we were so, I like to say spontaneous, but Bob and Punch might use the word erratic, Bob and especially Punch were concerned that we couldn't deliver the goods live. We tried this experiment where we recorded the live set in the studio, and then they were going to put in canned applause, so it would be us pretending to play live. But it was dead in the water because we really needed that interplay. Finally Punch backed down and we cut *Live Bullet* at Cobo in fall of '75.

Bob Seger (*Bob Seger and the Silver Bullet Band, Bob Seger and the Last Heard, solo, vocalist*): I didn't want to release a live album because I thought it was getting to be a camp thing. The performances were above average nights, but not the peak of what the band can do. Technically, it's far from perfect. But the next studio album wasn't finished and I decided we had to get something out.

Drew Abbott: Before we went on, Bob said, "Look, we've been doing this for a year here, and we know what we're doing." He said play to the audience—maybe the recording will be released and maybe it won't, but don't play it safe. Capitol didn't want a live album because it thought the market was saturated with live albums, like *Frampton Comes Alive!*, and Punch went around them and put it out anyway.

Tom Weschler: Someone said the live album isn't really live. I'm like, "Are you nuts? Of course it's live." "Oh right," all sarcastic. I said, "Listen fellas, I was there. I was even in the truck." They were amazed, just like I was. We were like, "How in the hell are they getting this so tight?" They didn't do that in a studio.

Drew Abbott: It was a live album. I don't personally know of any studio touch-up. I played one studio note on the second live album. I touched up one note, I will confess. They dragged me and said play this one note over. But not *Live Bullet*.

Charlie Martin: Money-wise, when I started playing with Bob we were all, including Bob, making $150 a week. Then that gradually went to $200, $225, up and up. I was with the band four years, and by the time I left I was making $1,500 a week. Out of that we didn't have to pay for hotel rooms or cars, but we had to pay for our own food. If we decided to eat lobster or Whoppers, we had to pay.

Drew Abbott: All of a sudden we were making pretty good money. It happened to all of us to a degree; it wasn't the fame or the music—it was the money. People came out of the woodwork who wouldn't talk to us before—well, it was about money. Bob was making a lot of money with those writer's royalties, and he started hanging in different socioeconomic circles, with singer-songwriters. So even though we were a band, it had changed. It was a band, and he was part of the band. But he went with people he could speak the same language with, who were successful. He was hanging with who he wanted to befriend. Also, becoming too friendly with your musicians wasn't going to work. He had to be able to direct them and tell them what to do.

Shaun Murphy: I left and rejoined Bob in '78. By then we were flying to gigs, commercial. We did some European dates, which were very few and far between for Bob. He doesn't like to go overseas. He says, "I don't like the hamburgers over there."

Dan Carlisle (*WABX, WRIF, DJ*): In interviews Bob was very personable. But if you set him up, like, "Here he is, Bob Seger!" he would not really talk. The last time I interviewed him—it was going to tape, a longer piece—and I told the production guy that when we get into the room, just start the tape, don't say anything. So I came in, and we're setting up mics and getting ready and making small talk, and Bob didn't even realize he was being interviewed. And it worked.

Bob Seger: I've always considered myself an antistar. I don't move well in a crowd, at cocktail parties, and such. I'm sure the Mick Jaggers, the extroverted rock stars do very well in that scene. But I'm an introverted person, basically. It's very tough for me to do it. And I try to stay out of it as much as I can. It has nothing to do with developing a mystique or anything like that. That's not the way I am. I just don't deal very well with people I don't know.

Charlie Martin: The year after the *Live Bullet* recording, we did a show at Pontiac Silverdome that was promoted by Steve Glantz with a guarantee of $100,000 plus 25 percent over breaking point. The day of the show, at about four in the morning, we went to sound check on this huge PA. There was this feedback loop that, no matter what, they could not get rid of.

Tom Weschler: The whole Silverdome roof is kept up by zero-pressure fans making the wind noise, so that's what the electrical hum was, was the fans. They were made in Japan, and they had a different kind of current. Instead of rigging the current for here, well, they had to redo that electrical stuff.

Charlie Martin: So at 4 a.m., with union stagehands working triple time, they had to strike the stage and move it back fifteen feet and set it all back up, and it just cost thousands of dollars. We had gotten $50,000 in advance and were supposed to get the rest on the night of show. But because of this fiasco, Steve Glantz did not have the liquid funds to pay us, and Punch was adamant that we were not going to play without it. Punch told him he was going to have a riot, so Steve had to call his dad, Gabe, who drove it out to him that evening and handed it over to us in a certified check. Glantz filed bankruptcy after that, and we never got the 25 percent.

Drew Abbott: I still rue the day of Charlie's accident. We were coming home from rehearsal and I saw Charlie's car at the side of the road and I almost stopped, but I had to get home for something. He had gotten off the freeway and was coming back with a can of gas and was crossing the street, and a gal came around and hit him. He was okay—his feet were moving in the hospital, but he got a blood clot and that was it. He could never walk again. After that Robin left, and we got David Teegarden after trying a few drummers.

David Teegarden: One day I was in Oklahoma at Dick Sims's house, and Jamie Oldaker drove up and said, "I just got a call from Bob, talking about Charlie Martin's accident." I was feeling awful for Charlie, but I was also down because they didn't call me; they called Jamie to take over. That's how it is—they forget about you. They had been on the Night Moves tour, and it had soared to the top and really took Bob to a new arena. They went out for the rest of the tour, and the last gig was in Tulsa. We were friends, and we went to eat, and then I took him to the gig, and we were in the dressing room and he tells me this is Jamie's last gig because he had to go back with Clapton. They were going to take a break and audition drummers. They auditioned dozens of drummers, but I got it. When I signed on, my pay was $400 a week, and I thought I had hit gold. It didn't take long to get a raise to $600, then Punch would pull me over to the side and say, "You're getting a bonus on this" and hand me $2,000 extra. I was seeing all kinds of bonuses, then I was up to $1,500 a week. The first album I did was *Stranger in Town*. At that time they didn't give me a full cut on gigs, but now I was seeing $50,000 royalty checks. I can't believe it happened. We flew everywhere. I never had to touch my luggage, and we'd get there and have three limos waiting for us and the road manager would make sure bags got put in the van, and we'd bitch if we had to wait for our room keys. We played in Oakland at the coliseum, and Bill Graham built a whole western movie backstage with girls wearing tights being cocktail waitresses and Eddie Money came up and did a comedy routine, which was pathetic. That was the *Against the Wind* tour. Then I was cut in on a concert take, so Bob would split the proceeds among the core members of the Silver Bullet Band. I was really making serious coin. When we started that tour, Drew Abbott—he was kind of an accountant, he was always talking about money—he said, "You know the ticket prices are going to be $15 a ticket. That's outrageous, people can't afford that." I said, "Well, I don't have to pay that." Drew bitched to Punch, and Punch said, "Shut the fuck up and play the gig."

Drew Abbott: Punch is a good businessman, and he's been right more than he's been wrong.

David Teegarden: We were setting attendance records; Punch could book Atlanta and sell out in ten minutes. Then we started just doing two nights in every city. That was the first time that kind of thing had been done.

Shaun Murphy: We would come back and do these great shows in Detroit. One year Mitch Ryder opened for us. Mitch came into the dressing room, and they're all glad-handing each other. So Mitch sits back at a table and is talking to Bob, and he says, "You know, there's only a couple great song writers in the world, and one of 'em's me." Bob didn't know what to say.

Drew Abbott: Craig Frost came and played keyboards, and then after the '89 tour David and I left. In any corporation you have to look at a band like this as just that. I was a cog that worked in the corporation up to that point, but where he was going musically—wanting to play everything like the record, including the solos played by session guys—it was difficult. It caused friction. I think he was right to do this, it was working, but we had been pretty damn successful doing things the way we had been doing them. Bob was going in a different direction, and I was just going to cause a lot of friction. We never got into that for the money; it was such a shock to me, that money. All I wanted to do was make enough money to get to the next gig, and when I was off the road I would still go down and play the blues off of Cass Avenue, but the other guys never played when we had down time. I don't know why.

David Teegarden: You know, protection is utmost in Punch's deal, Bob's image. It's very rare to find people that passionate about it, and he loves Bob like a son.

Drew Abbott: When we were opening for Bachman Turner Overdrive, they were hitting big, and I had breakfast with Fred Turner one morning, and he said here's how it happens: "You have to have the right material, the right record company, the right band, and the right manager all at the same time, and if any one of those is missing, you're not gonna make it." We were listening to him and thought it makes sense to us. So Bob had the right everything all at the same time.

Mitch Ryder (*Mitch Ryder and the Detroit Wheels, Detroit, solo, vocalist*): Bob is one of the greatest writers we've ever produced. When he was serious about his writing—and I use that in the past tense—he wrote some songs that can never be matched. So he clearly had a talent. The question still remains: Did he make Punch Andrews or did Punch Andrews make him? I think Punch has done a remarkable job handling his image, considering what I know about him. And he's done a remarkable job taking care of his money for him, which allowed him the luxury of going ten years between albums, to serve his fans as one of the upper class. I just don't feel he served his fans as well as he could have, and I don't begrudge him the idea of living the life of luxury, 'cause he earned it. He had a choice to make. He had to choose between fans or money, and he chose to "enjoy my life." Good for you, Bob. You enjoyed your life, but the fans could have been a lot happier.

David Teegarden: I still get my royalties, and I never signed a contract. They don't have to pay us shit. But they do.

Creem: *"They're No Good Since Lester Bangs Left"*

Robert Matheu (*photographer*): I met this guy David Tedds a few years ago; he was from Redford. He said, "Dude, I went to see Black Sabbath in at Cobo Arena, and my best friend made this big cross out of tin foil and cardboard." And I went, "It was on the cover of *Creem* magazine?" He goes, "Yeah, oh shit! You're right! How do you remember that?" I said, "If you go twenty-two pages in, there's another picture of the huge cross, and I'm right in the middle of the photo," and he goes, "No, really?" And I am. This is way before I was ever part of *Creem*. I've got a bad mustache and I got a Cody High School T-shirt on.

David Tedds (*fan*): I didn't put the Sabbath cross together. I went to high school with the guy that did. I saw it waving around at the front of the crowd, and he told me in school the next day that he'd made it. He was a trip; he was permanently stoned and drove around in one of those seventies custom vans with the shag carpeting. His eight-track collection consisted exclusively of the first several Sabbath albums. He'd just rotate them day in and day out and drive around blaring them as loud as possible for the populace to hear, whether they liked it or not. He lived in his parents' basement. The floor was painted black with a huge silver cross in the middle. His famous line to me was, "Dave, one of the reasons I love Sabbath so much is that they're so scientific!"

Bobby Hackney (*Death, bassist, vocalist*): We read *Circus*, but we grew up with *Creem* in the midseventies. Our hope was always to be in *Creem*.

Mark Norton: I was in the 27, and we opened for John Cale at Bookie's. Barry Kramer was there with his ex-wife, Connie, and we sat around doing coke at the table.

Robert Matheu: I'd see the *Creem* people at the shows—mostly Lester—before I was involved with the magazine. I'd see Lester at the Faces shows, and I snuck backstage. Actually, at that time you didn't have to sneak backstage: a 35-mm camera was better than a laminate pass. I was seventeen, and I'd see Lester and I knew who Charlie Auringer was, I knew who the *Creem* people were, and I had my 35-mm camera. After the show the Faces were always across the street to the Pontchartrain, where they were staying. And I could just keep taking pictures, because for them it was all about the party. Lester didn't give me the time of day. He'd be nice occasionally and go, "Did you get any good photos tonight?" I'd say, "Yeah, you want some?" He'd go, "No, not really." After a couple of the Pontchartrain parties he said, "Maybe I want to see a photo of that." It would be safe to say I did some blow off the back of a Ronnie Wood guitar with him once at the Pontchartrain. I think the beauty of *Creem*, of why the magazine stayed what it was for so long until Barry passed away, was because Barry never cared to play with the New York people, the big boys, real hard. He liked going to New York, but he liked coming back. Whether he was cognizant of it, I don't know.

Linda Barber (*journalist,* Creem *magazine*): What eventually doomed *Creem* was that Barry separated *Creem* from *Rolling Stone*. They were very similar publications, but Jann Wenner had the vision to see it on a more standard level, kid of a rock 'n' roll *Playboy*. He got political; he got environmentally conscious. He expanded into so many other realms besides just music. Whereas Barry was like, "No, we're just about music." I think that's what killed it, because generations grow up faster after us. They are smarter, younger, and they are hungrier for more. Some other things can relate to music. Something even as dumb as Bill Clinton taking up the saxophone.

Robert Matheu: I think that's what kept *Creem* so good for so long is that it stayed removed. I don't think it was a conscious thing on Barry's part.

Bob Mulrooney: I went down and met Lester Bangs at the *Creem* house when they moved to Birmingham, about close to the time he was leaving. I called down to the *Creem* office and tried to order a back issue that had some article on the Velvets I was looking for, and the guy on the phone goes, "Hey, I wrote those articles." I go, "What?" And then I knew who it was and I said, "You're my hero."

I was going nuts. So I was doing a radio special on Lou Reed a little later for this community college station, and I talk to Lester again. I wanted him to come on the show, but he couldn't, but he tells me that if I'm really into the Velvets and Lou Reed, call this guy in New York, and that was this Constantine Radulavitch, this famous Velvets collector and archivist dude. So I call him, and he sent me copies of all his stuff—four huge reel-to-reels of stuff, unreleased songs, Lou Reed playing on an acoustic at parties of Richard and Lisa Robinson, and he's drunk on his fucking ass, and then he'll get all scrambled 'cause he's arguing, and what else? Do the Ostrich was on there. The guy says, "Here, take these and just take what you want off of it for your special, but give them to Lester afterwards." So I took them to his house on Brown Street in Birmingham. Dave Marsh lived there; so did Ben Edmonds. I went there with a couple friends. I wasn't even a drinker at the time, and Lester's hands were shaking. It was, like, the early evening, but he was shaking when we met, and he goes, "Let's go get some beer." And we got loaded. We put on the tapes for a minute, and Lester goes, fuck this shit, let's put on *Raw Power*. So we played *Raw Power*, like, over and over and over, for hours. Only that and Blue Oyster Cult, the second album, *Tyranny and Mutation*. All of Lester's room was all albums—you couldn't even sit on the floor—and he had these huge speakers, but only one of them worked. It was weird to read how depressed Lester was when he died. He used to call me at my house, like, looking for Quaaludes.

Mark Parenteau: When they got the office in Birmingham, *Creem* was really becoming a glossy national magazine. Ben Edmonds and Dan Carlisle lived on Smith Street in Birmingham. It was just a suburban house directly across the street from the chief of police, and we were having so much stuff going on and then his kids, his son and daughter, tried to come over and hang out with us. I'm like, "Dan, this is the police chief's son. You may want to be careful." But stars were coming to that house because it was so powerful between *Creem* and WABX. I mean, it was really the house you wanted to visit if you were Bryan Ferry. Bryan came over during the heyday of Roxy Music, since *Creem* magazine had championed that music first and had written about it and inspired Dan and I into playing it on WABX.

John Brannon (*Negative Approach, Laughing Hyenas, Easy Action, vocalist*): *Creem* was like the bible to me when I was growing up. They had the Stooges, Lou Reed, Alice Cooper—all that in the seventies. I would find the old ones and just devour them.

Linda Barber: I was hired by Barry Kramer on the spot in 1976. I was from Michigan, but I had been working in New York for *Mademoiselle* and *Glamour*. He was very impressed with my résumé because even though he was into the Detroit scene, he wanted the magazine to be global. Barry was a great guy, but he had a huge temper, very short fuse. So my associate there, Sue Whitall—who took over as editor when Lester left—she told him what I had told her, that my father was very violent and abusive to my mother. Barry would always have these screaming tirades at the editorial meetings. I would just end up like unbelievably freaked out. Once he was screaming about the cover; it was Ted Nugent and he asked that we submit our headline ideas. We had the mock covers, and he just was outraged that this headline saying, "Poontang" was even typed on the markup. All he said was, screaming—he screamed so loud at Sue and everybody else, and everybody, you could see the spit flying out of his mouth I mean—he said, "Do you know what you're saying? Why don't we just put 'pussy' on the cover?" I froze because of the screaming. Then he put the cover down and he walked over to me and he kissed me on the forehead and he said, "I'm sorry for yelling."

Cathy Gisi (*journalist,* Creem *magazine*): Lots of people would say Ted Nugent could be aggravating, but he is who he is and he is true to himself, and back then he never hesitated to answer my calls when I needed something. I did a feature with him and spent a night picking him up at the airport and driving him back to his farm in Jackson. I had two vehicles I could use, one a real hot Camaro, and I thought, "No, he'll kill this thing." So I had just gotten a brand-new four-cylinder Chevette to run around town that top-ended at seventy miles per hour. Ted won't let anyone else drive. He found gears in that Chevette I didn't know existed. My mechanic husband wondered why there was straw in the undercarriage that night, and it was because we headed for town to get pizza that night and Ted drove through the field. His house was an old farmhouse, and I figured out the reason he wouldn't let anyone drive is because they might know how to get back. He took so many back roads and did it so quickly that I didn't pay attention how to get there.

Mark Norton: We knew how to rig the phone machine so you'd get a conference call going. You could call one person at A, one person at B, and the phones would ring and they'd both pick it up, and they hadn't phoned each other. So we had Nugent's number, so we hooked up Nugent with Billy Joel. Then we'd all listen in; we'd hear the phones ring, and then we'd hear "Hello?" And the guy who picks up says "Hello, who is this?" "This is Ted Nugent." "Well, this is Billy Joel. What are you calling me for?"

Dave DiMartino (*journalist, editor,* Creem *magazine*): People might have said about *Creem:* "Well, they're no good since Lester Bangs left." I never said those words, but I imagine others did. So I had to operate, as did Sue, who worked directly with Lester for a couple of years, in his shadow. I was hired as an editorial assistant in '79, so I sat in the desk of their departed editorial assistant, and it happened to be Lester's desk. While I was working at his desk I would find some great stuff, like memos between him and Barry Kramer. I said, "I can't believe I'm sitting in this chair." There's some YouTube clip I saw in the past three years of Lester Bangs being interviewed about Roxy Music, and it freaked me out because he was sitting at my desk, and I saw some of the same pictures on the wall right behind that are always there. That was kind of cool.

I think Sue Whitall felt massively in the public eye because she replaced him.

Mark Norton: I was hired in before Dave was, in August '79. I said, "Barry, I gotta tell you something: your magazine used to be great and it really sucks now." He said, "What's wrong with it?" I told him, "Look, it's 1979, and there's all kinds of great music going on, and you still insist on running these stories about these hackneyed dinosaurs that don't have anything to do with contemporary street culture." He said, "Do you think you could change it?" I said, "Hell yes, I could change this." And I discovered that Barry used to keep his drugs in a hollowed-out Bible.

Dave DiMartino: The first day I worked at *Creem* Sue Whitall, Linda, and I went across the street to a restaurant to talk about *Creem* and what it was all about. Mark, who was not working there at the time—he hadn't even freelanced—happened to be by, so they invited him over too. So we sit down, and I guess he needed to show his license or something like that, for drinks or something. We were all pretty young. He said, "Hey, check out my address," and he lived with his parents then, in Troy, and his address was 69 Hampshire Place, and he pointed at the 69 and goes, giggle giggle. I said, "Alright! This guy is such a jerk—I love it!" He did it on purpose just to be an asshole, you know what I mean? It was so great.

Mark Norton: One time Chrissie Hynde agreed to be interviewed, but when she found out Sue was going to do it, she backed out. I was hired there at *Creem*, and Sue Whitall was the editor, and then my brother decides to start going out with her. And when things got bad between them, things got bad for me. One night he just left for Ohio, not telling her—or me for that matter. And then it was just bullshit at work; she was always on me. Dave and I begged Barry to get rid of Sue.

Dave DiMartino: The first cover that I worked on was Zeppelin, the live shot, the yellowish tint. At that point U2 was starting to be big. I think it was just their second album, and we ran in to do a set-up with them for a photo. They didn't want to do it unless they could be on the cover, and at that time Robert Plant and Zeppelin was still massive, and Robert Plant was going to give away one of his only three interviews for his solo career to *Creem*, and I said, "Look, I've already promised the cover to Robert Plant." The U2 guys are like, "Anyone that would put fucking Led Zeppelin on the cover instead of us, fuck 'em."

Robert Matheu: My first photo published in *Creem* was Mitch Ryder with Lou Reed onstage at Masonic. Lou was not really real big at that moment, the Street Hassle tour. Even though the Masonic show was sold out, it wasn't really *Creem* fodder anymore. Mitch came out and they did "Rock 'n' Roll" together. On my way out I see Jean MacDonald, the Arista rep. The next day I get a call from Sue Whitall at *Creem* saying, "Hey, Jean tells me you got photos of Mitch singing with Lou last night. I'd sure like to see 'em." I said, "Oh, great. I'll print some up and bring 'em up tomorrow." So the next day I go up there about noonish or something, with the prints, and knock on the door and, I'm poking around, and I ask where Sue is. This guy says, "Well, she went out to lunch a little while ago and stuff, and I'm not really sure." I said, "Who are you?" He goes, "I'm Dave DiMartino." I said, "Oh," and I didn't say anything for a second. And he says, "It's my first day here." Because I was kinda thinking in my mind, "Well, I don't know that name. Dave DiMartino? Am I in the right office? Is this the dentist's office?"

Pretty soon Bill Holdship and John Kordosh joined, and *Creem* was real good with them.

Mark Norton: Dave had to go interview the Clash at Masonic, and they were just having a bad day. They were on the bus or whatever, Dave was smoking a cigarette and blowing it in Joe Strummer's face, and Joe was saying, "What the fuck?" He was really mean to Dave then at the end, and then he smashed his hand on the tape recorder and walked out.

Dave DiMartino: It started out okay, and then all of a sudden Joe got really pissed off because he said I was blowing smoke in his face. It's actually incredibly fortunate in terms of trying to document the dialogue, because you can tell he's getting more pissed at me and more pissed at me. Then all of a sudden, when he smashed it, it was like one of those piano-key cassette recorders. It totally sounds like he's smashing something because it didn't just go off. During our talk I was a little cocky, and he kept complaining about their deal with CBS to the point where, if I couldn't elaborate on aspects of the deal, it would just be uninteresting reporting. So I'd say, "What do you mean? What's the deal, what's so bad about the deal?" He could have just said, "We gotta do fifteen records. And I don't really give a shit." And I'd say, "Oh, that sucks." But instead, he's saying, "You're just sitting there blowing smoke in my face, blah, blah, blah, about to go on stage, blah, blah, blah." Paul Morley, the *NME* writer, was on the road with them too, and after the, uh, incident, he said, "Well, how did it go?" I said, "Not too good. It started out okay, and then all of a sudden Joe got really pissed off because he said I was blowing smoke in his face."

Cathy Gisi: We were also buying interviews from other writers. We relied on word-of-mouth recommendations. We used to get unsolicited transcripts from all over the world. This one came in that was so well written and so well done that we got on the phone to talk with the writer. We had never seen him anywhere, and he sent us this fabulous interview with David Bowie. It comes out, and Bowie's publicist calls and says David never spoke to this writer. This guy had sent us hotel receipts and his notes—everything checked out. The writer defended himself to the hilt. I don't know how, but we came to some sort of an agreement with Bowie. They didn't want us to issue any kind of retraction. They realized we had re-searched this writer, and it was a great article. We ended up paying the writer too.

Mark Norton: I did some heroin, and Dave and I went to interview Bruce Spring-steen. I always wondered if Bruce knew. I was barely awake.

Dave DiMartino: I talked with Michael Bolton one time. Just before that I inter-viewed Dionne Warwick of all people, and she said something basically negative about Bolton. So then like a couple months later I had to go out on the road and do a Michael Bolton feature because he was at the peak of his fame. Bolton and I were—it sounds like a such a cliché, it's almost laughable—but he and I were in the back of a limo. I knew I had to ask this because I was told by higher ups to ask it. I said, "Let me ask you something: what do you think about the whole notion of people saying you're ripping off black music? Let me read you something Dionne Warwick said." I read him something about him stealing music from black people. His eyes started watering and he was just really quiet, and I could tell I really hurt him deeply by asking him that trash question. My heart fuckin' broke.

John Kordosh: Arista got me tickets to see Dave Davies, who must have totally been fucked up the night I went to see him. That's all I can conclude. He had every reason to totally fucking love me because I was the biggest Kinks fan in the god-damn country and also a big Dave Davies fan too. I'm standing around and Dave Davies comes out, and so I figured, well, I'm not interviewing him, but I'll just go say hi to him, and so I did. I said, "Hi, Dave," and he's short, like most of the British rockers of that era. He kind of looks up at me and says, "You're a fucking insect." And I go, "What?" This was apropos of nothing. Nothing had happened. I hadn't been making a pass at his girl, trying to steal his drink, or anything. Then he had some security guy try to kill me. He did, he absolutely did, he grabbed me by the collar—I was wearing a jacket—and he grabbed me by the collar of my jacket and, like, lifted me off the ground. I'm like, "What the fuck?" He used my face to open the door.

Cathy Gisi: People took it all so seriously. Bebe Buell called, and we had run a photo of her and her husband at the time, Todd Rungren, and this other guy who looked like he was talking to them seriously. This other person was saying, "Dr. so-and-so assures the Rundgrens the only thing wrong with their baby is 'It's Alive!'" She called and said, "Do you know how hurtful that is?" And the longer she ranted and raved, the more idiotic she sounded. It was all we could do to keep from laughing, and then it was, "You know this is *Creem* magazine, right?"

Dave DiMartino: I wrote a caption of a paparazzi shot of Christie Brinkley. She was waving at the camera and she had her hand raised, you know, so I put in quotes: "Married to a moron? Why, yes, I am!" So it looked like she was saying that. Billy Joel called up, and nobody was really believing it was Billy Joel, and he was really saying, "Look you can say whatever you want to about me, but don't fuckin' get to my wife/girlfriend."

Mark Norton: When Barry was six years old, his father died at thirty-seven. When Barry was thirty-seven, he died in 1981 and his kid JJ was six. Really, really spooky. On deadline that night—we were supposed to ship in the morning—and Barry walked in and said, "You guys want some pizza?" So we ordered some pizza in, and everybody took a slice. We're all drinking, and it was getting on about 1:00 in the morning, trying to get the captions done or whatever the hell we had to do. And Barry walks in and he opened this pizza box and he said, "Who ate the last piece?" I said I did, and he stomped out of there, and that's the last thing I saw of Barry Kramer. He died at three or four in the morning.

Bill Holdship (*journalist,* Creem *magazine*): I was told they found him with a bag over his head and, you know, a band around the neck. So to me that sounds like suicide, you know, but I guess he was also way out of it at the end. You know Dave told me stories of him, you know, thinking that there were, you know, the whole cocaine thing, where you think there are bugs under your skin.

Cathy Gisi: As tragic as it was when he died, I thought he wouldn't have had it any other way. He died laughing. He had that nitrous tank in the hotel room and had a party.

Linda Barber: He was loved by a lot of people, but I don't think he realized how much. It was a packed funeral. It wasn't standing room only, but being Jewish, he had to be buried right away. I got there after the casket was closed, and I'm glad of that. I want to remember him behind his desk.

Mark Norton: I think people like Whitall say I didn't snort shitloads of coke and drink with Barry. Well I did. Fuck you all. Barry was really lonely. The bartender at the Lemon Peel was his psychiatrist.

Cathy Gisi: When you got Barry by himself he was deeply emotional about people and the magazine and the world he grew up in. His allegiances to people never wavered even if they screwed him. He felt Lester had done that, but he never wavered from his devotion to Lester. When Connie wanted a divorce, he was so afraid he was going to lose this one stabilizing thing in his life. I think he partied one step too far between the coke and the nitrous. I don't think he intentionally took his own life.

Robin Sommers: Barry was intense at all times. He had drugs that none of us could get. DMT, which is still the best drug I ever had; it looked like tree sap and you smoked it in a hash pipe, and as you inhaled, it took three seconds, and then you started to hallucinate. To take acid the first time I did, it was up over at Barry's. I looked at the wall and it looked like coral, then flowers, and everything modulated. Barry had connections all over the area with everybody. He had friends that would go to Europe all the time.

You're Gonna Die

David Keeps, aka DB (*Destroy All Monsters, manager*): In the midseventies there was jack shit going on around Detroit. The MC5 guys were in prison or trying some new projects with little success. Bands had scattered. A bunch of hippies. I was going to U of M in Ann Arbor, where it was a $5 pot fine, so there was a lot of weed. Christmas break in 1973 Alice Cooper played in Ann Arbor at Crisler Arena. I went with my childhood friends, Cary Loren and Bobby Epstein. We went to Berkeley High School, and Cary had drifted off in a more arty, drug experimentation thing. Bobby and I were more into drama and academics.

Cary Loren (*Destroy All Monsters, guitarist, artist*): I started going out with Niagara when I was a senior in high school; she was a year older than me. We left Detroit to live in a commune that her sister and her sister's husband ran in Washington, DC. I was a bike messenger going around Washington, delivering all kinds of shit to people like Kissinger. I got hit by a bus, and my bicycle kind of crumbled up, and my glasses were broke. It was during a rainstorm, and the bus driver just picked me up and threw me on the sidewalk. At that point I just said, "I gotta get outta this place." It was a good excuse to leave, and the commune really hated us. I think they were getting sick of Niagara and I. So right after the bus hit me, we got these Alice Cooper tickets and we moved back to Michigan, to Ann Arbor, where we decided to kind of stay.

David Keeps: So lo and behold, the show happened. Cary shows up with Lynn Rovner, or Niagara, as she was calling herself by that time. We all went to high school together, so I was aware of who she was. But by this time, 1973, she was a completely different creature. She had a fire-engine red bob and wore sunglasses all the time and was completely obsessed with old movies and knew all the right bands, like Lou Reed, New York Dolls—all that early proto punk. With drugs. I was just captivated by her. That was around the same era that *Pink Flamingos* came out, because Niagara did not look unlike, at least hair-wise, Connie Marvel. I had gone and seen *Pink Flamingos* at a midnight screening in Ann Arbor. We saw it and then walked out and turned around and got right back in line and saw it a second time. Because it was just like this life changer.

Niagara (Destroy All Monsters, Dark Carnival, vocalist, artist): I started going to U of M art school, and the first person I met was Mike Kelley. He sat down next to me on the bus because I wasn't wearing overalls, which everyone else was at that time. It's hard for me to believe now, but that's what people were wearing: blue jeans and overalls and stuff. That was "in" for a short time. I was wearing a lot of eye makeup, as usual, and he thought I was kind of a transvestite type, like a Warhol superstar, and so he sat next to me and we got along.

David Keeps: After the Alice Cooper show we all became tight. I really admired what Cary and Niagara were doing. So much so that I ended up conning my parents into sending me to England to go to art school. I thought that I wanted to be an artist or painter or something like that. I left in '74, and meanwhile Cary started in on all kinds of avant-garde stuff—mostly underground movies and Jack Smith.

Cary Loren: Jack Smith did the film *Flaming Creatures*, one of the great artists and filmmakers. I was learning about La Monte Young and a lot of the composers of New York and the Velvet Underground and all that stuff of the sixties. I got to meet Jack and stay with him over a summer in New York. I brought his aesthetics back to Ann Arbor.

Niagara: Cary and I were into music, and since he was a guitarist, we had to start a band. We were doing every kind of art there was, going in all directions, so the band was obvious. Mike Kelley was my friend, and I practically lived there after school, at this house he shared with Jim Shaw. They had this big sign there that said, "God's Oasis Drive-In Church."

Sue Rynski (photographer): I came back to Ann Arbor after a year in Paris and wanted to finish my art studies at University of Michigan. I wandered into the God's Oasis house where the band had its headquarters. It was next to my apartment building, and Niagara came up to me and said, "You're going to be in a movie.

Let me get you a costume." They were filming something, and she was in a bridal dress. Niagara was nice and arty.

Niagara: One day Mike said to me, "Do you sing?" I told him, "Well, we wanted to start a band." Jim and Mike weren't musicians per se, and I became the front person. We practiced one day and then went to a party on New Year's Eve and told them we could play. We plugged in and we just did it. The guy at the house said, "Well, what's your name?" We had no idea. Jim just said, "Destroy All Monsters," and it was like, fine, that's not bad. That night we just jammed on "Iron Man" for as long as we could until they unplugged us. We're banging on cans. "Is he alive or is he dead" is all that I said.

Cary Loren: It was at a comic book warehouse where they had these meetings and sold comic books and distributed them. It was a party for mostly young kids and people that worked at the warehouse. We thought, "Well, we look like a band." But we were just screwing around and doing our thing, playing noise, playing with records while we practiced. I think we started to play "Iron Man" or something like that.

David Keeps: When Cary was twelve he was a classical guitarist. He could play like Segovia. I used to sit and watch him play guitar when we were in grade school. Mesmerizing, brilliant guitarist. Then you've heard Destroy All Monsters, that period of music, '73 or '74. It sounds like he can't play at all. Certainly not that he has any classical background. So Destroy All Monsters had that same sensibility as the Stooges when Iggy was pushing around a vacuum cleaner. When Mike Kelley and Jim Shaw went to California to continue their art education, Cary found the Miller brothers, Larry and Ben.

Sue Rynski: With the Miller brothers, the music was spacey rock. Ben and Larry were trained musicians and added another dimension. Niagara had songs like "Bored." Iggy ripped that song off. It was clear he gets a lot of material like that. I was listening to this song from Party and he says, "I wonder if you'll hear this song." Then he mentions me in that song "Girls," where he sings "Hanging down with Susie." I get angry when I hear that.

Robert Matheu: Iggy had done this little rap and he said, "She's got big boobs and she's got high-heeled shoes," and he was singing about Sue. You know, because she was hanging out and he was watching her at sound check and making up this little thing. I'm not necessarily saying the song was inspired by her, but definitely part of the lyrics.

Niagara: Pretty soon after Jim and Mike left, Ronnie [Asheton] came back from LA after New Order didn't work out. I met Ronnie at the Second Chance in Ann Arbor at a Ramones show in '77. Joey Ramone was walking around backstage with a bag on his nose, and I was like, "You mean that glue thing is like true?" I know he did glue. You can't write about something that beautifully and not have done it. At least that night. Everyone that I've said that to has been surprised. John Holmstrom in New York was like, "What?" Listen, I saw it. If this was the only time he did it, I saw that time. Ronnie looked very dapper. He'd just come from LA, and he had on a white flight scarf with a couple rhinestones in it and a jacket and a vest and had a cigarette holder. His hair was perfect, Brian Jones–like. Aviator glasses. His jeans were pressed. He was really styling in a low-key way. We talked, and at the end of the night he was saying, "I can get you some German military women's jackets." I thought, "This is a come on that I usually don't get." Cary got his number and told him we have a band and we had the Miller brothers playing for us, these big psychedelic, twin, beautiful brothers. Cary was amazing after that; he didn't leave Ronnie alone.

Cary Loren: It had come into my mind to get Ron Asheton into the group, and we had a concert coming up at the Underground; it was built into this hill. I got Ron to come out to see us; I gave him a six-pack to come.

David Keeps: Which is odd. I don't know what Cary was expecting because his vision of what the band was going to be, or at least his vision of the band as it had expressed itself on stage prior to Ron and Mike coming to the group, would be baffling to those guys, who were in bands that had record label deals and wrote their own songs. They came from a place. They had seen the big time. Ron was fairly fresh from the big time, because this was '77. Ron must have looked at this and said, "What the fuck?!"

Niagara: Ronnie was pretty laid back. He didn't know what his next step was, and Cary just kept after him and said, "Well, come to a practice. Just practice one day." Cary finally got him to do it. Ronnie said, "At least I'll get a free six-pack of beer." You know, he didn't have any money. So he came to practice. We hit it off pretty much.

Cary Loren: He saw we had a scene; it was a freak scene. And we all looked up to Ron. He was a superstar of the area. He was living with his mom. I would pick him up and drive him to our practice.

Niagara: I was freaked because I was singing. I was a nervous wreck. I took a nice pill and I felt better. I never had stage fright because I knew I'd be high enough that I wouldn't care, so I never really got stage fright. In the beginning I had Tuinal. They were called rainbows; they were turquoise and red and in the middle they were purple. They were real pretty. I was into these beautiful pills. I also had Seconals that were bright red, and I got them at the free clinic where this beautiful doctor was. He looked like a gnome with the little glasses, but he was real big, and he was so slow and sweet. I'd say, "I have trouble sleeping." He'd go, "Have you ever tried the old-fashioned remedy, Tuinal?" I said, "No, but would it help?" So he was giving me all these great pills. There was nothing wrong with that. After a while that wasn't going on, and I started drinking some like everybody else.

Sue Rynski: Ron joined and brought in Michael Davis, who was just out of Lexington prison. Ron was important, but none of those guys took themselves for anything special. They'd done their thing and failed, and they were humbled and serious.

Niagara: At that time Ron was living with Ann. Ann, my Ann. That was one of my first questions to Ronnie when I found out his mother's name. I said, "Ann, my Ann?" He said, "Yeah, Iggy was trying to be funny and put that name in." Scott and Ron were both living there, and I had an apartment. Then when Ronnie and I got together, we were staying at people's places that were gone or something. I had a little job somewhere for a couple months, and I got food stamps. I didn't get money, but I got food stamps. After that I couldn't imagine spending money for food. We started to hang out with some of the MC5 guys along with Michael. Fred Smith was really fascinating, and he was a real trickster. He wanted to take people and just mess with their minds. He would do that with Cary when Cary was on the verge of losing his mind, and it was terrible. Fred would go, "I just had sex with Niagara in the back room." Cary would be like, "Is that really true? Did that just happen?" Fred was trying to pull all this horrible stuff. He didn't know that Cary was losing his mind.

Cary Loren: I broke up with Niagara earlier in 1977. She had become Ron's girlfriend. This stuff happens in bands; we were still playing. Then the end of summer 1977 I went to New York to promote the band. I went to see a show at Max's

Kansas City and I got dosed; I think it was PCP. I couldn't even find my car. I couldn't drive; I was lost for several days in the city. I got back and had to go in the hospital. I was sedated. Then I was going to practices, and I couldn't even hold my guitar. It was a Syd Barrett situation. I was voted out of the band.

David Keeps: I went to London for a while, and when I got back Cary had been thrown out of the band and Niagara and Ron were together. Niagara has amazing allure. I don't think she could be bothered to seduce anybody. It's like one of her paintings says, "I'm going to play with his brain like a drunk kitten."

Niagara: Cary had troubles before that, and then the guys agreed he had to go. Cary came over; I was crying. I was pretty shocked he was out of the band. We had broken up about that time. He was like, "I lost my job, my band, my girl, and my mind."

David Keeps: I was listening to the Stooges and the MC5, and it was kind of amazing to be involved in this group. Not actually playing in the group but being involved with a group of people like that. Just a couple years earlier we were smoking pot every day and every night listening to the same records: *Berlin* by Lou Reed, the New York Dolls, some Velvet Underground, Stooges, MC5, and doing artwork. Cary would be doing something, Niagara would be painting some kind of water color, I would be doing some kind of ridiculous, crappy collage. Now all of a sudden these people were in our lives.

Sue Rynski: Iggy came to town to visit one day after a Destroy All Monsters show at the Second Chance in July '77. Before he got there, I caught DB chanting to himself so he wouldn't be nervous. Everyone came over to my house to watch the video from the night before and we're sitting there, and Scotty came over, then Iggy walks in. That made me nervous. He thought Ron's band was nothing special, and who's this girl who can't sing, and he wasn't very nice. We went to another place with a good turntable, and he played us the test press for *Lust for Life*.

Hiawatha Bailey (*Stooges roadie, Cult Heroes, vocalist*): I was watching the video at Sue's, and people were all talking, and I felt this hush come over the room, and I just kept watching. And someone lays down on the floor next to me, and I turn around and it's Iggy. So I asked him what he thought of Ron's new band. He said, "Well, I always like Ron's guitar playing, but that singer is awful." And Niagara was standing right behind us. She had to hear, but she didn't say anything.

Niagara: It was in our coke dealer's house the first time he came to town. Iggy was nice and he said, "Call me Jim." I just thought it's too . . . I can't just call him Jim. I should call him Iggy because it's like calling someone like Mr. something. So when I called him Iggy he would just hate that, and I was like, "Oh God, that's not right."

David Keeps: Iggy mistook me for somebody that he used to know, so he would, like, sidle up to me and put his arms around me and say, "I haven't seen you in so long." I was walking down the street and I'm thinking, "Okay, Iggy thinks I'm somebody else and I'm not going to tell him differently. At least not right away." I mean, I've got Iggy's arm around my neck. I think I will stay this way for awhile. That was a moment for sure. My perception of that was that he and Ron were not cool. Like they were in contact with one another, but they hadn't reached the kind of rapprochement that happened when they finally ended up touring.

Niagara: Every time Iggy would get in touch, they were asking him, "Hey, when are the Stooges getting back together?" Iggy would call every year and say, "Yeah, we might do that." So every year he would put Ron and Scott through this thing like they're getting back together, and it never would happen. He'd be in town, and we'd hang out with him.

Iggy Pop (*The Stooges, Iggy and the Stooges, solo, vocalist*): Ron and I would run into each other once in a while, and I didn't get that vibe, but I didn't get a bad vibe either. Finally, when he became more active in something that was, what I thought was a step up from what he was doing in the Detroit area with . . . what's her name?

DJ Dianna (*Club DJ*): Poor Ron. It's never good to have your girlfriend in your band. But she couldn't sing and was fucked up. Her voice was atrocious, and she would start twiddling knobs on Ron's amp.

Niagara: DB was our manager and he wanted to take us to Europe. But it was terrible because he took the first offer. He liked the guy and made a gentleman's agreement that this guy would handle our tour. Then this other company came along and offered DB everything. Big posters, all that. And he didn't take it. We didn't know until later that he never signed anything with the first guy, that it was just gentlemen's agreement. So DB made a terrible tactical mistake, and at the same time we're finding out, we're not sleeping anywhere. And where were we getting anything to eat?

David Keeps: We were getting by okay, but one day we were driving along in the van, and I look over and Niagara is eating split-pea soup out of the can with a spoon. Which was weird on its own but also because she never ate anything but sweets.

Niagara: The shows themselves were great. Every time we played, people went berserk. I don't really remember a show we played at anywhere that people didn't go crazy, so I was thinking of it that way. There were some big shows and some little crummy shows. We played in Liverpool. We played across the street from where the Beatles played. The reviews were really funny. They would say that Ron had gained weight since the Stooges was their main thing. You know how in England their style of writing is being really bitchy and really laying it on. Ronnie stopped reading them. We were there a month and played almost every night. People were real nice, of course, and they were always saying, "I could have got you this tour" all along the way. DB was getting like more and more, like, to himself, like, he wouldn't talk to us anymore. He stopped touring with us eventually. He just hated us, I think. Mike Davis was starting to call him "snot finger" because he always had all these allergies and he was always gross. DB finally left us at the airport on standby for three days while we sat there with no money, no food. We were calling anyone we knew. DB was like, yeah, bye. DB thought he'd be making money.

David Keeps: The tour of England really wiped things out. There was absolutely no indication that anything was going to happen in the US. I had sent the first single to Sire Records and to Bomp and anyone else on the map at the time. I got no's. So we had two singles out. "Bored" went over to England as an import, and somebody at Cherry Red found it. Cherry Red signed us and they said, "We can put you on the road. We're going to release the single and put you on the road." American punk bands were cracking the charts in England in those years. We'll do it in England like so many other punk bands have. We had hotels. There was a road manager. It was proper, and we played a lot of places. We played in Sheffield, and the guy from the Human League came and saw the show. Lemmy from Motorhead was at one of the shows. Hull was like the most punk of all. Hull was people breaking beer bottles and lining the front of the stage trying to get Niagara to crawl into them. I kinda got held up by the promoters there, though. At the end of it all I had to call my dad and get him to wire me $10,000. I was told by the promoter, "Well, things really didn't work out that well, and the shows weren't really 'dot, dot, dot, dot' and it's going to cost you $10,000." I was shocked to be handed a bill for $10,000. And the tour agents were holding our passports, for "safe keeping." I actually had a moment when I thought, "I'm just gonna get on a plane and go home and fuck it. I'm leaving. Just let it be. I'm not going to pay the $10,000, this is bullshit." The band were never concerned about money that I owed or what I spent. I think Ron and Mike certainly wanted more and expected more.

Dave Hanna (*Ramrods, Space Heaters, guitarist*): David Keeps came back from England after the Destroy All Monsters tour with these singles. There were only a handful of people around town who knew what they were, these great 45s, the Sex Pistols and the Damned. That really started something. There was no form to follow. It was reckless. It was stupid. It was creative. There were no places to play. People were just starting to write music. We just came across each other from seeing the bands. It such a small group of people that whoever was playing, all the same people would be there.

We started bands and were just playing the history of Detroit music. We played MC5 songs and Stooges songs. New York Dolls. For as much good stuff came out of the seventies, the radio sucked. There was nothing. You had to look elsewhere.

Sweet Nothin'

Hiawatha Bailey: I was sentenced to prison for selling drugs. They busted everyone in town, it seemed, and I was one of them, although I was on the run for six months before I turned myself in. The music was over, the bands were gone, and there it was. When I first got sentenced, I thought they'd send me to Milan, a federal penitentiary in Michigan. The next thing I know, they put me in this van that was dropping people off at various places. First we were going to Alderson, and the next stop was where I was going—Lexington, Kentucky. You know the *Valley of the Dolls?* The women's prison in Alderson, Virginia, is called the Valley of the Dolls. They had all of these women in the van with me, and there was this pregnant woman who was saying, "I don't care what he is, I'm getting me some dick before they lock me up." I'm like, "Whoooa." I'm in this van with all these horny women, and I'm the only male. I'm scared, okay, let me out, please, help me, Jesus. So they get me to Lexington, Kentucky. It was an experimental prison for drug offenders. There was a place in Lexington called ARC, the Addiction Research Center, and they were doing all kinds of weird research. The prison was like a dorm, you couldn't leave and you are a number. Mine was 29750–117. I was in Younity unit, which was general population for cocaine and acid people. There was also a heroin unit. One day I'm walking through the lobby of the place, and there were people sitting in the lobby waiting to be assigned a room. This person sitting there waiting looks at me and I look back and I look again, and I think, "How cool could the fates be that that person looked like Michael Davis?" You're not supposed to talk to incoming residents, but I come over and look at him and said, "Hey, Michael." And he looks at me and says, "What?" He didn't recognize me—it was such a strange place to see someone. So I start walking away, and he said again, "What?" So I came over and I said, "I was just wondering. You look like Michael Davis from the MC5." And he says real low, "Oh yeah? What if I am?" I said, "Michael, hey hey!" And he remembered me, and it was insane. I had someone in there with me. One day Mike and I were sitting about, and he was reading *Rolling Stone*, and it says Wayne Kramer was busted and was being sent to an undisclosed location in the federal correctional system, and Mike showed me this and says, "Hi, I hate Wayne." And I said, "Michael, what would the odds be they would send him here?"

Wayne Kramer: Everyone who was in Lexington was kind of hipster. It was the end of an old program. End of the era of rehab in American corrections. It was built in the thirties as a public works narcotics farm. One of the first attempts to deal with drug addiction as a social problem, not a criminal one. We had therapy and behavior modification treatments. I went down in '75, came up in '78. When I caught my case, Michael told me he had caught one too. He figured, "Well, we'll be in Lexington or Sandstone." I had a terrific lawyer, but it didn't mean a thing. I went through the same trauma of being locked up, though. Had a terrible time. On the trauma scale it's right below losing a child, I'd say.

Hiawatha, being a gay man, it's not what people think, being in prison. Gay people have always gone to prison, and they find their space and learn how to live. I wasn't with him all the time, but we worked together for a year or so, and nobody beat on him or raped him or anything that I know of. Michael was pretty low key; he didn't play in the prison band or anything. He was discouraged about music I think; our relationship was strained in that way. We had history together, which was of value in those circumstances, but he was just disenchanted with the idea of music.

Hiawatha Bailey: After I got out I was living at this farm with Michael Davis and this woman, Pam. We had a practice space where Destroy All Monsters would rehearse, and Scott Asheton was living with Liz, his girlfriend for a bit. I had started my band, the Cult Heroes. Fred Smith was coming down, and him and Rock and Scott started playing songs in the rehearsal room. Which was the seeds of Sonic's Rendezvous Band. One night Michael and Fred had a fight at our house. Fred was coming over a lot, and Dennis would come over once in a while, and I thought, "This is great, I'm going to get the MC5 back together." Fred and Rock would sit in our driveway and drink. So one night I came home and just Fred was out there, so I asked him inside, and then I went to the store and got some Jack Daniels. I was trying to figure out this guitar chord, and we're all in the living room drinking—Fred, Michael, me. I was asking Fred how to play this guitar chord, and he said, "So you fancy yourself a guitar player now?" He takes my Melody Maker and shows me how to finger it and leans over and gives me a kiss on the head. And Michael says, "What do you think you're doing? You've turned into a real asshole." They stand up and look at each other—I mean, I'm scared, these are tough guys—and Fred goes, "It's your house. You take the first hit." Mike says, "You're the guest. You take the first hit." And Fred popped him one. Man, they fought all over this house; they flopped over on each other. We had this potbelly stove, and they knocked that over. It was the battle of the titans, this MC5 battle in my living room. I finally pulled them apart. Then they sat down and everything was okay again.

Gary Rasmussen (*The Up, Sonic's Rendezvous Band, bassist*): Ron Cooke was the first bass player. I took his place in Sonic Rendezvous. Ron had been playing with Mitch Ryder and selling his equipment and buying motorcycles. He had a thing with Scott Asheton too, where they weren't real tight. I don't know if Ron didn't think Scott was very good. But Ron would come to me and say, "Hey, can I borrow your amp this weekend?" Or "Can I borrow a bass from you this weekend?"

Ron Cooke (*Detroit, Sonic's Rendezvous Band, Gang War, bassist*): I only knew Fred Smith before that from passing. Quiet dude. How he ever got the name Sonic, I don't know, man. It would take a bomb to move that guy. I knew Scotty before that too. That was a Fred-and-Scott conscious decision to hook up for some reason. Fred just said, "Hey, Scott's coming over to jam with us." I always loved playing with Scott. Musically, Scott and I really played well off of each other. When I was there, the band didn't even have a name. So it was kind of like a band.

Gary Rasmussen: One day Fred called me and asked me if I wanted to play a gig with them in Bad Axe. So he sent over a tape, and I had three days to learn the material. Scott Asheton had been saying, "Ron's fuckin' out of his mind, and you should get Gary."

Ron Cooke: I'm not a type-A personality, you know, and where Fred is like not a capital A type. He don't want to move too fast. To get Fred to do something, man, was, like, I can go to the United Nations and get something done easier. And Fred was not a hustler in regards to taking care of his own professional image. I just got tired, and I just didn't think the band was going anywhere.

Gary Rasmussen: I drove everyone to Bad Axe because I had a car. I don't think anyone else did.

Scott Morgan (*Rationals, Sonic's Rendezvous Band, guitarist, vocalist*): Fred and I had been hanging out with Gary, establishing a relationship. Then he did that Bad Axe gig, and it was really good. The handwriting was on the wall, and we took Gary. Ron will tell you something different.

Ron Cooke: Bad Axe. Yeah, I wasn't in the band then. I had quit. I've tried to set this story straight a number of times because this always comes up. After I fucking had done all I had done in my career and I had played with some fucking drummers outside of Johnny Badanjek. I'm in the rhythm section, pal. I got impeccable fucking meter. So my musical mind at that time was, "Am I wasting my fucking time here?" Playing is hanging, and fucking playing, talking to each other musically, man. What do you think jazz cats do, man? They just have a bigger vocabulary, man. I probably said more words to you right there than I ever said to Scotty Asheton in my lifetime, man. God bless him! I'm glad that they got out there and they did their thing. That's fucking fine. The story of that, and I've set it straight that way a number of times. That's the deal. I did not leave that band because of Asheton. That is not the case at all. They were not trying. Hey, I'm from a working band, man.

Gary Rasmussen: We made very little money, ever. There were a lot of gigs we did where there was hardly anybody there. The people who were there hated us and said we were way too loud. I used to have to drive to pick up Fred in Detroit for practice because he had his license taken away for a while. He had been drinking all night, and it was like eight o'clock in the morning, and he just plowed into the side of a cop car. Lost his license for a while. Scott Asheton had these weird day jobs. A friend of his did tree work, so he was cutting trees; I had a friend who was doing landscaping, and he would hire me and my friends to come and do awful landscaping work. And he worked at a place called the frog farm for quite a while. It's a University of Michigan frog farm; actually they grow frogs from tadpoles to frogs for experiments—they send them to schools to be dissected. Then he worked at the tofu place in Ann Arbor for a little while.

Harold Richardson (*Gravitar, Easy Action, Negative Approach, guitarist*): Scott Asheton drove a cab in Ann Arbor the same time I did, and he was a disaster. He would take the cab back to his mom's and just sit. They fired him.

David Keeps: Scott Asheton was the person out of that whole thing that intimidated me the most because he looked most like the person who would step off a motorcycle and snap your neck like a pencil. So I gave him a wide berth.

Robert Matheu: The only time I ever got any kind of STD was from Scott Asheton's girlfriend of the time. She was sixteen, and I got crabs from her.

Scott Morgan: I was living with my parents at the time. Scott was living with his mom. Those guys would live any place they could. Fred stayed at my parent's house. Fred and Freddie Brooks, who was managing us, stayed at Gary's apartment. We were lucky to get Scott a set of drums. We went down to the local music store, and he picked out a set of Ludwigs, and we put them on a payment plan, and his mom signed for it. I don't know if he ever paid that back.

Gary Rasmussen: Freddie Brooks was managing us, and he was getting some of the gigs. Sometimes I think he took all of the money. For a while Freddie was living in my apartment hallway. The stairs came up and then this little hallway, and my door, and window—he kind of set himself up there outside the door. He would live there and get up in the morning when we'd get up and come in and use my phone to try to get work. There was a little competition between Fred and Scott Morgan, so it was a good thing for the band, because Fred would show up and go, "I've got two new songs," and Scott would go, "I got three new songs," and Fred would go, "Well, I've got another one too."

Scott Morgan: We both had songs. I would write something, and Fred would write something.

Chris Panackia: Sonic's Rendezvous Band was really not an Ann Arbor band, but they would play there all the time. They were the kind of band you really had to like to go see. They were just fucking boring. But you got past that because of who was in the band. You would not want to look at that band when they played. They looked like a bunch of fuckin' drunk hillbillies, God bless 'em. Fred's a great player, and Scott Asheton is a fucking great drummer. Never hit his rap tom or floor tom. He was always fixing his hi-hat and right cymbal crash. You look at his toms, and they never had dents, they were never dirty. Because he never hit them.

Gary Rasmussen: We had label interest, but Fred was bitter about being ripped off by the record labels. He made money, because at some point he had a Corvette and a motorcycle and a bunch of guitars and stuff. I think he lost it all. He didn't have shit.

Robert Matheu: Fred had already done that with MC5 and didn't want to play the game. I can say that this is why Fred didn't want a record deal. He already had a shot at a record deal and didn't want to fail again. He wanted to stay where Sonic's Rendezvous Band was and say we have a nice little thing here and it doesn't have to be big.

Gary Rasmussen: When somebody would come from a label, he'd be rude to them on purpose. He thought, "We're going to do this, but not now." Which was Fred's thing for years. He'd ask me, "We're gonna do this, what do you think?" I'd tell him, "I think this is gonna be good; I think we should do it. When do you want to do it?" "Well, not this week, but I'll call you next week," and that went on for years. It makes you nuts.

Scott Morgan: Fred met Patti when she came to Detroit on her first tour. We all decided to go see her play, and she was doing a meet and greet at the Lafayette Coney Island downtown. You could see the sparks fly. It turned out really well; they had a good life.

Robert Matheu: I was talking to Lenny Kaye that night at Lafayette, and I lost his attention because Patti walked over, and Lenny was saying something like, "Hey Patti. Fred Smith's here. Remember I was telling you about him? He's one of the guitar players from the MC5." It's not like she didn't remember. It always stuck with me that he was telling her who Fred Smith was. Because I thought, "Geez, everyone should know who he is." I thought later, "Do you think that there was a period of time, like after Patti retired in the eighties, that maybe Lenny just looked back for a second and kinda regretted introducing Patti to Fred?" You know, because they got married, and he was out of a gig and there was no more Patti Smith Group.

Gary Rasmussen: Patti and Fred were involved while he was still married. She really loved Fred. It was awkward sometimes too, because we'd be playing someplace, just a club, and then Patti would show up, and then here's the crowd watching us, and then all of a sudden the crowd is watching her watching us. She was making money. They were connected; they were on the phone together all the time. We played together, and sometimes we'd have rooms, and she'd be somewhere better.

The gigs with her were way good gigs for us, at Masonic Temple, the Aragon Ballroom in Chicago, she was on that level. And we were in the sleazehole clubs, doing whatever we had to do. Not long after that, Iggy approached us for his European tour. It was his last thing for RCA records. We went three weeks early to rehearse. They were great gigs, like three months' worth, three or four a week. I was three months behind in my rent when we went over there, but I was sending money home.

Scott Morgan: We had recorded "City Slang" and "Electrophonic Tonic," then Fred and Gary and Scott went to Europe with Iggy. Fred told me Iggy wanted them to go to Europe, and I told him that was fine; we'd put the single out when they got back. Iggy didn't ask me to go. Then the tour ended after three months, and Iggy wanted to keep the band for the US leg, but they had already decided they were coming back. They didn't just want to be Iggy's band; they wanted to be the Sonic Rendezvous Band. I don't know what happened on that tour though, because when they came back, Fred and I had a falling out. They started giving me a hard time because I had been in the studio messing around, doing other stuff, and they were upset about it. So I said, "Well, I don't want my song on the record"—"Electrophonic Tonic." That was the stupidest thing I could have said. It ended up a mono mix of "City Slang" on the other side.

Bob Mulrooney: We used to call Sonic's Rendezvous Band "Sominex Rendezvous." They would play for so long, and they had "City Slang," which was phenomenal, but they had ten other songs that were just like "City Slang." They kept giving Scott Morgan, who kind of turned out to be a not-so-great performer, a smaller and smaller role. Freddie Brooks said he was their manager, and he thought Fred Smith was God.

Gary Rasmussen: At some point Scott Morgan was kind of on the outs; he was not really involved in it anymore. Fred got so involved with Patti that we weren't playing and we weren't rehearsing and we weren't doing anything, although we talked about it a lot, and we went from actively doing things to talking about things, and then it got to be where Scott wasn't really involved at all anymore. Scott Morgan was a little miffed, I think, when we went to Europe to play with Iggy; Patti and Fred were living in the Book Cadillac Hotel before it was renovated. They had a mattress, basically, living this Bohemian lifestyle. Me and Scott Asheton would go to Detroit, and we'd go to the studio and not do that much, just sort of play some, and we'd end up going to the bar, and getting way wasted. I was stopped a couple of times, and the cops would say, "Can you get home?" I could not drink with Scott Asheton or Fred. They're serious, professional drinkers, and I'd end up trashed.

Scott Morgan: The band would have meetings in Detroit maybe once a week and just hang out and talk a bit. Then one day Gary called me and said, "You're not in the band anymore." I'm not sure why Fred didn't call me. I can't ask Fred.

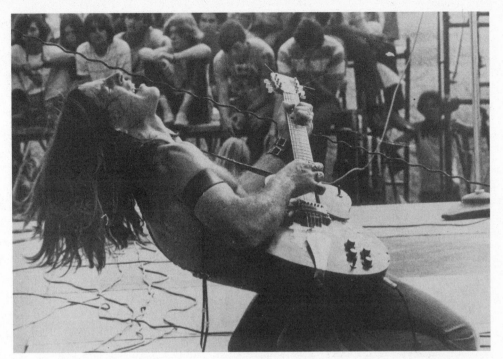

Mark Farner, 1969 Grand Funk Railroad publicity photo. Farner: "I always wanted to create this atmosphere where the only thing going was the music. That's why it was important to play really loud. I don't want people talking while we're playing." (From the collection of Jack Bodner)

MC5, 1969, Michael Davis, Wayne Kramer, Rob Tyner, Dennis Thompson, Fred "Sonic" Smith. Dennis Thompson: "We grew up with the same working class ethic, the same outlook and attitude towards music. It needed to have passion. It needed to have an emotional message. I think these were things that we understood well before our age." (Lee Short, from the collection of UHF Music Royal Oak)

SRC on Tubeworks 1968, Glenn Quackenbush, Scott Richardson, E. G. Clawson, Al Wilmot, Gary Quackenbush. Gary Q: "The cool thing about SRC was that we were always playing good shows for good money. For two years we grossed over a hundred thousand dollars a year. So that would be worth a quarter mill now or more? And we didn't put it up our nose." (Robert Matheu)

Rob Tyner with Davison Township Police Chief Ed Boyce, MC5 show at Sherwood Forest, October 1969. John Sinclair: "Tyner was a guy who went way beyond music. Music was his basis, but I mean he had a huge mind. We were a great pair, just flying mentally in the same orbit." (From the collection of Peter Cavanaugh)

The Frost playing the Grande Ballroom. Bobby Rigg, Donny Hartman, Gordy Garris, Dick Wagner. Bobby Rigg: "We recorded our second album there. It was 96 degrees outside. There was no ventilation in the Grande Ballroom. The roadies were pouring water over me." (Photo courtesy collection of Dick Wagner)

Brownsville Station. Tony Driggins, Michael Lutz, T. J. Cronley, Cub Koda. Lutz: "We had a van for the equipment and we bought a limousine from the old Cadillac Hotel down in Detroit. The limo was great for traveling in because it rode great. The four of us would ride in that and then our two road crew would be traveling in the van." (Lee Short, from the collection of UHF Music Royal Oak)

Goose Lake, Detroit's Woodstock, August 7–9, 1970. Freak flags flying high. Michigan Governor William Milliken: "I do not oppose rock festivals, but I do oppose and will fight drug abuse such as took place at Goose Lake." (Lee Short, from the collection of UHF Music Royal Oak)

Ted Nugent leading the Amboy Dukes at the Eastown in 1971. Nugent: "Tune in drop out, but I got news for ya, if what you're doing is causing you to drop out, you're not tuning in." (Robert Matheu)

Alice Cooper carries old school Michelob bottle and Glen Buxton carries bottle and SG to stage, Cobo Arena, 1972. Alice: "We were driving along to rehearsal one day and CKLW's pick hit was 'I'm Eighteen' and we stopped the car, and just sat there and listened to it and went 'Well even if that's the only play we ever get, we heard it on CKLW and a lot of people heard it.'" (Robert Matheu)

Detroit with Mitch Ryder. Left to right, Steve Hunter, Johnny Bee, Mitch Ryder, Ron Cooke, Brett Tuggle. Shot at local Channel 62 in April 1972. Mitch: "To start the band Detroit, I think somebody just fucking opened the prison doors." (Leni Sinclair)

Suzi Quatro center stage at Olympia, opening for Alice Cooper in 1975. Suzi: "We used to practice at the Alice Cooper farm when the neighbors got pissed off around our place." (Lee Short, from the collection of UHF Music Royal Oak)

Sonic's Rendezvous Band, Fred Smith, Gary Rasmussen, Scott Asheton, Scott Morgan, in 1977 at Morgan's Ann Arbor house. Morgan: "One single in six years of playing together. We weren't making any money, our touring was sporadic." (Robert Matheu)

Ron Asheton and Niagara on the floor of Bookie's, 1977. Niagara: "I love his solos because they're like a story, they start out and they have a middle and an end." (Robert Matheu)

Bob Seger and the Silver Bullet Band at the Pontiac Silverdome. Drew Abbott, guitar; Chris Campbell, bass; Bob Seger, piano; Robyn Robbins, organ; Charlie Martin, drums. Drew Abbott: "We were guaranteed a bunch of money, over $100 grand. A lot of money back then, pocket change today." (Tom Weschler)

Don Was, leading the Traitors, Bookie's, 1978. Was: "The punk stuff out of Bookie's was mostly influenced by New York." (Robert Matheu)

The Romantics at Bookie's, 1979. Mike Skill: "We're playing all these clubs everywhere and there's an energy right in front of the crowd. The crowd's right there and you're playing off the crowd, real close." (Robert Matheu)

Cobo Arena, from the stage outward. Robert Matheu: "Until '77/'78 there was no such thing as a photo pass. Detroit crowds were notorious for rushing the stage within the first three or four songs, so it was about position and hoping to get a good spot while you remained salve to the crowd." (Robert Matheu)

Bookie's, a former burlesque/gay bar turned into the city's punk rock joint in 1978. Scott Campbell: "They had these different managers running Bookie's. They would play Donna Summer while we were trying to set up for the night. I would get there early with my PA and they would bitch at us." (Courtesy of Scott Campbell)

Mark Norton, singer for the Ramrods, at Concord Castle, an apartment building off downtown Detroit. Gary Reichel, Cinecyde: "I just sat there and shouted and went 'Oh my God. This stuff is great!' And it was like brothers-in-arms. I couldn't believe it. There was someone else who's doing it." (Katy Hait)

Gary Reichel, vocalist for Cinecyde, at the Kramer Theater. The band led off the Detroit wave of late seventies New Wave bands with a DIY single, "Gutless Radio." Mark Norton, Ramrods: "You can't talk about seventies punk in Detroit without talking about Cinecyde." (©2013 S. Kay Young Photography, LLC)

Iggy singing "Empty Heart" with Sonic's Rendezvous Band, November 1979, at the New Miami in Detroit after Iggy's *New Values* tour show at the Masonic Auditorium. (Robert Matheu)

Nikki Corvette, leader of Nikki and the Corvettes. Nikki: "I went every place when I was a kid, they all thought, 'There's this crazy sixteen-year-old girl who's at all of these shows.'" (Robert Matheu)

Crowd, Negative Approach at the Freezer, 1982. Corey Rusk: "The Freezer was like a sort of hippy, poetry slam, sort of place." (Davo Scheich)

Corey Rusk, the Necros. Rusk was a driver of the hardcore movement that Detroit predictably did better than anyone else. Touch and Go Records founder Tesco Vee passed the baton to Rusk, who took the label To Indie Valhalla. (Davo Scheich)

The Laughing Hyenas, Kevin Monroe, John Brannon, Larissa Strickland, at Staches, Columbus, Ohio, 1989. Monroe: "A guy came out to look at this house we were renting in Ann Arbor, he was thinking about buying it. He said the owner told him we were a cult." (Jay Brown)

The White Stripes, Jack and Meg White, backstage at the 40 Watt in Athens, Georgia, September 1999, opening for Pavement. The headliners loved the Stripes enough to give them a bonus of $500, which covered the minivan they had to rent for the weekend. (Photo courtesy of Ben Blackwell)

Human Eye: Bottom, left to right: Brad Hales, Johnny LZR. Top, left to right: Timmy Vulgar, Hurricane William Hafer. (Lindsey Muliolis)

The Go, John Krautner and Bobby Harlow, at the Beechland Ballroom in Cleveland, second US Tour, 1999. Harlow: "If you take young guys with shaggy hair and tight pants and baby faces and leather jackets and put them in front of teenagers I think that it just kind of works." (Keith Marlowe)

Mike E. Clark's mom bequeathed him $500 on her deathbed so that he could take some classes in audio production. He's the go-to producer for Insane Clown Posse. Kid Rock is lucky to have him. (Photo courtesy of Mike E. Clark)

The Dirtbombs ending their set at the Detroit Institute of Arts, October 2006. The show was a party for the film *It Came From Detroit*, which documented the Detroit music scene in the late nineties. Pat Patano, Mick Collins, Ben Blackwell, Ko Melina. Obscured by Patano, Troy Gregory. (EWolf)

The Dirtys play the Shelter, 1996. Joe Burdick: "We eventually realized the backlash of all the shows we had played in Detroit and all the shit we had broke. We had destroyed the whole back room of the Magic Stick doing body prints in the dry wall. We had to give up our whole pay that night." (Amy Cook)

Bantam Rooster at Zoots. Eric Cook, drums, and Tom Potter, guitar. Potter: "Girls didn't even have jobs then, except for being secretaries. In our day and age women can have real jobs cause I've lived off plenty of them." (Amy Cook)

Rachel Nagy, Detroit Cobras: "They were trying to find singers and nothing was working out. I was always there, watching the *Simpsons* and drinking beer and passing out. Finally they got me drunk enough that I could get up and sing." (Jay Brown)

Demolition Doll Rods, Margaret Dollrod, Dan Kroha. Margaret: "We had a number one single in *Rolling Stone* magazine. Nobody ever knew about it because we never went around going, 'We're in *Rolling Stone*.'" (Jay Brown)

Nothin' to Do in Detroit

Jim Olenski (*Cinecyde, guitarist*): I went to this party in late '77 in the basement of an apartment building off of Jefferson on Grand Boulevard. In the basement we saw these white kids, late teens, early twenties. One of them was Mark Norton, and he was putting on these rubber gloves and wearing a garment bag. He was getting ready to play with his band, the Ramrods. They were great. They had originals; they were doing songs off of *Raw Power*, and doing them well. It was like brothers-in-arms. I couldn't believe it: there was someone else who's doing it because Gary and I had already pressed a 45. No one would buy it.

Gary Reichel: There were these black people down there that were against the back wall. It was like that scene in *Apocalypse Now* where the band was playing "Suzie Q" and there were the Vietnamese at the cyclone fence watching. I was struck by the whole thing. I talked to them and gave them a 45. Later on we went to Greektown, and it's bumper to bumper every time you go down that Main Street in Greektown. Suddenly Mark comes out from nowhere—he recognized us in the van—and he jumps on the bumper and he's screaming. That's when our friendship began.

Mark Norton: The party was in the Concord Castle, right down East Grand Boulevard in this shitty apartment building. It wasn't much of a party; there were like twenty people down there. We knew the manager of the building. He was just this total drunk. He said, "Yeah, you guys get some beer. You guys go practice down there." So we played and invited some people over. Cinecyde came to our party. They did a record before anyone, and they were into the same things that we were into. We didn't know there were other people into what we were doing, but really, how was I supposed to appreciate Bruce Springsteen in 1978?

155

Gary Reichel: I had written this song called, "Gutless Radio." We loved what rock and roll was, and we hated what was happening in rock-and-roll radio, so "Gutless Radio" was sort of a poke in the eye to the industry. The Ramones album comes out, and they don't play it. I had discovered that there were bands that made their own stuff; they didn't have managers and all that. So I showed the song to Jim, and we recorded it and found a place to press records, Super Disc in East Detroit. It was the old General Motors studio. They contracted it out; you would listen to the acetate, then they sent it to a pressing plant in Scranton, Pennsylvania. And you would get records back. We made our own sleeves. This was really radical back then. We didn't have enough money for the printer to run the sleeves, so he let us operate the fabricating machine ourselves. So we issued this 45, "Gutless Radio," and the flip was "My Doll." A couple months later we put them into some stores. I sent some out in the mail and places like *Trouser Press, New York Rocker.*

Bob Mulrooney: The Ramrods were me, Dave Hanna, Mark Norton, and Peter James. We played a sixteen-year-old's birthday party in Birmingham in '77. I think it was Dave's little sister. We played my old junior high. Dave and Mark had to act like real punks, acting like they were the Damned or something—spitting drinks on the stage.

Scott Campbell (*Sillies, vocalist, promoter*): Pete, Norton, and Mulrooney and I were sitting over on Mack Avenue at a Jack in the Box, and as soon as Norton left to go to the bathroom they said, "Hey, you're gonna be our singer." They wanted to get rid of Norton because Norton was an endless problem. Mark was terrible. I mean, he learned as he went along, but Mark was terrible. He couldn't sing. He couldn't actually breathe. He got beat up at a show, and I was trying to save him. I had the Sillies at that time, and we were playing the Velvet Hammer with the Ramrods. After the show these bikers were, like, dragging him by the hair, and I was trying to get these guys cooled down. I was doing okay, and then Mulrooney stepped in like an idiot, and then they started punching him. I'm standing there, 120 pounds, and no one's throwing a single punch at me.

Bob Mulrooney: I told this guy that was beating up Norton that he wasn't going to fight back, then he started beating on me. These bikers were huge.

Mark Norton: I walked out on stage at the Velvet Hammer, and there was this big biker and his girlfriend standing next to the stage, and I look at the biker and then his girlfriend and said, "Your woman just gave me a great blow job in the parking lot." He jumped on me, and it was a massive fight. We never even got to play. I got the shit beat out of me. Me and Jerry Vile were the only ones who would ever fight when the shit went down. And we got murdered.

Jerry Vile (*The Boners, vocalist, artist, editor, White Noise, Orbit*): The Ramrods were at the Velvet Hammer, where the bikers just pounded the shit out of Norton and Mulrooney. I didn't want to get beat up by bikers. I don't got your back. We snuck out and picked Bob's carcass out of the parking lot that night. You'd think bikers would love punk rock, but they don't. Bikers like gentle music.

Scott Campbell: We booked two nights, so the next night practically everybody pussied out except me, Tom, Michael Profane, and, I think, Steve Sorter showed up because Mulrooney was too scared to show up. We just played the second night and nothing happened.

Steve King (*The Pigs, Boners, bassist, producer, Aretha Franklin, Eminem*): Norton was digging at the biker girls. It's like a surefire way to get beat up. Everyone was, like, all nerved up, like "We better get the fuck out of here." The bikers aren't going to really know the difference between us and the Ramrods—they're just these punkers, and they're just going to kill us all.

Andy Peabody (*Coldcock, vocalist*): Mark got beat up at a lot of shows. He punched out one of the ceiling tiles at the Red Carpet one time, and their crew just came right up and dragged him off the stage and pounded him around and threw him out of the club in the middle of their set.

Paul Zimmerman (White Noise, *editor*): We were always looking for new places to play. One night we went to the New Miami, this crazy place where Vietnam veterans hung out. Norton went in there and pretended he was a veteran, talking about his days in 'Nam. So one of them asked him where he was stationed, and he was like, "Uh, Danong" or some such thing, and the guy was like, "I should kick your ass for making this stuff up."

Mark Norton: Willem de Kooning said the only time an artist is free is when there is utter indifference in his work. The Ramrods basically pulled from the art crowd and from the music crowd. We were so over the top for the guys that were playing the Silverbird and doing bar-band standards and all the rest of it; they were just going, "Look at us." They still had hair down to here and they looked like seventies hippies, and we were like motorcycle jackets, our hair was all fucked up, and, you know, we weren't accepted. We were bête noire. It's like this shadow following us; they hated us. We played a set, twenty minutes. Some of the shows would start and end in about two minutes into it if there was a fight. Sometimes the fight didn't come till later.

Paul Zimmerman: Some of these shows would be held in halls like a Moose Club, and to get people you'd have $5 for all the beer you can drink and some bands. The people that wanted all the beer they could drink were not the kind of people that would like those bands. They'd get drunk and then get pissed about the bands.

Steve McGuire (*Traitors, bassist*): There were bands around like the Ramrods, and we wanted to get in on it. I was a bass player, and I was jamming with this drummer Terry Fox, and we saw an ad for a guy who had songs. He was a guitarist, and he wanted to put together a new kind of band, like a punky kind of band. It was a guy named Don McAlpine. We started playing originals with him, and it hit me that it doesn't matter how good you play, you don't have to be a virtuoso, but rather the confidence you have in what you play. So then we heard about Don Fagenson, who turned out to be Don Was, and how he was looking for a band, so we connected with Don and a guy named Jack Tann. At the time Don was playing bass with Lenore Paxton, and me and Craig Peters and Terry were living in a condemned, abandoned farm house at Novi and 12 Mile. No heat, no hot water, but we pirated electric. All we did was practice and do drugs. We were starving and used to go to the grocery store not to shop but to eat; we'd just chow down in the aisles.

Don Was (*Was (Not Was) bassist, vocalist; Traitors, vocalist, producer; Rolling Stones, Bob Dylan, Bonnie Raitt, Iggy Pop*): From about 1971 to 1981 I worked with a piano player named Lenore Paxton, who was a very well-known jazz musician. I learned more about music from her than anybody else in my life, really. We played mostly at a place called Bobbin' Rob's Lounge in Madison Heights, right in the shadow of the Warren Ford factory. It's like a cheater's place for the executives. She'd play these songs that I never heard, and I'd have to watch her left hand and listen, and I got one time through a verse and a chorus to learn the song, and she was off soloing. When I was going to University of Michigan I used to drive to Madison Heights to play the gigs, and it went to the point where I was a father trying to support a family on $150 a week, which ultimately I couldn't do. I started engineering for Jack; this is the late seventies. Jack came from a family of entrepreneurs. When I met him he and his brother were marketing mood rings.

They were the first ones on that, and they made a killing on it. Jack was a sweet guy, and he had Sound Suite Studios, and he loved music. So in the seventies I used to read the *Village Voice*, and I started seeing the ads for CBGB's and these bands with the crazy names, and I told Jack about it: "There must be some way to create something like that here. There must be bands like this here." I formed a band called the Traitors, and Jack became a punk rock promoter, which wasn't the way to approach music like that. It was supposed to look cooler than to go in like P. T. Barnum.

Steve McGuire: When we hooked up with Don and they had this whole floor of an old Westinghouse factory at I-94 and Trumbull, with all this old equipment from United Sound and Sound Suite. It was our rehearsal place. I had quit high school and started living there and experimenting. When I first met Don I thought this was our ticket; we're going to make it. I was so naive. There were blurbs of the Sex Pistols, and I thought the Traitors and the Sex Pistols were in a race, and whoever won would be kings.

Scott Campbell: This was the new breed coming in. Stevie McGuire had come in and taken Don's place in the Traitors. Don was moving into a managerial role.

Bob Mulrooney: Don was the lead singer of the Traitors, and it was wild. He had this wife who thought she was a groupie or something, and they had, like, this open marriage, so she was always hanging around, picking up punk rock guys, and he was always at his studio picking up black lead singers and shit.

Steve McGuire: We didn't play that often, but what Jack Tann did, which was very smart, was he had a complete show. So he could book his little Motor Town Revue of three punk bands into an evening.

Scott Campbell: The Mutants were making fun of the Traitors at the Red Carpet one night, and McGuire was like sixteen years old, and he was feeling bad; I could see it on his face. I said, "Believe me, I know these guys, I know them well. I went to the band leader's bachelor party, and if they're making fun of you, it's because they're old, jealous assholes. So you're doing something right just by them making fun of you."

Steve McGuire: We were the band that was gonna play all of Don's songs, and he had all these cheesy recordings that he had done demos on. We went on a dance show on Channel 62 and lip synched one of our songs, and the host came over to interview us, and me and Don McAlpine grabbed his arms and punched him in the stomach. And Don Was took over the set, and because of that, during the nine o'clock movie, rolling across the scene, the rolling bulletin at the bottom of the screen said, "Punk rock band takes over local TV station, details at eleven." But we staged the whole thing, planned it ahead of time. For another show at this theater in Taylor, to create buzz, we staged a protest—"no punk rock in Taylor"—and had our friends' parents come out and protest.

Gary Reichel: The Traitors went onto a local black dance show called *The Scene*. It was all set up. The host was given a preproduced thing about what punk rock was. They played two Motown songs, "Money" and something else, singing to pre-recorded music. When they got done, the host comes up and says, "That's kind of freaky." So Don and Stevie McGuire come off, and they're kind of being aggressive and start arguing with the host and push him down. Then they had all their friends call all these various TV stations and say that these punk rock guys took over the show. There was only one station that bit on it, but they led off their 11:00 newscast with "Punk rock hits Detroit and it packs a punch." They interviewed the host. The newscaster says, "Needless to say, they won't be invited back." It was very funny.

Mark Norton: All those guys from the west end—the Traitors, the Pigs—those guys are all from Livonia. So they were all way west side guys, and they all came to know each other through Don, who got these guys to come down and form this deal with him and Jack Tann. Don was starving at the time.

David Keeps: It was three bands Jack Tann and Don had for this concept—the Traitors, the Niggers, and the Pigs. Everybody thought they were ringers and in-authentic posers and that they were to be despised.

Steve McGuire: The Niggers were a jazz fusion band, and Don wrote some songs for them and put them in leather jackets.

Scott Campbell: The Niggers were all hired; they were not a band. Don put out ads, and then he picked people and hired them; this was like the Monkees. They gave them the songs, they told them what to play, what to sing, what to do, and told them who was going to be in the band, and they named the band. So they were employees that they could change like Menudo.

Gary Reichel: They basically hired the bands and marched them down to one of the Birmingham salons to get the punk rock haircuts. They had a slick flyer to give to club owners. "And we'll handle everything. The three bands will all tour. We'll use the same equipment. You don't have to worry about time between bands." That's how they were selling it. And they had bigger aspirations than that. They wanted to get them signed.

Steve McGuire: Jack Tann was considered to be an interloper, a phony. Don's stage name was Prez, and they came out with signs, like the Ramones.

Rick Metcalf (*creator of Detroit! Motor City Comix, artist*): Don was throwing chicken bones and holding up signs that said, "I hate you." People yelled back, "We hate you."

Mike Rushlow (*Pigs, Rushlow-King Combo, guitarist*): I was in the Pigs, and we had these songs I wrote—"Stay Away from Janet," "That's What Summer Is For," "You're Nuts."

Jerry Vile: They had this one song called, "You're Nuts." "You're nuts. Ask anybody, I know they'll agree, you're nuts, I don't want you hangin' around me." Really.

Mike Rushlow: Then we saw this ad Jack Tann and Don Was had placed in the *Detroit News*: "Punk rock band wanted." We answered it, and Jack Tann came over to watch us practice. I handed him a lyric sheet, and he sat down in a folding chair and read along. So he says he'll get back with us, and he called a couple days later. So next we go down to this place to meet Don, and it was where the Traitors practiced, in this downtown Detroit area. It was really decrepit, with broken windows, pigeon poop everywhere. I couldn't believe there were even businesses in there, but there was a photography studio and this practice place. They also had electricity.

Jerry Vile: The Pigs had to wear these old suits; they were supposed to be like Elvis Costello.

Mike Rushlow: Don told us what he envisioned, and it wasn't like this formal thing, but he said, "I see you guys wearing ill-fitting suits." And we all had glasses, so a lot of people thought we didn't really need glasses, that was our gimmick.

Paul Zimmerman: They were fake geeks.

Mike Rushlow: We signed a contract with Don and Jack. Later on, when we moved on, we had to get out of the contract because we wanted to sign with another management group. And Don wrote that up, this end-of-contract document, and it was all this legalese, then at the bottom, in really small print, were the lyrics to the *Gilligan's Island* song.

Jerry Vile: People would hire me to go on tour with them if they were playing Chicago or Cleveland. Don Was hired me for something, the Pigs or someone, and we went to play Cleveland. I got really drunk after the show, and Don says, "We're going back to Detroit tonight," and we were like, "Fuck that." But Don insists, "No, this equipment's really expensive; it could get stolen." So I'm driving back drunk. It was supposed to be in a convoy, but we just said, "Fuck it, forget it," and pulled over in a rest area and went to sleep. A few hours later the door opened up, and Don Was has got his fists balled up: "Hey motherfucker, we've stopped at every rest area between here and Detroit! I'm a Golden Gloves, and I don't care how big you are." I was so sleepy, I was like, "Whaaaa—?"

Mike Skill: The Romantics played with the Pigs and the Traitors, with Don Was. It was some place in Oak Park at the school where Don's dad was the principal.

Don Was: Yeah, my dad was a counselor at the junior high in Oak Park. We got him to book the Traitors and the Romantics just to have a chance to get out and play somewhere. It was disastrous. We got to play, but it was a huge incident for my dad.

Mike Rushlow: There was going to be this Motor City Revue tour, and this was before Bookie's opened in Detroit. So the Traitors, the Pigs, and the Niggers did the Motor City Revue tour—three cities: Philadelphia, Boston, and New York. I don't remember getting paid very often, but we got $10 a day and each band got a hotel room.

Paul Zimmerman: Don and Jack put together these glossy brochures for the Motor City Revue.

Scott Campbell: Don and Jack Tann also had this idea to produce an album that nobody would release after getting advance money and spending all the money over at Jack Tann's studio. They would just basically scam the record company to get the advance money out of them. That never happened.

The Voice Box
and First in Line

Billy Goodson (*scenester*): In the midseventies I went with a friend to this place in Detroit, Frank Gagen's. I had no idea this place existed. It was great, with the drag queens and the mime syncing and all the coke and the pot and everything all over the place and everybody dressing up in glam. One guy looked like Marc Bolan from T. Rex. It was called Frank Gagen's, but a guy named Bookie owned it. He was a real bookie, and he had this voice thing where he had to put a little microphone up to his neck to talk. Everyone was going there, sort of underground. Queen came in there after a show, and Freddie picked some kid up and bought him a Maserati.

Vince Bannon: Bookie had his vocal cords cut, but he would talk, although with difficulty, with no voice box. Most of the time he talked, like, in this almost, like, this really, kind of like, slurred whisper. He was in his late sixties.

David Keeps: Vince went in and found Bookie sitting on a bar stool with the trach thing, the cancer mic. Bookie would sort of quack like a duck—that's what it sounded like. The only person that could really understand him was Vince.

Stirling Silver: I used to go to Bookie's when it was called Frank Gagen's. It was a gay bar, and I went there for the express purpose of meeting so-called fag hags. There were girls that were beautiful and wanted to dress up but were sick of men hitting on them. They wanted to be around good-looking, well-dressed men that complimented them and had no agenda. I met so many beautiful women there. I went there a lot with Andy Peabody, who was later the singer for Coldcock. We went to Gagen's all the time. He looked a lot like me: was very gayish looking, good

163

hair—he was a hairdresser. One night we walked in and to our immediate left was Freddie Mercury and the Queen band.

Billy Goodson: My aunt used to go to Frank Gagen's when it was a restaurant in the twenties or thirties. I tended bar there for a few months in the eighties or so. It used to be drag shows before it was punk rock. There was an oval circle of booths, and you could walk around and on each table see a pile of coke or smack or anything you wanted. This was during the drag scene in the seventies.

Hiawatha Bailey: Bookie's had been this gay bar I went to where we could dress like the New York Dolls and there were all these six-foot drag queens. It was one of the rare places you could go in Detroit dressed like that and not get your ass kicked. It was just a pick-up joint. Bookie freaked me out with that thing on his neck. Next thing you know, Scott Campbell and Vince Bannon were hanging out with these rich old homos so they could put bands in there.

Michelle Southers, aka Bambi (*scenester*)**:** It was a gay bar during the day; it always stayed that way. He was actually a bookie—that's how he got his name. I was at Bookie's for the bands at night when I could, but the gay guys adopted me during the day when I could be there. The first modeling I did was for a hair magazine called Flair. My hairdresser was Danny Smith; he was a Sassoon-trained guy. This was 1978. I was dancing with a fake ID, I was a sixteen-year-old making $3,000 to $10,000 a week. I had whatever money gives you.

Scott Campbell: I met Vince Bannon at a party. He said he was rhythm guitarist for Bowie on the Diamond Dogs tour, who turned out to be Stacey Hayden. He said he had a band and didn't. He basically lied about everything, but I liked him anyway. He was the one who had scouted out Bookie's when people like Alice Cooper hung out there. They had an after-party for Alice in '75 for the *Welcome to My Nightmare* tour at Bookie's. Everyone knew it as Frank Gagen's. You go down to Frank Gagen's da da da, you don't want to pay to get in, da da da da, beautiful cruiser, at Frank Gagen's. Even though it was a gay bar, it already had people from the rock world hanging out at it.

Vince Bannon: I went in there with Scott Campbell from the Sillies and Andy Peabody and just said, "Hey listen, we're going to try and do shows in here." He'd lost a lot of his business because a better gay bar had opened next door called Menjo's. He was at a point where he didn't really care about the business, but it would be great if he made some money.

Kirsten Rogoff (*Algebra Mothers, Sillies, bassist*): You had Bookie's and then Menjo's on the other side, so I mean a person really, if they were so inclined, had the best of all three worlds there. You had Menjo's, you had another place, the Glory Hole, and then in the middle you had Bookie's, where everything in between went on. So if you're bisexual and you wanted to buy sex, you had that; if you're trisexual and you want to try something new, you could try that.

Rick Metcalf: I was studying to be a lawyer and started liking other music like Blue Oyster Cult and Hawkwind. I read about them in *Creem*, like I read about a lot of music. The first time I had seen that magazine was when it was a tabloid, and I saw it at this biker house in Birmingham near Southfield. It was amazing. The writing was really cool and had some leftist politics and some at the time I didn't get—half the reason I read the *Fifth Estate* was the comics. I was like, "What the fuck are you arguing about?" But the comics were really funny. In May '78 we went to the Hash Bash, this annual stoner event in Ann Arbor. They had it at the U of M gymnasium and first had a jam band playing, and all these stoner types; we probably looked like late-seventies stoners, but we had some bikers with us too. We got kicked out of the show for trying to resell tickets that we found in the trash. Then we found a flyer for this sex bash, at some kind of hooker bar that was within walking distance from the Hash Bash. It was such a contrast to these hippies bragging about the best Thai weed and people depantsing each other to slouching all cooler-than-you with a feather boa. The Sillies were playing at the hooker event, so it was even better. I'd never seen stuff like that. And they had fly-ers for another Sillies show at Bookie's. I called Bookie's the weekend of the show and I asked, "Is this a bar?" "Do you sell beer?" Really stupid questions.

Tesco Vee (*Meatmen, Blight, vocalist, editor,* **Touch and Go** *magazine*): I was the little suburban kid at Bookie's, and I would be, like, going in the bathroom to take a piss, and there'd be, like, a bunch of, you know, like, sluts in the boys room. I was like, "Oh my God! What's going on? These girls are in the men's room!" Mom warned me about gay guys, but she didn't warn me about girls in the men's room. What do I do now? I just hid my penis and peed.

Dave Feeny (*Hysteric Narcotics, the Orange Roughies, keyboards, guitar, founder,* **Tempermill studio**): Bookie's was like that PSA, "Your brain on drugs," come to life. For a suburban kid—we were from Livonia—it was like an amusement park.

Gerald Shohan: When Bookie's started, it was basically Vince and Andy Peabody talking Bookie into letting this kind of thing happen to his club. They talked him into doing Wednesdays or Tuesdays. Then it got into another day. Then it was bringing in money and people. Finally we got the weekend nights. Sunday was still left for the drag shows. So Sunday morning we would, a lot of times, we—being Coldcock, this band we had with Vince and Andy and me and Bob Mulrooney— were rehearsing there in the basement, and the drag show would go on at night. We'd stick around for the drag shows.

David Keeps: Vince and Scott had the whole relationship with Bookie. Vince booked Bookie's. It couldn't have been a more fantastic venue for punk rock. It was like a grown-up supper club let loose. It had a black-and-white tile floor and these fake leather booths. Bookie's was special. Bookie's was, like, basically being allowed to go in this place—you know, like, parents would have the living room that none of the kids were allowed to be in? It was like having access to that and rigging it up. It was really key to keeping things alive in the city during that period.

Tex Newman: Bookie's had these great old lights that had, like, eight different colors. It was like a ballroom with these ornate ceilings that formed an arch, a dome, antebellum, and these huge booths that were handmade and were just great to sit in. It had the room upstairs with the secret door, and the basement was a real basement, and the kitchen was down there when everyone first started playing there. There was a big sign over the bar that said something like, "Help those that can't do anything about what they are." It was a transvestite bar, gaudy but really cool. It made you feel like you are in something. The fact that it was also a gay bar, and many people hadn't been to that kind of thing, gave it an element of voyeurism. But really, it was the bands that pulled everyone in at Bookie's, because without that there was no excuse to go.

Chris Panackia: The only people that could stand punk rock music were the gays, and Bookie's was a drag bar, so they accepted them as "Look at them; they're different. They're expressing themselves." Bookie's became the place that you could play. Bookie's had its clique, and there were a lot of bands that weren't in that clique. Such as Cinecyde. The Mutants really weren't. Bookie's bands were the 27, which is what the Ramrods became, Coldcock, the Sillies, the Algebra Mothers, RUR. Vince Bannon and Scott Campbell had this Bookie's because it was handed to them basically. You know, "Okay, let's do this punk rock music. We got a place." To get a straight bar to allow these bands that drew flies to play at a Friday and Saturday night was nearly impossible. What bar owner is going to say, "Oh yeah, you guys can play your originals, wreck the place, and have no people?" Perfect for a bar owner. Loves that, right? There really wasn't another venue.

Mike Skill: Bookie's would have us play one night on a weekend and then Destroy All Monsters the next. There were a lot of really good bands playing by then. Things had moved out of the kind of show bars, those places with three sets a night.

Bob Mulrooney: There would always be a bigger variety of people when the Romantics would play anywhere.

Tesco Vee: You went to see the Romantics because all the hot girls would go.

Scott Campbell: First Romantics show at Bookie's was early '78. The Romantics didn't draw anything. They were signed at Diversified Management Agency, and they were working a lot, but they didn't draw until early '79. Then they got backing at WWWW for their single, "Tell It to Carrie." Rich Cole had been a roadie for the Mutants, and I knew Jimmy Marinos 'cause I'd run into him over at the music store at Eastland. They wanted me to produce their first single, but I didn't like what they were doing.

Mike Skill: My main impetus was getting in the studio and recording music—that's what I wanted to do, and be a songwriter. I wrote, "What I Like About You" on a summer afternoon. My dad had a quarter acre in Fraser, real nice out there at the time. I just had an acoustic guitar and one day jumped on the picnic table and wrote it. I had to go to rehearsal that night. I had no car, and I was always late getting to practice. But that day I borrowed my mom's car and I got there early, and it was just me and the drummer. I said, "I got this thing," and we played it.

Chris Panackia: The Romantics eventually would play three nights at Bookie's and sell out every night. They played the Silverbird on a Monday night and didn't announce the show until just before doors. This was right when "Tell It to Carrie" was starting to hit and people were just waiting for them to explode. When they announced it on the radio, 6 Mile and Telegraph became a parking lot. There were probably a thousand people outside there that couldn't get in.

Bill Kozy (*Speedball, guitarist*): I was real young, and my pals from Warren Avenue took me to the Silverbird when the Romantics did a surprise show. Beers were 25 cents. It was this rowdy rock crowd, but things were different than that. The Romantics' fans looked like late-seventies rock people.

Cathy Gisi: The Romantics played at this little tavern in Hamtramck in this residential neighborhood with wartime-era houses and families. The Romantics were gonna play this corner bar. The cops were called four times because the neighbors couldn't stand the noise, and they kept shutting them down. They'd wait ten minutes and start all over again. Finally the cops came back and shut the power down on the bar itself. So the drummer ended up doing a fifteen-minute drum solo until finally the cops took his drumsticks and broke them.

Mike Skill: We started creating our own look, our own vibe. Being into rock music, we liked dressing up more. The natural progression was to do the leather because, well, the Dolls used it. It was much softer. It breathed better than vinyl. We made it more like sixties, and theirs was more like Rolling Stones.

Irene DeCook (*makeup artist, leather fashion designer*): I was doing stuff for gay S&M people in Detroit. I was making leather clothes, leather chaps. I started out with fabric when I was sixteen when I was designing and modeling. I only knew how to make women's clothes. Then when I was eighteen or nineteen, my instructor said, "Why don't you put your clothes into one of our fashion shows?" which was a drag show. So I got into the gay community making drag clothes. Then got into the gay leather scene. The Romantics had this idea for red leather, and the owner of a leather company who I was friendly with called me and said, "I got this little band in here. I'm asking your permission to give them your number" and gave them my number. I had never heard of them. The Romantics were a big thing in the city—lots of hype and their managers were sure they were going to be huge.

Mike Skill: Our suits were wearing out. We had vinyl, but it was too hot and we couldn't afford leather at first. Then we were about to get signed, and we happened to meet Irene DeCook. So we got together with her.

Irene DeCook: Their managers, Joel Zuckerman and Arnie Tencer, called me, and they're like, "I want you to meet these guys. It's the Romantics, and we'll give you an album cover." They're acting like big shots. I'm not impressed. They thought I'd be, "Wow! It's the Romantics!" So I went to meet them, and it was in their rehearsal hall in Gratiot, and they were all, you know, the four guys sitting cross-legged on the floor, had been rehearsing all day. They didn't look like rock stars. They just looked like little kids. They were a few years older than me. And we met and I said, "Yeah, we'll do it." Before this they didn't have any money for leather, but they had finally gotten this record deal, and they'd gotten an advance and got to get some real clothes. And before then they were wearing pants that were made of table cloth material because that's what they had the money for. It was fake vinyl, and it gave them all rashes. They were just so excited they would get some leather. They'd seen some of my work. But the main thing was that they had to be so tight that they had to lay down to put them on. So I'd have to fly out and do fittings and take in their clothes for the four years that we did this, regularly. Then as they got money, they got more and more and more.

Mike Skill: We went for fittings. She'd come over to the studio or rehearsal hall, and she'd do a fitting. Then for the final fitting you'd go to her house, and if you needed anymore, you'd go again. She would get them tighter and tighter and tighter. At her apartment there were kinds of collars and stuff on the wall and in her room and stuff too, because you'd change in her room.

Irene DeCook: The Romantics did an interview on WWWW, and Jimmy talked about me wearing all leather clothes and spiked-heel boots, and how strange my apartment was with whips and chains and weird sexual devices hanging on the walls.

Mike Skill: She was a character, and it added to the whole allure of the Romantics. She was part of the whole thing.

Irene DeCook: But the main thing was that they wanted these fucking pants so tight they had to lay down to put them on. So I made the pants; we fitted them, and they go off to Florida to do the album. I sent them down the pants, and they called me and said, "Well, we can't put them on!" It's like, "You gotta lay down." And they laid down and they put on those fucking pants. That was the first time, but I was flown out to many different places. As they got money they got two or three made of everything, and leather does stretch. You have to take it in every so often so that it fits right. Jimmy would have to have four of everything, with him sitting down and sweating like a maniac. And I actually have a gold album from the fourth album. At the time my daughter was five, and Rich's pants looked about the size of hers. They were just tiny, tiny little boys. I mean everybody was super-skinny. The waists were like 26. That first album hit, and they ended up going to Australia and Japan before I could make them a wardrobe, and they ended up having to wear one pair of leather pants for sixty dates. They were soaking wet. They would take them off and turn them inside out and they would sort of dry, if they could. And that's all they had. Then they'd put them on and wear them the next night. They'd still be damp from the night before. When they came back they were like beef jerky. Pubic hair–encrusted beef jerky.

Mike Skill: When things started happening we were already thinking, like, "Man, get a record deal, get a record deal, get a record deal." We just kept pounding it and meeting all the people we could. Our managers—even though they were inadequate as far as business, they didn't know business, they were learning it as they went—they would really keep us financed. "You guys go rehearse; you guys go write songs. We'll take care of all the other stuff." The only problem with it is the managers were our friends, and we ended up firing them because they were hiding money from us. It turned out to be a sour, sour thing, unfortunately. What they did is they tried to keep us from getting—this is not my words—but to keep us from getting spoiled, they would dole out checks.

John Kordosh: I didn't know Arnie and Joel until they were managing the Romantics, and then, of course, we ran into them a lot. I thought they were slimeballs. We were concerned for the Romantics' sake. Then they got signed through CBS, and it looked pretty good for them. It wasn't until much later that I realized they were really getting ripped off on their own songs, which is a pretty damn old story.

Tom Morwatts: The Romantics had a couple of really knucklehead managers that were always pulling some shit. I told Wally the first time I met those guys, "Look, I'd be real careful with these guys. I personally wouldn't work with 'em." I got such a bad vibe from them, but who knows? They may have gotten nowhere without those guys.

Irene DeCook: I think about one incident that really sticks in my mind, and this was the first hint that something was rotten. I give the managers credit for believing in this band. Although they were managers at Big Boy before they took on the Romantics, believing in this little band that they were fans of so much that they were going to invest a lot of money and really push them and promote them and make them famous and basically tell them what to do. But of course, the Romantics, they wanted to be musicians. They didn't want to do the business. And they didn't look at their accounting for four fucking years. When they finally did, they saw that the management was flying first class and letting the band pay for it and taking 20 percent and this or that and taking all of their publishing. I talked to Jimmy about it, and this was very early on—maybe the second album—and they were getting ready to go on tour, and they all come over and we're doing fittings and they're ordering up all these clothes. I called management to get money to pay for materials, and they're like, "What are you talking about? They don't have any money." I said, "What?" Arnie goes, "Well, maybe we can loan them some money."

I went and told Jimmy about it. The Romantics weren't watching it. It was after the fact that they really found out, you know, four years later, when they started looking at shit. Then it was, "Wow, you've been screwing us all this time." So it's like they don't have any money, but maybe we can loan them some. The Romantics were still living with their fucking parents, and Arnie and Joel, of course, had their own condos. They were driving better cars while the Romantics are driving twenty-year-old cars. At the end there was no money after being, you know, famous and traveling the world. Where is the money? Well, Arnie and Joel took all the money.

Mike Skill: Coming off *In Heat* and a couple years after that I'm going, "Look, this doesn't seem right. We're not getting paid what we're supposed to be getting paid." I wanted to change management. I talked to Wally and we split and that was that. And then over time we looked through records and files and followed down this, follow the money, follow the money. There was discrepancies. We took them to court, and, you know, no one wins in that situation. But we won in that we got our copyrights back. And when you have the copyrights then you can sell off, you can sell out, license your copyrights and that, so we did make some money on that after that.

Tex Newman: When this whole thing was starting, the Romantics had the most money because of Arnie and Joel. They thought they were the Beatles playing this homogenized power pop. I think people were jealous because they were successful; they wore the leather suits, and I mean it's Detroit—they do well with that in New York. They were outsiders, because pretty soon really big bands started coming to Bookie's. So instead of having a weekend of local bands, you'd have these big out-of-town bands.

No Hands Clapping

Kirsten Rogoff: The Police played at Bookie's for maybe forty people.

Vince Bannon: The funny thing about it is you'll probably talk to two thousand people in Detroit that said that they were there that night at Bookie's, but there were no more than forty people there. We might have paid them $200.

Scott Campbell: We were dealing with one of the Copeland brothers, who ran the booking agency for the Police in '78. He wanted us to take his brother's band, which he said was called the Police, and he sent us a 45. They wanted $300 first, then $200. Nobody played the "Roxanne" single outside our club. I DJed at Bookie's and played the hell out of it. We booked the Police for a Sunday night, and Andy Peabody was going to run the PA—he had this little thing. The band showed up and was bitching about the PA right away because he had these small speakers. They were pissed off, but it was their fault—they were too loud. The Police were too loud—imagine that. They weren't adjusting themselves for the room, and they didn't set up right.

Vince Bannon: The Police invented the touring model. I will hand that to Sting and Andy and Stewart. They basically came over here and forced their hand, where it used to be that, you know, you had to get on a big tour, you had to have a lot of air play. They just came over here and played. It was them, their road manager/ sound man, and roadie. And the band had a station wagon. You remember that Andy Summers had played Detroit before when he was in Soft Machine opening for Jimi Hendrix.

Chris Panackia: I rented the Police my soundboard when they played Bookie's. I'll bet there were thirty people there. They all bitched about Bookie's sound.

Vince Bannon: After the show I was having a beer with Andy Summers, and he was explaining to me that they were a reggae band and asked if we promoted the show in the black areas of town. I had to explain to him that black people in Detroit didn't know what reggae was. But you know he was probably living in London, and he goes to Brixton and that's all they're listening to: reggae. He figured, "Well, gee, it must be the same thing."

Scott Campbell: The Police were traveling in an extended Dodge van, so it was like a standard van but it was like a B350, where they weld on an extra two feet at the end. Ian Copeland told me, "It's only a three-man band; it's not expensive." Maybe that's why they took the $200. They came back late '79, and Vince goes, "This is my show, this is my show." We had a battle over who was running the Bookie's. So I just go, "What the fuck." I guess they got the door, and he oversold the tickets to the point where he sold five hundred tickets, and he knew he could only hold four hundred people, tops. I didn't have a deal with the cops, but Bookie did.

Cathy Gisi: The Police played Bookie's twice, and the second time was just amazing. They must have paid off the local police not to shut the place down; it was packed that second time, about six months after the first. For Vince to book 'em once was amazing and twice was better.

Tesco Vee: We'd go to see everyone at Bookie's, like the Revillos, Johnny Thunders and the Heartbreakers, Gang of Four, the Effigies, and the Misfits many times. You know it's funny—all the Detroit bands would warm up all those national acts—the Mutants, the Algebra Mothers, Flirt, the Cubes, the Sillies. We talked about them a lot in *Touch and Go*. It was like new wavy stuff, but still it was new music, and we covered new music, and it was probably just to fill up the pages. That's not very nice is it? In retrospect Coldcock was just okay, but really. What do we like about Coldcock? They played like every show because Vince managed Bookie's, so he put them on the bill. But Andy was a good front man, and Vince had a backwards haircut way before Justin Bieber came on the scene. So what's not to like?

Scott Campbell: Everybody started coming through. The Cramps were there a couple of times. The first time Tom Ness, the guitarist, was watching Bryan Gregory, and he goes, "I know that guy. I went to high school with him." Sure enough they went to Redford High, they both graduated, and they were talking to each other afterwards. They both went to Redford High, and they both played Flying

Vs, but Tom played the shit out of his Flying V and Bryan's playing was very limited.

Skid Marx: There were all kinds of people around Detroit who were "managers," and with all these national and international bands coming through, more people came along. We were in Ann Arbor getting ready to play the Second Chance opening for Sonic's Rendezvous, and this guy comes up and says, "I really like your band. You know, you should be playing all the time." Then he said, "I worked with Aerosmith," and I'm thinking, "Okay, here we go—bs." This guy says, "Go check it out on the *Bootleg* album. My name's on the back." I say, "What's your name?" And he says, "Gary Brimstone." I check it out, and sure enough. We got together, and he paid for our first trip to New York, where we made only like $36 at Max's. Yeah, it was great. We became good friends, and it turned out he was in the import/export business. Gary Buermele was his real name. People called him Brim.

Chris Panackia: Brim looked almost like John Oates from Hall and Oates. Little black mustache, curly hair. Had gold chains, the whole thing. Brim managed Flirt and was the drug runner for Aerosmith. When he booked Flirt in New York I went, and Skid kind of took me under his wing. I was eighteen years old. We were at Max's Kansas City playing in front of Johnny Thunders and the Heartbreakers. We did two nights at Max's with the Heartbreakers, and after the first show Johnny handed me his guitar and said, "Bring it back tomorrow," because he would have pawned it. We had been talking during the evening, and he figured out I was this straight kid and I wouldn't fuck up. He trusted me because I didn't do drugs. There was a real Thunders/Detroit connection. Jerry Nolan was a good guy that I really got along with. He was much older than those guys. I was at Thunders' loft that trip, and he goes, "Do you want to buy those drums?" It was Nolan's original Dolls set. The pink fuckin' premiere set. He goes, "Give me two hundred dollars you can have 'em." They were in a fucking closet. And it was the fucking 10 by 14 rag tom. It was his set. The pink Premier. It had two floor toms, a rack, and a kick drum. Two hundred bucks, and I had no way to take it home.

Ron Cooke: I knew Gary Brim from him showing up. I was living in Ann Arbor, and we were at the Second Chance, hanging at parties, and Brim was always engaging, a real musicologist. He loved the *Beverly Hillbillies*; we used to smoke dope and watch the *Beverly Hillbillies*. He was quite the guy. We used to hang out at the Whiffle Tree, this bar in Ann Arbor. I don't know if that was the real name or not—we called it that, it was a real cocaine hangout. We're in there drinking one night, drinking champagne. Brim was not a very big cat, and these two big thick-necked assholes were sitting at the bar, and one of them said something to Brim, and he says, "You know what? I'm gonna crease your forehead with this bottle." And I thought, "Oh shit, these are some big motherfuckers we're going to be rolling around with in here." A crease in his forehead? Thankfully those guys left us alone.

Skid Marx: I was at Brim's house one night in Ann Arbor, and we were listening to the Rolling Stones *Some Girls* album without vocals. He got that kind of thing— he knew people. We're smokin' some joints, and there's a knock on the door. And he goes, "Skid, I'll be right back. I got some business to take care of." I'm like okay. Then he stops and he says, "You can come along." I get up and walk out to his garage, and I wanted to go home. There were bales of pot out there. I didn't want to be around THAT. I mean, you know, an ounce or something is great, but bales? But he took care of the band for a while. He eventually got murdered. You hang out with people like that, and it's going to happen. When you're dealing in such big quantities. He was the one that actually brought Johnny Thunders to Michigan. He was very good friends with Aerosmith, and I met all the Aerosmith guys through him. Yes, he did import/export "finer powders." That's how he became friends with Aerosmith and Johnny Thunders.

Scott Campbell: We booked Johnny Thunders one night in the summer of '79. We thought it was just gonna be Johnny and some pick-up band. He didn't say it was going to be the Heartbreakers, with Billy Rath and Walter Lure and Jerry. A great surprise. After they did a check, Johnny was sitting around the bar, and he kept saying, "A band with me and Wayne would draw." That's when he met Wayne, who I knew. When he was just out of prison. Wayne used to call me up and ask, "Do you want to go to the beach?" or "Do you want to go shoot baskets?" or whatever. I'd interviewed him for a magazine, and we just became friends. So they met that night.

Skid Marx: Up in the dressing room that night, just before the Heartbreakers were ready to go on, Jerry was passed out in one of the stalls. Everyone's going, "Come on, Jerry. We gotta go, we gotta go." Brim came through, and he had a big baggie full of white stuff. I don't think it was coke, but I took a snort of it anyway. Then they went into the stall. I don't know how much Nolan sniffed and snorted, but I tell you what, he played the best I ever saw him play. Wayne Kramer got up there at the end and did "Do You Love Me" with them. They used my car to go to the club, and all four tires got slashed outside Bookie's. So Brim had to buy me new tires.

Ron Cooke: Johnny Thunders is coming to town. Bookie's, that Heartbreakers show, that's where I first met Thunders. Brim says, "We should get Wayne, man, and it will be a great band."

Wayne Kramer: I knew Johnny was a heroin user, or I certainly figured it out pretty quickly. Rushing into toilet stalls, "No, gimme the spoon, man, ahh mother-fucker, yahhhhhh." He said, "You wanna come over to this drug dealer's house with me? He's got coke." I said, "I don't think so. I just got out." And he said, "Well, he's got kilos!" Through sheer self-will I was able to say no that night. But eventually I went up to Ypsilanti, and of course I'm an addict, and how long does will power last?

Ron Cooke: Next thing I know we're in rehearsal as Gang War. In the hands of Wayne and me, Johnny Thunders was a pliable fuckin' baby. Because we were tough guys. Wayne had been in the joint. Johnny ain't never met no real hard guys before. We used to fuck him up hard, man. I whipped him once. I slapped the dog fuck outta him. He just deserved an ass whipping; we were in Toronto or something. The money we had to record and do some other weird shit came from that dope Brim was selling. I whipped his ass too. In the end someone did more than that. He went downhill fast; that blow just ate him up. Him and Thunders, I saw them go through $60,000 worth of dope in a week. Not gonna live like that very long.

Skid Marx: Brim brought Thunders here, and he stayed at our house for a while; then his wife and kids came, and they moved over to Brim's. After Gang War started, that's when things started changing for them. December '79. I think it started happening then, because Johnny would get his royalty checks for the Dolls and they'd be gone. Nothing for the family, just for his own pleasure, and he was getting maybe ten grand every quarter, plus publishing. It was heroin-ed out. We were just having a Christmas thing, and there's a knock on the door, and it's Wayne Kramer. Yeah, Wayne, you can come in. So we're doing the thing, and then about one o'clock in the morning this guy comes knocking on the door. He's like, "Is Wayne here?" "Yeah, I guess, come on in." It's Christmas Eve; I didn't know him. We're all smoking pot, hanging out, and Wayne, Johnny, and this guy take off. They went to a different part of the house. I didn't know where they went, but they came back. Then I go into the bathroom, and there's blood all over my walls and shit. I told them, "Get the hell outta my house!" I kicked them all out on Christmas Eve. I told Julie, Johnny's wife, and the kids to stay—all the rest of you guys get the fuck outta here. I don't want this shit in my house. That next day was actually the last time I actually talked to Wayne, to this day.

Kirstin Rogoff: We did some shows in Canada with some version of Johnny Thunders, but they weren't doing real well. We had to draw straws to see who would sleep on the mattress versus the box spring. You know, that's a way to make one room bigger for a number of people. So I got Johnny Thunders. So we're sleeping in the same bed, but, trust me, nothing interesting happened there except that he was trying to watch TV, smoking a cigarette, falling asleep. The cigarette would float down and he'd burn himself. He'd wake himself up and smoke some more, and then he'd run to the bathroom and throw up. I said, "You're going to die in ten years," and he did. I took Johnny to the hospital at least once. He would shoot up in his hand, I think, and his hand would just blow up and get infected and the circulation would stop. I carried him off stage once and had to go to the hospital and sign for him. He couldn't even write his name. I would hear him talk about his ex-wife. He said she was tall and blonde and had big feet. I thought, "Big feet?" He had a couple kids, and he said that they like listening to his music. I said, "Why aren't you with them?" So he didn't say anything. He seemed like he was very sad about that loss. He chased after Niagara, and she played very hard to get.

Wayne Kramer: One of my points in my narrative was Gang War as a stepping stone to New York. I knew Detroit was a slippery slope for me. Everyone I knew was in prison to some degree.

Ron Cooke: Wayne and I went and played this big show in New York with Thunders. These guys busted into the motherfucking warehouse, tapped into the electrical system. There were twenty thousand people in the fucking warehouse, man. And they were probably selling forty pounds of heroin in the motherfucker. So we get all done, and we were counting the money up, and I go, "This is fucking bullshit, Wayne. Let's go see these motherfuckers, man. We want some dough out of this gig, man." Wayne goes, "Alright, let's go." So me and Wayne go down the hallway. There's this big fucking guinea motherfucker standing out front of this door. He goes, "What do you guys want?" We go, "We want to see the boss, man." He goes, "What for?" "We want to talk to him about some money." He goes, "Who are you? Where you from?" I said, "My name's Cooke. This is Wayne Kramer.

We're from Detroit." The guy goes, "Hold on a minute." Goes to the fucking door, the door closes, he comes back out and says, "Who'd you say you were? Where you from?" I said, "My name's Cooke, that's Wayne Kramer. We're from Detroit. We're from the band, man. We filled this fucking place. We want to talk about getting some more dough." He goes back in and comes out and says, "C'mon." So there's this fucking dude sitting in there with a thin T-shirt on. Stone Italian mother fucker. He's really a bad ass. Count the fucking money, man. He goes, "Who are you guys?" We have to go all the way back through this fucking thing. He looks at me, goes, "Cooke, you from Detroit, eh? You know what, man, you got fucking balls, man. And your buddy here." He goes, "Frankie give them $2,500 bucks apiece." We fucking hustled the fucking mob cats, man. Thunders? Who knows where he was at?

Vince Bannon: I booked Iggy at Masonic and then brought him back to play a week of shows at Bookie's. That was a really big five sold-out days.

John Kordosh: The Mutants opened for Iggy that week, one of the shows. Bookie's was really kind of poppin' then—all sorts of national acts were coming through: the Stray Cats, bands that were really getting big. So it was definitely a happening scene, as they say.

Iggy Pop: That was at a time in my life that I was the most completely insane. What I love about looking back on that was I was having a very hard time with my career, with my health—it was all bad. But my motives were pure. I would do these crazy things. I had an idea that all the one-night shows you would play in these weird theaters, the promoters would rig the whole thing so nobody could have a good time. It just wasn't happening—it wasn't cool; it wasn't a connection. So what I was trying to do was like what people would do back in the days of the Dorseys or Sinatra—you'd go and play a stand. I did a week in Atlanta at a place called Richard's, and I did a week at Bookie's and one other, and it was a great idea. The things that stand out about it all for me are the things happening offstage. Particularly how disgusted I was and how weird I felt because there was a band called General Public at the time. It was created by the leader of a band called the English Beat, and at the time they were all the rage; they had big hits doing this horrible fake ska. They were playing a bigger venue in the area, and they came down in their tour bus to watch, to hang out or something. I went onto the guy's bus, and he was going to be a cross-over, to be above all music scenes, you know—"I wanted to be a real star," like Elvis or something, "for the general public." I just remember his snotty attitude and just how smart he thought he was. It just disgusted me and I also felt, "Well, oh gee, here I am doing this, things don't look good." In Detroit I got really nervous when Jimmy McCarty came down, the guitar player from Mitch Ryder. Johnny Bee came with him. Those guys were and still are musicians that I really respect. That was like, "Oh shit, oh shit, here comes McCarty and his guys." I was a little star struck. It's pretty funny: there's a compilation out there on me called *Roadkill Rising*. And I was singing "One for My Baby," the blues jazz song. And there's a recording of it from that stand at Bookie's, and people wouldn't shut up. You know the trouble with people if they're out having a good time. I stopped like five times saying, "Shut the fuck up!" The whole tour was kinda like that; it was real rough and ready, and I'm real proud I did that, but on the other hand it was, like, it was a statement to me and it was pure.

Tex Newman: We opened one of those nights, and he was bad. I walked out and people waiting out back were offering me $100 to let them in the bar.

Kirsten Rogoff: Zion Stooge, this girl, changed her name and had Iggy tattooed on her. She was just in love with Iggy Pop and just saw herself as that. There were a lot of people who had severe mental problems around there, and they dressed the way they did because they had a mental problem, not because they were trying to be something. One person might go with a crash helmet or a soldier's helmet into the club, not because they're trying to dress up for it—because that's how they dress all day long.

Michelle Southers: When I first dated Jim it was after he was in Germany with David Bowie. He was pretty clean, and I actually met him at Bookie's. I had come in from LA; I was modeling out there. I was working for Richard Tyler, and a designer friend of mine from Australia had given me all these crazy clothes that he had made. I walked in and I was the prodigal daughter. I had this spacesuit-looking thing on, with a really tightly woven full-body stocking, fishnet, and then I had this silver—looked like aluminum foil—big shoulder-pad thing, micromini—like if I bent over, my ass was out—with all these fake gemstones all over and glitter and heels this high. I walked in, and it just so happened that Iggy had played there for how many nights. He wasn't playing that night; he was just hanging out. Iggy walked up to me, grabbed me and kissed me in the middle of the club, and told me he was at the Briarwood Hilton and he would be there for X amount of days, and he gave me his room number. Of course I didn't call until the very last day. I had probably just turned eighteen. I did meet with him; I had lunch with him in Ann

Arbor at the Briarwood. It was just one of those things, a couple times, when he was in Michigan type of thing. If he'd see me, you know, whatever.

Paul Zimmerman: There was this guy, Tom Mitchell, once we all started hanging out at Bookie's. He was so into "We should not all look the same. There shouldn't be a punk uniform." So he went down to Army surplus and came back with a silver fireman's jacket that weighed, like, forty pounds, and he used to wear that around. There was a horrible liquor store about a block and a half from there with the ghetto glass and everything. When you couldn't afford the liquor in the bar, you would go get a six pack and drink it in the parking lot. In fact, the big thing at Bookie's was to get there before ten and drink for an hour and a half in the parking lot. Sometimes the parking lot was as much fun as inside. So these guys went to get a six pack, and there were some girls and there were some guys, and they went over, and Tom slaps a $20 into the little ghetto tray, and this little kid came in, a little brother, grabbed it and ran. And Tom made the mistake of going after him. As soon as he went into the street he got circled, and they punched the girls and he got stabbed in the stomach. I'm inside at Bookie's, and one of the bouncers comes over to me and he goes, "Hey, you gotta go check on your buddy. He's bleeding out in the street." I went out, and Mitchell's sitting up against the wall, and he's just gray. He shows me the stab wound, and the girls are frantic. One of the bouncers goes, "An ambulance will take forever. I'll take you now." So we jumped in his car, and we piled him in and went down McNichols doing about eighty to Ford Hospital, about three miles away. And, you know, that's not a road you can go thirty or above. We're roaring into this hospital. And we get there and Mitchell's girlfriend is like, "F'n N word, f'n N word." And we're in the waiting room, and I'm like, "Would you chill? We got him some treatment." So the hospital comes and tells us, "Well, somebody's gotta call his parents," and then they all looked at me. So I had to do this call at 1:30 in the morning: "You need to come here. Your son's been stabbed." They ended up messing up his treatment, and he was in the hospital for a month.

Keith Jackson (*Shock Therapy, guitarist*): I always carried a gun, a little .45. Only once did I get caught with it, and it was at Bookie's. One night I power slid my car up to the front of the club; I was going too fast and bumped against the curb. I got out and a cop had seen me, just down McNichols. He said, "Do you have any weapons?" I said, "Yes, I do. I have a gun in my pocket." So they put me up against the car to pat me down, and his partner reaches into my leather and pulls it out. He slides the clip out and puts it in his pocket. So they run me and I check out okay, and I said, "Can I have my clip back?" They said, "Nope. Have a nice night, Mr. Jackson."

Bob Mulrooney: I lived right around the corner from Bookie's with Vince Bannon. It wasn't even a ten-minute walk from the place, and across the street was Highland Park, which was really rough. We were in Palmer Park, which was okay; it was mainly gays. The black people wouldn't go over and rob the gay people, at least, but later on, when they could see the crowds coming in to Bookie's and there was more nicer cars and shit, then they started paying attention. I know somebody got killed in the front part of the parking lot. I think the heroin really started in the end of the Bookie's days, and I wasn't into it. I had done it once or twice during that time, but the richer kids, the ones that were, like, doing tons and tons of coke and after that, what else can you do except something to calm down? There was this one coke dealer from New York; he used to come in, rent a limo, and sit with the car running while this Louie guy was inside getting everybody high. It was the best coke I ever did. It was so pure, but actually in a way it kept me away from the street garbage in Detroit for a few years. The bouncers from Bookie's started working with those guys. They moved the product in Detroit. Before the airlines tightened down, everybody was making some good, good money.

Jerry Vile: We started a magazine to talk about the scene, whatever it was, and we called it *White Noise*. Paul Zimmerman and I started it. First, though, we drove out to the West Coast in 1978 to see what was going on there. We'd go to shows and tell people we were from *Punk* magazine. That was the magazine that made journalism understandable to me. It was *Mad* magazine with, like, cartoons and hand lettering. So where everybody else like Legs McNeil might be the influence to some, John Holmstrom was the influence to Paul and me. We were in LA and we bought a copy of *Slash*, which was impossible to get in Detroit. We didn't even think about selling ads; they had to tell us, "You sell ads in a magazine, and that's how you make your money." We were trying to make our money by selling them for a buck apiece. Don Was and Jack Tann bought an ad for Sound Suite. But we didn't have a business plan. It was printed on newspaper, like how *Slash* was. Paul went to journalism school, and I never even took journalism in high school. Paul's like this really handsome, nice, baby-faced kind of guy that girls love, and the guy's got, like, with this really twisted brain. So our first issue we put Niagara on the cover, and she drew the back cover. The first reaction was from Sirius Trixon from the Motor City Bad Boys, who wanted to beat me up.

Paul Zimmerman: We did a "Welcome to Detroit" double truck. We had all the bands that we liked, and we were just about to go to press, and Jerry said, "Something's wrong with this picture of Sirius." And he goes, "I know!" and he takes a flare out and he goes on Trixon's face, dot dot dot dot dot dot.

Jerry Vile: He had really bad acne. He said, "What the hell did you do to my face?" I said, "I was trying to make it look more like you," and he grabs me. At that time I was shoveling asphalt for a job, so I picked him up and threw him against a pinball machine. Sirius never bothered me after that. But that was the one reaction I remember well. They had benefits for *White Noise* at Bookie's. It was pretty popular. I also had a band, the Boners, that I started. Then I had even more excuses to be an asshole.

Paul Zimmerman: The Ramones were playing in East Lansing, down the road from Detroit at this preppy place called Dooley's. We went to see them and maybe interview them for *White Noise*. So we went backstage for this interview, but Jerry and I realized that we didn't have paper. Or pen, for that matter. But Mike Murphy was with us and said, "I'm gonna write everything down and let me go with you and be the transcriber." So we get back there, and they're all eating pizza, and we start talking and doing this interview. And so one of our first questions was, "Where is Tommy?" This was July 1978, and Marc Bell had just taken over. Joey said, "Well, we had to let him go because he was walking around clucking like a chicken!" I knew this is going to be a good interview, and I looked at Mike, and he was not writing anything down.

Mike Murphy (*The Denizens, the Rushlow-King Combo, the Boners, Hysteric Narcotics*): I think I wrote stuff down. Or at least I wrote an article on it for *White Noise*. I could have made it all up. Johnny did most of the talking, and Joey just stood in front of a mirror and played with his hair. Dee Dee was too messed up to talk.

Paul Zimmerman: At the time Jerry was into this thing where instead of interviewing people he thought it was cool to give the band a McDonald's application and have them fill that out, which isn't a terrible idea. But the last thing a band wanted to do is homework, and the Ramones didn't want to do it. Finally, I was dying of hunger, and we were wrapping it up and I had on a *White Noise* T-shirt, and Joey was looking at it, telling me how great it was and that he wanted one. I said, "I'll trade it for a piece of pizza." He said, "Deal." So I took off my shirt—literally the shirt off my back—for a piece of Ramones pizza. I kept waiting for him to wear that shirt, but it never happened.

Jerry Vile: We had this place called the *White Noise* Mansion. It was in a hillbilly area of Detroit.

Paul Zimmerman: The first one was on Fielding and Old Redford, and it was two bedrooms, a stand-alone house. It was just Jerry and I originally, and then later Steve King moved in. The landlord had fixed the place up pretty nice, but something had happened and there was a hole in the wall in the living room right away. The landlord came over one day unannounced, and he was looking at it and saying, "What?! What?!" I go, "We were moving a couch." He didn't kick us out.

S. Kay Young: You walked into the place and the first thing that hit you was the stench of old fast food, and it got worse. In the basement, where people tend to have a washer and dryer, they had a wash tub piled with dishes that were crusted with food. They didn't wash dishes; they just put them down there. The beds had no sheets and they had been pissed on.

Katy Hait (*Sillies, vocalist, photographer*): I was Jerry's girlfriend for twenty years, including then. There were definitely no sheets on the bed. I don't think you cared how creepy it was at that time. There were fast food bags piled up so thick that you couldn't see the carpet.

Jerry Vile: If we didn't announce a party after Bookie's, we would come to our house, and people would break in and already have a party started. You'd try to bring a girl home, and there would be a party going on at your house that you hadn't planned on. A lot of gang bangs happened there and bad, bad stuff. There was one girl named 747, and one night she got grain alcohol in her eyes, and I tried to wash it out in the bathtub and she fell. I heard her head hit the bottom of the tub; I can still hear that sound in my head to this day. I'm thinking, "I've fucking killed her," and I'm fucking around with just a leather jacket, no clothes, and a naked girl in my arms.

Steve McGuire: I lived at this place called the Earth Center in Hamtramck. I was in the 27, which was Mark Norton's band after the Ramrods. We played at Bookie's, and I had never done coke, and this guy named Tommy Ballantine came up to me and Craig Peters and told how he liked our band and offered us some blow. We did a couple lines and went back to his house and sat up in his attic and did blow for two days. He told us he was going to buy this place in Hamtramck, and it has a hall with a stage and we could practice there, so we said, "Sure." Craig and I lived there, and there was a stage and there were these two little rooms over the stage, and we each took one. After 27 broke up, I met Ahmet Ertegün's niece and married her. He was the founder and president of Atlantic Records. I was nineteen, and we got divorced pretty quickly.

Mark Norton: Of course there were shitloads of parties. One thing the Zimmerman and Vile excelled at was peeing in the shampoo bottles of our host.

S. Kay Young: There was this after-hours place on the East Side, where you walked in and it had these huge fish tanks, and they sold really bad coke. You'd go in and sit down at a table and there were playing cards on the table. And you would turn them over if you were there to score.

Kirsten Rogoff: The Chili Sisters had parties all the time after the bars closed. They'd make chili, and we all knew that it was going to be a really good time. The night my mother died I went to a Chili Sister party. I ended up at the basement stairs in a wheelchair covered with confetti.

Diane Koprince (*Chili Sisters*): It was me and Karen Parapata; they called us the Chili Sisters. We had parties all the time, and we knew there would be a lot of drinking, so we made food so people wouldn't drink on an empty stomach. Plus a lot of those guys in the scene had no money.

Sue Rynski: The Chili Sisters were friends of mine from high school, and they had a house at 13 Mile and Woodward. They had parties for all the guys and gave them beer and chili.

Kirsten Rogoff: There was always a lot of drinking and rooms where people would screw each other. I'm surprised they weren't raided.

Diane Koprince: They were all costume parties. We kept a big box at the door that had things you could make a costume out of if you happened to show up without a costume. In the box we had my old waitress uniforms, with frilly aprons, party masks, clothes from Salvation Army. Jerry Vile came as a sofa one time, with cushions stuffed in front and back.

Jerry Vile: The Chili Sisters would have chili parties that were also acid parties, and I remember taking a whole bunch of acid because I wasn't getting off, and then getting off really bad. That's one of my bad mistakes in life: these drugs aren't working, get me more, and then getting off, and then getting instantly paranoid, because I have a paranoid personality. One time I was tripping and I made myself throw up all this chili, seeing trails in the chili and going, "That's not where I want to see trails, I want to see them on my hands, not on my puke." Sometimes there'd be costume acid parties too.

Paul Zimmerman: One time we were coming back from Bookie's, and Jerry was passed out in the backseat. When we got home I tried to wake him up. No luck. So I left him there and went to bed. In the middle of the night he woke up, felt sick, but his foot got stuck under the front seat and he puked all over the car.

Jerry Vile: I woke up in the backseat of Paul's Maverick, and I was throwing up and my feet had gotten pushed under the seat and I couldn't get up, so I'm throwing up all over myself, in the backseat of a Maverick, and I shredded my legs; they were all bloody from pulling them out from the springs. I just managed to get out and left his car door open as I passed out on the lawn. He found me the next day. His whole car is full of puke, and the smell never went away.

Paul Zimmerman: He cleaned it out a bit the next day. Still stunk. Finally he said he had the solution: Locker Room, that chemical in a tiny container that disco types used to inhale on the dance floor. He stuck that in the car and rolled up all the windows. It smelled better, but on hot days it still reeked of refried barf.

Rick Metcalf: There used to be a place on the east side of Detroit called the Meet Market, and Jerry and the Boners would play there. The guy who booked the place loved the Boners, and he'd bring them in on a weekday and hardly anyone would show up. They paid them in dope and booze, and we were completely incoherent after that. They had these small tables, and one night Jerry jumped from one to the other, four or five in a row, and people were sitting at them, and people had pitchers of beer spilling on them. But he made it all the way across before he fell in a heap. Another time a black street dude walked in and starting singing Otis Redding, and we turned it into "Otis Otis / he's the way / Otis Otis has a big dick and liked to play."

Paul Zimmerman: Bookie's was like the clean up, then, after Bookie's you'd frantically try to find an after-hours party. So sometimes it was in Palmer Park— Mark Norton had a place there; Vince had a place there. In Palmer Park, these apartments—we had this thing called tumbling. It's where you'd pretend to throw yourself down a flight of stairs but you'd actually hold the railing carefully, and pretend to roll down the stairs, but that would entice someone else to try it. So one night we had Stiv Bators from the Dead Boys with us, and if you've ever been in the Palmer Park apartments, they're metal, the stairs. And so we showed Stiv how to do it, and he just did this swan dive onto the stairs, rolls down, smashes the bottom, hits this door. This old lady comes out like with this horrified expression like, "What are you doing?" And he just goes, with this big smile, "We're tumbling!"

Jerry Vile: During one of our parties Steve King started up a chainsaw and cut the coffee table in half. Another time we got up one morning and saw Steve's car on the front lawn and the wheels were all that was left. The tires looked like those little drill things with the squares of sandpaper on it. We couldn't believe the car was drivable, three out of four tires were like that—they weren't flat tires; they had turned into these, like, sanding wheels. I don't think he was purposely sideswiping cars that night; I think he was sideswiping because he was drunk. We used to purposely sideswipe cars when we were driving home drunk anyways because we drove such shitty cars. I don't think Steve was doing that, but the cars on the street were dented pretty bad. Bootsey was so mad that we were evicted from one place that he broke the toilet upstairs and it flooded for a couple days; it destroyed the house and all this art on the walls, and it ruined all my art. Our equipment was in the basement, and that's where all the water ended up. We lived at 8 Mile, right by the State Fair—we were a block off of Woodward. Frisco's, that's where Bambi danced at. She was good looking; she was hot.

Stirling Silver: I called her Michelle, and I went out with her off and on for at least two years. I went and saw her strip a few times. She was beautiful, sexy, and liked to have sex. Plus she liked rock 'n' roll and all that. The Talking Heads came over one time to my house after playing in town at the Punch and Judy. Four guys lived in that house, and between us we had ten thousand albums because we all worked in record stores. So the Talking Heads came over, and Michelle was there. David Byrne sat in this big chair, and he never moved all night and barely talked to anybody. Jerry Harrison wandered all around, talked to a lot of people. Tina and Chris were conversational. Michelle was walking around; she was always wearing, like, something up to here. She had a body. She would wear this one satin dress a lot; it was like, "Jesus Christ." So Jerry Harrison started hitting on her. She wasn't my girlfriend. I didn't want her to necessarily be my girlfriend because I knew she'd break my heart, so he was flirting with her, and I think they went off for a while. The next day party's over and Michelle was there, because she would stay there for a couple days with me, then take off. The next morning there's a ring at the doorbell. I opened the door, and it's fucking Jerry Harrison. By himself. And he goes, "Is Michelle here?"

Michelle Southers: I was a fifteen-year-old runaway. At first I was a live-in house-keeper for this young couple with a toddler in Warren. I'm from Milford, the boondocks. I met this couple at one of our field parties, and I decided to run away from home. They let me live with them because they both worked and had a lit-tle child, and I got to live there for free and babysit. One of the woman's friends was a topless dancer, Diana. She'd pull up in this big convertible, and she'd be all, like, just so flashy and blingy and all that, and she was probably all of twenty. I always lied about my age, so she thought I was seventeen. Diana wanted to hear my story and my problems and everything, and I told her the altered version, and I said, "I'm just trying to get a job," and she said, "Well, if you lived with me, I have a beautiful place." She had a gorgeous, huge apartment. She said, "You can just stay with me and clean my apartment and I'll give you $150 a week and you don't have to babysit kids." So yes. One day her car wouldn't start, so the owner of this topless bar she worked at on 7 Mile and Woodward came to pick her up. He saw me and said, "Who is this? Bring her with us. We'll buy you lunch, sweetie." So I go to the strip joint, and they asked me if I wanted something to drink. I didn't know anything about drinks, so I wanted something ridiculous like Annie Green Springs or Strawberry Hill or something they didn't have. He sent the bouncer to the corner party store to accommodate me, and I had a couple glasses of wine. Then the owner offered me three $100 bills to do one song, to pick a song and go up there, and I'm like, "No, I can't do that—dancing." "Oh, come on. I have so many costumes, and you only have to take your top off just for like thirty seconds. At the end of the song, just flash 'em." So I did it. And while I was up there, I also made $200 in tips. I had them play "Brick House." The rest is history.

Bob Mulrooney: She lived at the apartment where me and Vince were. She lived in the front room on our couch for a few weeks. It turned out, she gave like five guys from Bookie's VD, and then she ended up moving somewhere else, and she might have moved to LA for a little bit, and then she came back, married this punk rocker. I remember them at parties; they were always doing a ton of coke. I saw them at some little Chinese restaurant; they were ordering food right around that time of the killing.

Michelle Southers: I was making so much money, and I would only go out with rock stars. Then I met this guy, he was gorgeous. He was six-foot-four, Russian and Italian—Joseph Bazzetta. I met him at the Red Carpet at a 3-D Invisibles show, and after that we were together constantly. After eight months he murdered his stepmother. He was living at his parents' house, and she was looking to get rid of him and get him out of his father's house. They had been on vacation for a few months. She came back first because she wanted to make sure she had everything prepared for her husband's return. We were at the City Club, and it was late, so I stayed there at his house. His bedroom was in the refinished basement, and she would never know anyway. I wake up to this loud noise. Like if somebody dropped something on the roof, like a loud, loud drop, like bam, thud. And he's not with me, and I'm waiting to hear another noise because I'm not supposed to really be there, and I don't want to front myself off; so I threw my clothes on and I started creeping towards the noise, upstairs. I keep going up the stairs, and I walk into the kitchen and he was strangling her. It was a horrible thing. I was frozen. I can't even explain it. It was like being trapped underwater and you can't move and you can't scream. I was paralyzed. Eventually I screamed. And he turned around and he looked like a monster. I was standing in front of . . . there was the stove here and the refrigerator here, and like a little bit of a counter top, and he was in front of me this way by the sink area, and he turned around, he stood up, and he came to me and started shaking me and said, "Shut the fuck up, bitch, or you're next!" This is my boyfriend. So I help him. I went with him while he buried the body in a wooded area in a shallow grave in Oakland County; it was a place where I was from. When you're dating somebody and you show them where you grow up, and this is the place where we used to party, big gravel pits, way out off of Hickory Ridge Road, and he said, "We're going to that place." He stopped at a nursery on the way there, with a dead body in the car in broad daylight, to buy foliage to plant over and make it look like it's not a fresh grave. But he bought forsythia, which is ornamental. It has no place in a forest, but he didn't know, because at the time it was green. He was always a suspect, and I never told. With this guy, and his reign of abuse, and "If you ever leave me, I'll kill you and your family." I was a classic battered woman.

How he got caught was really a fluke. This was in August of 1983 when the murder happened. There was an article that came out in the newspaper in early '88 about this drug dealer that went to federal prison in the fall of '83 from that area. It was found that he had buried a half a million dollars somewhere in the woods out there. So this hunter guy who lived out there, he reads this article in the paper and thinks about when he had seen this forsythia, and he thinks that's a marker that was put on the money. And of course what they find is a skeleton. She was identified by her dental records, and her jewelry was all still on. I got to court, the prosecutor was saying, "She didn't tell for five years. That means she's just as guilty as he is." I got fucked. I got totally fucked. He got found guilty of first degree but mentally ill. I got second-degree murder with a life sentence. I was in prison for twenty-one years.

"You're Not Punk Rock"

Paul Zimmerman: There was a point where Bookie's became a victim of its own popularity. They gutted it; they wanted more space. They also opened up this thing downstairs that used to be storage and made it a second bar. It wasn't Bookie's as much anymore.

Scott Campbell: After two years Vince decided he wanted to run the place all by himself. Some drug dealer was financing his attempt at doing concert promotion. That dealer eventually got shot by some rival drug dealer. That was the guy that got killed in the parking lot in '80. I didn't want to deal with those people. I was doing everything except sitting there and drinking with the old man.

Vince Bannon: I didn't know what I wanted to do, to be perfectly honest with you. Scott was really focused on his band, the Sillies. I'll give it to Scott—he was so focused on the band. I was a haphazard musician. The funny thing about it is that I ended up becoming, say, the more mature person out of all the kids around me. One day it just occurred to me that this putting on shows is working. We're getting people into this place. I'm making it where I can pay for an apartment and other things.

Bob Mulrooney: Scott Campbell has his own version of the whole history of Bookie's, that's for sure. He started it with his money, but then Scott was incompetent in a lot of ways and Vince ended up firing him. I can see both sides, but Scott was just a really unusual person, and he doesn't really have a lot of common sense. He's just a weird person. I was the drummer in the Sillies, so I know.

190

Katy Hait: I joined the Sillies as a singer after Sheila left to go to Los Angeles and join the Screamers. I'd never sung before in my life, but I knew everyone in the band, so there I was.

Chris Panackia: There were more places because there were more bands finally. It was Bookie's. Now Monday and Tuesday at the Silverbird would do the same bands. The Dead Boys, Destroy All Monsters, Wayne Kramer played there—same bands that would play Bookie's. Johnny Thunders and the Heartbreakers at the Silverbird, they would have gone to Bookie's before. Wednesday you would go to the New Miami. All those bands would play there Wednesday and Thursdays. Now you could take six nights a week and find that music at that time.

Paul Zimmerman: That's when the shift turned to places like Lili's and Paycheck's. The only problem with Lili's was you couldn't get far enough away from the band if you didn't like them; there was a little alley entrance, so you could go out there; that's no good, up front is no good, up front there was a pool table. But if you didn't like the band, you would still be too close.

Brian Mullan (*sound man, promoter*): During the week Lili's was a regular bar, and you would walk in off the street and musicians would hang there. Almost everyone and a lot of the time bands from out of town would be directed there.

Paul Zimmerman: After the Clash played at Masonic, they were directed to Lili's. We had already been introduced to the place by Art Lyzak; it was a cool little joint in Hamtramck. You go in and get a Stroh's and a Chrysler, which was a beer and a shot of Kessler's. We were hanging out there, and the Clash came walking in, Joe Strummer and Mikey Dread. We walked over and started talking to them, and I showed them the latest *White Noise* and said to Strummer: "Buy an issue of this magazine." Dread goes, "Do you know who that is, man?" and I went, "Yeah, I know who it is, and I know he's got enough money to afford a dollar." Strummer was very cool, and he said, "Oh, I want to pay" and whipped out some money. These guys were so polite. Somebody offered them some blow and Strummer said, "That's so nice, but no. We've got our own, thank you."

Art Lyzak: My mom started Lili's 21 in Hamtramck in 1975. My mom was Lili— she was twice divorced and had five sons. In the early seventies, late sixties, the second husband who fathered my four half-brothers wasn't giving her any dough. So she was a barmaid in a place called the New Dodge Bar in Hamtramck. She was a beautiful chick, and she liked working the bar and found out about a bar called the Columbia Bar, which eventually she changed to Lili's. She got some dough from my dad, who she still got along with. It was a nice place, just as a shot-and-a-beer place. If I was doing a gig and or hanging out, I'd be like, "Hey, my mom's got this bar. Let's go over there." When we started having bands, for a good eight or ten years my job was, like, the booking guy.

Jerry Vile: I got banned from Lili's. It started because I had put Locker Room on their towel machine and was sniffing it and then I put my lighter on it to dry off the towel machine. When it caught fire, I ran out to the bar to get a glass of water to put it out. They were pissed, but I told Art, "I just saved the whole bar from burning down. You should be thanking me." So he's mad about that, and weeks later I'm in there with Sailor Rick, who's Paul's brother-in-law. He's, like, six-foot seven, and we got our feet on the jukebox and we're, like, kickin' back, getting drunk, and they got pissed again, and it was, "All right, fuckers, you're out of here!" On our way out Rick takes a bottle, throws it through the window, smashes their Lili's neon sign. The fucking bar erupted, and everybody wanted to kill us. Rick was surrounded by, like, eight guys, and I was always getting into fights anyways, and I'm surrounded by a whole group of people. But Art cooled it down. That could have been life changing. I could have had no teeth—it was like thirty-five to two. A couple weeks later the opportunity to play a show at Lili's came up, and I started thinking about how fun it would be to do because I'm banned there. So I came up with the idea of doing it from the van. We were called Free Beer for the Boners that night, and we ran cables from the van into the club into a TV onstage and the mic cable into the van with a camera on me. I had a series of disguises in the van, so I had, like, a bag over my head, hand puppets, whatever.

Art Lyzak: I thought, "Well, he may be banned, but not his image."

DJ Dianna: There was a cool place called Nunzios. I was already going to Bookie's, and I had been through the Grande and the Eastown. But Nunzio's was four blocks from where I lived in Lincoln Park. All I knew is that it had huge disco parties. So I go to this place, and the guy who was the DJ, who was buying these cool new records, was a guy we all called Twig, who liked to get high. So Nunzio, the owner, said "If you are going to hang, why not work the door?" It was inevitable—every evening Twig would start out the night fine and get higher and drunker, and by the end of the night he couldn't work. So one night he got drunk and Nunzio said, "Okay, you're the DJ." I said I didn't know how to do that, and he took me to the booth and showed me how, and it went from there. It turned into me and Twig cospinning records, and eventually it worked itself into me working. Nunzio's was picking off some of the bands from Bookie's. Twig eventually died.

Glenn Johnson (*Mr. Unique and the Leisure Suits, drummer*): There were these weird shows all over the place even during Bookie's. We went to see Wild Man Fischer at the Latino Ballroom in Pontiac; it was this ballroom with plastic folding chairs and a stage like a church basement. The promoter bought Wild Man a bus ticket and had him come out. About forty people showed up, and I had just gotten out of the hospital from a car accident, and I had both my legs in casts. Fischer walked out and says, "Is there a drummer in the house?" So my pals carried me up in two leg casts and I played drums for him. They had a kit from the opening act, so I just came up and played the worst drums ever. He learned "Night Moves" by Bob Seger just before he got up there, figuring he was in Detroit and had to play something like that. There was this great network for bands starting about this time. Not just for people like Wild Man Fischer, but it was becoming more possible to do shows in other places.

Nikki Corvette: Since I've been going to shows as a kid, I made friends with bands. Even before I was ever in a band I made friends with everybody. I was pen pals with bands from all over the world back in the days of letters, which is great because I have letters. When bands would come to town I would do what I could to help them out. "Okay, but when I'm coming to play your town, you help me out." I'd meet people, and they'd hook me up with shows. We'd play the East Coast. We played down South a lot. We'd play the Midwest. Los Angeles. We played with the Ramones at the Second Chance in Ann Arbor at one point. A couple days later they we were doing a show in Toronto, and the opener canceled and the promoter called and said, "Do you want to open for the Ramones?" Yes, we did. After the show Johnny Ramone came up and introduced himself. And, well, he really pursued me after that. A year later, after *End of the Century*, Johnny called and said, "This is where we're playing. What shows do you want to open?" They were playing a venue on the west side, but I didn't really want to go because the promoter, Gail Parenteau, did not like me. She thought that I was going after all of the guys she was after. Johnny just said, "We'll put you on the guest list and make sure you get in." And I'm, like, it's just going to be a hassle you know. And then he said, "We won't play if you don't get in." "Oh, I am there." You know I want to be there for that conversation. After that Johnny used to call me every day from the road. It was really uncomfortable when I would go see Johnny on the road. Years later I realized that the reason everything was so uncomfortable was because he was going out with Linda. And not only was he going out with Linda, but he was having me come to shows and used my band to open shows.

When I saw *End of the Century*, I figured out the dates and I went, "Oh my god, like, okay. No wonder everybody hated me." I still have letters and cards from him.

Don Was: You know all I wanted out of life was to not have to go to work, get by playing music. I had to take this gig repairing copy machines; I didn't know anything about it. The first week on the gig they said, "Well, you know, when you're out on service calls, we want you to learn to sell toner and paper to the clients, so you have to take the Dale Carnegie sales course." I really thought I had bottomed out. I went to the class; it was after-hours in some office building, and it was me and seven Willy Loman kind of characters. I wasn't quite suicidal, but I was depressed. I really thought my life was over. The first night of the class they said, "First thing we're gonna do is we're gonna make a list of your goals: where do you wanna be a year from now? Where do you wanna be five years from now? Where you wanna be ten years from now? What do you want to be doing?" I roll my eyes. It's actually quite a challenging thing, if you're gonna be honest and do it right; it's a little embarrassing to get up in front of a room of strangers. But I tried to take the proper attitude. I read mine to the class: "One year from now I don't wanna have this fucking job anymore." That was my one-year goal. It got the big laugh of the night, because everyone was there in a last-ditch attempt to save their job. I went on: "Then five years from now I want a record to come out, and ten years from now I want a hit record with someone who's nationally established." At the end of that first class I thought, "Wow, fuck that. If you just look at this list, how hard can this be?" I started applying the methods that they taught, and within a month we had a record deal for Was Not Was. David was living in LA as a freelance jazz critic for the now-defunct *Los Angeles Herald-Examiner*. He arranged an interview with Michael Zilkha, who owned a label called ZE Records in New York City, and they had the Waitresses, King Creole, the Coconuts, James White and the Blacks, Material with Bill Laswell—it's a very cool label, man. David interviewed him. He talked to him, and twenty seven minutes in he said, "By the way, there's this band out of Detroit you really gotta hear; they're perfect for what you're doing." He said, "Oh, wonderful, have them call me." So I called. We conned our way into our first deal. We sent him "Wheel Me Out." Then I used my Dale Carnegie on him: "If I could show you a way. . . ." What actually happened was that "Wheel Me Out" became a very big club hit in England and had nothing to do with the Dale Carnegie scam like that.

Steve King: I was playing music and working at the Kingsley Inn up on Woodward and either hitchhiking or taking the bus home down to 8 Mile and Woodward. If I worked too late and missed the bus, I'd have to hitchhike. I never got robbed, but lots of perverts. It was like, "Oh no, I missed the bus. Not again." When it got on my nerves I'd say, "Just drop me off here." This one guy said, "I got *Playboys* in the glove compartment, and it makes me hard just kind of thinking about them." I'm like, "Okay, pull over. I'm getting out. I'll just walk, thank you. I think I'll catch a cab here." I was walking through some terrible neighborhoods. I was living on the first street south of 8 Mile. Then Mark Norton told me Don needed some help at his studio, Sound Suite. I was just trying to do that anyway—get studio work. Don was great to me. He showed me how to align the tape machines. Back then you had to calibrate the tape machine and check them all. It was ground-level money. I used to get paid by the night, and sometimes we'd work two weeks in a row when Don would be gone for a couple weeks. He was gone to New York to make something; he was starting to take off. And I was meeting these pretty big music names—Sweet Pea Atkinson, Dave McMurray, Luis Resto. I would sleep on the couch in the studio, and in the morning somebody would come in and say, "Can you do a session?" My first session was with Aretha Franklin at Sound Suite for a car commercial. Here I was with all these uptight ad people, and I was like this little white guy sitting there sweating. I was so fuckin' nervous. I thought I was cool and had it all together. The good thing or the bad thing about Sound Suite was nothing ever worked, so I was always like, "Ah . . . which mic? So which channel should I use to get this working right?" That sets you off on a bad foot if you can't get the stuff to work. But the session went great. The studio assistant took the lyrics from the session that Aretha had sung and framed them for me.

Mike Murphy: No band got famous out of that whole era except the Romantics, and that's freaky. People kept saying someone will discover Detroit at that time, like they did in New York and Los Angeles, and it never happened. Then the bands imploded or were erratic, and it was kind of strange that nothing ever happened out of that whole time, the first wave of punk rock. Bands were going to New York and playing shows and showcases.

Katy Hait: These bands from other cities would come in—Teenage Head from Toronto, Skafish from Chicago—and we were just as good as those bands. We joked about it because Detroit was such an underdog. Bands from LA and New York would become famous even though they weren't that great.

S. Kay Young: The music was really good, but no one hit like the Ramones or the Cramps did because Detroit was not New York. There were no record label scouts here.

Jerry Vile: The whole Detroit punk thing—nobody made it, and there are a lot of reasons. The record covers always looked like shit.

Mike Murphy: I would say it's not that the Romantics weren't Detroit, but they were not representative of that scene at all. But maybe that's why they did get signed. When they were first working they were getting on all the good bills and paid for a rehearsal space and they were on salary, which sure isn't like the rest of the bands. We were poor. I was working at a 7-Eleven.

Vince Bannon: The Romantics were the only ones to pull out of Detroit in that era with any kind of substantial deal. You know it's interesting: Jerry Harrison of the Talking Heads told me that all these bands rolled into New York City because there were so many clubs besides CBGBs that they would play. They could actually afford to live in the East Village and build a buzz. So you're an A&R guy in New York, and this band is playing various buildings, and there's a big buzz. Same thing in LA. The thing you have to remember is, what big bands came out of LA? The first punk rock bands were all signed to independents. It was out of New York where at that time the record capital was, and if you were to make it, you had to go and live in New York and do it. Also, anybody who really made it—from the biggest pop star to the rock-and-roll guy you think is totally underground—their ambition is through the roof. A lot of these guys that were from Detroit, they lived at their parents' house, they go and play a gig, they come home, and Mom would make them breakfast in the morning.

David Keeps: Bands from Bookie's didn't break out. The bands that did do something had heavy management, people who were willing to invest money in them to get them out of Detroit, like the Romantics. Also in Detroit you didn't have these bands with money or commitment. You had to have both, and many didn't. I don't think anyone was poor; I think that they were mostly suburban kids living in their parents' houses and didn't have jobs. They weren't like dole kids. It wasn't as if you went to Bookie's and all these people were from the projects or got ADC. There were kids who wanted to move out of their parents' and lived in shitty neighborhoods. People like Steve King got out because they had a talent for other things—in his case, recording.

Steve King: I worked for Aretha Franklin a few times after that commercial, worked on a lot of R&B stuff, Anita Baker. I kept moving up the ranks, doing a lot of sessions. I ended up at the Hit Factory, and we were working on the fuckin' same Neve that John Lennon was working on. I was in New York working for about a month and a half. Finally I came back here. And I got a new car.

Vince Bannon: In 1981 we architected what we were going to do and how we were going to open Clutch Cargo's. Bookie's was, I don't know, getting done. I was in business with another guy, and he took good care of everything, from what our security would look like and so on. But again, we were under the radar. We would have grown exponentially if the media in Detroit would have been supporting what we were doing. In cities like LA you had like KROQ, so you talked to the promoters. It wouldn't be economic reasons; it would be media reasons. But we couldn't influence radio. When we moved away from Bookie's was the same time radio became really corporate. The stations were owned by corporations; Lee Abrams and those guys came in and said, "If you want to grow your radio station in Detroit, play much more Rush and much more Bob Seger and much more Journey."

Skid Marx: There were newer bands coming along, and there was a little bit of friction going on between the hardcore, younger punks and the Bookie's crowd. There were new metal bands, too, that weren't really Detroit bands or playing Detroit music.

Mark Norton: We went through what I think is called the Middle Child Syndrome. As the middle child, we were fucked anyway. Ezra Pound said, "Make it new." Our younger brothers, the third son, the hardcore guys came along and ripped the torch out of someone's hands—it certainly wasn't ours. We never had the torch in the first place. No one was interested in what we were doing. Everyone looked everywhere, but in their own city or state for the latest trend. "Punk rock sucks." It especially sucked coming from Detroit. I know where the Ramrods stand: we were and are the lost children between generations. We didn't exist then, and we don't really exist now—never did in the first place. We were a chimera, beat-down motherfuckers who knew right from the start in mid-'77, that knew every card in the house was stacked against us, and we liked it. The Ramrods set the stage for those who would know how to navigate the entire mess—hardcore. Bless you guys.

Stirling Silver: I don't like hardcore because I don't like that they can't sing. It's yelling.

Paul Zimmerman: One of the first hardcore bands I saw was Black Flag at Clutch Cargo's. My wife-to-be and I had gone to a wedding, and we were dressed super-normal. We went in there, and their audience were all in uniforms, and we were like, "Uh oh." They were all in black, and I've always liked black. I wore black to weddings, but that night I didn't. So that night we were getting some funny looks, and finally she went to the bathroom and I heard this ruckus. These two girls in the bathroom go, "Look at Barbie. Come on, Barbie, huh, Barbie," and she finally kicked one of the bathroom stalls open and went, "You want to fuck with Barbie? Come on, fuck with Barbie!"

Bob Mulrooney: There were a few hardcore shows at Bookie's, and people were just going around grinding their heels into my shoes and just wanting to cause trouble. And they were all guys, and I don't go out for that. I go out to look at girls, and there was no girls there. Hardcore was too negative. I like the look of the Gothic scene—not so much the records, but the Gothic chicks.

Jerry Vile: Part of the reason for punk rock was pussy. Man, if I was gay, I would have really been into hardcore. If you go to gay bars now, it looks like they're into hardcore.

Gary Reichel: You'd hear that we were the old people and that we were resisting the new breed. But they never tried to be cool with us.

Dave Rice (*L-Seven, guitarist, producer*): Black Flag played Bookie's in summer '81 with Dez singing. The front was full of new kids. The back was where the older people stood wondering what was going on.

Brian Mullan: Bookie's introduced me to what led me to hardcore. Actually it went backwards. A high school teacher of mine was sitting around with me and my twin brother after school doing an extra credit project. We went to school in a pretty shitty area, Benedict at Outer Drive and Southfield, so we were not having a whole lot of fun. The Catholic schools back then were about as good or bad as public school—no real difference. We grew up at 6 Mile and Greenfield. After the great white flight the house across the street was empty and a moving van pulled up one day and we were all happy: wow someone is moving into that house. The next day we woke up, and all the bricks were gone from the house, so we had to stare at a tar-paper shack for the next year. We all had paper routes for the *News* and *Free Press*. The *News* route was an afternoon route, and it was brutal because on Friday, they all knew you were out collecting. So some Fridays you'd get robbed and others you wouldn't. Then we got smart and would collect Monday, Wednesday, and Friday, so when they caught up to you Friday, their take wouldn't be so great. So this teacher presented the question to us that day: "You guys aren't having much fun are you?" "No, not really." My brother and I had each other, but that was about it. He goes, "You didn't hear this from me, but I think you guys need to go to this place, place called Bookie's. It's on 6 Mile before you get to Woodward." My brother went before me, and he came back all jacked up and excited. "Man, I went to that place he told us about. It was crazy, man. The guitar player was wearing a wedding dress." It turns out that it was the Damned. I went a couple weeks later, 'cause I lived on 6 Mile, took the 6 Mile bus. This guy Rob was working the door, and I'm thinking that I looked like I was twelve and there's no way I'm gonna get in. But the guy just says, "Hey, man. How's it going?" and he opens the door for me. There weren't too many people around, and I didn't know a soul. I was real nervous about going to this new place, and I looked up and there's Gloria Love, who I didn't know at the time, had never seen her. She was clad head to toe in leather, and she looked up at me, and she's like, "Darling, we've been waiting for you." She runs over and grabs my head and buries it in her breasts. I was still a virgin at the time. That's very much a night that changed my life. That's why I started going to Bookie's, which pretty soon introduced me to hardcore when they booked Black Flag.

Dave Rice: The upstarts were coming into the old guard's headquarters. I use the image of the old guard being kind of crowded into the back half of the bar during a hardcore show looking like somebody farted, you know like "What is this horrible . . . oh my God." Where the bald kids with bandanas on their legs were right up front. The hardcore thing was just deliberately nihilistic. And homophobic as fuck. Which, I mean—rightfully so—rubbed people the wrong way. But there were hilarious aspects, you know, I mean just the old punk scene was taking place largely at Bookie's, which was an old gay club, so there was a lot of cross-over there.

A lot of those people would come from that kind of *Rocky Horror* mind set, where even if you weren't gay, you acted it. Then little reactionary kids come in and call everyone dick smokers. It didn't go over so great.

Tex Newman: There had always been a rivalry between the Elvis Costello people and us. And the big rock bands were also the enemy, and then the bands that wore their tiger-print pants. Bookie's was punk rock, and the Freezer was for the hardcore shit.

John Brannon: You want to talk about punk rock, I'm gonna go Stooges, MC5, real Detroit rock. Alice Cooper. The only thing that really carried that on after that was Sonic's Rendezvous Band and Destroy All Monsters, which were all my heroes from the other bands. Anything else that claimed it was punk rock in Detroit was just a joke. So I lived through that whole '79 to '81 thing where new wave took over. So you got all these old Bookie's bands, you're all coked out, you're wearing suits and skinny ties, doing Animals covers or some obscure Brit-sixties shit, and you think you're fuckin' punk rock. No, you're not. No, you're not.

The Big Three Killed My Baby
(1981–2000)

Vengeance

John Brannon (*Negative Approach, Laughing Hyenas, Easy Action, vocalist*): Larissa and I were living in the City Club, the old women's club on Elizabeth downtown, and it turned it into a squat. These little boys called the Guardian Angels moved in, which kind of turned into an abandoned building in the middle of Detroit where the crack industry started. It was the basis for *New Jack City*. As time goes on, people get greedy, you know, and all the cousins start moving in. And the thugs. Everybody's like, "We're taking over this building." All the dope gangs moved in. Everybody in their right mind moved out. Me and Larissa were like, "Fuck it, we're squatting." The owner had bailed. He lost all his money and moved to Puerto Rico. Negative Approach practiced there on the third floor in a ballroom. We lived up on the sixth floor. Then it kind of came around, you know, "You're cool, white boy, but you're going to have to start paying us protection." Larissa goes up and goes, "Fuck you, motherfucker!" Okay, that didn't go over in the 'hood. They were shooting up the halls with shotguns. She had the gun down in her face. We were cool with the main dudes, but when the cousins and the thugs moved in, they didn't have any respect for the scene. They were going to kill us. They blew the door out with a shotgun after Larissa told them to fuck off.

Chris Moore, aka Opie (*Negative Approach, Crossed Wire, drummer, guitarist, vocalist*): This guy pulled a gun on us and said, "I'm sick of you guys making all this noise." John cooled him down by talking to him.

John Brannon: I was cool for a minute holding off some of the dudes, and then it became a whole ten-story building full of thugs wanting to kill us.

Chris Moore: Before that, John and Larissa lived at the Clubhouse over in the Cass Corridor. But in the City Club they had this cool apartment. The windows were always open and this city noise was coming in, and they had all these records and artwork. I loved hanging out there and them showing me this great art and different music. I got a great education from both John and Larissa.

Rob Michaels (*Bored Youth, Allied, vocalist*): One time I was over there and there was this guy and he had some cocaine. He was trying to get me to shoot it. I was like, "You're not a fucking doctor."

Dave Rice (*L-Seven, guitarist; producer*): Larissa was into shooting cocaine. She just thought it was cool as fuck. It was really ostentatious—shoot up right there in front of people, you know, the great shock-value thing. We were not planning for the future.

John Brannon: I started doing speed and using needles in '81. At that point it wasn't heroin. The Necros told me before I met Larissa, "Oh, yeah, she does that dope." They were all straight edge. I was, whatever, you know, drink a 40, smoke a joint. Do some speed. The shit was highly available. I always had good weed.

Marc Barie (*scenester*): Larissa was an addict from the day I met her. She told me right off that speedballs were the greatest thing and she showed me this piece of art, the plaster of Paris thing of a hypodermic needle. I checked it out for a little while; Larissa turned me on to shooting dope. I could see where that was going. It got to that point, for them, that the needles were just appearing regularly, and it was about shooting up several times a day.

John Brannon: Me and Pete Zelewski would go to whatever punk gig, and we're always like, "Who's this chick?" Larissa stood out. Then we started going to see L-Seven shows. We had Negative Approach together, but they were doing all these big gigs. They opened for Bauhaus at Bookie's. We met them at some big outdoor gig and, we got along. Then my mother kicked me out of the house. Fifty cents, I take the Jefferson bus, come downtown, walk about three miles over to the Clubhouse from Jefferson, knocked on her door, and was like, "'Sup?" And I'd only met her twice. I'm like, "Um, I need a place to stay." She says, "Come on in." I had nowhere to go. I lived with her for about a year first, but we were best friends at that time. Then we actually became a couple.

Sherrie Feight (*Strange Fruit, Spastic Rhythm Tarts, vocalist*): You'd go to Detroit for a show, you never knew what to wear. So you'd kind of wear what the guys were wearing. The first time I saw Larissa, I was like, "Oh my God." She was in a slip and combat boots, her hair bleached out, with this milky white skin and those eyes. I wanted to be like her, but there was no way. I was this rich kid and she was from down on Cass; we were from different worlds.

Andy Wendler (*Necros, McDonalds, guitarist*): We went to see the Clash at the Motor City Roller Rink, and Joe Strummer kicked his roadie. He was pulling the typical rock-star nonsense—kicking his roadie in the chest because his guitar was messed up. We said, "Okay, this is cool. We love it." When we saw hardcore, it was right away the idea that this is our thing. We were seven years younger than the guys from the Clash, and the first punk wave and stuff. We played little shows, like basement shows and party shows, then actually started playing real shows with the Fix in Lansing at Club Doobee before the Freezer happened. As record collectors, we had all the 27 and Coldcock singles, the Bookie's bands and all that stuff. We liked it, but it wasn't us. The one thing that set us apart was that we wanted to do our own thing, and that was always very clear to us. We weren't gonna try to get in on the end of the Bookie's thing; we were just gonna do our own thing. We were also too young. There were many times playing Bookie's and other places with the Misfits, where we'd meet with the manager and he'd say, "All right, just come in right before you play, or whatever, in the back door or something." It was always that hassle.

Chris Panackia, aka Cool Chris (*sound man at every locale in Detroit*): Hardcore kids were cool because they didn't bathe and they had no hair on their head. A lot of them squatted. The hardcore kids played the Freezer, the Clubhouse, Cobb's Corner. They played places that were just inferior in every respect possible. Even a bathroom was a luxury. The bands wanted beer and to sell a few T-shirts, and that was good enough. They didn't have any high hopes. One more thing about that whole hardcore thing is, who would have thought John Brannon would be revered by every punk rock, hardcore kid in the world as like the greatest punk rock lead singer ever? I was the only sound guy that helped those punk rock guys out. They would always say, "Yeah, Cool Chris always treated us good, man. You were always really good to us." I didn't want to be that rock sound guy—I was one of them.

Rob Michaels: Dave Rice and Larissa took me to see the Necros, and the next thing I knew I was friends with all those people. At that time if you saw someone who looked punk at all, you would cross the street to talk to them—it was a fraternity.

Corey Rusk (*Touch and Go Records, owner; Necros, bassist*): I was younger than the other guys in the Necros, so from the time they had driver's licenses, we were going to Detroit, going to Ann Arbor to get records, or going to Detroit to try and sneak into a show, because we were underage. I quickly realized that my fake ID didn't work all that often. Once I had a driver's license, I could go on my own. It really wasn't ever like I wanted to be a promoter. It seemed like if I put on a show at some rental hall, then it's all ages and I get to see the band that I really wanna see. So I started renting out halls in the Detroit area when I was seventeen to put on shows of bands that I wanted to see.

John Brannon: It was all promoted on the phone. You call up one dude. He'd call up six dudes. We'd pass out flyers at the gigs. All this shit was word of mouth. No Internet. No MTV. No radio play. Everything was done with cassette tapes and letters, so you're talking about creating something out of nothing. It started with fifteen people. We know the first five bands that began it all: the Fix, the Necros, the Meatmen, Negative Approach, L-Seven. You got another scene out of that scene when a bunch of those kids following those bands started magazines and bands and that shit became national. "Okay, we're bored, we live in Detroit, we're going to create nothing out of nothing."

Tesco Vee (*Meatmen, Blight, vocalist, editor,* **Touch and Go** *magazine*): The Freezer is where a lot of the next part of Detroit music started. It was about fifty feet by twenty feet wide—just a shit hole. A beautiful shit hole. It was like a frat boy fraternity for hardcore. There were a few girls, but for the most part it was guys.

John Brannon: We never expected anything out of it except to write those songs and play the shows. The fact that Negative Approach were able to make records through Touch and Go Records and get the exposure through *Touch and Go* magazine was just great. We didn't know it was going to turn out to be this whole thing.

Keith Jackson (*Shock Therapy, guitarist*): That scene had girls, but they all died. It's weird when you look at it, like these chicks that were hanging around all seemed to pass away over the years.

Hillary Waddles (*scenester*): There were girls, but we were all people's girlfriends. It just wasn't the time for that yet—girls didn't get in bands; you didn't get the sense that you could be anything but a groupie or a girlfriend.

Gloria Branzei (*scenester*): It was a little dick fest, and they didn't like girls. They were too cool for that shit; it slowed them down.

Hillary Waddles: Those kids that got into the straight-edge nonsense really didn't like girls, some of those guys from Ohio. I was terrified to be down there in that area, but we went. I was a bougie girl from northwest Detroit, and here were all these suburban kids with no survival instincts. I mean, I may have been from there too, but I still grew up in Detroit, and you pay attention.

Gloria Branzei: It was a really violent scene. I would kick someone's ass for the hell of it. At that time girls and punk rock did not go together at all. It was just rock-and-roll chicks.

Tesco Vee: Washington, DC, had more girls in its scene, but it was a similar scene. In Detroit there were a hundred core kids that made up the entire scene.

Sherrie Feight: Going to shows in Detroit meant you were gonna get hit. I still have a scar on my leg from being in the mosh pit.

Jon Howard (*scenester*): There were a lot of people who knew about these older clubs before but couldn't get in because they had ID checks. I knew about these places when I first started shopping for records at places like Sam's Jams, but I was fifteen. My dad lived in San Francisco at the time, so the winter of '81 I went to the Mabuhay and saw Dead Kennedys, Husker Du, Church Police, Toxic Reasons—all these great bands. I came back here, and we had the Freezer for all ages. It opened the door for music for a lot of people, so kids could see live bands now. And hardcore was the music that was their first experience.

Andy Wendler: The Freezer was on Cass and Willis in downtown Detroit. The guy who ran it was a speed freak, and we could get away with anything we wanted. It was right around the corner from where John and Larissa lived in the Clubhouse at that time, which was right between Cobb's Corner and the old Willis Art Gallery.

Hillary Waddles: The Freezer was a crappy place. We went over to the Burger King to use the bathroom. No way I was gonna use the Freezer.

Corey Rusk: Even though it was so inner city, and at the time Cass Corridor was really, really bad, it seems to have gotten cleaned up over the years. At the time all the people living in the slummy areas where the rental halls were at were not accepted. Punk rock was not accepted and was not mainstream, and if you looked like a punk rocker, you weren't cool; you were a freak. It's amazing that all these white kids invaded all these inner-city neighborhoods for these punk rock shows, and whatever violence problems there were, were usually between the white kids.

Keith Jackson: A lot of us were from the suburbs, and we all wanted to be downtown where it was tough. And it was. There was no interference, which was fine. Cops never came around, and you were really on your own going to see bands. That stuff out of LA seemed phony to us; they would hang out and then go back to their parents' homes, and it seemed pretty easy. But at the time in Detroit you could go to a show at a place on Zug Island, and there were no cops, no security. You would bring in generators into a burned-out building, and that was your club. I stabbed a dude in the ass one time at a Subhumans show at Zug Island. There was this huge fight that broke out, and I mean it just kept on going for most of the show. He punched my girlfriend and I had a four-inch blade I carried around, and I stabbed him in the ass. He screamed like a little girl.

Corey Rusk: We were probably mildly entertaining to the residents. They just looked at us like we were freaks too, and we weren't the white people that they had problems with. We had no race problems.

Brian Mullan: Roaming the Cass Corridor at whatever ungodly hour, we all wore jackboots, had our hair cropped or shaven. I had this kid from Amsterdam came to visit one night when Marc Barie and I were living at this funeral home down there. We were going to see a show at the City Club. So we're walking down there, and all of a sudden there's this big shiny gun being pointed at us with the guy holding it yelling at us, "Suck my black dick, white motherfuckers." It was a miracle, because you never saw cabs down there, but a cab pulled up and we dove through the fucking windows. Nobody really got hurt down there because nobody had money. At the time I was taking the Jefferson bus to Nunzio's to run sound. I made like $15 a show, and then I sold loose joints. I was just surviving.

Andy Wendler: There was the Rayis Brothers place, the party store, right down the street from the Freezer. Everyone went there; they were Chaldeans who ran it. It was a safe zone. They just didn't take any shit. If there was anybody lingering around outside, they'd just go out and confront them with a weapon because they were making the business turn away. They'd just handle the weapon and tell them, "Get the hell out of here." The other thing about Rayis Brothers: the store had a two-inch plastic bullet shield, like other places, but the bullet shield was around the entire store, so when you went in you were like in a gerbil cage, and you'd say, "Give me that, give me that" and all of the product was behind the plastic shield. Say, "give me some Fritos and a quart of Bud," and they'd go around the actual store and get it. The customer was in a little booth buying stuff.

Tim Caldwell (*artist*): I was in jail one night, and a guy told me the cops came into the apartment building right by the Willis Gallery because he had let loose from the rooftop with a machine gun. He hid on top of the elevator while they searched the premises.

Dave Rice: I lived in a few different buildings around there, briefly in the Clubhouse with this guy Darryl. Darryl and his brother and this friend of ours, Jenny, were there, and a couple of guys came in with their shotgun and just, like, cleaned the place out of as much gear as they could carry. Okay, gotta get a new amp. Gotta get a new guitar. I always played like this slap-together pawnshop crap anyways, so it wasn't like I lost a '59 goldtop or anything.

Andy Wendler: We'd get fucked with occasionally, but we had numbers on our side. We were never there alone. There would be forty kids skateboarding down the middle of the street. John and Larissa had respect in the neighborhood, back when thieves used to abide by that kind of thing, because they lived in the neighborhood. So if you were with John and Larissa, you got a little bit of a pass. It was a big heroin neighborhood in those days, and they were amongst it. The guy who owned Cobb's Corner got shot in the backroom one night. That was a money thing—he had it. One time the Detroit police pulled up at the Clubhouse and said, "What the hell are you kids doing? Go back to Roseville, you idiots. What are you doing down here?"

Gloria Branzei: Those guys thought they were scaring the people in the neighborhood, but they were fooling themselves. I was in the shooting dens, and I knew what they thought; they just thought we were fucking crazy. But they sure weren't scared of us.

Corey Rusk: The Freezer was the all-ages reaction to the City Club situation. Somehow we managed to get into a lot of those City Club shows, though we were underage. But the Freezer was just so cool, it didn't matter.

Brian Mullan: City Club was the old woman's club off Elizabeth right downtown, a block off Woodward. It was one of Vince Bannon's big to-dos. Any time there was a big show, whether the Dead Kennedys or the Exploited, the Cramps or whoever, the security guys would always beat up on the punks. So there was a backlash. Bannon was the Establishment, a businessman, and in retrospect I don't begrudge him that.

Rob Miller (*Bloodshot Records, cofounder*)**:** I had a humiliating night at City Club. I got a fake ID at the Lindell AC bar and tried to get into a Fear show with it, and the door guys, they laughed at me.

Chris Panackia: Vince was booking bands at City Club before it was opened. And he still was running Bookie's. The fucking agents went crazy. He goes, "Oh, I got this great place," and he wouldn't tell them until they got there. About four or five hundred people in the ballroom could see the band at City Club, but you could put a lot more people in it. In a two-month span he did the Dead Kennedy's, the Fear, the Cramps, the Rockettes, the Stray Cats, Duran Duran, Haircut 100, Killing Joe, Gun Club, Human League, Circle Jerks, Sparks, the Flesh Eaters, and Orchestral Maneuvers in the Dark. It was the best place to be. The Circle Jerks show was during the Grand Prix downtown, and you got in free if you brought a helmet. One guy brought a helmet.

Vince Bannon (*Bookie's, City Club promoter, Coldcock, Sillies, guitarist*)**:** In '81 we architected what we were going to do and how we were going to open Clutch Cargo's at the City Club, which is what it was. Clutch Cargo's was the name of the production, and it was at the City Club.

Rob Miller: The Dead Kennedys was oversold, and it also brought to bear the uncomfortable underbelly of Detroit hardcore, which was how right wing it was becoming. You had skinheads goose stepping, these National Front guys.

Keith Jackson: One night I was with Kirk Morrison from Dead Heroes. City Club had just opened, and we were outside and we heard gunfire, which wasn't unusual. But a bullet went through my jacket and shattered my collarbone. Some guys dragged me into Detroit Receiving by my arm and said, "Our friend got shot." The cops actually came to the emergency room and talked to me. They said, "Were you returning fire?"

Corey Rusk: We'd go to City Club because they got bands we wanted to see, plus we would be on some of those bills; Negative Approach played there a lot. The Freezer wasn't there to put those larger places down.

I would help organize those bands at the Freezer, though, and we started getting out-of-town touring bands that were open to playing different places. Like when the Misfits played at the Freezer. It was just such a huge time for music. At least to us.

John Brannon: We were writing the soul music of the suburbs, and the Freezer was perfect. If you want to nail what soul music was for that time, the scene—even though it's basically a white scene—it is our soul music, man. We're creative, we're bored, we've got nothing going on—man, we're creating this shit. The whole thing about being in a band at that point, there was no separation between the kids and the audience and who's on stage. It was music for the people.

Rob Michaels: There was no consciousness at all of "Hey, this is the town that the Stooges and MC5 were from." There was this Stooges residue, and there were people we thought of as that. It wasn't like people didn't know about those records, but there was no sense of "Hey, this is Detroit and this is what came from here." It was this sense of "We made this."

Face Forward

Tesco Vee: Dave Stimson and I started a label, Touch and Go, named after the magazine we had. We had friends that were in the Necros and the Fix, and these bands were so fucking good and nobody's going to put their records out, so I have to put them out. I felt like it had to be done. We were part of something that was great, and we weren't deluded into thinking our own little thing was great; it really was great. We had some really good bands, and the world needed to hear them. The Necros and the Fix were the two big bands, and then Negative Approach.

Andy Wendler: In the fall of '80 we ran into Tim Story, who is now a Grammy award–winning producer and composer. But at the time he had a four-track in his basement, and that's where three songs on the Necros' first single came from. He just came over and brought his bike and his four-track over and a little mixer, and we just laid it down, and then that was it.

Tesco Vee: Those first records by the Fix and the Necros records sat in various shops. We'd drive them down to Ann Arbor and we'd run and look and, yep there's still five. Still five Necros. Oh, we sold one Fix for $2. Now those records go for a couple of mortgage payments.

Corey Rusk: The first two Touch and Go releases, the Fix and Necros, were so limited, two hundred of the Fix and one hundred of the Necros. And that seemed like so many: we have five friends. You know, "We don't know anybody beyond our five friends who would want this."

Marc Barie: Corey took it from those two releases, the Fix and Necros, and Touch and Go became one of the biggest indie labels in the world. That doesn't happen accidentally.

Corey Rusk: Sometime in late spring of '81 I got a job at a lumberyard, specifically because I wanted to make some money so that the Necros could record another record. I had the idea of the *Process of Elimination* EP too. So I have to get some money together so I can record all these bands to get a compilation out documenting what's going on. I was just an amped-up kid. I wanted to do shit. So I worked all summer, loading trucks and saving my money.

Tesco Vee: I officially handed Touch and Go Records over to Corey when I moved to DC in '82, but he was handling it before that. The *Process* EP was when the passing of the torch went down. Corey called me up one day, and I realized that I had no interest in running a record label. I was doing it out of necessity, as a companion to the magazine. Corey was like, "I want to take it over," and I said, "Go for it." We were friends, and he thought, "This is what I want to do." And this was a perfect, already established name. I was getting ready to pull up stakes and go to DC. I lost my teaching job, unemployment in Michigan was 16 percent, and I didn't have money to pay the rent, much less put out records.

Chris Moore: People made fun of Corey behind his back because he was so serious and ambitious. He had such a drive to make something of this music that was happening. He wasn't much fun, but he really looked out for us in a lot of ways.

Gloria Branzei: Corey Rusk was one of the best fucks I ever had.

Marc Barie: Corey's dad was really interesting. He manufactured something for the auto industry. One day we were all around Maumee and he took us over there. The line workers looked at us like we were demented. We had all the punk rock chains and boots, and Todd Swalla had a Mohawk. I think Corey got his business sense from his dad, who made a lot of money.

Corey Rusk: I was living with my grandmother in Maumee, Ohio. I had a little recording studio in my basement and so I started recording bands for Touch and Go. All the crappy sounding records were recorded there—the Meatmen EP, the Negative Approach EP. The Blight thing was recorded there, and that was one of the better-sounding things that was recorded there. That was one of the first things that I did there that I thought, "Wow, this sounds really heavy and great."

Chris Moore: We had the run of Corey's house, and we had a skateboard ramp we built in the front yard or the driveway. We would record and skate all day and burn ourselves out on that. No one was into drugs or anything. The older guys drank beer, but we just skated.

Corey Rusk: I put bands up all the time, even when I lived with my grandmother. I brought Flipper back to my grandma's house, which sounds like a potential disaster. But they were so nice to her; we all hung out and had pizza. Suicidal Tendencies also stayed at my grandmother's. We all went swimming in the river, since the house was on the banks of the Maumee River.

John Brannon: We started going on tour, and we'd have to sneak Opie out of the house because he was fifteen. Opie, Graham—those kids were still in high school. I'm sure, looking back, the parents probably realized what's going on. Opie would tell his folks, "Oh, I'm going to spend the night at Graham's house," and then we'd go out. DC, Philly, and New York, and then be back in time for him to get to school.

Chris Moore: My parents worried, but they knew about my friends. I didn't tell them what went down.

Andy Wendler: We did our first real tour with the Misfits. We had made great friends with them, and Corey and Barry were pestering 'em like, "Hey, can we get on those bills?" I don't really know why we got along with them so well, other than the fact that Jerry and Doyle might as well have been from Ohio. They were just such great, good-natured guys, and we really hit 'em off with it. Glenn, for whatever he's become now, was incredibly articulate and artistically talented and had an eye for just really clever, almost iconic graphics. I don't know—that really appealed to us. We were like, "Wow, they're like the Ramones but scary." On the Misfits tour we took Corey's dad's ratted-out old Suburban. It was tight, and we had to sleep on top of the gear in the back. It got horrible gas mileage, but it was cheaper than buying or renting something.

Corey Rusk: You essentially had to sleep standing up.

Punk Rock Sucks

Russ Gibb (*Grande Ballroom promoter*): One of my ex-students came to me and said, "Have you heard Negative Approach?" I said, "No." He said, "Well, there's a place called the Freezer Theater." So I went to see them, and they were rehearsing in some fucking little place on Cass somewhere; it looked like a little storefront or something. I saw them and I said, "Wow, this is interesting." They're doing things that the MC5 were doing. Now this is fifteen years later. You know, click, click, click, click. Of course I saw money!

Corey Rusk: Russ started showing up at the Freezer. He was hanging out and absorbing it all. Maybe it reminded him of his youth in the sixties. He saw that I was involved in some of those shows at the Freezer. Honestly, I'm socially awkward, and it was more enjoyable to me to have a sort of take-charge attitude and be more like, "I'm gonna do a bunch of the work to make these shows happen, even though I'm not making any money from it." You know, it's not my club. I'd do a lot of the flyering, and Russ saw that in me and started trying to talk to me. I totally blew him off in the beginning, like, "Is this dude a cop, or what the fuck is he doing here? Why is there someone this old here?" I was sort of suspicious of him.

Russ Gibb: We started a show my students did, *Why Be Something That You're Not?* It had a lot of the bands playing at the Freezer on it. I owned the cable company, and we did that. So when I saw the Freezer, it was just about the same time that that I was getting involved deeper and deeper in cable. I needed the programming.

Corey Rusk: I'm sure, being seventeen years old and full of testosterone, I was a total dick to him. And he just kept hanging around and being cool, and eventually

215

I lightened up. He started telling me who he was, what he had done. The fact that it involved the Stooges seemed cool enough. He saw this all-ages thing happening and was like, "We should open an all-ages club together." So Russ and I spent a long time trying to find a place.

Russ Gibb: We didn't get rich off it, but it was okay. It was an experiment, and we brought in a lot of people to play there. The one that really closed me up was the Graystone. But Corey was this terrific kid, and he made it work.

Corey Rusk: We couldn't find any place, and I had been regularly successful at doing shows at this place on Michigan Avenue, the Graystone. It was more than Russ wanted to spend to get a building, but it was also in a better location and a nicer place. He was more likely to get his money back out of it in the end than from some of the really fucked up places we were looking at in the Cass Corridor. Russ ended up buying the Graystone, and the agreement was that he would put up the money and buy the building and he would buy a PA. I would agree that I was gonna run the place and do whatever the fuck it took to make it work and that he wasn't going to put in any money beyond that. He wasn't going to make the club pay rent right away, but as soon as we got to the point where it was actually making a little money, then we needed to start paying some rent. But it never became profitable.

Russ Gibb: I made a few bucks. I didn't lose on it. By the time I sold the building and everything, I made money on it. I would go there but not often. I was still involved in booking, but by that time Corey was directing. I've always said you go to the people that know it. You get them involved, not people like myself. We're the business end of it. Our end is to put the numbers together to see if it can make a buck.

Corey Rusk: I ran that place for a year and a half before I moved to Chicago at the end of '86. I've always worked hard my whole life and slept very little, but that was the hardest I ever worked and the least I ever slept. Because on top of doing the Graystone, Touch and Go was doing pretty well. We were working with the Butthole Surfers, and Big Black, and Killdozer. I was also delivering pizzas for Domino's. Running the Graystone, I probably wasn't a good enough business person on behalf of the club. I never made a dime personally from running the Graystone. I felt a duty to do the best possible job I could because Russ had put up this money. I'm gonna bust my ass to find out because Russ has put his faith in me, basically.

Mike Hard (*God Bullies, Thrall, vocalist*): At the Butthole Surfer shows at the Graystone there were people selling acid inside the door to help enjoy the show. With the Buttholes it wasn't like coke or fucking heroin at the door before you could walk in there. I mean, you could score it. But for the Surfers it was everybody through the crowd, "Hey, you wanna buy some acid?" The whole place was tripping. It almost was part of the price of your ticket. You gotta get acid with it, you know?

Corey Rusk: The Buttholes broke down one time somewhere near Cleveland, and they had a show at the Graystone the next night. So I had double interest in their situation, in that they were both on my label and we had this big show at the Graystone. We needed the headliner to show up. My dad lived between Toledo and Cleveland, so I got him to drive half an hour to an hour east, get them, and then drive them up to Detroit. I was busy, and when you're younger you don't think about those things as much; it's just like, "Thanks, Dad, I'll see ya later."

Tesco Vee: We played the Graystone once when Corey was booking it and then once with Scary Cary, who took over after Corey left. Scary pulled a gun on us. He shorted us on our guarantee. He offered us a certain amount, and then he couldn't come up with the whole amount. So my genius band members decided to steal the microphones. They stuck the microphones in their trap cases and we were loading out in the rain, Scary came out to me and put a gun to my forehead and said, "You better give me my microphones back or I'm gonna kill you!"

John Speck (*The Fags, Hoarse, guitarist, vocals*): I heard a story from one of the guys in a local gang that was friendly with Cary that blew my fucking mind. They went over to Cary's house to hang out. And my buddy Chris asked where the bathroom was, and it was like, "Down the hallway, blah." He opened a door and Scary went, "Hey! What are you doing there?" Like he peeked open thinking it was the bathroom, and he said that in that room from floor to ceiling was ammunition.

Tesco Vee: I was surprisingly calm about the whole thing. I was like, "We'll get your microphones back." So we had to tear everything out apart out in the rain and get his microphones back. I was, like, "You guys are a bunch of idiots." Turns out now Cary's in prison for armed robbery.

John Speck: These were some hardcore guys. Cary is a one-percenter, which is a biker outlaw. There were a few people out of that scene who ended up doing time.

I used to work for another guy who was in the Iron Coffins, Bird. Went up for gun running and drugs. I know another guy who's been in and out of prison for a long time, Darrel Maniac, who was a big deal dude. He was an original Detroit Skin. That guy makes me more nervous than anybody else in the fucking city scene ever did. And he's a tattoo artist, and I was trying to get a job at Eternal Tattoos, so I had to do a tattoo in front of the boss to show him what I could do. I get done with it and he's like, "Well, why don't you go hang out and watch Darrel, and if you've got any questions, ask him." So I go walk over to his workspace, and I'm standing there at the doorway, and he's got his back to me and he's bent over tattooing. Darrel's like, maybe, like, this tall and just a brick shithouse and covered in tattoos. He had a big Manson tattoo. Just a dude that's been in the fucking prison culture for a long time. He turns around, and the hair on the back of my neck stood up just as he started looking, and he just looked at me and said, "Don't stand behind me." He said it in a way that was just fucking chilling. And obviously I'm like, "I'm sorry." We had some badass dudes around.

Don Kirshner of Detroit

Corey Rusk: While I was doing the Graystone, the Butthole Surfers records just took off, and Big Black and Die Kreuzen were selling a lot of records too. There was this big staircase at the Graystone that was four and a half feet wide, and it ran up from the club to the apartment, where Lisa and I lived for free. That staircase was our warehouse for the label. We didn't have enough room to store all the records that were coming and going, so we'd get a big shipment of records, and we'd be stashing 'em in every little storage room in the Graystone and in our apartment.

Andy Wendler: Corey had to quit the Necros to focus on Touch and Go. It was becoming very clear that it needed full-time stewardship, and he was the man for the job. He's another one of those guys who went crazy from all the time in the van. That was before cell phones, so you couldn't even do business.

Corey Rusk: I got Big Black on the label as soon as I could. The second EP, *Bull-dozer*, there was a limited edition of two hundred that were in a galvanized metal casing. That eventually led to me getting in touch with them. We had been talking to the Butthole Surfers about putting out their records, and they were coming to Detroit, so Lisa and I got them a gig at Paycheck's. We were trying to think of an opening band, and we were like, "That Big Black band's really cool. I wonder if they'd come from Chicago and do it?" They were cool and opened that show. Big Black and the Buttholes both stayed with us, and Steve Albini and I got along really well, and we've worked together ever since.

Russ Gibb: By the time we started the Graystone, I was also deep in television production, so I had a crew.

Corey Rusk: I don't think Russ needed to make a living teaching school. And here he was in 1981, teaching media at Dearborn High School. He put a bunch of his own money into helping fund Dearborn High School having its own high school TV studio and station that was probably as good as the local public television station set-up. You look at how forward thinking was this fucker? Nineteen eighty-one was the year that MTV started, and the bulk of America did not have cable TV then. You know, like MTV is a household word now, but it was just like this bizarre upstart concept in 1981, and so for Russ to really see that the future of music was in music video in 1981 and to put his money where his mouth was—to say, "I want the kids in my class to have this experience, because this will prepare them for what is gonna be the future."

John Brannon: We did those TV shows with Russ Gibb. He locked onto the scene and saw something that was going on, and he was really into the idea of the youth presenting their art. He had his students come out and tape all these TV shows, and they became the first kind of public access TV shows. And they were doing it on this extreme hard core punk.

Corey Rusk: *Why Be Something That You're Not* was Russ's thing in his high school class. Russ would get this huge mobile studio and set up in the Graystone and film. Marc Barie and I tried to film four bands a day, and on a Saturday each segment was thirty minutes. We had Necros, Negative Approach, Meatmen, Misfits, some other Detroit bands of the era that didn't put out records. We did twelve episodes. It probably owed more to *Don Kirshner's Rock Concert* than anything on MTV.

Doc Dart (*Crucifucks, vocalist*): We did Russ's show with the Misfits, but I didn't know they were the Misfits. They came with these guitars and these outfits. It looked like they'd shopped at K-Mart for Halloween stuff. Little Doc did not like costume parties, first of all. He did not like Halloween costumes, because Halloween's about something much deeper than anything a human could do. He did not like mimes. He hated clowns. He did not like street theater, puppets, or theater in general. So you know where I'm coming from here. If the theme is "Why be something that you're not," the dress-up thing—I'm not sure how well that gels.

Mutiny in Hardcore

Mike Hard: Before the Graystone was up and running, Birthday Party played Detroit, 1983. Everyone was there, and it was the night Detroit hardcore changed forever. John and Larissa were hanging out with Nick, and L-Seven and the Necros opened. It spawned the Laughing Hyenas.

John Brannon: I have the board tape. I don't want to get sacrilegious here, but seeing the Birthday Party was better than the first time I ever saw Alice Cooper or Iggy. Because it was so fresh. It was the month they just put out the *Bad Seed* EP. Larissa and I had all those records, and I was writing what would be *Tied Down*. I'm listening to *Junkyard* and *Prayers on Fire* and thinking, "this is the shit, man!" I realized then that what you play and what you listen to can be two different things.

Dave Rice: L-Seven opened, and I shook Roland Howard's hand afterward. But Nick Cave was out of it. He came off stage and came by in tears, all freaked out. I thought, "I'm not going to bother Mr. Cave." He ended up hanging out with Scott Schuer and Larissa. Scott was driving Nick Cave around, looking to score, and Cave was searching under the seats. Scott had a seventies Impala, and Scott's like, "What are you looking for?" And Cave says, "Where's your shotgun? Doesn't everybody in Detroit have a shotgun?"

Scott Schuer (*L-Seven, guitarist*): We ended up bringing Cave back to Larissa's apartment in the Judith on Willis Street. We both lived in that building at the time, but in different apartments. I think Cave had just broken up with his long-time girlfriend and seemed genuinely heartsick. I think we were just in the path of the train.

John Brannon: Opie from Negative Approach played drums with L-Seven that night. We shared a practice space, and Opie knew all the songs, and Kory Clark had quit. That night I told all those Negative Approach dudes, "This is the future of rock and roll." They all told me, "John, that band sucks. I hate this band."

Margaret Dollrod (*Demolition Doll Rods, guitarist, vocalist*): L-Seven were pussies. They called the cops on me one time because I wanted to get this guy's attention and he was dancing with another girl. I took my clothes off and I got on the stage thinking that maybe that would work. He was like, "What the fuck are you doing?" L-Seven called the cops, and they came to arrest me. The cops thought that I was dancing for the show, and they gave me a T-shirt. I went outside, and L-Seven was talking, "Yeah, we showed her. We called the cops."

Dave Rice: Larissa hadn't played guitar much before the Hyenas, just toward the end of the band when she just was hanging out with John and clinking out some Alice Cooper stuff or whatever. The next time I see her she's just killin'. Her tone, man. They were putting the Hyenas together, and L-Seven was done shortly after that. Around then I auditioned for PIL while I was living in Detroit, playing in the Linkletters. PIL were planning to do this tour, and he got me the audition in Pasadena at Perkins Palace. I flew myself out there. At that point it was an excuse to get out of Detroit, and I had a brother out there to stay with. I headed over to the audition, and here's Johnny Rotten in the front row with a big can of Fosters. When it was my turn, he said, "Dave from Detroit, play us some rock and roll." So I played "This Is Not a Love Song" and "Swan Lake." Martin Atkins was on drums, so it was pretty fuckin' cool. I didn't get the gig, and I don't think that tour ever happened. They were gonna do a tour and it got postponed, and then they did *Album*, so I can say I got bumped by Steve Vai.

EWolf (*photographer, Dirtbombs, drummer*): There were so many different bands and so many different scenes by the mideighties. You had hardcore, and there were bands playing variations on it. Even some bands doing the more metal end of it like Ugly But Proud. There were bands that defied classification, like Sleep and Private Angst, Vertical Pillows. We did the *Angry Red Planet* EP for Corey when Touch and Go was still nothing. He had just started to do some things with the Butthole Surfers. Then he picked up the Didjits, and Big Black. I had been shooting music photography for some time, but without having any real plan. The Didjits came through town, and they stayed at my house. The next morning they got up and said, "Hey, you shoot pictures, don't you?" I said, "No. Yeah. Kind of." They said,

"Well, we need some new publicity shots. Can you hook us up?" So I did it just as a favor. We did a session, and the photos came out great. I sent them the proofs, and Corey called me and said, "Man, we really liked the photos. We want to pay you for them so we can use them." He just offered me some money and I figured, "Money? Okay." Through Touch and Go once these photos went out, I guess anybody who was shooting photos who wasn't Charles Peterson or Michael Lavine at that point must have been shooting total shit, because everybody went gaga over these shots. I shot a lot of bands and record covers—Jesus Lizard, Atomic Fireballs, Iggy Pop, Lee Harvey Oswald Band. Stuff for Atlantic. I stopped counting at sixty-five covers.

John Brannon: The next time Nick Cave came to town he stayed at my place at Cass and Willis across the street from the Clubhouse. I missed it all because I was doing the Tied Down tour with Negative Approach. It was '84 and *From Her to Eternity* has just come out. Larissa scored for him. He was like, "Fuck my band. I'm hanging out with you. Your boyfriend won't mind that I'm here?" She's like, "Oh, he's cool. He'd get a kick out of the fact you're even here."

Sherrie Feight: I saw her that night, and it really made me sad. She was all fucked up. I hated to see all that talent being wasted, and I knew that's where it was going.

John Brannon: She's telling him, "This is like the area where you can walk a block and, you know, you could get a blowjob from a one-legged hooker. You cop dope two blocks away." He looks through all my records and he put all the records into stacks, the ones he liked and the ones he didn't like. He put all the Detroit shit in one stack. All my Alice Cooper, Stooges, and shit. I get back and Larissa said, "I do remember he put all the Bowie stuff in the bad stack." She said, "He pulled out your Ted Nugent first solo. That was in the good stack." That was the start of the next phase for me. There wasn't a whole lot going on in Detroit other than hardcore. Nugent and Seger were no longer really part of Detroit and hadn't done a good record for years. There was a hair-metal scene, bands like Seduce, that didn't even sound like anything remotely Detroit.

Andy Wendler: We came back from a tour, and a guy named Ken Waagner was in Detroit making a ton of money producing shows. Waagner started managing Seduce, but at first they were skeptical. They were doing live concerts on the radio, a local band at Harpo's thing, and they were making $300 to $400 a night. But they were selling out Harpo's and being on the radio. So Ken's like, "Well, let me be your trial manager." The very next night Ken comes out of the box office with $3,000. Wagner just went in there and said, "There are a thousand people in this club who paid five dollars a head to get in here tonight. You're not paying my band $300." This is what the club scene was going like. There was money. The bands sure weren't making it.

John Brannon: It was like everything had kind of hit a dead end, and there's this guy coming in first with the Birthday Party and then with the Bad Seeds, showing everyone what was going on. And we took that for sure. That Bad Seeds show was at St. Andrews, which was by then the big place to play in the city.

Chris Panackia: Because you gotta remember, Bookie's, people just partied, and it was just fun and all that kind of stuff. But St. Andrews, it went to another level.

Vince Bannon: We didn't make it to '83 at City Club. The guy who I had the joint venture with wanted to change the entire deal, so we walked out. We took everything to St. Andrews Hall and had a wonderful relationship there.

Chris Panackia: Now you're talking about a twelve hundred–seat club with St. Andrews. You're talking about way more people to get involved in debauchery rather than seventy-five or one hundred. More money. It was the place to play. It was the number-one hall in North America all those years.

Andy Wendler: We went on the *Tangled Up* tour that summer of '86, and we were finally making money. It was four months with Megadeth and four months with the Circle Jerks. We made anywhere between $5,000 and $25,000 a night. It was like, "Hey, here's some money." Somebody would be like, "Oh man, my sneakers are bad," and we'd say, "Okay, here's a hundred bucks. Go get sneakers and socks." We played arenas. A week before this tour I was playing a gig in an eighty-seater. When we got back to Detroit the Hyenas were happening, and there was a whole new wave of hardcore: Almighty Lumberjacks of Death, all those guys. You know, all these new young hardcore bands were around, and I'd see 'em, and it wasn't my thing.

Jon Howard: ALD, Feisty Cadavers, Son of Sam—I mean it got more into this like dirtbag, white trash, punk thing. It was more like what Scary Cary was doing at Graystone. It was like a little more chaotic and fucked up. No, it was more white trash, like Sex Pistols-y. The clubs were like Old Miami, Blondie's.

Mike Hard: The clubs in Detroit had really gone in a direction. At the Old Miami you could score at eight o'clock and ten o'clock. The coke man is there. You go there at eight o'clock. You walk in, and there will be all these dudes sitting at the bar. Then the coke man will walk by them and he'll go into the bathroom. Then one at a time each guy—right into the bathroom. And the bathroom at fucking Old Miami was bad.

Margaret Dollrod: I pissed in the street rather than use the bathroom at the Old Miami. Which wasn't really a stretch.

Mike Hard: Or even do lines in there. But these motherfuckers are doing lines. There used to be a piece of wood in the Old Miami bathroom with, like, tile on it above the shitter? The guy who was running the place took that off and he put a piece of stainless steel there so they could do their lines without getting it fucking caught in the grout.

Charlie Wallace (*ADC, vocalist*): We played the Hungry Brain, which was the basement of a retail store. The store was closed, but you go down to the basement and it was this huge, open floor. We pulled up and jumped out of the car and were swarmed by undercover cops, who were screaming at us, "Where are the needles?" We told them we're playing a show down the street, and they're like, "You guys are playing a show down here? Man, you're nuts." These are the guys who just ran up to us asking about needles telling us this. They were sure the only reason four white guys are getting out of a car down there was to buy heroin.

Brian Mullan: The Hungry Brain was this shithole to go hang out at after the Graystone closed, getting to the late eighties. Scary Cary took over booking shit at the Graystone and then did stuff at the Hungry Brain.

Norm Zebrowski (*Disinfect, vocalist*): The Hungry Brain was one more Detroit venue in a really bad place. West Jefferson and Dearborn in Delray. Fucked up place—lotsa violence inside and out.

Mike Hard: We played a place called the Bank one New Year's Eve. It was on Michigan Avenue. It was one of those big huge Detroit granite fucking banks that these kids bought, and right on top of the bar there were big old fucking nitrous tanks, nitrous balloons everywhere.

Lacy X (*Son of Sam, Hillside Stranglers, vocalist*): There were bands like us, Son of Sam, that weren't in the Touch and Go clique. There was the Feisty Cadavers, Beer Whores, Almighty Lumberjacks of Death. The bands from '81 to '83 got more attention, but there was a big divide between that older scene and the one that had started.

Keith Jackson: My pal Itchy and I were coming into Detroit from Farmington Hills, and it was hard to be accepted because there was this group of hardcore guys we called Russ's Army. It was after Russ Gibb. He might have been a legend for what he did with the Grande, but he was also a teacher and had all these students from Dearborn getting into the punk scene. Later he bought the Graystone, but those kids were just sort of his acolytes. I had already been hanging around at Bookie's, and I dug all the music there. But this was sort of a cliquish kinda hardcore thing, and the people in it were really clannish.

Lacy X: A lot of the newer bands were inner-city, working-class Detroit, and the other ones were suburban kids. People were getting killed, people in bands.

Andy Wendler: It was a lot of Detroit, south-side skinhead dudes. You know, a lot of access to fireworks and guns and that kind of thing. John and Larissa were hooked up, and they had a house in suburban Ann Arbor.

You Just Can't Win

John Speck: I was just fucking blown away by John Brannon. The Laughing Hyenas inspired me even fashion-wise. The way he looked. The way he carried himself at that show, and of course he was just fucked out of his fucking mind and totally oblivious on heroin. I knew and revered Negative Approach, and so it was weird to see him in this new band, the Laughing Hyenas. He comes out, and his hair was long and all in his face, and he had a straight mic stand. He comes out, and he's got long, like, button-up work shirt and jeans and engineer boots, and he had a six pack with him, and he set the six pack right at the base of the mic stand and never fucking said anything or looked at anybody, and the band was playing, doing some sort of, like, instrumental opening thing. Larissa's guitar is a killing loud Fender Twin in a buzz, and the band's playing, and he reaches down and he never looked at the audience, and he fucking cracks a beer, and he just fucking starts pulling off it, and he just drains most of a beer, and just fucking plants one foot on the base of the mic stand and his hand and just never opened his eyes and just fucking, "RRRAAAAAAH." You could tell he was just fucking doping and out of his mind. Then I would hear the stories about, like, you know, Brannon was at Off the Record in Royal Oak, flipping through the records in there, and there's some little kid in the hardcore section, and Brannon's a couple of aisles or rows away, and he sees the kid, and the kid is looking at the Negative Approach record, and Brannon's like, "I was in that band." The kid looks at him and he's like, "Fuck you, hippie."

Rachel Nagy (*Detroit Cobras, vocalist*): I used to live in the house Kevin Monroe's dad owned in the Cass Corridor. But that motherfucker. I guess there were talks to turn the place I was living in into a coffee shop but no one told me. So Kevin kicks me out. He's a piece of shit for that. He had a bunch of his mom's antique sofas and stuff in there. I bought five 40s and I peed on everything. I peed in every

227

sofa, corner, everything—everything I could pee on I peed on. Fuck you, dude. You know what? You think I'm going to go live on the street in the Corridor? Well, there you go, bro. And then he fucking locked up my shotgun to make sure I didn't try to steal anything. Meanwhile, his dad works for the Detroit Symphony Orchestra and has a beautiful, beautiful house in Indian Village.

Kevin Monroe (*Laughing Hyenas, Mule, bassist*): I grew up at 6 Mile and James Couzens until I was eight. Then we lived in Indian Village. My dad was in the Detroit Symphony Orchestra for forty years. He started there at a young age, like in '68. We moved into the city when everyone else was moving out, like six months after the riots. My parents were very optimistic.

I got into the scene—well, I had a good friend, Veronica Webb. She became a model later on and was in some Spike Lee movies. She used to go to shows with Negative Approach and L-Seven. Then the Graystone. I knew Mike Danner, who was playing drums for the Hyenas at first. Mike was from Milford—way out there. At least John and I had some Detroit roots, but a lot of the kids were from the suburbs. You can't choose where you come from, of course, but they were from West Bloomfield and Royal Oak. Mike asked me if I wanted to try out for bass in this band he was in. The whole thought was that bass wasn't all that important and that whoever they got was just going to leave and they would replace him anyway. Mike told me this at the beginning. It was an honor to be asked, and I thought to myself, "Wow, I would love to be in this band, but I can't play. There is no way I want to be disposable." So I gotta compete with some of the coolest bass licks I could come up with and have my own, like, totally original sort of sound. Not that that was—you know, I could not do that necessarily, but that was my thought, anyway—was to come up with something that would make me different enough that I would stand out as being a crucial part of the band. They were in Ann Arbor already, and I had moved to Ann Arbor. Danner and Brannon and Larissa had moved to Ann Arbor only because you could get a practice space without having to worry about getting your equipment stolen. I mean, Detroit in the seventies, eighties—we were broken into at least eight or nine times at my father's house.

John Brannon: We came outta Detroit in 1984. We didn't find any place to live right away. Me and Larissa, we just loaded up all our shit, a suitcase and a guitar. We just drove to Ann Arbor. We were like, "We're going to live in Ann Arbor." We'd just find out where there's a party, park the van out there, and live there for a couple of days and move on to the next place. Then we discovered these things called frat houses. So people would come up to us: "Do you guys know anybody here?" And we were like, "Oh yeah, we're with John." There was always a John, you know. They would have these community kitchens. We'd go in there and make our food and drink all their fucking beer and go to the next party. We lived out of the van for about two to three weeks. We didn't give a fuck. We were twenty-five years old, we had no money, so we just lived in my van. About two or three weeks into it we all got jobs. I worked at Harry's Army Surplus, and we rented out this big country house. It was $500 a month and belonged to this old doctor in Ann Arbor. It was out where the Stooges used to have their place. It was right out on Packard and Platt. Two acres of land, three-car garage, six bedrooms—so we all moved into that bitch. We were like, "Alright, we're setting up shop here, man." Then we pulled in Kevin Monroe.

Kevin Monroe: When I met John I had never played bass. I had played guitar, but the bass was new to me.

John Brannon: The only song he knew how to play was "Hell's Bells" on guitar. I'm like, "Alright, this is a start, dude. You can go from here to here." Kevin and Larissa learned how to play from scratch together.

Kevin Monroe: They were concerned because I had combat boots. They were worried that I was going to be dressing too trendy at that particular point. They didn't suggest anything. It wasn't that. They weren't trying to insult me. Larissa was like, "Well, we weren't really sure, because you had a uniform." I didn't have a uniform.

John Brannon: Mike was not the best drummer but I figured this is everything I need to make the greatest band in the world. We moved to the land of the Stooges, and we're going to start from scratch. We're going to get a house, which was about half a mile from where the Stooges house was. There were people hanging out around us by then, and it was cool.

Kevin Monroe: I started driving a cab, which was a little rough. I was just seeing the nightlife. It was like being a cop or something. You see the underbelly of society in such a way that, at first, it was very exciting. It was more of an adventure than a job. But was it a healthy lifestyle? I was young, and I was kind of . . . I thought I was Travis Bickle. I got a lot of fares that wanted to know where to score, and I knew.

Preston Long (*Wig, Mule, P. W. Long's Reelfoot, solo, guitarist, vocalist*): I met Kevin Monroe at the cab place in Ann Arbor. He introduced me to Touch and Go music. I knew nothing about punk rock, and I was in my midtwenties, and I was flunking out of the university. I thought he was kind of a dandy and an asshole and a smartass, and we got along. Next thing I know he was crashing on my couch. I had been listening to country blues and this stuff, and then I ended up in Wig. I didn't feel too good at the time. I wasn't perceiving the world correctly, and the music came along as a therapeutic outlet. It wasn't a form of art exactly for me. I had roommates, this one guy who played guitar, and we ended up seeing White Zombie. They played one song and the cops shut the whole thing down; this was the *Soul Crusher* tour, so it must have been their first tour. That was cool, so I joined Wig. We shared a practice space with the Hyenas.

Kevin Monroe: Before we moved to the real Hyenas house, we had a place near Packard that they sold out from under us. This guy shows up wanting to buy the house. He told us that the owners thought that we were a cult. Finally we got the Platt Road house, which was the Hyena house for years.

John Brannon: One day I'm walking down the street, going to the party store, and I hear this band. You know, coming out of the basement. I'm like, "God damn, that sounds like Ron Asheton." Sure enough, like two houses over, Destroy All Monsters. That's where Michael Davis lived, and I ended up becoming great friends with that dude.

Jim Magas (*Couch, Lake of Dracula, vocalist, electronics*): I was working at Harry's Army Surplus, and Brannon called me and said, "You wanna meet Michael Davis?" It was during this Ann Arbor Art Fair, some street fair thing. I went down, and Davis was shirtless, wearing a bullet belt and sunglasses, standing in front of Schoolkids records. We were drinking 40s, and he was still looking like a revolutionary.

Rob Miller: Michael Davis was one of my stage hands when I was helping run the State Theater. I would pay him $40 a day to hump gear, and this was when the MC5 had yet to have been rediscovered and appreciated. At some point Michael Davis was selling U of M painter caps on football days in Ann Arbor.

Gloria Branzei: He was picking up cans. He was doing anything for money. It was sad. Ron was living with Niagara, and they were all pissed about Iggy all the time. He left them, or at least that's how they felt. Those older Detroit bands didn't do very well for a while.

Dave Feeny (*Hysteric Narcotics, the Orange Roughies, keyboards, guitar, founder,* **Tempermill studio):** I became tight with Rob Tyner and he would bring these bad, young rock bands to produce in a studio I had in my parents' basement in Livonia. They paid him $500 a pop. That was it.

Jim Magas: Scott Asheton would come into Harry's and talk about shit. I'd ask, "Are the Stooges gonna get back together?" and he said, "Yeah, we want to, but Iggy's not into it," and he was all, "How great would it be?" GG Allin and Dee Dee Ramone was living there too at the same time. Dee Dee came into Harry's; he was holding these tie-dyed shorts up to the mirror, and he asked me to go clothes shopping with him. I said yes, but he never came back.

John Brannon: Michael Davis had his motorcycle parked in my garage for two years when he was going through a split with his wife. We were drinking together, and I was doing a lot of dope. He was banging this chick that was living with us at the time. Out of those couple houses we had, that's really where my Monkees vision came full circle. When I was growing up it wasn't about the Beatles or the Stones; maybe my sister was in that shit, but I was at that period where my first vision of rock 'n' roll was the Monkees when I was six. We all live with the band in a house where we jam, and we can't pay our rent. We started writing songs immediately. The first Hyenas song was "Stain." I would come up with the riff to a song even before this all started, and I was sure somebody could play it better.

Preston Long: I don't know how they got by. They never worked. They had people bring them pot and beer and whatever else.

Kevin Monroe: Pretty soon we needed a drummer, and we put out an ad in the paper that Jim Kimball answered. He was an athlete. He used to be a diver, like his brother the Olympian, Bruce Kimball. Bruce Kimball won the silver. And his dad was a diving coach. So he worked out and he liked to party, but not on the same kind of level that we did. He was always into staying in good shape. He became more physical on the drums once he joined the Hyenas. He became a monster.

John Brannon: The whole time that Jim Kimball lived with us, he never knew what was going on with the dope. He would just take acid and go wind surfing with his dog. He had his room, but he kept it locked. He wouldn't even keep his Campbell's soup in the kitchen. He had it all up in his bedroom. We were like, "Jim, we're not gonna eat your soup."

Peter Davis: Kimball was a Popeye-looking motherfucker. He was batshit crazy, but he stayed away from the drugs that everyone else was doing. He had some kind of accident in diving before all this. He was on his way to being an Olympian, and he got hurt and he never really recovered. Jim was a pretty clean and athletic guy, driven and really talented, but a few bricks shy of a load upstairs.

John Brannon: We get out of Detroit, and as soon as we moved to Ann Arbor that's when the horse kicked in. So we drove to Detroit to the same block we had lived in every day to get dope. We were aware of all the dealers. When we lived in Detroit that might have been like a once-a-month thing for Larissa. It was just a matter of time before that got worse. She wouldn't string out, but it would be like a pick-up now and then. Then the dope just eventually caught up with all of us—Kevin, Larissa and I. Of course I was already a derelict before I met her. But heroin didn't really come up until about '85 to '86.

Kevin Monroe: I'm an adventurer. I like music as an adventure, and the drug thing was an adventure for me. I was into it, and I'm not afraid to do anything. I probably, in a lot of ways, revived a spirit in John and Larissa that probably shouldn't have been revived. Larissa didn't really introduce John to dope. Maybe on a small scale. It didn't go crazy until we were all together. I feel as much to blame if not more so as being an influence for that particular excursion. I was at least an extremely effective go-between. It wasn't Larissa with the connections at that time. Later on, yeah. Working with them, I started showing up with a lot more quantity of things and quality of things. Then it was different. Clearly different.

MC5:
Are They from Detroit?
Fresh Blood and Garage Innocence

Rachel Nagy: My dad worked for Ford; he was a heavy truck engineer. They moved him around, so I went to kindergarten in Australia, which was fucking awesome. Then we came back to Detroit and I went to school there. I was in second grade the first time I saw a *Hustler* magazine. It was in my school playground, which didn't have swings; it just had chains. And we used that picture for our little playhouse. It was great. I mean, it was disgusting. It was some girl with her legs spread. Welcome to Detroit. We lived different places in Detroit: 7 Mile, Evergreen, Woodbine. I went to church and school at 10 Mile and Nevada. It was a majority black church and school. Ford Headquarters is in Dearborn, so we eventually moved there, and that's when I left. I missed Detroit. I knew how to function there. There was, like, no rules. You could set your car on fire and nobody would give a shit. I mean, they'll rape you and murder you, oh well. But at least you can do what the fuck you want to do. When I left home it was, "Oh, she's not gonna graduate. She's gonna become a loser, blah, blah, blah." I walked from the Cass Corridor to Edsel Ford, down 94, every day. I also caught rides, and then guys would pull down their pants and then I would stick a switchblade in their crotch. And then they would drive me all the way to school, as opposed to just part of the way. I graduated with honors. I didn't go to my graduation ceremony, either. Fuck all you all. You gotta remember you're fucking sixteen or seventeen years old—you can't get a decent job. So I stripped. I stripped on the seedy places on Michigan Avenue, where they didn't give a shit. Gold Diggers, Show Bar 51 or 52—you know, it was just run by old Jewish ladies. As long as you didn't drink, they didn't care. You know what is really fucking pathetic? Those were the days when you could work a day shift and make $13.50 an hour. Cash. There was no contact. You didn't have to sit on anybody's lap. It was all tips. It was all just these regulars. It eventually turned into guys fucking girls in corners and you having to pay to work.

Mick Collins (*Dirtbombs, Gories, Blacktop, guitarist, vocalist*): I was born in 1965 into a family with absolutely no musical background. And I'm talking about extended family: aren't any musicians or artists or anything. My first show was Bo Diddley at the Michigan State Fairgrounds. It was at around two o'clock in the afternoon, and I was about eight years old. My dad used to work on cars at an auto shop across the street from the state's largest record distributor on 6 Mile and Linwood. He worked on the car of a guy named Mr. Angott, who was part of this record distributor. Mr. Angott found out that my dad had five kids at the time—this would have been the midfifties—and he started giving my dad a box of records from the week. So when I came along a decade later, we had a basement full of rock 'n' roll 45s. We had hundreds of them, if not thousands. And by this time, you know, that kind of rock 'n' roll was totally outdated. So there was a record player down there, and what I did, when I was in kindergarten or whatever, I would sit down there and play records all day. By the time I was twelve I was spending my allowance on disco 12s. There was a record shop literally around the corner from my house. And when punk rock rolled around we were like, "We can do this! Let's give it a try," and we gave it a try. I was not aware of any Detroit rock-and-roll legacy at that point. We didn't discover those bands for another decade probably. I didn't even want to lie about it—you know everyone wants to claim they were listening to the Stooges and MC5 before they were born. But I didn't hear about those bands until I was eighteen or nineteen.

John Szymanski, aka John Hentch (*The Hentchmen, organ, vocals*): The legacy of Detroit rock and roll didn't affect us at all, me and my friends in high school. As far as music goes, it was hearing oldies radio, sixties stuff. Our parents were not rock and rollers, and that whole Detroit music thing didn't impact us at all; we were just aware of Motown.

Rachel Nagy: I mean, there's this crowd, when you grow up in Detroit, your parents listen to shit. You hear it at house parties; you see people dancing in your house and that . . . entire "Well, that's what old fogies listen to." It's not until later on that you get into punk and metal and whatever else and then at some time, it dawns on you: Holy crap, this is where this all came from and this is way better, you know?

Jason Stollsteimer (*Von Bondies, Baby Killers, guitarist, vocalist*): The MC5— did they ever actually live in Detroit? Because they're Downriver kids. That was always like a rumor in the younger people like, "They weren't even from Detroit."

Dan Kroha (*Gories, Demolition Doll Rods, Rocket 455, guitarist, vocalist*): From '82, '83, when I was seriously starting music, to play and really listen, to about '86, I wouldn't listen to the MC5 or the Stooges. I thought that was, like, hippie music, because anything from the late sixties to me was hippie music, and any guys with long hair were hippies. When hardcore was going on I was discovering, like, the sixties garage scene that was, like, concurrently popping up. Gun Club was the first punk band that did blues kinda stuff as far as in the late seventies, early eighties. I was really into the Who and stuff like that. *Quadrophenia.* I started trying to find other people that liked that music, and I started reaching out. I met these guys in Madison Heights that liked sixties stuff. They hung with some Rochester people, and one of them was Tom Lynch. He was at Hart Plaza one time for a show, and he was wearing a Martha and the Vandella's T-shirt. Mick Collins saw him with one of these shirts on, so Mick came up to Tom and said, "Hey man, where did you get that shirt?" They started to talk and they exchanged numbers.

Mick Collins: I was wearing the Martha and the Vandellas T-shirt. King Sunny Ade played Hart Plaza in 1984. So my friends and I, we had to see that. We rode our bikes downtown, and there's three thousand people down there, so you can people watch. We were walking around Hart Plaza, and we see this guy in an English Beat T-shirt, and it wasn't the stock one; it wasn't the one that you see in all the magazines and catalogues—it was a different one. I was like, "Oh my god, we have to meet this guy and find out where he got this shirt from." My friends were like, "No, do not tease the white people. Let's keep going and stay out of trouble. Let's keep walking and check out King Sunny Ade." I went up to this guy and asked him where he got this shirt from, and he liked my Martha and the Vandellas T-shirt.

Dan Kroha: One day I came over to Tom's, and he was talking on the phone to Mick, and he said, "You know this guy that I'm talking to on the phone lives in

Detroit. He might not live very far from you. You should talk to him." I got on the phone and talked to Mick.

Peg O'Neill (*Gories, drummer*): Growing up I was really into the sixties stuff. My mom was always playing music in the house, Motown and all that. We'd always listen to the oldies stations— Fats Domino and stuff like that—because it sounded different than anything else. I first saw Dan walking home from high school. I used to walk down Livernois on the way home from high school heading to Sam's Jams. He'd drive by on his scooter, and I was kind of this Who freak. I got this big book on them and started reading about mods and shit, and I started painting targets on my clothing. Then I see him on his scooter cruising down Livernois.

Dan Kroha: I found a '73 Vespa in the paper. A little 125, and I went out and looked at it. It was in perfect condition. It was bright orange. It wasn't really the *Quadrophenia* thing I was looking for, but there weren't any others. It was a '73; it wasn't a '63. I bought it anyway and decorated it a little bit, and I wrote, "The Face" on the side of it. Peggy was walking home from Ferndale High, and she'd see me buzzing around with my Vespa, and I kinda caught her eye. Then we started on Saturdays to go to Dearborn to Off the Record.

Peg O'Neill: I met Mick not long after that. Dan kept telling me, "You gotta meet this friend of mine." Because you know how it was back then: if you saw someone that looked like you or might be into the same stuff you're into, you're just like, "Oh my God. It's someone just like me." Dan was like, "Oh, you gotta meet my friend. He's really cool. He's into the same stuff we're into. He DJs, and he has these bands."

EWolf: Mick would DJ at places and use the moniker James McDermott. He wore a suit, looked very natty and almost ska-like. I caught him once at Cobb's Corner spinning, playing Mod stuff and old garage records.

Peg O'Neill: It's hard to forget Mick's DJ name—James McDermott. So mod. One night Dan and I walked into Paycheck's and Mick played "Boom Boom" by John Lee Hooker. I was like, "Holy shit, this is gonna be great." I just kept coming up to him, requesting it over and over. He probably thought I was annoying.

Mick Collins: When we started the Gories, it was totally influenced by *Back from the Grave* comps. We heard those bands and that really was the moment we said,

"We can do this." We heard *Back from the Grave* and *Nuggets*, and I think *Pebbles* was just coming out. And we thought: you know the goal was really just to say that we'd done it and maybe made a couple 45s, and you know, like, years down the road maybe we'd do a comp that was like *Back from the Grave*. That was the idea.

Dan Kroha: *Back from the Grave* had just come out, and all other comps were coming out. So we'd sit around and listen to them and drink Budweiser. We were beer drinkers, a little bit of weed. Some acid now and then. Very sixties style. We were hanging out in my bedroom, listening to records, and Mick was like, "Man, these songs only have like three chords in them." He goes, "We can play this stuff." I'm like, "Well, let's do it! We should do it then!"

Mick Collins: We decided to start the Gories, and Peg was the drummer because she was sitting there. Peg and Dan were boyfriend-girlfriend and she was there while we were having this conversation. And the person we called wasn't home. Fred Munchinger from Fortune Maltese—we called him to be in the band, and he happened not to be home that night. So we got Peg to do it.

Dan Kroha: She said, "No way, man, no. I've never played anything. I have no desire to get up on stage and do anything." "No, you gotta do it," we told her. "We're going to be the worst band you ever heard in your life."

Peg O'Neill: It took a while for them to convince me.

Dan Kroha: Peg and I broke up before we ever played and almost never started the band.

Mick Collins: When Dan and Peg broke up, that was the end of the band, and this was still 1986. We hadn't played a show yet. Peg announced that they just had broken up and that she was leaving the band, moving to Pittsburgh. So around July I get this phone call from Peg going, "Hey, when's practice?" and I was like, "What do you mean practice? You quit the band!" And at this point she was back in the band, and I was, like, bugged about it.

Dan Kroha: Rob and Becky Tyner started this thing called the Community Concert Series. He was still, at that time, pretty well involved with the Cass Corridor scene. For the first Gories show we went down there and signed up. I had never even heard the MC5, and as far as I was concerned Rob Tyner was just some old fucking hippie with a gut and a huge afro. Rob at that time had this solo thing where he played autoharp and sang. He was singing songs about Vietnam and sixties stuff. We were just like, zzzz. He was just going on and on. Meanwhile we're just getting drunker. Mick and Peg were drinking Thunderbird. Peg had taken some mushrooms. They were getting fucked up. They were scared about getting on stage.

Peg O'Neill: Doing mushrooms will make your stage fright disappear. It was this place that was really supportive of local bands, and they let bands play there who couldn't get a show anywhere else—like us.

Dan Kroha: Finally he gets done and it's one o'clock in the morning. I think Rob probably introduced us. He was like, "Alright, we got a brand new band here. They're called the Gories," as he's looking at a piece of paper. We played four songs and barely got through it. After that we'd get shows then, but no one would show up. We'd get like twenty people or so, you know. Hysteric Narcotics would get a good crowd, and they could draw like seventy-five or a hundred, so when we opened for those guys we would have a good crowd. But if we were headlining, not so good.

Dave Buick (*Italy Records, founder, the Go, bassist*): As stupid as it sounds to say, you saw the Gories and you walked away thinking, "Anyone can do this," or at least they made you feel something is possible. There was this fucked up innocence to the Gories.

Tim Warren (*Crypt Records, founder*): Danny was sending me tapes starting around 1986. He wanted me to sign them. Later on, around 1989, they played in New York at the Knitting Factory with Alex Chilton, and I was going to go see and sign them, but I decided to do Billy Childish and Thee Headcoats. I gave them the $1,500 advance instead of the Gories.

Dan Kroha: We recorded an album, did shows. Then Dan Rose, a friend and fan of ours, was a huge Alex Chilton fan. He went backstage one time after one of Chilton's shows and had a tape of the Gories' first album. Dan just put the tape on and didn't say anything. After a little while Alex was like, "Who is this?" Dan was like, "Well, there's this band who are friends of mine from Detroit." Alex was like, "Do they have a record deal?" Dan's like, "Well, they put out a local album, but they don't really have the record going right now." Alex was like, "Man, these guys are doing like for R&B what the Cramps did for rockabilly. This is cool." We drove down to Memphis to record with Chilton; he had gotten a $6,000 budget from New Rose. We were to stay at Tav Falco's house.

Mick Collins: We're sitting on the porch just hanging out, and this car pulls up. And this girl gets out, and she's kinda walking to the door and said, "Hey, excuse me for just a moment." And she busts the window and then reaches around and opens the door. We're like, "What the fuck?" Then she's in there and we're sitting there, like, "We're from Detroit, you know. It's not like we haven't seen this before."

Dan Kroha: So we drive up to Tav's, and the first thing we see is Tav's recently ex-girlfriend, Lorette Velvette, climbing out of the window of the house. She had broken into the house to get back some of her stuff. We said, "Hey, how's it going?" She's like, "Hi!" We were like, "What's going on?" She's said, "Oh, I'm Lorette." She had a bag of potato chips. She goes, "You guys want some chips?" I said, "What are you doing?" She's like, "Well, you know, Tav and I just broke up, and I was just getting some of my stuff out of the house."

John Szymanski: We had all heard of the Gories but didn't know any of them, but I knew we were all inspired by the *Back from the Grave* compilations on Crypt. We had a ska band at the time. The ska band opened for the Gories at Finney's Pub. Then we saw them at an after-hours club, and it was nothing but technical difficulties. Maybe when we saw the Gories, we felt that we could do that too.

Margaret Dollrod: I met Dan when he came to my dorm room at University of Detroit. I was supposed to room with his sister. I had left my dorm room open, and he was in it rummaging through my clothes basket, and I'm like, "Who are you and what are you doing in my dorm room looking at my clothes?" He's like, "Oh, well, you just have such nice clothes." So I was like, "Well, I'm glad you like them." He looked around and said, "Why do you have pictures of sixties *Playboy* chicks on your wall?" I said, "Well, you don't? Sixties *Playboy* chicks are hot, you know. I like having hot things on my wall." Then I realize this guy is kinda wanting to be open and wild and stuff but was kinda like, "I don't know, I can't," and I'm like, "Oh, I like this."

Dan Kroha: I peeked in the room and was like, "Wow! Sixties *Playboy* pictures in a girl's room?" I had broken up with Peggy shortly before we did that first show anyway, but it was tough.

Mick Collins: There were many moments if I had the opportunity to walk away from the Gories, I would have. Sometime between our second breakup and the European tour, Dan started going out with Margaret. And that was bad.

Dan Kroha: When Margaret first saw the Gories she fell in love with the Gories. She had a crush on Mick too. Not only did she think that me and Mick were cute, but she really genuinely loved the music. She would get up on stage and, like, run between our legs. She already went out just wearing a bra at that point. Like, she didn't have to take her clothes off. She was already half undressed. Peggy hated that. Hated it. It was stressful, but, I mean, my life was just drama. It was just nonstop drama.

Margaret Dollrod: Yeah, I loved them. I traveled with them. I carried their equipment. I sold their T-shirts. I was the roadie. I was the hot roadie. I would travel with them, and I thought they were so great. So I wanted to dance. I wanted to dance, and the way that they played kind of freed me. I would be like, "Yeah, taking my clothes off!" You know, okay, so maybe some people do that for Guns 'n' Roses, I understand. Peg hated it. She had a meeting in the middle of Europe and said to them, "If you don't send her home, then I'm gonna quit." I'm like, even if they send me home, I'm not going home. I got money. I will rent a scooter and follow you, and you'll really hate it. Because I will dance.

Mick Collins: When we did the Europe tour Margaret flew over there on her own. She got the tour schedule from Dan and got a Europass and followed us around on the tour. Which didn't bother me none—I mean it was Dan's girlfriend. Peg was really bugged about that, even though her boyfriend was with us at the time; he was our roadie.

Dan Kroha: We did a show in Holland where Margaret was dancing crazy, and it was pissing Peggy off, and she just started playing really slow and then just barely hitting the drums. She ended up dropping her sticks and walking off stage in front of a packed house. Peg disappeared and we didn't know where she went. We sent her boyfriend to find her. She came back and she was okay. We did a few more shows, and we go to France and for a show. There weren't a lot of people at that show, but Margaret was dancing, and it was pissing Peg off. Peg throws her sticks down and leaves again. Walks out right in the middle. It was the worst feeling in the world—people are digging it and she walks out. Mick said he felt like bashing Peggy on the head with his guitar. He said, "I felt like hitting her on the head and letting the little people out." Finally we all decided that we could continue the tour. Margaret toned down the dancing a little bit. Peggy bit her lip and got through it.

Mick Collins: We finally threw Peg out in France. We were obligated to do these last few shows, however many shows it was, but I said, "When this plane touches down in the US, don't call."

Tim Caldwell: The Gories had great out-of-control R&B, and no one cared. As much as Moe Tucker got beat up in the Velvets for primitive style, I don't believe Meg White would have gone over if not for Peg having laid down the basics in the Gories.

Troy Gregory (*Witches, Dirtbombs, bassist, guitarist, vocalist*): With the Gories, it was typical Detroit. Not too many people got them, but all of a sudden when they found out that people in New York liked them or they were selling records in Europe, they like it. It was the industry people in Detroit who were the real fuckups because they had these bands around and didn't see it.

Karen Neal, aka Queen Bee (*Thrall, bassist, vocalist*): The Gories opened the door to all kinds of new stuff in Detroit. We went to Europe, and the Gories were huge.

Cool American

———————————

Andrew WK (*solo, the Pterodactyls, Mr. Velocity Hopkins, vocalist, drummer, keyboards*)**:** I didn't get into music beyond piano lessons and whatever records my mom would buy me until junior high school. I had no older brothers or friends, not even kids in my neighborhood. No scheme for me to learn about things except cable TV. It wasn't until I was thirteen and the friends that I had that we were able to branch out in music. To me at that point music didn't seem as exciting to me as a guy freaking out in front of me making sounds that I'd never heard ever before. First guy that did that was John Zorn. It was, "Oh, this is going on in New York." But around the same time there was this local guy, James Johnson, who just blew my mind. He lived on his own while he was sixteen years old, and there was this scene. It was a cross between Ann Arbor radical tradition—very political, an anarchist movement—crossed with a crushed punk style, crossed with a colorful new-age hippy vibe. No Mohawks and spikes, but yarn and twenty different kinds of clothes at once, like a clown. The whole vibe was to be as crazy as possible, which often depended on the quality of drugs. It was all living on their own crime, not having jobs, insane vandalism, truly crazy people living together at these sort of flop houses. It was a big street scene, and these dudes that would hang out for years, drifters, would become local legends. I would go to these houses where people were crazy; they would do stuff like try to pee on you. And it was all about mushrooms and acid. I was terrified to do that stuff, seeing how these people lived. These were my idols in high school. The first show I saw was in the basement of the Unitarian Church in Ann Arbor. It was Scheme, and bands related to that scene, and everyone was in their underwear, and all the windows got broken out, and the cops came and shut it down. I thought, "This is what it's all about."

Aaron Dilloway (*Wolf Eyes, Couch, Spine Scavenger* **vocalist, guitarist, tapes, electronics):** That was the Nautical Almanac show, and my band at the time, Galen, played. Twig Harper had a rope or string tied around his dick, and he ran it under the handle of a little Peavey Bandit, and he was standing on a table lifting the amp up.

Andrew WK: I'd go downtown and stand outside the Huron House. This place had mattresses nailed to the outside walls, a swimming pool dug in the front yard, and bicycles in the trees. The doors were pulled off of the rooms, and people would be playing music at all times. The smell was so god-awful, and there was a lot of darkness to it as well. It wasn't this cheerful happy place. It was like a haunted house crossed with a fun house. Through my friend Moralis, I finally had an older guy to show me stuff; he introduced me to new music. He took me to Schoolkids Records to see this guy Jim Magas from Couch, our favorite band, and we were too scared to talk to him. I had heard MTV, I liked a lot of other stuff, but nothing compared to Couch for me. To have your favorite band in the world be around and to see Jim on the street—I would have butterflies in my stomach every day hoping to see these guys.

Jim Magas: I was working at Schoolkids when Couch had started, and everyone hated us. But we had played a couple of shows, and young kids started to get into us. No one our age was into it. I was twenty-six, and most of these basement shows, the kids were eighteen. These teenage kids came into the store and asked me questions about Couch, and they were like, "You have to meet Andrew." The first time he came into the store he was real shy. His hair was bleached LA style, dirty blonde, and had a painted jacket. They had to pull him into the store. He was turning red.

Jon Howard: There were all these bands that were based on noise around Ann Arbor because Detroit was so bad at the time. They'd go up and play Detroit, but it was just a crappy place to live.

John Szymanski: We played with Monkey Tailed Skink, but we were kind of innocent kids; we didn't get too deep into the Ann Arbor scene. We went to the parties but were probably too nervous and shy. They were all at least five years older than us.

Jon Howard: The noise scene was a little intimidating. It was kind of cliquish. I knew people, but they weren't openly looking for friends. They had their own thing going. Bulb Records was early—Andrew WK and Wolf Eyes—and they had the real DIY thing going with make-their-own tapes, their own vinyl. Everything was super limited and handmade.

Andrew WK: Wolf Eyes originated with Nate Young and Aaron. Nate went to my high school. I was blown away by him; he was one of the people I idolized. He got kicked out of high school, so he was a sophomore when I thought he was a senior. Later he met Aaron, around the same time I did. Aaron had a band called Galen, and he moved into the Huron Street house.

Harold Richardson (*Gravitar, Easy Action, Negative Approach, guitarist*): Huron House was this place where punk rockers lived in and they had shows in the basement. Lotta shit broken, kids puking on the steps as people were walking in to see the show. It was a place that if you were claustrophobic, you weren't going to be into it, because the place would be packed tight for almost every show.

Aaron Dilloway: Jim Magas and Geoff Walker from Gravitar were this bridge between noise and rock. One day I went into Discount Records and saw the Couch seven-inch, and I thought, "How did they get a record out?" This was a month or so after the show with the Hyenas, and I asked Jeff what else was out there like this, and he had other things to show me. Caroliner, this SF band on Subterranean that was huge for us. We wanted to do this stuff. Put out fucked up records.

Harold Richardson: I spent my senior year in DC after ten years in Germany. My dad was an Army officer; I was a Eurofag. I moved back, and Springsteen was really popular, and I'm still into going to discos—we made fun of all the kids going to the 9:30 Club. I went to the disco, and it was all Miami Vice—we were doing blow off girls' stomachs, and these other punk rock kids were all sober and straight edge. We thought that was weird: they were pacifists and always getting in fights and getting their ass kicked.

I had to go to college, and Central Michigan, it was the only place that would accept me in the States because I was a terrible student. When I got there in '86 Cliff Davies from Ted Nugent was living there at Mt. Pleasant, where Central is, and we both washed dishes. He told me he used to play with Nugent, and I said, "Sure you did." Then he shows me his gold records and shit; I was like, "Wow." He said Nuge never paid him off, so there he was, washing dishes and getting some kind of percussion degree at Central. I moved to Ann Arbor—it was more happening for music—and then I joined Gravitar. Jim Magas and Pete Larson—man, they knew shit. I was in a band with Jim called the Browns, which Aaron Dilloway was in. Andrew was a really sharp dresser. He would make his own suits even then, and he was a shy and quiet guy; it was when he did music that he was pretty abrasive. It was a noise punk rock scene that wasn't punk rock at all. It wasn't hardcore like it was in Detroit, but more of punk rock kids that were into noise instead of just punk rock.

Aaron Dilloway: Wolf Eyes were all in that Huron House; Nate, I and Solomon, Sol Meltzer from Nautical Almanac lived there. One morning they tried to wake me up—there was a KKK rally in Ann Arbor, and they were gonna go protest against it. I was hung over and I went back to sleep. Nate woke me up and said we have to hide Twig because the cops were looking for him because he threw rocks at the cops at the rally and he had to move to Chicago for a while. Nate made this tape of Robert Redford reading Peter and the Wolf on one side and wolf howling on the other and he took the wolf sounds and played an organ over it. He wanted me to come in and play guitar on some tracks he was working on, and he had done a show under the name Wolf Eyes—him and a keyboard that he had messed with.

Andrew WK: We all moved to New York, where they lived with me for two months with the idea they were moving out too. We were all gonna do Wolf Eyes together, maybe call it Mini-Systems. I wanted it to be my band, and we played songs that eventually became Andrew WK songs. But they missed Michigan, and it all eventually became clear that it wasn't in the cards. And I was so sad when they left; I was back to knowing nobody. It took them being out there to make me play shows in New York. And when they went back, that's when they focused on Wolf Eyes in earnest and added John Olson not too long after. Once Wolf Eyes blew up, Wolf Eyes in my mind still has the potential to be as big as they wanna be.

Aaron Dilloway: Andrew left, and we were constantly on the phone and sending tapes back and forth. Andrew was recording under the name Wolf Eyes at the same time as Nate and I, and eventually the plan was to get together for Wolf Eyes. But he was in New York and we were in Michigan. We moved out to New York and stayed a couple of months, but by that time he had his own thing going and we had ours. We wanted to get weirder and he wanted rock and roll. He basically said he was going to get signed to a major label and make music for as many people as possible.

"Warm Beer and Bestiality Go Together"

Rusvelt (*Blondie's, owner*): The cops hated me, man, oh yeah. I said I always got busted there; they didn't want the club to be there. There were always problems: the neighbors would always complain, the noise, the kids. There was a guy who used to climb the trees next to the apartment buildings by Blondie's before the show, during the show, after the show. And he would toot this horn. The neighbors would always complain. They always used to say, "That's the devil's place" and all this, and "The devil lives there and satanic bands play there." Vice would come all the time and bust me; I was always in court all of the time. Mostly the underage drinking. The young kids came to drink. There was this kid's birthday one time, and two of his buddies are drinking and he wasn't drinking. So I went over to him and said, "Why aren't you drinking, man?" And he says, "I'm not old enough." "So if you're not drinking, how old are you?" He says, "Well, I'm nineteen." So I said, "If you're not drinking, then get the hell out of here." I served everybody man. I trained everybody at the door outside if a vice cop pulls in—I trained them—all I said was, "Take all your drinks at the bar." They all rushed to the bar, and nobody had anything at the table. We got busted, don't get me wrong; we got busted more than once for serving minors.

Bill Kozy: Blondie's was our hangout, man. I didn't light candles and listen to Venom as some kind of ritual like a lot of the people there did. We'd go to see these wild-ass bands. That was our scene; it's where you went most nights, and there hasn't been a club like it since then.

Karen Neal: I pulled a knife on this guy at Blondie's who was fucking with my friend, this guy Mark DeWitt. I don't remember cutting him, but I pulled. I had a straight razor in my boot, and I just like, shook it in his face, and I was fucking pissed off. He told people that I cut his hand, and I don't remember it. Later on Inside Out was playing a show at Blondie's with Heresy, and my bass got left up by the stage, so I jumped into the pit to grab, to get my bass, and DeWitt's friend came up and just—boom!—tried to break my nose. There was blood everywhere. Chuck Burns was such a gentleman. He gave me his towel to bleed on.

Rusvelt: I opened Blondie's in 1984. It was all local bands at first, not doing much. Then this booking agent from Ann Arbor calls me and says, "We got this band from LA called Slayer. Would you be interested? $500." So I'm like, "Let me ask around and give you a call back." I ask the kids around, and they go, "What is it? Slayer from LA?" I said, "Yeah." "Okay, get 'em, get 'em, get 'em." I booked the show. I moved the stage on the other side; I knocked all the coolers out, the wall—just for that show. I was by myself, waiting for the band, and they pulled in, and the fucking tour bus is bigger than the bar. I said, "What the fuck is this?" One of them walks in and says, "I ain't playing here." Tom Araya, the singer, says, "Oh man, this is cool. We're going to rock the house. We're going to fucking yeah yeah!" Good energy and good attitude and shit. Sound check comes, and everything's shaking; all the bottles from the bar fell down on the tiles. I had some air conditioning, and it fell right on the fucking floor, and they blew their whole PA system. I says, "What is this?" Their manager goes, "We have a better system in our basement. Are you kidding me?" So I'm on the phone going to get a better system. I was on the phone all day long, and I got a new system for the show. I had to. I didn't even have any opening bands. I charged $6, and it was packed. It was a Saturday night, and I go to the guys, "Do you want to play another night?" "Well, hell, we're off. Don't tell the agent." So another $500. And the second night was fucking even busier. I asked them, "What do you guys need?" They go, "Man, we heard of this White Castle." So I brought them bags and bags and bags; they got sick and were fighting it on the stage. Slayer was the beginning, and everybody started calling me—everybody in the world; it was like a snowball effect. It really started a lot of that metal scene in Detroit.

John Speck: Blondie's was an eye opener, because fairly soon after starting to go there I realized that there were kids my age drunk at the shows, and I was underage. How was this happening? So I watched this one kid one day, like, barely peek over the bar, walk up and buy a pitcher, and I was like, "Where's this at? Did his dad send him there?" So then it became one of those deals: walk up, and Roosevelt's at the door, and he's like, "Five bucks, kid. ID." I'd be like, "Oh, I left my ID at home."

"Ten bucks." He wouldn't stamp you with the underage, and you'd walk over to the bar. "I want a pitcher of beer, please." It was $6 for a little minipitcher. They were making a killing off of suburban punk kids getting shit-hammered and then driving drunk home with the first alcohol of their lives in their systems. I drove me and my buddies home when I was old enough to borrow my mom's car. I came to at the rumble strips while going into the center of 75 like bumpbumpbumpbump. I'm like, "UGH! Ugh!" and all my other buddies are all passed out in the car, and everyone's like, "Oh! Fuck."

Rusvelt: Guns 'n' Roses came to town early on, opening up for the Cult somewhere in Detroit. I'm working the door at Blondie's, and this guy comes in on crutches. I had Diamond Rexx in from Chicago, and this guy on crutches moved the chair onto the stage and gave hell to the band. He's yelling, "You guys suck! Get off the stage!" So I went up to him and said, "Listen motherfucker, you got one leg broken, and I'm gonna break the other fucking leg! Shut your fucking mouth!" It was Axl Rose. Someone had to tell me, because I had no idea. He was a pain in the ass.

John Speck: GG Allin show at Blondie's. My friends were all like, "Dude, this guy throws shit and shoves the microphone up his ass, and so you gotta go." Everyone was waiting for him to go on and waiting for him to go on. I was standing kind of back because I didn't want to get shit thrown at me, and he comes out, and he comes out all "Grrraaah." Getting all aggro with poop, and everybody starts trying to get the fuck out of the way. But there's nowhere to go because it's fairly packed. And people start trying to get where you are, and you're like, "Get the fuck away from me, motherfucker!"

Steve Nawara (*Electric Six, Detroit Cobras, bassist, guitarist*): I was in eighth grade, and I went to see GG Allin at Blondie's. He came on, and he shit, and he started running after everyone.

He started running up everywhere. The whole place broke out into a riot. This skinhead came and hit me in the face. He was too big for me to fight back, so I looked around and there was a smaller skinhead, so I started hitting him in the face. And then, like, I'm sitting there and just didn't know what the hell was going on, and GG Allin seemed like he dropped out of the sky and landed about five feet away from me, threw his cowboy boots up on the table, and I was just like, "What the fuck?" I was terrified.

Bill Kozy: I ran out the door, and Rusvelt was cowering with a trash can lid, saying, "GG, what are you doing?" The barkeep, Skin, after the show, I remember him with his mop bucket just going, "Just another night."

Rusvelt: Oh man, when GG Allin played, it stunk. Two fucking days, the place stunk, and you could not get that smell out. I could not open the club. I threw the shit in the pitcher, and every time somebody bought a pitcher of beer I said, "Hey, you know what? That was GG Allin's pitcher." I'd just fuck with them. GG, he comes up to me, he tried to shake my hand, and I goes, "I'm not shaking your hand," and he goes, "How about giving me a twenty and I can go lick your toilet seats?"

Greg Schmitt (*photographer*): Everyone had run out the front door, and Rusvelt was running around telling everyone the show was canceled. He thought everyone had left, but they were just in the parking lot. They wanted to see the show, but they were scared. So someone goes up to Rusvelt and tells him, "You have three hundred people out there in the parking lot, and they are going to be a lot harder to deal with than GG Allin." Rusvelt had gotten married a couple weeks before that show, and she was working the bar. After the show she went home and locked him out of the house. She told him, "You let the devil play."

Steve Nawara: While GG was doing all this, a band called Cum Dumpster that was playing behind him, just playing the most awful shit. It was the most, like, depressing music I had ever heard in my life. I have actually never heard anything that depressing since then either. In was sludgy and dark. In a way I wanna hear it again.

David B. Livingstone (*God Bullies, guitarist; producer*): Cum Dumpster was the later project of Bob Madigan, who was the guy behind Slaughterhouse. I recorded Slaughterhouse, and it was like a week-long abortion. It was like the blind leading the dead. Nobody really knew what was going on. It was like, "How much noise could we possibly make if everything else was turned up?" Then it was, "Let's play this three different ways and keep all three tracks, and we'll bounce. We'll do some more tracks of the same thing." My most vivid memory of that is when we were mixing, and it's like, "More this. More treble in that. More treble in that. More treble in that. More bass in this." It was like, "Okay fine. Whatever the fuck you want, you know? You're paying." Then they came with, "It all sounds really good, but, ahhh, can you make it more clear?" Oh, yeah. I'll just press the fucking clarity button. Then every time Bob sang, he had to throw up first. So he just starts throwing up on the carpet. It was like, "No. You're not throwing up on my carpet. Go get a tarp and come back. Put your tarp down. Then you clean up after yourself."

Charlie Wallace: The guitarist from Slaughterhouse had ten delays, and I saved all my money to buy one. They must have had jobs or something. He turned it on, and it was like whaaaaa. We went to Bob's house one time and watched GG Allin videos. Then Bob says, "Ever wonder what a pig's dick looks like? Well, check it out." And he puts on a video of a girl fucking a pig." And he's got beer, but it's warm, and he says, "Warm beer and bestiality go together."

I'm Hell

John Brannon: Me and Larissa had a Sonny-and-Cher show going on for a couple years, only it revolved around drugs or lack of drugs. We would play New York a lot and always called ahead and had little girls pick some dope up for us. You know that record cover for *Paul's Boutique?* We stayed on the second floor. It was by this bar where we used to hang out with the Dust Devils, over by Max Fish. The Puerto Ricans were all out there, so dope was easy. We had money and we stayed close.

Kevin Monroe: When we first landed in Amsterdam on our first European tour, I told Larissa, "Listen, if you need to get something, please do not do it on your own. Just let me do it, okay? Do not do anything by yourself." We got picked up at the airport and were taken to the hotel in Amsterdam, and five minutes later our guitars were being thrown down the stairs because she asked the owner of the hotel where she could get off. Killdozer was with us and were like, "What in the hell is going on?" Nirvana got kicked out of the same hotel for the same reason.

Jon Howard: The Hyenas, except for Kimball, were longtime, hard-working junkies.

Peter Davis: I started booking them around the time *You Can't Pray a Lie* came out. Their stuff was going pretty good; they were getting dates with Sonic Youth, and they were well on their way at that point. But they were using, and people on the business side got a whiff of what was going on.

John Brannon: Nirvana came and played Ann Arbor and stayed at our house. Kurt crashed on my floor and he was sick. Me and Larissa didn't know. At that point we had just met him. But we had shitloads of heroin on us, and we could have gotten straight. Kurt pulled out all my blues records, and of course he's play-ing my Lead Belly records. I kinda felt like he was, like, in the bathroom getting sick or some shit, but I didn't put it together.

Rachel Nagy: Kurt's not a girl, so he couldn't have fucked John. John would never give up his dope to anybody that wouldn't suck his dick. I like John and I think he's a great musician, but he is a user.

Kevin Monroe: Before that, Dave Grohl and Scream played a show with us in Detroit and stayed at the house in Ann Arbor, about forty-five minutes away. One of the guys in Scream sat their gig money in one of those rubberish sort of zipper bags on top of the gas pump in Detroit. They left it, drove to Ann Arbor, and they couldn't find it. Then they remembered. It was three in the morning, and they drove back to get it and it was still sitting there.

Rachel Nagy: I used to sell weed to Nirvana and Soundgarden because I knew all those guys at St. Andrews and I was always hanging out in back. "Hey, Rae, you got some weed? 'cause there's these guys that need some." Of course, it was, "Oh, I love those guys. Sure, here." My good girlfriend, Jenny Youngblood, married Dave Grohl. She was kind of a bougie northern suburb girl, and Dad was all telling Dave, "You need to grow up and be a man." And Dave's like, "Ah, nah. I think I'll go on tour. See ya!" It was like, "You know what, sweetheart? Your daughter is walking around in pink rollers, so shut the fuck up."

John Brannon: We toured all the time and always hooked up with all these crazy people, especially crazy chicks. We'd stay at some place; it would turn out to be a meth lab or some shit. One of the chicks from this one meth lab we picked up, and she ended up going out with Kevin. And then when he dumped her, she later ended up with the bass player we got to replace Kevin, whose name was Kevin Reis. She must have liked Hyenas' bass players named Kevin. Kevin Reis ended up ODing.

Peter Davis: I never got any complaints about the Hyenas getting there, playing well, or anything. Just complaints from promoters about not being able to get into the bathroom after the show because things were occupied.

John Brannon: We always attracted the nuts, for sure, then they'd end up on tour with us. We'd be in LA, someone would say, "Could you drive me to, like, wherever?" We'd do it. What the fuck? We were bored and we never had roadies, so we figured, "You got some gas money? You got some weed? Yeah, you can roll with us." Or it would be like some kind of kid who was some young cool kid. They'd always freak out, like, hanging out with us or, like, you know, we were kind of shady.

Grace Kennelly (*LA scenester*): The Hyenas came to LA and took it over. I got to know the Hyenas through my ex-boyfriend, who was in Lubricated Goat, and I would put up bands. John stayed with me. I saw right away that John likes to tell stories, and half the time they aren't true. He put on this badass front, but he was one of the sweetest guys I ever slept with.

Peter Davis: They were getting the reverence on the street and they were drawing, but the money was just okay; it wasn't barnstormers as it should have been.

Charlie Wallace: We played with the Hyenas in Montreal at the Foufones Electriques. I was big L-Seven fan, but Larissa was junked out of her mind. I wanted to talk to her about L-Seven. First she disappeared for two hours, then I tried to talk to her when she got back, and all she could say was, "yeah yeah yeah." Kevin Monroe was weird too. He used to go out with this girl Xiola in Ann Arbor. She inspired the Jane's Addiction song "Three Days." I met Xiola at a Detroit show, and she invited me to come to Ann Arbor and visit—she paid for my bus ticket. It turned out that she was a bad junkie; I was only eighteen and had no real idea what that meant. But Kevin was there at the house in Ann Arbor sometimes when she wasn't living in LA, and I'd see him. Xiola went back and forth to LA, and she finally died of a heroin overdose.

That night in Montreal we were talking, and Kevin remembered who I was. It was one of those conversations about a girl we both knew. We talked and he says, "Yeah, she passed away last year." Which I didn't know. Sort of out of nowhere, he says, "If I ever find you had anything to do with that, I'll find you." I said, "Dude, I don't even do heroin," and he said, "Okay, you say that to me now."

Preston Long: Wig played on a bill with the Hyenas at CBGBs, which was one of the first times I played with the Hyenas. We did "Public Animal #9," which we later recorded for the Alice Cooper covers thing on Sub Pop. But that night I went up there and it was abysmal. Larissa was a half step off the whole song, playing an E flat while we were playing an A. Wig toured with the Hyenas for a while, and Larissa would book the shows, so we'd play one and then have nine days off. We'd get kicked out of wherever we'd be staying, and no one was taking care of shit, and we'd just kind of be out there. That's when Kevin and I sort of thought about putting something else together.

John Brannon: It just got to a point that we had never stopped touring. We didn't live anywhere; nothing else is going on in our lives. I was staying with whatever chick I was with when we were home.

Preston Long: I had a guitar with four strings on it, and so I learned this stuff and was playing more country stuff, old-time stuff. Kevin was around, and we were talking about doing something. It kind of evolved that we wanted to play country music really hard.

Kevin Monroe: Preston and I had already started working together just as a side project before Jim and I decided to leave. John wasn't real happy about it. We told John, and Bill Metner was there, a longtime friend of John's, who is dead now. We were picking up some equipment, and John was trying to strong arm me. Bill found me in, like, some closet trying to hide from John.

John Brannon: The *Hard Times* tour lasted five weeks, and I was off drugs at the start, but I broke down by the time we got to fucking LA. Some fucker gave me a bunch of black tar dope. Of course I shot it all up and fucking ODed in the van. They're carrying me out to do the gig. Eric Erlandson from Hole was there with this, like, little girl. He's like, "John, I want you to meet my girlfriend, Drew Barrymore." I looked at her, said, "What's up?" and threw up all over. She was terrified. That tour was the whole quitting/stopping, quitting/stopping. Over the years I went through every methadone clinic in this fucking town. We got off the Hard Times tour, and I went right into rehab. I had enough; I was tired of being like this. After twenty-seven days Larissa came by and broke me out. We went and scored. Rehab doesn't work. I had to do it myself.

Anthony DeLuca (drummer for Boston bands Swirlies, Blake Babies): There was a show my friend hooked up at his loft in, like, the south end of Boston with the Laughing Hyenas at like 2 a.m. And it was a big deal—everybody who was into music in Boston went to this show. So it was like two, now it's like two-thirty, and it's like quarter of three, and everyone's kind of late. There's, like, a lot of people there, like two hundred people, maybe more, and everyone's like, "What the fuck?" You know, "Where are the Laughing Hyenas?" Finally Larissa and Todd Swalla, the drummer, walked in, and they were kind of like, "Oh, yeah, alright, yeah, cool. We're ready to play, whatever." And they went in the bathroom for awhile and came out a little bit later together, looking really antsy. I was talking to a friend of mine a little bit further away from where everybody walked in, and there was this commotion, and I remember, like, looking up, and the next thing you knew, like, what had happened was they stole the cash box, and they just split, you know, like they just split. There were probably, like, you know, a thousand dollars in there. They never played the show. But that was kind of what they were; that was what they were known for. And John was the leader of this pack of criminals, right?

Harold Richardson: John was already a local legend in Ann Arbor. I was working at a pizza place and doing a delivery one night and saw John having sex with a chick; he had her bent over a car by the Blind Pig downtown. I went back and told the guys at work I just saw John Brannon fucking some chick, and we all jumped in my car and went back, and he was still fucking her. Of course we yelled at him. Heroin was everywhere around Detroit and Ann Arbor in those years. I started driving a cab, and I'd always have people jumping in the cab looking to score, and I always knew where to take them. Most of the cabdrivers I worked with were junkies and crackheads. Right before they put her away, I would take Eminem's wife, Kim, from Ann Arbor to Detroit so she could cop. Usually it would be a round trip, and I would wait around and she would call me. She was a pretty tough lady, and she would complain to me that white guys were never into her.

Preston Long: Kevin, me, and Jim formed Mule and toured on a demo tape, with flyers that said Ex Hyenas. That was a time when you could play anywhere and people would come out. One of our first shows was in East Lansing with Urge Overkill somewhere on campus, and we didn't know what the fuck we were doing. We had borrowed amps, and I probably had a borrowed guitar, and by then Jim and Kevin were a pretty respected, established rhythm section, and there I was out front with this borrowed gear, and I sucked. I knew I wasn't a front man and I wasn't a guitar player. I heard about that shit for years, how bad I sucked. So I came back to Detroit and went down in the basement by myself and practiced the songs over and over and did all the stuff I couldn't do, like standing up and singing and playing. We had no ethics before that MSU show; I was like, "Fuck this. I am not showing up like that again." When we worked on our first album with Steve Albini, Kurt Cobain had died about that time, and Albini had mostly good things to say about Kurt. He has a lot of bad shit to say about people, but he was smart enough to rein it in about Kurt.

We toured in a Volvo station wagon that had 220,000 miles on it that my sister had given me. Jim had this shitty little Chevy Monza. We toured in two cars, and we spent more money keeping the Volvo running than we were making. It broke down in Montreal, Baltimore, Ohio somewhere, and I'd have to be the one to get up at six in the morning and find someone to fix it, and we would be puttering up to a gig, and it would die in front of the club. Inside we had to travel with all these hoses and things to fix it; we collected parts and had them in the cab, and the radio didn't work. A few gigs we showed up after everyone had left. That was the demo tape tour.

On the Corner

Jack White (*White Stripes, The Dead Weather, Raconteurs, solo, guitarist, vocalist*): I didn't know anything about Detroit music—its identity—until I worked with Brian Muldoon and he was playing the Gories for me. My brothers weren't even into the Stooges or the MC5 or Motown. They were into a lot bigger stuff, like the Rolling Stones, Beatles, Led Zeppelin, the Who. The Muldoons lived next to us; they were a family of like seven or eight kids. We had a bunch of big Catholic families on the block. I'm the tenth child in my family, seventh son. So he was doing upholstery in the basement of that house, and I ended up doing upholstery in the basement of my house later on. As a total side note, there was a third upholsterer on the end of the block, this little German guy named Klomp, and he had been the first one. So that's why I named my upholstery shop Third Man Upholstery. But Brian's family was into all the punk: Iggy Pop, David Bowie stuff, Television—they were into all that. I had gotten the Stooges record out of the dumpster in the alley. His brother had gotten hold of the family house and threw a ton of records from the attic out in the garbage, and I just happened to be walking home that day and saw those, and I got the first Stooges record out of that trash and fell in love with it, you know. I recorded "I Wanna Be Your Dog" on a four-track—it was hilarious. It was sort of like, "Oh, okay, so that's supposed to be Iggy Pop, when he was younger or something?" I had known a little about Iggy Pop, but it was kind of funny. It was sort of one of those things people thought I was making it up later on, you know? A little too perfect.

Bobby Harlow (*The Go, Conspiracy of Owls, vocalist*): I was born in Miami and lived with my mother until I was twelve. Then I was raised by my grandparents. I was supposed to be named Robin after Robin Trower. I was going to get beaten to a pulp in school, so my grandparents talked my parents out of it. I could sing

257

all the Beatles songs when I was a kid. One day I got really high on acid and put on the *White Album*. I only had the first half, but I listened to it that day and something clicked.

Jack White: When I was fourteen we skipped school and went to Harmony House at Trappers Alley, and I bought the *White Album* by the Beatles. The Robert Johnson box set was up on the wall; Columbia had just come out with that box set, and that picture of him on the cover legitimately was scary to me. I thought, "I have no interest in listening to that music; that's very scary." So it took a couple years for that stuff to siphon through. When I got older, in my twenties, and all my friends worked at record stores, and all these record collectors and garage rockers, you know, a lot of them worked at record stores, so they had the ability to listen to so much music. I was jealous of them because you just don't have the time in the day to be able to do that, and when you have a job at a place like that, well, I started thinking maybe I should work at one of those places. That's when I made the decision to be careful of myself, to be careful collecting things like records and emulating other people.

Dan Kroha: I met Jack hanging out at the Gold Dollar. At that point I was renting an apartment on Prentis. Doll Rods were kinda old hat by that time. When I first met Jack he's like, "Wow, you're Dan from the Gories? Wow! Really?!" He looked up to me so much that I didn't even notice that he was, like, this much taller than me.

Jack White: I was sort of fumbling my way through, and I didn't know that the Gories still lived in town or whatever; by the time I skated into them, I was really impressed. I didn't know you could go to a show and maybe see one of them.

Margaret Dollrod: After the Gories broke up, I told Danny, "I could do a band with you, but it's an all-girl band." Because he was always going through my clothes, I was like, "Maybe you, like, want to be more flamboyant in your dress, maybe you want to be a girl." He used to tell me when he was little that he'd put his hair behind his ears and wrap a towel around his legs like a mermaid. If we're friends, we help each other's dreams come true. So I said, "I don't know if I want to be the mermaids. But I wanna be your friend. So I'm having a girl band. You wanna be a girl in the band, you can be a girl in the band, but it's an all-girl band." That was the Demolition Doll Rods.

Tom Potter (*Bantam Rooster, Dirtbombs, Detroit City Council, guitarist, vocalist***):** Dan was one of those guys where people would be like, "Dan's got to be a total fucking fag—he dresses like a girl." I'm like, "No way, man. That dude gets more fuckin' ass than a toilet seat." He always had chicks.

Dan Kroha: Before that I had Rocket 455. I was one of the founding members of that band. It was named after a car that Margaret had, an Olds '88, a humongous two-door with the 455 engine. But Margaret came to me with that idea. Good name. Crazy, cool, weird song titles. Wants me to be a girl in it. This is something different. So I said, "Yeah! Alright, let's do this." I'd wear her clothes. We would go to the thrift store almost every day. She had really good taste in weird stuff. We made a bedroom of the house we were in into a closet. All our clothes were together because I was really into clothes. I would start picking stuff out of her stuff and be like, "Okay, I want to wear this, I want to wear this." It was the early nineties. There was a lot of freaky stuff coming out.

Jack White: I went to a Doll Rods show up in Ferndale at Magic Bag, and I came outside, and I had bought the album in there, *Tasty*, and I was walking outside, and the Hentchmen were right there. Somehow I started talking to them, and they said, "Let me see the cover," and they were laughing because it was Mick eating a hot dog on the cover. I said, "Oh, I didn't know that was Mick." I didn't put two and two together. And then John Hentch asked me what I did, and I said, "I do upholstery," and he goes, "Give me your card. I have some work for you." That ended up with the White Stripes playing our first gig—we opened up for the Hentchmen the next day.

John Szymanski: We met Jack and Meg outside, and we were playing at the Lager House a few weeks later and needed an opening band. So he told us about the White Stripes and it sounded cool. They said they had never played out, so this was their first weekend playing.

Jack White: It was just baby steps and learning; it wasn't my scene. I'd only been in one band as a drummer, Goober and the Peas, and they weren't really part of that scene. They were part of a different part of the music scene. At the same time I was playing in coffee houses for a couple years there in Hamtramck, which is totally different from all that scene as well. Dan and the Rocket 455 came in there. Kroha had a Rocket 455 patch on the back of his jacket, and someone had mentioned something having to do with the Gories, and I didn't know who he was or whatever. Later on, when I had met him, I remembered him from being in the coffee house with that jacket on, which was pretty funny.

John Szymanski: Jack knew Neil from the Gold Dollar because of Goober and the Peas. I think the White Stripes played its first show there, then with us the next night at the Lager House.

Bobby Harlow: The Gold Dollar was initially intended to be more of an art rock kind of thing. That was what it was supposed to be, but then rock-and-roll bands took over. Neil Yee, the owner, wanted, like, stuff that was a little more left field, a little more left center, and then what he ended up with was the Wild Bunch and the Hentchmen and the Cobras and the White Stripes that were doing more direct music.

Neil Yee (*owner, booker, Gold Dollar*): I saw the building, the Gold Dollar, in 1994, and it was just this empty place that needed plumbing and electric, which I did a lot of myself with some friends. Still, it looked destroyed when I bought it, and it looked destroyed when I opened it.

There were people around there who were fighting against the bar, and I went in thinking it was going to be a losing proposition. I wasn't expecting big crowds, but I ended up doing better than the numbers in my business plan.

Harold Richardson: People always talk about the Gold Dollar as this place the so-called garage thing started in Detroit. But they started by booking noise bands from Ann Arbor and shit.

Neil Yee: I didn't picture the place as getting big. But it did get best known as this place for "garage" in Detroit, this focus on one style of music. But a lot of what I liked wasn't for the masses.

Jim Magas: I played at the Gold Dollar as Magas and set up the first two US shows for Peaches. I had just started doing solo electronic stuff, and someone said I should meet Peaches because she was doing stuff like me. I e-mailed her and brought her to Chicago. Then I decided she'd be great to play in Detroit, and by now Brannon and Harold were doing Easy Action. I called John and he said, "Does she have a demo?" I told him, "Just trust me on this." I put her at the Gold Dollar with Magas and Easy Action. We got $50 each. A couple years later Peaches and I played at the Magic Stick, and Marilyn Manson was there. She didn't need a demo.

Neil Yee: Within weeks I got a call from Elvis Costello's keyboard player, who was in town doing a show at the Fox Theater, and they wanted to check the place out. I don't think he showed up. One of our door guys almost didn't let Alex Chilton in—we were strict about that. One of the guys from Sponge came around and said, "You know who I am. We have a top-ten song." He says, "Well, then you must have $5."

Harold Richardson: We were one of the first rock bands to play the Gold Dollar. We moved to Detroit after a bunch of shows at the Dollar, since John and I were banned from the 8 Ball and the Blind Pig in Ann Arbor anyway. We were drugged out dudes, and John had a thing for one of the waitresses at the Pig, and she thought he was stalking her. Not long after we got back to Detroit our drummer, John LeMay, got busted for dope and so did Brannon. Brannon was living at the Beethoven Apartments on Third and Prentis, and he was copping over by Masonic, and he got busted with the dealer. They put him in the cell they called the David Ruffin suite because he had guitar picks in his pocket. The cops were like, "Oh, you're a musician? We'll put you in the David Ruffin suite." At that time, late nineties, the Detroit scene was small, and everyone was excited that something was starting to go down. Eventually we got left behind when everyone else got big. The White Stripes were just starting, and no one liked them. But pretty soon we were doing tours, and people were asking about them. This was after that first single on Sympathy, and I got back and said to Jack, "You should go on the road; everyone's asking about you." He was like, "Okay, okay, yeah." He wasn't crazy about it at first. But in a few months they were huge. Once they got huge, everyone else did with this garage thing, and we were left with the rock thing. We weren't so popular.

John Krautner (*The Go, Conspiracy of Owls, guitarist, bassist*): The Go wanted to open up for the cool bands, the bands that were pulling in people like Cobras and Rocket 455. Those were the big bands in our eyes.

Rachel Nagy: The Cobras were all into doo-wop and shit, doing only covers. We weren't trying to do it verbatim; we're not some Motown revue. I heard the songs and would start to change them. We weren't like the other bands, really, at all.

Jason Stollsteimer: Bantam Rooster was the first band out of that Gold Dollar scene that toured. And they were on Crypt, which made them extra cool.

Chris Fuller (*Electric 6, manager*): Tom Potter from Bantam Rooster was important in all this. He came to Detroit in 1997 as Bantam Rooster with records you could find in stores outside of Detroit, or even outside the country. There were bands in Detroit already, but they didn't do records or tour. It was no accident that Tom Potter came to town and things started happening.

Tom Potter: Bantam Rooster played its first Detroit show at the Tap Bar, and a couple of people from the Detroit Cobras were heckling us. We were outsiders. Detroit had already started something like what we were doing, but we were like, "Fuck you, man." They were probably pissed because we had gotten signed to Crypt. I had sent tapes out to a couple labels. I got a letter back from Larry Hardy. I didn't know him at the time, but he actually sent a letter back: "We really like it, we're full up right now, but keep sending me this stuff." I just gave up hope on the other ones, and a month after I'd given up hope I come home and there's this call on my answering machine, and it's Tim Warren: "Hey, daddy. What's going on? This is Tim Warren from Crypt records. I really like this tape you sent me. I was kinda thinking, like, maybe we could do a single or, I don't know, fuck, maybe an album, I don't know." Just going nuts on the phone.

Tim Warren (*Crypt Records, owner*): I'd spent a lot of time in Michigan when I was compiling the *Back to the Grave* comps—that state had such great old sixties bands. So I knew Detroit. And Tom sent me that tape, and I said, "Hey, this shit's really good."

Tom Potter: Coming home and getting that on your answering machine, like Tim Warren wants to do a record with ya, it's like, "Fuck, yeah, all right." That was huge for us, because we were from Lansing, not Detroit. That started things. We started playing Zoot's, then the Gold Dollar a lot when we weren't touring. We made money.

Matthew Smith (*Witches, Outrageous Cherry, the Volebeats, THTX, vocalist; producer*): Before the Gold Dollar there was a club called Zoot's.

Troy Gregory: Zoot's was the place that had noise bands, surf bands, and some guy with turntables all playing on the same bill. It was where all the people who couldn't get booked anywhere else played.

Matthew Smith: It was like a house in the Cass Corridor that used to be a whorehouse in the old days. The Gold Dollar became the whole nexus of everything. Between that and the Magic Stick, it was like all the bands were playing there. But that was a real interesting atmosphere. It just felt like Weimar-era Berlin or something.

Troy Gregory: And when Zoot's went down, Neil Yee was getting the Gold Dollar going, and at the same time Jim Diamond was moving in with his studio. It all came together.

Neil Yee: The thing about Detroit at that time, there were so many small scenes that had great music, and everyone focuses on the garage thing. And we had touring bands play to no one. Godspeed You Black Emperor! played to eight people.

Tom Potter: They had prom nights at the Gold Dollar. Just get really drunk and pretend it's your prom.

Matthew Smith: They did, like, this prom night for all these kids that were these rock-and-roll outcasts and apparently never did proms. But it kind of felt like being at The Rocky Horror Picture Show or something. It was just really, I don't know, it kind of felt like you were at CBGB and Studio 54 and the Warhol Factory all at the same time.

Tim Caldwell: Tom Potter was always at the Gold Dollar. One night they had some kind of prom, like the Gold Dollar prom, and Tom was MC, and he was fucked up beyond all control, like Foster Brooks fucked up. Rachel Kucsulain, the bass player from Slumber Party, walked by him while he was raving, and he jumped off the stage and started playing bongos on her ass. Yeah, seventies-porn prom-emcee Tommy was in rare uber-obnoxious, randy, foul-mouthed mode that night. I expected a vaudeville-style hook to yank him at any given minute. Later that night I was leaving and there was this little grassy patch behind the Dollar. It would have been a great picture.

Martin Heath (*cofounder, Rhythm King Records, Lizard King Records*): Parties with the Wildbunch and the Go. For an English music geek, it was full of amazing beautiful women who, after a slurry hello, turned around and threw up in the sink. Meanwhile there's a banging on the door as the bass player ran in complaining about how he was sitting in his car with a friend having a quiet joint when a dude pushed a shotgun through the window and fired it.

Tom Potter: Heath was in Detroit—I think he was scouting the Detroit Cobras—when one of us was doing a coke deal outside on Trumbull while we had a party. Some guy taps on the window and puts a shotgun in and demanded they turn over the drugs. The dealer jumped out the car and gets shot in the ass and everyone runs. They bring this guy into the party, clean the buckshot out of his ass, and Heath is petrified.

Chris Fuller: He was buying coke, and the dealer pulls up to the curb, and someone comes from another side, and the dealer gets shot in the ass. Heath was saying someone should call the cops.

Tom Potter: When he said it everyone kind of stops everything and, after a pause, started laughing.

Bobby Harlow: Why is it that people always act up when we have visitors here? It's like they know they're here and they bring out the guns.

Troy Gregory: You'd have after-parties at the Electric 6 house on Trumbull, and there would be fights and drunk people and drugs. Cocaine came in real heavy. You added that into the mix, and you had people fucking each other's girlfriends and boyfriends, and that fueled fights. You know, someone is in the bathroom with someone's girlfriend, and it's bad blood from there.

Eddie Baranek (*The Sights, guitarist, vocalist*): Potter, in this town, is the original two piece. He's the original go out there, do it, figure it out later. Neil was cool about getting us into the Gold Dollar even though we were underage. I'd go down there with Ben Blackwell. Neil tells us, "Don't fucking drink." So twelve minutes later we were in the women's bathroom slamming cans of beer because the women's bathroom had a door on the stall that locked, and we're like, "Neil's not gonna go pee in the women's bathroom. He'll pee in the men's bathroom. He's not gonna come in the chick's bathroom." So we would go in there and just chug them and then walk out. Well, he caught onto it, and he's like, "Okay, you guys can't be doing that shit."

Ben Blackwell (*Dirtbombs, drummer, Jack White's nephew, honcho, Third Man Records*): They'd let me in and they would say, "We're going to draw like thirty Xs on your hand." I'm exaggerating, but they're like super, super cautious about it. After a few times Neil Yee came up to me and said, "You really don't drink, do you?" I was like, "No, I really just want to see the show." I wanted to do nothing to jeopardize seeing any of that stuff. People like Eddie Baranek from the Sights or my wife, who was my girlfriend then, Malissa, they were getting in saying, "Oh, I'm not going to drink" and hammering beers. Then they started putting Xs on their hands. I've been told that I ruined it for everyone by not drinking.

Rachel Nagy: It was a dirty little place, and everybody knew each other, and the drinks were cheap. There was a security camera, black and white, so you could see who was out back. We never got paid much there. We could play the Magic Stick and do much better. There were never that many people at those shows.

Tyler Spencer, aka Dick Valentine (*Wildbunch, Electric 6, vocalist*): Neil Yee, who ran the Dollar, liked us, and we played there at least once a month starting shortly after it opened. We were the yang to the yin of what Detroit was at the time. We weren't a garage band—I never owned a jeans jacket in my life—but people coming to see us were taking a break from what was happening in Detroit.

Timmy Vulgar (*Clone Defects, Human Eye, Timmy's Organism, vocalist, guitarist*): A buddy took me to the Gold Dollar for the first time. The Gore Gore Girls go on, and the only thing I could think of, I was like, "These guys are like the Damned's first album. This is exactly what I'm looking for, this kind of punk, this kind of rock 'n' roll." I was sick of hardcore and that kind of stuff, and I wanted to hear balls-out rock 'n' roll, seventies-style, punk rock.

Neil Yee: The only person that we had to ban repeatedly was Timmy Vulgar. And he'd some back in disguise, with sunglasses and stuff sometimes. We'd let him back in eventually. He would try to apologize, and it would be so primatively ignorant. One time he commented on my racial ethnicity and then apologized by saying he really liked Japanese punk rock bands. I'm not Japanese.

Timmy Vulgar: One night, it might have been that same night as Gore Gore Girls, the Cobras went on, and Rachel pulls her pants down, moons the crowd. We were up in the front, and her butt's right there, and it says, "Eat me"—like "eat" and then "me" on each cheek—and we're just like this, "Uhhhhh." We look at each other, and we're like, "Okay."

Bobby Harlow: Rachel is Amy Winehouse, but she's like the dangerous version. Amy Winehouse was tragic but was, like, this, can't walk straight, and she's singing, she's a wreck. Well, Rachel Nagy will kick your fucking ass. You know she's real dangerous, really out of control. And check out Winehouse's tattoos—same place as Rachel's.

Chris Fuller: She was scary. One night she got into it with Joe Frezza from the Wildbunch and had his lower lip gripped in her teeth. He had to beat her on the head with a beer bottle to get her to let go.

Tom Potter: You could drive as fast as you wanted to in Detroit. Getting pulled over for drunk driving was really rare. That story—you know, "Really, they pulled you over on someone's lawn?"—had a lot of truth to it. It was a drunken rocker's paradise, and the only fee was having your car broken into every couple months and possibly being held up at the ATM.

Chris Fuller: You could drive up Woodward doing 110 with a straw up your nose.

Tim Warren: In Detroit, stopping at lights is optional; the place is just down and dirty.

Timmy Vulgar: There would be great parties after the Gold Dollar closed for the night—people getting drunk, running around naked, falling down stairs. Not the dudes. Well, maybe I just was doing that. One time I came down the stairs at Dave Buick's house, and all I had was a condom on my dick, and I just peed in the condom.

Dave Buick: Very true. There was this period of time that people were going completely crazy. There were parties four or five nights a week at various houses, either John Hentch's or the Wild Bunch house, first in Hamtramck and then the place on Trumbull.

John Szymanski: We had a record release party at the Lager House, and a limo shows up and it's [former Detroit Tigers] Kirk Gibson and Dave Rozema, and I guess they were married to sisters. So they're in the bar digging the show with about a hundred people. When the bar closed, my girlfriend at the time was a party girl, and she just invited them back to my house for a party. They accepted, and she jumped in their limo over to the house.

Tom Potter: The Dirtys would bring down coke from Port Huron. It wouldn't even be like a natural color. It wouldn't be a color found in nature; they'd just be like, "Yeah, I'll do this. It's made from the bones of old people."

Ko Melina (*Ko and the Knockouts, Dirtbombs, bassist, guitarist, vocalist; DJ on Sirius Radio's Underground Garage*): Our friends were at the Gold Dollar, but that's about it. Just everybody that you hung out with. Anybody who was in a Detroit band ended up going to the Garden Bowl or the Gold Dollar.

Jason Stollsteimer: There was no way for us to check out what was going on in Detroit because we were too young to get into the shows. So I threw house shows at my place in Ypsilanti. The Go played. The Clone Defects played. The Rapture played our house. We had Wolf Eyes play. Wesley Willis played at my house. All these Detroit punk rock bands played, and we paid them in beer.

Ko Melina: I don't think anybody was really making a huge effort to be known. Tom Potter with Bantam Rooster and the Hentchmen were the only bands that were really touring. Everybody else was playing Detroit and that's about it. This was before Jack was in the Go and he was doing Two Star Tabernacle. The bands didn't begin with this great idea to become national and tour. People were in each other's bands and it was a community.

Bobby Harlow: I didn't really care about the White Stripes, but then I saw Two Star Tabernacle and saw Jack play the role of a member of a band versus a character, like Jack White. He was an amazing guitar player.

Jack White: Him and Johnny came after the show; they came backstage and said, "Man, you are a conquistador."

Bobby Harlow: We were forming the Go, and I told John Krautner, "Look at this guy play." I know, but Jack was already prepared to join somehow. I think he wanted to be in a rock-and-roll band. I called Dave Buick, who Jack was hanging out with, and I said, "Do you think Jack would be interested in playing with the Go?" Dave said, "He's right here." So we went over to Dave's house, and before we even asked, Jack said yes.

Dave Buick: Jack and I were hanging out every day together, so it was a pretty simple issue. It was a really good idea.

Jack White: It was something I'd always wanted to do, just be a guitar player in a band. And there was the gang mentality of it. As a drummer you almost sometimes don't feel like you're part of that gang, and I'd done that before in a couple of bands, and so it was a novelty for me to play the guitar and not have to sing or be a songwriter, and I could play solos, and so I was part of the mob, you know?

Bobby Harlow: We practiced on the third floor at Jack's house—a big, big old Detroit home. It was decked out in red and white. He already had an idea of the White Stripes. Meg was his wife, and he was calling her his sister. He had the whole thing figured out. Jack was less involved in the White Stripes than he was the Go for a short period.

Matthew Smith: We did a three-song demo for the Go in Jack's living room in Mexicantown. He already had the red-and-white theme going on there, and he was really into the recording process.

John Krautner: We got a deal with Sub Pop from Dan Trager, who was an A&R guy for them from Michigan. That was the first time we could tour. We had finished recording *Whatcha Doin'*. Dan flew into Detroit and took us to dinner at the Cajun place in Ferndale. They gave us $5,000 to buy a van, and we bought a shuttle bus from Farmington Hills hospital.

Dan Trager (*former A&R, Sub Pop*)**:** I grew up on the east side of Detroit and the Go were friends of my friends from high school. I moved up at Sub Pop from publicity to A&R, and I was digging through demos to sign my first band. I was in Detroit in Thanksgiving 1998, and people were telling me about the Go and the White Stripes. I got a tape of the Go, and I realized I was in love with this band.

Jack White: It was kind of shocking, having Sub Pop interested. We had dinner with Jon Poneman, and it was all great. I was so surprised that they cared about a Detroit band. I didn't know that much about the music business. I also had the White Stripes going, and it just shows you that nobody cared about the White Stripes, really; that band was already happening, and so was Two Star Tabernacle. I was in three bands. The Go was the one that people were talking about at that moment.

Dan Trager: The Go was a real baby band, a very green developing artist. But I was knocked out by the songwriting and the guitar playing, which was a lot of Jack White.

Matthew Smith: There was a little debate about what was going to happen next, because we had to have a series of meetings to reassure Jack that he would be able to do the guitars the way he wanted to do them. I think he would have rather been producing the Go. He was used to running things. When he came into the Go thing, it was difficult for him to just step in and be a part of it.

Jack White: There were other recordings of songs that they chose alternate takes of. There's a song "Meet Me at the Movies" that was recorded in my living room by Matt Smith, and there was a studio version done of it that I thought was very superior to it. I kind of lost breath arguing with them about it. I think it was a turn-off to them that I was actually so—me and Buick together, actually, so adamant about certain stuff like that. But it's sort of like, it was their band, so . . .

Dan Trager: Soon after we got them in the studio it was like, "Jack is going to be out."

Jason Stollsteimer: There is a version of that first Go record where there are so many Jack White solos, it sounds just like the White Stripes. And they were real good solos. They ended up taking a lot of them out.

Jim Diamond (*Ghetto Recorders, producer; Dirtbombs, bassist*): There was some weirdness between Jack and Matt because they had very different aesthetics. They were doing the recording at Ghetto, and we set them up, and they played the songs live, and Jack's doing his solos. After we get done with all these songs, Jack said, "I'm ready to over dub on my solos, now." Matt's like, "No, you just did your solos. No." That was just the practice, and then you're going to do the real ones, the serious ones? I don't know. I was the engineer, going, "Ooohhh," looking at the clock.

Dave Buick: It was a long mixing process, and yes, there were some disagreements.

Bobby Harlow: There was the White Stripes thing with the Sub Pop deal. Is Jack able to do the White Stripes if he signs?

Dan Trager: Sub Pop was really all about contracts at that point. So we got the contract, and everyone else signed, but Jack was reticent. Soon I got a call from Jack, and he said, "Do I have to sign this? What do you think I ought to do?" I knew it was a classic moment, and I knew Jack was a major talent. I know I was supposed to strong arm him into signing, but I just didn't think that this was the time to be strong arming. I said, "Do what you want to do," hoping I'd get a chance to work with him again.

Bobby Harlow: He decided not to sign the contract, and I suppose maybe if he would have, it would have allowed Sub Pop to have their grip on the Stripes as well.

Dan Trager: We would have had right of first refusal for the White Stripes. But Sub Pop never ended up making a pitch for the White Stripes.

Jack White: By the time they were going to kick me out of the band—which was the only band I've ever been kicked out of—they had a contract, they had another contract there that I didn't sign, and I just happened to be un-naive at that second to actually look through this other paragraph, and actually something caught my eye and I thought, "Maybe I better to hold off on this for a second." I'm glad I didn't, because if I had signed another contract, Sub Pop would have owned everything the White Stripes ever did. It was just like a little paragraph thing, and I saw it later on. No lawyers were even around, it was just something—I just don't even know, they must have hired somebody, I don't know—but I didn't have one for sure. Maybe God just kind of held my hand back there for half a second. Because I didn't know they were kicking me out. They were just saying, "You've got to sign this stuff." So I signed one of them; I said, "I've got to look at this other stuff," and they go, "Oh yeah, and by the way we need to talk—you're not in the band anymore," so it was sort of funny. I really didn't know what to think. It was a really, really bad time because I had just quit Two Star Tabernacle because it just wasn't as fulfilling as I thought, and the White Stripes was taking up so much more of my time. I was trying to concentrate; I was just between the White Stripes and the Go, so it was kind of a depressing time.

Dan Trager: You're talking about immense egos in the studio. Matt Smith couldn't be a more influential person in that first Go record. Jack disagreed with Matt's approach, and Bobby's ego was just as strong or stronger than Jack's.

Matthew Smith: That was the beginning of bands getting on bigger labels, the Go on Sub Pop.

Tyler Spencer: The Go signing with Sub Pop made it frustrating for a lot of other bands; there was definitely some jealously on my part.

John Krautner: Detroit wasn't accepted as a city worth of bands yet. It was just us that got signed to Sub Pop; a year later Jack is getting some recognition in the UK, and then his whole thing started up, which in turn made bands like the Von Bondies get big.

Chris Fuller: The image being drawn of Detroit was that everyone spent all day listening to *Back from the Grave* comps and came out at night in their Prince Valiant haircuts. It wasn't true; the scene was really varied, there were all kinds of different bands.

John Szymanski: I bought everything I could out of the Crypt catalog.

Dave Buick: I don't know that anyone ever managed to dispel that image, but it was irritating.

Chris Fuller: You could go between the Magic Stick and the Gold Dollar and see all these great bands, and it would not be accurate to say they were all garage bands. And most of the people who were in bands really knew a lot about music. At that time you couldn't half-ass it and work.

Joe Burdick (*The Dirtys, bassist, vocalist*): Tim Warren came to town to see us after he heard the demos. He had a rental car, and we took the car out with him, and we started doing lawn jobs with his car. We were trying to run people down on Jefferson, trying to make him believe we were out of our minds.

Tim Warren: They were all over the fucking place; they were totally fucked up.

Joe Burdick: We were acting like junkies even though none of us were at that point. We told him we needed an image to get him to spring for jackets for us. Then we took him to an after-party at Jim Diamond's and he fell asleep with jet lag, and we were all in his ear trying to do some osmosis on him telling him to sign the Dirtys. He woke up the next day and said, "Something tells me I should sign you guys."

Tom Potter: The Dirtys were from Port Huron, and Bantam was still living in Lansing, and in Detroit they're like, "Oh, these cocksuckers from Lansing and Port Huron get deals?" Both bands moved to Detroit pretty soon, though.

Joe Burdick: Tim gave us $5,000 to record the album, which we did at Ghetto. It was supposed to cover a lot of stuff, a van and more. It didn't, but we did make sure we never ran out of beer. We ended up calling Tim a week before we left on tour and said we were out of money and said we needed another $1,000 for a van. We left a month before the album came out, so no one showed up at our shows. And there we were, splitting 99-cent Whoppers. That tour our van broke down at least ten times. We missed a lot of shows. We also crashed the van. Me and Marc had just smoked a joint, and we were driving at night through the middle of Wyoming. Marc says, "Hey, put on our record again." You know, "Let's listen to ourselves again because we're awesome." Marc's driving, and he goes, "Man, we rule," and right when he says that we're going sideways on black ice on the highway. We ping-ponged between guard rails, and there's steam coming from the engine. We popped a tire. By the time we got to LA everything was going cool. We knew Rick Hall, who was editing *Leg World*, a Larry Flynt magazine. We played Al's Bar, and after the show, Rick says, "Hey if you want to, we can have you guys check out Larry Flynt publications." We had already gotten an offer to check out Universal, but Larry Flynt, sure. So we went there the next day—no naked chicks. On the way out Rick goes, "Here, take this, and try and cover it up," and it's this box full of porn magazines and video tapes. Before we left I knew this girl who worked at the health department in Michigan who give me a bag of condoms. They were in a brown paper bag, and of course it ripped the first night out and it spills condoms all over the floor of the van. We get pulled over one night in Birmingham, Alabama. The cop shines his light in the van, and here's this box of porn and rubbers all over the van, and we try to tell him the story. "Yeah, we know the editor of a porn magazine" and so on. He didn't know what we were talking about, but he let us go. We also bartered some of the porn for chicken dinners at this chicken place in California. The guy's name was Hector or something; he was this gang-banger with a scar running from his ear to his mouth. We invited him to the show, and he comes up and says he can play. Larry gives him his guitar, and we're like, "What can you play?" He doesn't know, so I say, "Johnny B Goode." He plays nothing even close, just racket, and we looked at each other and he's all into it, thinks he's a rock star. At the end he even put a towel around his neck. So we're hanging out behind the club, and he starts getting mad at us. He goes, "You're gonna forget me," and he pulls out a knife and starts waving it around. We're like, "Listen, we're sure not gonna forget you now."

Steve Nawara: The Electric Six toured for three years straight it seemed. We did Europe a lot. We were in Edinburgh, Scotland, and were hitting these vodka bars with some girls. We come back to the bus, and people have their drugs out, and this girl is like, "Hey, you want some ecstasy?" And I, of course, say, "Oh yeah," and she hands it to me, and I grab a bottle of Jack Daniels and pull on it to wash down the X. And the whiskey hit my stomach in a weird way—you know how that happens? I lost the fight with it and projectile vomited, sprayed everyone in the back of the bus. These girls are covered with puke, and I look on one girl's shoulder, and there was the hit of X I had just taken. I just reached over with a finger and pulled it off and took it again.

Jim Diamond: I joined the Dirtbombs at the end of '97; Mick always had this rotating cast. Tom Potter joined in '99, and we toured a lot. Potter would run off all the time. Someone would say, "Hey, I got some speed." We were in Melbourne at the bar owned by Bill from the Cosmic Psychos. We didn't go on until 2 or 3 a.m., and we had to leave for the airport at seven. Tom takes off with some locals after we get done playing. I said, "Tom, don't leave. We gotta leave here at like 5 a.m. and go back to the hotel, then go to the airport." He's like, "Fuck you, Diamond. I'll be back. Fuck you. Quit telling me what to do." And lo and behold, he doesn't come back. I told the driver, "Go. We're not all missing our plane because he's not there." So we go back to the hotel, and we're sitting in the van, and the driver says, "What do you want to do?" I said, "Leave. We gotta go. We're not all paying extra money to rebook our flight because we're waiting for Tom." I said, "I don't know what we're going to tell Katy," his wife.

Ben Blackwell: There was a saying in the band, which was "DTK": Don't Tell Katy.

Chris Fuller: She grew up around drugs and was really down on them. Which made it tough for Tom.

Jim Diamond: Right as we're leaving—I mean the driver had the engine on and was starting to pull away—Tom gets out of a car and runs up. He was out doing drugs with someone. I wasn't the boss of the band, but I would deal with the booking agents and the drivers and the money and all that stuff. Mick didn't have to. We just made sure he could sit in the front seat all the time. Tom and I always called driving around Mick driving Miss Lazy. Tom came up with that one.

Dave Feeny: Mick is a genius, but when I worked with him I'd have to pick him up for the day's session. It would always be "My aunt has the car." Of course, I'd say, "Sure, I'll come get you."

Tom Potter: We practiced at Diamond's studio, and most of the time I'd be giving Mick a ride home because Mick didn't have a car. Yeah, I was driving Miss Lazy. On the route to drive Mick home we'd go up Cass Avenue and it would take us through a little drug dealer district. Driving a gunmetal gray van with a white dude driving a black dude in a van through the drug district, we'd get pulled over. A lot. We're in a van, so the cops would pull us over, and they'd be, like, on the speaker, like, "You need to step out of the van. Put your hands behind your head. You have to back up." So you'd get behind the van, and then they would come up, and they'd go through the glove box to make sure there wasn't a gun or anything. "Do you have any drugs on you?" We'd be like, "No." And they'd say, "Okay, you can go." I think every time it happened I was actually holding.

Mick Collins: I don't know what they're talking about. I had a car.

Ben Blackwell: In 2002 we're driving to Toledo for a show in Tom's van, which has become kind of the de facto Dirtbombs van at this point, and we're going southbound on 75. We get a flat tire and we don't have a spare. So we get taken to the Detroiter Travel Plaza, and it was a process. The Sights were opening for us, and they—it was one of those things you see in movies—they were told, "Keep going. Play some more songs." Because it's a nearby show, I have a bunch of family there. My mom and dad are sitting, waiting in Toledo, wondering where the hell I am. We get back on the road, we're driving down, and we drive past Toledo. No one had a map; it was just, "Oh yeah, Toledo! We know where to go." Everyone was oblivious to it. At some point in all of this, Tom Potter's driving, and the drummer for this show is Nick Lloyd from the Dirtys, filling in for Pat Pantano. Nick has cut up some lines of cocaine on a CD, and we're on the freeway, we're driving, and Tom looks back at me and says, "Safety first," and does a line. And we're lost. I was like, "Okay, yeah that's funny," you know. Fucking Potter. We finally get there and play. After the show I'm just gonna ride back with my mom and dad. I just had to grab my stuff out of the van, and my mom walks over to it with me, and I turn around and she says, "What's this?" She pulls out a rolled up dollar bill that she finds. I've never done any drugs, and she knows that, so she says, "Whose is this?" and I went, "Well, it's Potter's." She's like, "What should I say to him?" She goes back, finds Tom, and she has the rolled up dollar bill in her hand. She goes up to Potter and hands him the dollar bill and says, "Safety first." Walks away.

Ko Melina: The Dirtbombs had three or four shows that Jim couldn't do; he had some recording commitments. Mick gave me a tape to hear and learn and I said, "When are we going to practice?" He said, "Well, the shows are on the Fourth of July, so I guess on the Fourth of July we'll meet you on stage."

Troy Gregory: I got off a plane from Los Angeles after playing a gig with the Volebeats and went right to play a Dirtbombs show at the Stick, doing all new material. He had given me the disc to listen to, but we never played it together. That was just a roadmap—everyone has the map; you just don't know if it's going to be freezing rain. Being a good band is dealing with chaos.

Ben Blackwell: I'm at Jack's house and Mick calls Jack and he's talking about the Dirtbombs needing a drummer. Subsequently Mick has told me that he was kind of hoping Jack would play drums, but I was standing right there, and Jack said, "Oh, you should talk to my nephew Ben. He's right here."

EWolf: I was drummer number four in the Dirtbombs. Mick was a furry, and that was just starting to come out when we did the *Horndog Fest* cover. Mick said, "See, there's this whole scene like furry fandom, and so I've got this artist, and he's this big furry, and he's going to do the cover." He may as well have been talking about cocaine for all I knew. How would I know it was some kind of sex costume thing? Some people dress up like Captain Kirk. Whatever.

Eddie Sights, aka Eddie Baranek (*The Sights, Ko and the Knockouts, guitarist, vocalist*): The furries would come on tour with us when we toured with the Dirtbombs. We were in Ottawa at the Dominion Tavern. But the crowd was all those normal-looking white guys in their 40s with collared, tucked-in white shirts, and they would walk up to Mick and talk with him, and we would go, "What the fuck is this?" Ko and Jim, they'd be like, "Oh, it's the furries CD, *Horndog Fest*." There was a subcollective of them that would come to the Dirtbombs/Sights gigs when we played.

Mick Collins: The art for *Horndog Fest* was done by a guy named Joe Rosales. It's not totally a sexual thing, but essentially it's a comic for media fandom offshoots for people who are into touching animals. But yes, I am into furries. And I do go to the conventions.

Eddie Sights: The Dirtbombs were in Las Vegas playing the Shakedown. It was Potter, Diamond, Mick and Ben, and Pat Pantano, and there was always the band hotel room. Tom Potter's like, "Well, I'm going to get my own hotel room 'cause I'm going to party." Jim Diamond's like, "Well, I'm an adult, so I'm going to get my own hotel room." Ben Blackwell has his own thing. It broke down that Mick was left out in the cold. Mick's like, "Well, uh, where's the band hotel room?" I'm thinking, "What do you mean? You're the leader of the band." But out of the blue, this little nerdy white guy in glasses walks up to him and says, "Mick Collins? I've loved your work since Blacktop and the Gories." This nerdy guy goes, "I can't stay for the festival. I can't see you play, but I'm going to buy you a hotel room because I love you so much. You're my idol." And that's Mick Collins. Shit falls in his lap because he's so damn good in a way that people will take care of it.

Jack White: Mick Collins should be bigger; he's just brilliant, it boggles your mind. Detroit had all that stuff, and people said that about Brendan Benson too, especially because of the pop nature of his stuff. Brendan should be massive, and same thing as Mick. Funny thing is, even with the Gories, that was royalty to everybody in Detroit, but this is a sub-sub-genre of rock 'n' roll. You would go across the country, and nobody knew who you were talking about, all these Detroit bands. It made me, even more so, say we have this burning, volcanic scene going on, and we're so far away from everybody else that if it had happened in San Diego or Chicago, it would have gotten picked up and maybe ruined, and so it was a beautiful thing about it too.

The Same Boy
You've Always Known

Bobby Harlow: I'll tell you something about Jack: Jack would leave; Jack would disappear. He'd come in, and he'd do his show. He might stand around for a little while. Everyone else would get completely plowed, and Jack would be gone. In retrospect I think that's a pretty interesting thing. That's actually the way to do a show. When you're drunk, you think you're really good, but you're not. So Jack was always sober.

Jack White: I had little to no interest in anything but the music and the friendships, the family of it. Other than that, when everybody was doing anything else, I guess I just wasn't interested. It was just a little bit boring to me. I also thought girls weren't into me, so I wasn't pursuing that. And if you're not trying to get laid, I mean, hanging out after 3 a.m. in the bar, it's kind of pointless almost. I also had girlfriends, too, at the time. I wasn't really a drinker. I've never done drugs. I'm not anti that they did drugs; it didn't matter to me. I just never did it.

Tom Potter: Everybody keeps saying that Jack was checking us out, trying to get our moves. I don't think so. I get sick of people who are, "Oh, the White Stripes were a two piece." Our album came out before those two even started. As far as I know, he was busy listening to Rage Against the Machine. Seriously, you'd get in his car and look through his CDs in the car, and it was like Rage Against the Machine and that kind of stuff.

Jack White: I checked out any music, and it wasn't just obscure stuff. I would watch any documentary on television about any band—I didn't care who they were. I would watch the stupidest hair-metal band. I was always interested in how people were doing this, because you could learn so much of what not to do from things too.

Ben Blackwell: I went with Jack and Meg for a weekend early on. I played drums in Two Star Tabernacle, filling in for Damian in November of '98. They had a sweet gig lined up in Chicago opening for Jeff Tweedy's solo act at Lounge Ax. Two Star had just put out its first seven-inch, which was them and Andre Williams doing "Ramblin' Man" by Hank Williams. Damian had broken his foot. I did a handful of practices, but I had never played a live show before. It was a Thursday night show, then the next day we had off and we just hung out in Chicago. Saturday the White Stripes played; it was their first time playing Chicago, also at the Lounge Ax. Jack wanted to stay at the rock-and-roll Days Inn. Jack knew that all the rock bands stayed there. He told us when he was in Goober and the Peas they stayed there, and they saw Oasis's tour bus there.

Dan Kroha: When I heard that Jack and Meg broke up and Meg was working at Memphis Smoke, I went to there when Meg was working. I don't know why I was compelled to do this. I said, "Meg, I heard you and Jack broke up." I said, "Keep the White Stripes going. You got something good going on. I've been through this before with the Gories and Doll Rods. We kept the band going. It worked out. Keep doing it."

Ko Melina: They got a divorce, and at that point it was the band or the marriage, and they went with the band.

Jack White: There was a moment where she wasn't interested anymore for sure. We had one gig booked left, and I said, "All right, well, what do you want to do? Do you want to play this show, or do you want me to cancel this?" And she said, "All right, I'll play it." It was the Metro Times' Blowout in Hamtramck thing, and all of our friends came, and everybody sang along with the songs, and it was quite shocking. It was very unlike all those people. They're all nice, kind people. But it was unlike them to emote in that way. I'd never felt something like that. It was kind of a gruff time, and it was a gruff kind of scene—jaded—and it can be harsh feeling. So it was a beautiful moment that not only did they emote to us and say, "We love what you're doing—don't stop," that it affected Meg enough to keep her in the band. Sometimes Meg is very stubborn and impenetrable, but she would maybe say, "Uh-huh, thank you, uh-huh, that's very sweet, but I'm not doing this anymore." But it did affect her, and maybe those people talked to her too. I don't know.

Chris Fuller: One of the best White Stripes shows ever was at the Magic Bag shortly after Jack and Meg had broken up. Jack played a lot of piano that night, and he was staring right at Meg. It was frustration and anger.

Eddie Baranek: One of the first times I met Jack White was at the Magic Stick, and he asked me, "Can I record your band?" I was kind of weird with him because I was like, "I heard, like, you have to play guitar on the recording. Is that true?" He said, "Yeah." I said, "In that case, no."

Jim Diamond: I mixed the first White Stripes 45. He recorded it at home and then brought the tapes over here to mix. They had a really good look. They were more conscious of that kind of stuff than everyone else. Everyone else is walking on stage, looking like they just got done weeding the garden. People didn't really have a look. The Dirtbombs had a look because they had a black guy and two drums. That was the look. Jack and Meg came to Ghetto to do their first album, and we had to do a lot of takes because she wasn't a drummer. He taught her how to play the drums, but he didn't play any of the drums—he let her. We had to do take after take after take, because she would fuck up.

Marcie Bolen (*Von Bondies, Baby Killers, guitarist, vocalist*): I started dating Jack in '99. He still played in the Go once in a while at that time, and he was still married, but they were separated. She moved out and I moved in. They had been separated for a while. We dated right when they started doing some random touring. They were traveling in a van together and going around, and he was calling me and said, "You know we play these weird small towns, and people are kind of rude to us beforehand. But after we get done playing people treat us totally different."

Ben Blackwell: Early on the White Stripes did three shows opening for Pavement, which would probably be the first real touring. That was in Towson, Maryland, someplace in North Carolina and the 40 Watt in Athens, Georgia. The album came out in May, and this was September. We had an album and a single on Sympathy and two singles on Italy, a smaller label.

Larry Hardy (*In the Red Records, founder*): One of the big regrets of my career is that I missed the White Stripes. Jack sent me the first single with a really nice letter asking me if I wanted to work with them. I was working with the Doll Rods and Andre Williams at the time, and they both had releases where I was going to employ a publicist, and I thought, "Well, I'll get back to him." Mick and the Doll Rods were strongly urging me to work with Jack, and I had heard nothing but good stuff. But I just didn't, and the next thing I knew they were with Sympathy with Long Gone John. I felt like the guy at Decca who lost the Beatles. I still have the letter from Jack. I have collectors asking me to trade them for the letter, but I don't want that out there as a testament to my badness.

Ko Melina: Long Gone John was doing records with all the bands in Detroit; he was really ahead of it all. He knew something.

Dave Buick: As far as anybody outside of Detroit, Long Gone John put out a Cobras record and through Steve Shaw and myself, we got him copies of the White Stripes singles on Italy. And he just realized that they had something. I encouraged Jack to put stuff out with Sympathy because I knew it would get out there more. In hindsight, I wish I hadn't done that.

Long Gone John (*Sympathy for the Record Industry, founder*): Later on there was a movie, *It Came from Detroit*, and someone said I offered these bands $5,000. It was unheard of for anyone to give someone money who didn't have something going on.

Rachel Nagy: Long Gone made it possible for us to even exist. I mean, if we had $5,000, we could have done this all ourselves, but he had it. He did it. The guy is kind of a scammer, but at the same time anytime we need anything, he's there. So he's also pretty much a peach.

Long Gone John: I had always done records with Detroit bands. I did a single with Ron Asheton, Destroy All Monsters. I love Niagara.

Ben Blackwell: I was working for Italy Records, trying to move records. It was fun talking to people and asking, "What's going on there?" or "What records you got coming out?" The closest I had ever come to that before was doing phone orders with people at Sub Pop when I was still fifteen or sixteen and trying to tell them about the White Stripes. I'd say, "There's this really good band in Detroit." I'm just short of saying, "Should I send in a demo or something?" They said, "Oh, you know, the best a band can do is just put out their own records and tour." That's really cool, because the White Stripes ended up doing a single on Sub Pop basically through the power of putting out their records and touring. After *De Stijl* had come out was the point where Meg quit her day job. They were touring strong; there's only two people, so it's a lot easier when you're playing $500 a night gigs. So when I heard that, I was kind of like, "What? Meg doesn't need a day job? She can get by just on the band?" I knew the money from being around and seeing day sheets and knowing what their take for shows was. I was selling the merch too, so I definitely knew that. But I was a kid; I don't think I knew in real life what a person needs to get by.

Marcie Bolen: Von Bondies were playing in Buffalo, and they were playing in New York. I took a train down to New York and met him at Grand Central Station and then went on a tour with him and Meg in their van. There was me, Jack, and Meg. I drove once in a while. Then the White Stripes and Von Bondies toured together, first in the US.

Jason Stollsteimer: We knew who Long Gone John was because he put out a record by the Makers, who were one of my favorite bands. I knew he was at the Magic Stick one New Year's Eve. He looks like the beast from Beauty and the Beast, hair-wise.

Joe Burdick: Von Bondies weren't on Long Gone John's radar until after the White Stripes. John did the Cobras then the White Stripes then Von Bondies. He had come from LA to a New Year's Eve show in Detroit to see the Cobras and the White Stripes. Steve Nawara went up to Long Gone—he never saw him before and didn't know who he was—and he goes, "Sammy Hagar, what up?" Steve was trying to be funny, but no one wants to be called Sammy Hagar. We were like, "Ah, shit man."

Jason Stollsteimer: John—which is how he gets away with murder, bless his soul—helped a lot of bands that weren't very good at the time. We were just sloppy rock 'n' roll. There were certain things that he required from bands. If a band had a girl in it, there was a 90 percent chance he would put it out. One girl—it doesn't even matter if they play tambourine, if they're the singer, or the main song—he doesn't care. One of the opening bands was the White Stripes. We played by the men's bathrooms, with a little PA system with one microphone, and we're on floor level, so all you could see is me. He had no idea there were girls in the band because they were so short. The only thing he can see is from my nose up. "I really like

the sound and I really think you could put out a record with this. I'm Sympathy
Records. I'll sign you for $2,500." He was a mix between Seymour Stein and some
cartoon character. He gave us the $2,500. We spent $1,300 making the record and
took the rest of the money and got a van. Jack produced it, and we recorded at Diamond's. The album with Sympathy came out in 2001. Jack produced it, and they
were going on tour and invited us. The White Stripes weren't big yet. In Montana
there were 45 people. Chicago, 200 to 250 at the Empty Bottle. For the Detroit
scene they were the biggest band by that time, late 2001. Kid Rock was bigger, but
we never had seen him at a show in our lives.

Marcie Bolen: Jack would call me when they were starting to break and say, "Oh
my God, we played this show, and all of a sudden I looked out, and I could see
these people singing all the words."

Ko Melina: The White Stripes went on tour with Sleater-Kinney, and that was
a huge deal for anybody in Detroit. They also got offered to do an ad for the Gap
for something like $75,000, and Jack turning it down. I thought, "Man, they're a
really big deal now."

Jack White: I think that was one of the first offers we got for some money, and we
turned it down. The funny thing was, a lot of those things, we really didn't know
what to do. We needed the money, but we said no to it.

Tyler Spencer: One of the biggest solids I've ever had done for me came from Jack.
He sang background on our song "Danger High Voltage" and never asked for a
dime. His involvement in that song was a big part of us getting a deal, and my life
changed dramatically. He could have reasonably asked for money, and he didn't.

Timmy Vulgar: When the Stripes made it, Jack invited Clone Defects to come on
a few shows and open for them. We played six shows with 'em. We played for two
thousand people. He took a few bands from Detroit on the road with him. Totally
cool. You know, support your buddies with what you got. When we did that tour,
they were on tour in a beautiful, nice, rock-star bus, and we were in a rusty, old,
shitty minivan, following 'em. We had all our equipment stored underneath, inside
the bus. We'd get to where we were gonna play at 6:00 p.m. We'd set up, do a sound
check, and go backstage and drink a bunch and hang out with Jack and Meg. They
weren't ego'd out at all. They made sure we were taken care of. When we played our
set, we didn't have to set up our shit—there was crew. Then the crew would help

take our shit down. Then we'd go on our way. Every bar we went to afterwards we got kicked out of. After playing in Milwaukee, we were still at the hall, and I went up to a cop, that was like a security cop. Aren't those real police that do the security? I took a Clone Defects button and I went up to him and I pinned the Clone Defects button onto the cop. He's like, "WHAT ARE YOU DOING?" I'm like, "That's my button, man." And he says, "Walk away. Walk away." I walk away and I go towards the backstage, and I started breakdancing in this little area. Then I fell over and knocked some shit over. Then I went back in the backstage area, passed out on the couch, and they had a security guard watching the room to make sure I didn't come out and fuck any more shit up.

Jim Diamond: The first White Stripes record didn't do much at the time. But they always had a good gimmick with the color scheme and the way they looked. And they toured a lot; they worked really hard. I did their second record, which they recorded at Jack's house and mixed it here. I asked, "Why?" Jack told me the first record cost $2,000, including the tape. The second record, he said, "Yeah, all those drums, all the time it took, we wasted too much money, doing all the takes. So I'd rather do it at home." So the second record probably cost $1,000. Who knows what I charged him to mix the whole thing. Probably nothing. The third album, that was the one. They recorded that in Memphis.

Marcie Bolen: I went to Romania when Jack was doing the film with Renee Zellweger. He was talking about Renee a lot, but we had already broken up and got back together a few times. It was toward the end of our relationship. He was talking about how cool Renee was. He found a skull in Romania in an antique store, and he's like, "It's a skull, and Renee could tell how old the skull was just by looking in its mouth." I said, "You guys have become really good friends." He said, "Yeah, she's really cool. Talk to her on the phone." I talked to her on the phone, and it was like, "Hey, how are you?" Next thing I know they're dating. We were broken up, though. We were on and off, the last five months—we were like on and off. He'd bought a new house. I don't know about their breakup, but she got married to Kenny Chesney right after him.

Larry Hardy: Fat Possum offered $25,000 for that third LP *White Blood Cells*. Sub Pop was in there too, and I understood Jack didn't want to work with them because the Go had released a record with Sub Pop, and he didn't like the way it was handled. Bobsled wanted to do a record with them too, but Sympathy came up with the $25,000.

Long Gone John: I licensed and put out their records and paid for all of that. I just didn't make money on it.

Jack White: We were involved with all the other small labels because of their knowledge of Sympathy and Long Gone John. And I think they all kind of just backed off, like, "It's Long Gone's project; he's gotten a hold of these guys" or something. But he didn't really have a hold of us. We were loyal people, me and Meg, but there were no contracts. There was no mainstream major label, real label interest, until our third album was already out.

EWolf: Jack was really open and friendly at the start of everything. I did some photos, and it was all fine. Later, though, after they got signed to V2, they wanted to relicense the photos. I'm used to doing things with just a handshake, and all of a sudden I've got their management and legal team on me, demanding possession of the negatives. I didn't know if it was Jack, because initially I had to get the negatives back from him, after he had used them for the graphics, and he was fine. But now their management was coming back, and they're trying to demand possession of them and all the rights and everything.

Marcie Bolen: Jason said something to me about Jack being jealous, but I didn't see it. Not of me and him but, he told me that Jack got jealous of me and Meg, but I never saw it. If anyone's going on tour with their ex-wife, of course it's a little weird. They were on tour, and we were on tour, and we'd talk on the phone. I liked Meg, and I wanted to know that I could trust him with Meg. What am I going to do? I'm not going to say, "Don't be in a band with her." They were doing really well. I could either break up with him or deal with it.

Long Gone John: I went on an East Coast tour with the White Stripes and the Von Bondies. The Von Bondies record had just come out, and there was real severe friction between Jack and Jason. Jack did not like that guy, and he was jealous of Jason's relationship with Marcie. They were just friends, but they were in a band together. Even when Jack had nothing to do with Meg anymore, he did not like anyone else to be with Meg.

Jason Stollsteimer: At the Magic Stick there was never a fight. I got sucker punched. I didn't go to the police. Because there were so many witnesses, it was the state of Michigan that filed against him. I never sued him. I never took Jack White to court. How many times in history have two people from the local scene been that well documented? Within twenty-four hours he went to the police and said that I attacked him, which later he admitted he lied about that. He's, like, six-four, and I don't know how to throw a punch. I'm six-one, but he outweighed me by 70 pounds. He was, like, 210, like, six-four, and I was, like, six-foot-one, 140. It's like if a high school kid beat up a middle school kid. I've met more people that say there were witnesses to it than physically could have been there. "Oh man, I was there." "No, you fuckin' weren't. You actually were playing a show that night in another city. I know you weren't there. Stop being an idiot."

Jack White: It was a bar fight with somebody who is very manipulative, and that's why everyone heard about it. Had I gotten in a fight with Dave Buick, you wouldn't have heard about it. Or John Krautner. He had a history of manipulation with everybody on the scene and especially me.

Marcie Bolen: I was at the Magic Stick that night talking to Jack. We were broken up, but I gave him a present, a little stuffed baby duck, but he didn't want it. I was like, "All right. Fine. Whatever. Whatever. We're broken up. That's fine. I'll keep it myself." Then he started going over to Jason. He was pissed, and I was like, "Oh man, something's going to go down." I just knew he was in such a bad mood, and I was going over to Jason, "Stop. Don't do it." Jack was yelling at him and I was hitting him on the back, "Don't, don't, don't, don't." All of a sudden they were fighting. I had to walk away. And after that night Jack and I have never been friends again. He's like, "You didn't stick up for me. You told the lawyer that, what I did." I'm like, "I just said what I saw." What else can I do? He's like, "Fuck you. You should have stood up for me. That guy never stuck up for you." I have been caught between Jack and the Von Bondies.

Tom Potter: Shit, a year earlier no one would have cared about that whole thing.

John Krautner: It was just a bar fight. Nothing more.

Jason Stollsteimer: The only other thing that happened that night was press related. And everybody knew this. The next morning I had a cover of *Spin, Blender*—a four-page article in *Blender*—and *NME*. This was Von Bondies coverage, for advance of *Pawn Shoppe Heart*. They all got canceled because of the incident, and we never got them back. The record came out, and they were supposed to give me all this coverage. Our record review in *Spin* was five out of five. All the reviews were great, but every press blurb about it was only about the incident, not about the band. Our record had already sold thirty to forty thousand copies in prerelease, and it actually killed our record sales. It did not help. It's a total lie if anybody says it helped. We were supposed to have a cover on *Blender*. And instead of having the photo that they were gonna have of the band, they had one of me with a black eye. All of our interviews turned into that. The thing that sucked—we had mutual friends, local guys, who said he knew that I had all that press. So for him to pick that day, the day before our biggest press day ever, still irks me. I still have my press sheet from *Sire* saying what all of our interviews are, and they all got canceled. December 13 or whatever it was. I couldn't do them. I couldn't see. I was still in the hospital. My whole face was swollen. I was unconscious after the first punch.

Jack White: It took a while for me to understand that guy. I let him rehearse in my house for a long time. They asked me to produce their album, and I did, but they didn't want to put my name on the album. It was sort of like, "Well, we don't want people thinking. . . ." Well, why did you ask me to produce the record? That kind of stuff. Which, in its own essence, I don't give a damn about, but when someone starts getting insulting and saying things about you in the press, you're kind of like, "Wait a minute, dude, I did that for free, and you guys rehearsed in my house for free, and I took you guys on tour, and I could have picked some other band. I got you guys signed to Sympathy, all of that." Stuff I wouldn't even have said out loud because it sounds so self-serving. I didn't give a damn about that until it came back negatively to me, and I was like, "Wait a minute, hold on a second, get out the scorecard here for a second." It's also winning the fight, you know what I'm saying? It's like, I saw someone a couple days later who said, "You should have given yourself a bloody nose."

Rachel Nagy: Jack White is the only person in this whole scene that I'm glad he has made it. He is ambitious, he's clever, and he lifted up everybody in Detroit. Every interview he did, he lifted everybody up, including us. He helped a lot of people along the way, and a lot of people feel bad now, including Jason Stollsteimer from the Von Bondies. What did Jason do? Turned around and said, "Jack didn't do nothing for me." Ahh! Fuck you, you dick. I would've fucking gutted him like a fucking bitch. Jack, when he started getting successful, everybody had that sour grapes: "Well, I could have done that. I should have done that." Oh, really? Well, you didn't. I don't like everything Jack does, and quite frankly, I don't really enjoy his music. But I respect the fuck out of him.

Ko Melina: I thought the Von Bondies were going to be the next big band, because Jack had heavily promoted them so much and taken them on tour so much, so it kind of seemed natural that they would be the next to get big.

Jason Stollsteimer: I never defended myself in the press—what was the point? He was just becoming huge right then. You can't stand up to the local god. My lawyer said to me immediately, "Minimum $250,000 in damages because you were about to break. Your record just came out and you had all this press, and we can prove it." I said, "I wanna make my own money." I really didn't want his money. He went to court for criminal stuff; it wasn't civil. When they said, "Do you want to settle?" I go, "Settle what? I want him to say that he did it." I've never said his band is bad. People say, "What do you think of the White Stripes?" I think they're an amazing band and very unique. I don't like the guy. After the album came out the interviewers asked about it every time. And if you notice, 90 percent of the interviews I never answered. The 10 percent that I did I regret.

Jim Diamond: The White Stripes made it huge and then, to a much lesser degree, bands like the Cobras, the Electric Six, the Dirtbombs, out of that whole scene. The only thing that went awry with that was I felt that I should get a royalty off the first White Stripes record. Jack was like, "You're not getting a fucking dime. You didn't do shit." I had some legal counsel that had some dollar signs in this person's eyes. So I sued, and my lawyer convinced me, "No, you don't want to just go after royalties. What we should do is, you are involved with copyright here. You are a coauthor of the sound recording." He showed me all this case history and said, "No, you are a coauthor of the actual sound recording." Not the writing of the song but the physical sound recording. I said, "That's not what I'm interested in. I just want, like, a fucking two points off the sales." I spent $5,000 on depositions.

Eddie Baranek: I was deposed. I called Jim and I said, "I love you Jim, but don't fucking involve me in this shit." Friends of mine went down there to be deposed, and I said, "How is it?" They said, "There's a little pudgy guy who's a real asshole, and you do not want to be in a room with that guy. You will be there for a few hours, and he will just kill you." That was Jack's lawyer. I didn't want to go down there. I don't have anything against Jack. Jack got successful. Like, whatever—he got his and that's good, you know. And it helped everyone else in this town.

Tyler Spencer: I ran into Jack one day at Eastern Market and we had lunch. He told me he had two ideas about being sued. One was putting up billboards in Detroit that read, "Jim Diamond Sues His Friends." The other was buying the building that Jim has his studio in and evicting him.

Jim Diamond: I wish someone had sat down and said, "You know we shouldn't do this, Jim. It'll fuck up your reputation. It will make you look like a jerk. We shouldn't go after copyright." No one took into account this guy's a superstar and a millionaire and a very powerful person at this point. It shouldn't have been a jury trial. I was watching jurors sleep when I was there. I'm thinking, "Oh my God, this doesn't bode well." Then they just saw this star who won a Grammy. His lawyer kept saying, "Well, this is a Grammy winner who worked with Loretta Lynn and such luminaries." I was on some entertainment show called *Entertainment Justice*. It was one of those like 1:30-in-the-morning shows on Channel 50. My sister called me up and told me they had a picture of me and they described me as this worm crawling out of the woodwork, just some guy hanging around in the studio. It made me look like a schmuck to most of the public. I saw shit in the *NME* about how "Jim Diamond claims he wrote the songs now" or "He claims he created the White Stripes." They don't know what coauthorship of a sound recording means. After I filed that lawsuit, my business just went, pssht. I mean garage rock was kind of done and then that. People didn't want to work with me.

Eddie Baranek: I know that in his heart to this day that Jim didn't give a fuck about the credit. And the town was already divided in a way, and that just completely drove the stake. It was one of those things, "Oh, and you're still recording at Jim's?" This was from people who would be in a band with Jim. That would tour with Jim. Certain people. I would go, "You fucking lowlifes." That's what I thought. They were siding with Jack because they don't want to get their little piece of the pie ruffled. So we still go into work the next day at Jim Diamond's. We still go to our studio because that's where I go. That's what I do.

Jim Diamond: The jury determined that in August of 2001 Jack and I had a conversation, and he said I was never getting a dime. And that's what I basically lost on.

Jack White: Jim Diamond was paid in full for the job he was asked to do, and that job was engineer our record. I have a paid receipt for it which was the only evidence we needed to show in court. The camera man for the film *Apocalypse Now* doesn't own part of the copyright of the film.

"It Was Raining
Faggots on Me"

Mike E. Clark (*Insane Clown Posse, Kid Rock, producer*): I didn't have a dad. I grew up in government housing on government cheese. My mom drank, a lot. I never got in trouble as a kid because I was afraid that if they called the cops, I knew they would call my mom, and I wouldn't know what condition she was in.

I got a job at GM and got laid off. I took some computer-assisted design classes and got a job and got laid off again. Then I saw recording courses, and I had already had all this shit downtown, and I just wanted to do live sound. That's what I wanted to do—a record or whatever. Music was my whole thing anyway. My mom was dying of cancer, in hospice at the time. I was like, "Mom, I'm going to take these recording courses." She knew I was trying to find a job. She's like, "Do it." You know, she wanted to be a singer when she was a kid, but she was too afraid to try. Now she totally had my back. I said, "I'm gonna do it. I'm gonna do it. I don't know what's going to happen." I hated the automotive industry. I hated the nine to five. I hated everybody in it, you know. She asked, "How much is it?" I told her, "It's $500 to get in." That's all she had left like in her account. But she's like, "I don't need it." She gave me fucking her last $500 to get into these recording courses. I started learning and I would always go to shows and approach the bands, "You wanna record?" The first thing was the Viv Akauldren thing, and then the second one was Gangster Fun. We were in a little closet practically, recording at this place, the Disc, where the main studio was upstairs. They wouldn't let me up there. Eventually I started working the main studio. It was a rap studio, though, and the rappers didn't want to work with me.

Although one day I came in and there was this woman waiting to record. She looked like a homeless lady, in the lobby. It turned out to be Patti Smith, recording an extra track for an album. Eventually there was this group called the Beat Boys, and Marvin Lewis was the guy who everyone wanted to record. Marvin was sick one day, and he said, "Mike, Beat Boys are coming in. You gotta do the session." I'm like, "No way." But I was it. They show up, and I'm like, "Marvin's sick and I'm doing your session." They just laughed at me, and they're like, "Bah hah, ain't no honkey gonna da, da, da." So I grab this LinnDrum machine and I'm starting to try to program a beat for them, and they're laughing at me. They finally just ended up leaving—laughing. I was so humiliated and so mad that I just looked at that fucking LinnDrum machine, "Okay, I will show you motherfuckers." And that was the beginning. I started learning that drum machine, then I learned the next drum machine, and I started this and this. I got a sampler.

Violent J, aka Joseph Bruce (*Insane Clown Posse*): When we met Mike, we couldn't believe his efficiency. Our first session with Mike was insane in how fast he moved.

Shaggy 2 Dope, aka Joseph Utsler (*Insane Clown Posse*): We had been working with this other guy, Chuck Miller, who took forever.

Violent J: We'd have a sample, and Mike would loop it up in thirty seconds. We'd be staring at each other with our jaws dropped. And he'd say, "Do you want some drums behind it?" And we'd say, "Yeah," and he'd just start putting drums behind it. Two minutes later he'd have a beat under it.

Shaggy 2 Dope: Oh yeah. He was on it, you know.

Dave Feeny: By then Mike was at Tempermill, before he set up at his own house, and ICP we're Mike's guys. He didn't think they were very good. But those guys, they were selling cassettes out of the back of their car. They always had money; they would come in and pay in advance—no one did that. It was, "Hey, we want to do another record—here's the money."

DJ Dianna: Violent J and Shaggy were part of the crew at St. Andrews for a while. They were like Mutt and Jeff, following each other around.

John Speck: I worked with them both at St. Andrews. Shaggy was a bar guy. Those guys were high school dropouts, but they really knew what they were doing. They were hard workers. They were total white trash.

Violent J: And we go to know the Detroit rock scene. We worked at St. Andrews Hall, and we knew everybody. We were right there in the middle of it. We were getting turned on to all kinds of music working there. Bands like Sick of It All, Helmet. We put guitars in our songs. We learned that early, you know what I'm sayin'?

Shaggy 2 Dope: It started out straight rap, you know but then it started morphing and morphing to what it's become. Initially we were rappers, that was it. But you know then once we saw what was going on, the bigger picture, we broadened our horizons a lot more. We both had such deep rock influences.

Violent J: At St. Andrews, we were mostly bouncers.

Shaggy 2 Dope: Mostly I would check IDs at the door.

Violent J: I'd work the pit where the people would come crowd surfing, and I'd work the between the stage and the barricade. We were definitely assholes at some points, but on Friday nights they had Three Floors of Fun, and it was nuts.

John Speck: It was a Friday night, three floors of fights we always called it. Three Floors of Fun.

Violent J: We were just really getting ICP going, you know, we had jobs and shit, but we were forming all this music. We got into all kinds of things then. The Faygo.

Shaggy 2 Dope: Run DMC had Adidas. Beastie Boys talked about White Castle. You know what I'm sayin'?

Violent J: Everybody had their own little thing in rap. So we just, at the time we always had a two liter of Faygo in our hands and—

Shaggy 2 Dope: It was real because all we drank was Faygo.

Violent J: We'd walk up to the store with no money and by the time we got to the store we'd have found enough returnables to buy a two-liter. We'd come back with a cold two-liter and we'd pass it like it was a fucking 40. So we had it on stage to drink. Somebody was flipping us off in the crowd, and Joey took a two-liter and opened it up and threw it at the kid.

Shaggy 2 Dope: Not the whole bottle.

Violent J: And the fucking whole place blew up. Yeah, so we started doing that. We started grabbing the rest of it and started spraying it on the crowd. The crowd went from sitting there to jumping around and going crazy.

Violent J: We got signed to Disney down the road. That's when *Great Milenko* came out. Slash played on it and he was totally cool. That's the one thing we argued with the label about at that point. You know we wanted Slash in the video, and Slash volunteered. He's like, "I want to be in the video. I want to do all that." And the label's like, "I don't think that's the right image for you guys." You know they were saying, he's yesterday's news. You guys are something new. And I'm like, that's fucking Slash, man. What're you talking about, "How you gonna tell Slash no?"

Shaggy 2 Dope: And he didn't even charge. He wanted a fifth of Wild Irish Rose.

Violent J: A fifth of Wild Irish Rose. Killed it right there. And then he wanted us to come to the titty bar with him and we couldn't even do that. We were like, "Oh we're going to stay and work the song." I wish I'd have went now, more than anything. He called the next morning and was like, "Turn the radio on. I'm about to do this interview." He told me what station to go to. We tuned it in, and he's sitting there talking all kinds of fresh shit about us on the radio, you know, giving us love, saying, "This group ICP is awesome." Then he called us to the concert that night, or the next night, and he wore a *Riddle Box* shirt when he was playing with Alice Cooper. Alice did a vocal part on *Milenko*, too. We flew to Phoenix to record it. He came right from the golf course, you know. He actually had on a golf outfit with the fucking spike shoes. All he talked about was getting back to the golf course. He was sitting on a bench, and I sat down next to him, and I said, "I just want to explain to you what this is that you're talking about here." And I gave him the quick one minute version of what the Dark Carnival is. And what the *Great Milenko* was because he did the spoken word intro. If I could have translated the look on his face it'd have been, "I could give a fuck less."

Mike E. Clark: We finished all the post-production on *Milenko* and the label, Hollywood, came to town. I was in Royal Oak in a bungalow. I had it all cleared out and I just had everything, like I had like cinder block shelves, cinder block boards. They wanted to see the studio that we recorded *Milenko*. They thought we were fucking with them because, we're in a basement. They're like, "You did not make this record here." They got an amazing record. It's almost double platinum right now.

Violent J: When everyone started freaking about *Milenko* and it got pulled from stores because of all the folks getting pissed about the lyrics and Disney and all that, they went to Alice Cooper and said, "How do you feel about that record?" And Alice Cooper said, "If I'd have known what the content of the record was, I wouldn't have done it." This is Alice fucking Cooper, okay? And we said, "Fuck him." We dissed him. We were younger, too, and we said, "Fuck him." You know what I'm sayin'? We got a call from his camp or something, I don't remember exactly how it worked, but they were like, "Please stop burying Alice." And we told them, "Tell him to grow some, grow a set and have our back."

Eddie Baranek: Halloween '99 me, Ben Blackwell, and our buddy Mike, we dressed up as Catholic school girls and played the Garden Bowl as the Little Dolls. The same night the Majestic Theatre next door had a sold out ICP Halloween show. Never before was I called faggot more times in my whole life than that night, dressed as a Catholic school girl. The Juggalos went crazy. It was raining faggots on me. I was very proud of that.

Jack White: For the blues series at Third Man, we were talking about different acts that come in, and I said, "There's one band in the whole world," and I swear to God I still believe this. There is only one band that you can say, "We're doing a record with blank," and people would say, "Are you serious?" I could say any other band you could think of and nobody would say are you serious? Death metal, Christian, gospel, anything, people would go, "Oh, okay, sure, sure." But you say Insane Clown Posse and people are like, "Are you serious?" And that reaction alone makes me definitely want to do something with them. And they lived in southwest Detroit, too, when I was a teenager. I saw their graffiti all the time, that said Inner City Posse. In the studio, they were like yeah, that was us, that's us; we were laughing. I thought that was a gang of like, twenty Mexican guys or something.

Devil with a Cause

Rob Miller: Kid Rock was one my stagehands at the State Theater, and I had to fire him. He was walking around handing the bands his cassette tapes when he was supposed to be working.

Karen Neal: Cathy from Inside Out was walking around backstage at the Latin Quarter, and Kid Rock asked her about her jacket, kind of hassling her. She was really proud of her jacket, and she said, "Yeah, it's a Brooks." He's like, "There's something on your lip." She picked off this little piece of lint and said, "It must be your dick."

Kenny Olson (*Kid Rock's Twisted Brown Trucker Band, guitarist*): Those Brooks jackets were great. I was going from St. Andrews to my place one night, and someone threw a rock at the back of my head and hit me. These guys ran up on me so fast. There was blood in my hair, and all I was worried about was them stealing my Brooks leather.

Ruzvelt: Way before he got big, Kid Rock played at Blondie's, opening for Insane Clown Posse. He came to the door and gave me a hard time. I was checking IDs and he said, "You're not going to check my ID." I said, "What are you talking about man? Are you going to drink tonight?" He says, "Yeah." So I says, "What the fuck? Give me your ID." He showed me the ID. He goes to my wife, who was bartending, "What the hell was that?" "That's the club owner." Not such a good guy.

Mike E. Clark: Kid Rock came into the studio when he had nothing out. He had a little Casio drum machine with all his beats programmed, and he had turntables and records. He had all his shit ready to go. He goes, "Play the first beat—okay, I'm

294

going to record that." He knew exactly everything he was going to do, and I'm like, "Hell no." Then he's like, "Okay, now I want to put cuts all over this." He was just killin' it on the turntables. Kid Rock knew exactly what he was doing.

Chris Peters (*Black Eyed Peas, Kid Rock, guitarist, Electric 6, songwriter, producer*): I met Kid Rock when I was the music editor at *Michigan Review* at U of M. He was trying to figure things out, moving from a hip-hop career into rock. Hip-hop didn't work for him. He'd do shows and come out in his pimp suit and charge people to take pictures of him. I gave him cassettes of the MC5 and the Stooges as he was segueing into this rock thing.

Kenny Olson: When we started in the midnineties, it was just a bunch of people getting in cars and going to closer markets like Chicago and places in Indiana and Ohio. It was just us.

Chris Peters: Rock couldn't have come from anywhere but Detroit. He came from hip-hop and made it rock.

Mike E. Clark: Kid Rock was in that studio to cut the demos to go to New York, to Jive. He had a posse, for sure. I knew he was going to get a deal. Sure enough, he goes out to New York, calls me, "Yeah, we got a deal with Jive." I'm like, "We're doing the record, right?" "Nah, I'm going to New York to do the record." Son of a bitch. He got dropped pretty quick. Vanilla Ice comes out and makes a bad name for everybody in the business because nobody wanted a white rapper on their label. Vanilla Ice just became a joke for some reason. When ICP got signed to Jive, Kid Rock called ICP and told them, "Man, don't do it," because he had just gotten burned off Jive.

Violent J: Rock's parents were rich. They paid for shit, you know what I'm sayin'?

Shaggy 2 Dope: Every time he bumped into us, it's not like he was living in a mansion. He had just a little shitty apartment.

Violent J: But when it came time to press the album, he had the money, you know what I'm sayin'? He didn't work a job nowhere. He had the money. He'd go to his family and get it. There's nothing wrong, if we had the family we'd have done it too. But we just . . . at the time we were like, "It ain't fair."

Shaggy 2 Dope: But he deserves everything that he had gotten. He was fucking here forever.

Chris Peters: Before he made it he was sleeping on my couch and hit on a woman roommate I had. With no success.

Kenny Olson: When I was playing with Rock and those guys, I started putting together the Twisted Brown Trucker Band. Our first shows sold out the State Theater in Detroit, and all of a sudden all these labels started coming after us. We went with Atlantic to start doing *Devil Without a Cause*. Seriously, we had no idea that this mixing the rock, hip-hop, funk, twang was some sort of big seller. And at first people were telling us we couldn't get away with putting all these genres together and make it work. We did our first album in the White Room in downtown Detroit. We took some of our advance and put a hot tub in the studio. There were two Detroit bands that came out with same shock value as Iggy and Alice: Eminem and us.

Aspiring and Achieving
Lowly Dreams

Ko Melina: The whole scene was always just us and our friends. But the friends grew. There were more and more people who were not necessarily musicians getting involved. More people who were just getting into the music. There became a point where you could do package Detroit tours. There were a couple New York things where it would be two or three nights in a row of all Detroit bands at the Bowery Ballroom. Ko and the Knockouts did one of those. White Stripes/Von Bondies. Bantam Rooster did like a Bantam Rooster/Dirtbombs package too.

Mick Collins: Suddenly all these balding, pony-haired dudes are around looking for the next White Stripes. It was laughable. People were moving there—like whole bands were moving there to make it. It was gonna be like the next Seattle, the next big rock scene; all these people were rolling around. In 2000 you might go see a band, and you could get a table, and you knew everyone else that was in there, and you'd start making rounds like, "Hey, what's up? What did you think of that record?" A year later you couldn't get into the show because it was packed, and if you could get in, it was people from out of town that you never saw before in your life. That lasted for a summer. Suddenly they were there, and suddenly they were gone.

Neil Yee: A reporter from some out-of-town newspaper asked me if Detroit was going to be the next Seattle, and some of the bands were even saying that, but I said, "If the corporate powers decide so, it will be." When this garage thing was becoming popular, I found myself being less experimental in what I was booking.

297

Tim Warren: You had the irony of these writers from *New Musical Express* interviewing these bands squeaking by on $25 a gig, turning them into superstars on paper that didn't translate to sales.

Jeff Ehrenberg (*The Starlite Desperation, drummer*): We moved from Monterey, California, to Detroit in July '99 and broke up in June 2000. We started doing national touring and had an album with another on the way. We thought we could make a living as a band by touring and making records. By that time San Francisco was dot-com and more expensive than New York City, and we knew we couldn't be a professional band in Monterey. The summer we wanted to make this decision we got stuck in Detroit, and we had all these shows canceled. We played a show at the Gold Dollar, and some friends from San Francisco were among the eight to ten people at the show. Then shows kept getting canceled, and there we were in Detroit. And we fell in love with Detroit, and that's where we decided to move. I went first and found us a place in Woodbridge on Commonwealth Street. We had a huge house; it was beautiful—place to rehearse and record. We were the first people to move in after it was taken over by a landlord; it was a former crack house. It got trashed real quickly; we had parties and so on. When we moved there it felt like *Cheers* where you go to a bar or a party and everyone knows your name. We had these great shows and people came out, and the after-parties. I don't think anyone expected the Stripes to break like they did. But pretty soon it was Seymour Stein and Japanese tourists. You would see tourists taking pictures of the Gold Dollar and some other venues. It seemed like a stop on the rock tour map for a while. That tour wasn't just Hitsville anymore.

Dave Buick: Eventually Jack and I were at the mall, and we saw they were selling "garage jeans" at Hot Topic, and at that point we stopped caring about any of it.

Mick Collins: Seymour Stein saw the Dirtbombs play, and he fell asleep during the show. Tommy Boy Records was looking at us for a signing. Tommy Boy Records? It was ridiculous in 2001; it was the summer of stupidity.

Tom Potter: I got a free lunch from Seymour. Like most major labels, they just wanted cute and young. Me and most other musicians in Detroit were just not fitting the bill.

John Szymanski: That whole thing came to an end on its own. A lot of us moved on; it was a good time for some people to get jobs and get married. But some of the bands are still hitting it hard.

Eddie Baranek: Seymour came out a few times. "I want to see these bands." And we were one of them. He took us out to dinner before our show, and he ended up leaving his credit card on the floor at the Magic Stick. Then we got the report back from Seymour. "Those Sights guys, they jam too much." Seymour was sleeping sometimes when bands were playing. He was gluttonous, fat—you know, just kind of, "I know what I like and that's what I do." Same thing with Little Steven. When he came to Detroit he came to Jim Diamond's, and he played the new record for Little Steven. He's like, "Those guys got to quit smoking pot." We jammed too much for Little Steven.

Ko Melina: Little Steven had heard the Ko and the Knockouts record, and he had just started the Sirius satellite radio thing. It was that year, 2001. He told me what he was doing and that he had Kim Fowley, Joan Jett—these names in music. He asked me, "Do you want to do a show for my station?" I said, "Yeah, of course, but why me?" I had never done any radio. He wanted, like, a younger voice at that point because everybody else was the sixties and seventies. I went to New York and did some demos for him. I did a test session, and he said, "Here's a tape of it. Go back to your hotel and listen to it." I listened to about five seconds of it, and I sounded horrible. I kind of had a nervous breakdown. It was really scary, and I think I cried. So he gave me a really great pep talk. The next thing I knew, it was like, "Now you have a radio show."

Rachel Nagy: In a way it was cool because maybe some starving people could make some money. And at the same time, what sprang out of it were people trying to emulate it in a horrible way.

Jim Diamond: There were people from England coming here, interviewing us. I never thought anything of it at the time. I was just doing my job; I'm like, "This is great." More bands are coming through. I'm getting people from out of town. This is good. I never thought anything of it, like, "Oh my God, these are special times." Gregg Kostelich at Get Hip came here to talk with a band called the Paybacks. He'd put out their first two records. Greg told me later that it seemed to him like some people were getting big heads and talking like they were going to explode like Seattle and all this shit. He told me later he thought it was kind of "Eh, don't let your heads get too big." It might not happen like you're envisioning. And lo and behold, it didn't.

John Krautner: It was a goal of everybody to just live the dream: be a band and hang out. It wasn't about big cars and big labels—just to be free, to go out any night you wanted. Tuesday night just might as well be a Saturday night. We were all smart enough to know that it was not the new Seattle. Maybe some of us were optimistic about it going somewhere. But nobody knew what it would seem like if it did go somewhere.

Chris Fuller: Detroit had been over before, but then Jack left; so did some other bands.

Jack White: I left Detroit in 2005. I felt horrible; I didn't want to be alive anymore. I felt like I just didn't have any friends and I couldn't do anything that I loved. I loved my hometown and I loved music, and I felt like I couldn't even go out and see a show anymore. It felt like everything had just turned completely upside down, and I couldn't even figure out why or what I did to make that happen, and I just turned it all on myself, thinking it must be me, that I am not a nice person, or I might think I'm doing the right things but I'm doing the wrong things. I have no idea. I know it's just a complete negative mess around me, and I can't be here anymore. Either I just die, lay down and die, or I go away. And I thought a lot about different things. Maybe I need to go live by myself in Colorado or Mississippi and not have anybody around me for a while. Maybe I need to move to Europe or something. The problem is, I've never had any appeal for large cities like LA or New York, which is what you're supposed to do, you know? I was trying to also be really loyal to Detroit. Like I said, White Stripes made a lot of money in 2001 but I stayed in the city of Detroit. I didn't move to Birmingham or West Bloomfield. I stayed in the city and wasted a lot of money on taxes doing so. You don't get any points for that, but you get attacked for leaving. It was almost like, "You guys left me, man. I didn't leave you." So it was a very bitter time for me at the time. I didn't really know who to trust anymore or why I was even doing what I was doing, 'cause it was that kind of feeling like, well, this is what happens? This is the payoff? I would rather have my friends and the Gold Dollar instead all of this, if that was the choice.

Eddie Baranek: It was the Stripes and then what else can the major labels pick up? The manager of Fall Out Boy wanted to meet us; he said he wanted to manage us. We took every wrong turn; we were good at mismanaging ourselves. We're in New York; we gotta go meet with this guy. "You wanna hit this joint first?" So he says, "Where do you want to go eat?" We were little boneheads. "Pizza." At the same time was Rick Rubin. We were on our first tour of England, and we got this call from one of Rubin's henchmen that we need to come back to the states, that Rick

Rubin wants to fly us out to LA for a showcase. And we're like, "Isn't a showcase when you, like, play in an empty room at 5:00 p.m., and he sits at the end of the room and you're on display like a fishbowl? Yes? We don't do showcases." And we're like, "Yeah, we got Rick Rubin, man. We're bad asses." But he agrees to book us on a bill and puts us at the Troubadour with Johnny Polanski and Jesse Malin. Minnie Driver was there. It was the Ryan Adams-y Troubadour. We get in, and his minion takes us out to Dan Tana's. We're ordering a hundred dollars of this and that, and they're feeding us drugs and everything—tons of blow. Next day we play our show, and Rick Rubin floats into the Troubadour. You know the upstairs balcony? He just floated in with a fucking cape on. I'm thinking, "Okay, what the fuck? Where is he? When's he coming fucking shake my hand?" No, with Rick you get the call later. Another minion calls. "Rick enjoyed the show. Rick wants to meet you, Eddie, up at his house in the Hollywood Hills. You can't take a cab. I'll take you there right now, if you only say the word, 'I shall be healed.'" I'm like, "What? This is fucked up." I said, "No way, man, because this is my band. What is it—Eddie and the Chumps?" This is the fucking Sights, man. That's weird man. Not weird like he's going to touch my balls, but weird like, "Why can't you talk to my friends? Why can't we all have beers?" This was awkward. So I turned him down. We were Detroit; we weren't LA.

Ko Melina: The question you always get asked is, "What is it about Detroit? Is it something in the water?" "Yes, there is something in the water here. You just have to start drinking it, and you're going to be really good." John Peel became a big champion of White Stripes and sent his producer, Anita, over to Detroit for a few days to do, like, a radio documentary about Detroit. I took her around; she stayed with me. I thought she did a really great job. So I thought—maybe naively—that all journalists are like that and everybody is, like, looking out for your best interest, and they were going to paint you in a positive light all the time and not really take you out of context or anything. I think that soon after the White Stripes started getting really big, I was getting mentioned in *Billboard* magazine and had one record. Why were they even talking about me? Yeah, it's good, but at some point you realize that people aren't necessarily out to get the truth. At the same time the local press didn't really care about us at all.

Margaret Dollrod: I didn't see it coming, and I'd like to know what other part of Detroit exploded. Please tell me what other person exploded other than Jack. Eminem? Kid Rock? They weren't with us. Kid Rock saw us play and he told me, "You guys are crazy" in a complimentary way. Later I was at a party for WRIF, and

I had come up with this great idea that he should go on stage with your stripper people and stuff and have your Little Joe come out. And you know the cartoons that have the dynamite TNT thing? Little Joe could do TNT dynamite thing and the girl's tops will fly off and there will be fireworks behind it. Well, I never got to tell him the idea because Kid Rock said, "I don't want anything to do with you." When people would come to town to talk to the bands, no one would tell them to get in touch with us. We were kind of older and not really part of it by then.

Rachel Nagy: Let's face it: the Stooges, the MC5, Motown—that's the fucking shit. This is where it all comes from. And yet we're the fucking apocalypse personified. I've been hearing ever since I was a child that "Oh, yeah, it's gonna get better, and we're gonna make Detroit better." Yeah, that'd be great, but you know what? I don't want it to change. It's Detroit. I've watched all the cities in Ohio. I drive through Cleveland and even Toledo, and it's like, "Whoa! What happened? Look at this. It's amazing. It's a real city." I don't really know if I want to see that happen in Detroit. Detroit is Detroit. It's this beautiful place where you sacrifice your safety for a shitload of freedom.

ACKNOWLEDGMENTS

In the early-eighties punk rock days, where I come from, the Thanks List was a vaunted place that usually included every bathroom attendant and half-girlfriend. My favorite reaction to that was always the Brit band Discharge, which simply put on the back of its first single, "Thanks to No Fucker."

I like the sentiment, but that's not the case here. I have some hearty thanks to give to both connectors and connected.

At the top of that list is any and everyone who spent their precious time with me both in person and on the phone, and this includes the accomplished stars, the aspiring artists, the promoters, producers, fans, record store workers, roadies, sound people, DJs, and scenesters who created and cultivated the Huge Deal that Detroit music was and is. You collectively created this book with your generous contributions.

Thanks also to Ben Blackwell, Brian Bowe, Robert Matheu, Dan Carlisle, Rich Tupica, my editor at Da Capo, Ben Schafer, and my agent, David Patterson, at Foundry Literary + Media.

I can be reached by e-mail at avalanche50@hotmail.com.

Hit Facebook.com/Detroitrockcitybook and my website, Avalanche50.com.

If necessary, corrections will be made in subsequent editions of the book.

THE PLAYERS

Dan Carlisle: Disc jockey. WABX, WRIF.

Russ Gibb: Promoter, entrepreneur. Opened and booked the Grande Ballroom, Eastown Theater, and numerous other Detroit venues. Funded the Graystone Ballroom in the eighties.

Mitch Ryder: Musician. Vocalist, Mitch Ryder and the Detroit Wheels, Detroit with Mitch Ryder. The white James Brown.

Stirling Silver: Scenester. Record store guy, brought the New York Dolls to their first Detroit in-store.

VC Lamont Veasey: Musician. Bassist, guitarist, Black Merda, Detroit's pre-Funkadelic psychedelic black rock band.

Robin Sommers: Artist, scenester. Friend of *Creem* founder Barry Kramer. Deceased.

Ron Cooke: Musician. Bassist, Detroit, Gang War, Sonic's Rendezvous Band.

Don Was (Don Fagenson): Musician, producer. Vocalist, the Traitors. Cofounder, bassist, vocalist with Was (Not Was) with David Weiss. Grammy-winning producer with credits that include the Rolling Stones, Bob Dylan, Iggy Pop, and Paul Westerberg.

Mark Norton: Musician, journalist. Vocalist Ramrods, 27. Writer for *Creem*.

Hiawatha Bailey: Musician, scenester. Vocalist Cult Heroes. Only black man to work for the White Panther Party.

Brian Pastoria: Musician, producer. Drummer, Adrenaline.

Tom Morwatts: Musician. Guitarist, Motor City Mutants, the Mutants.

Dave Leone: Promoter. Booked the string of teen clubs called the Hideout with Punch Andrews and later formed Diversified Management Agency, which handled loads of Detroit acts.

Jerry Bazil: Musician. Drummer, Dark Carnival with Niagara and Ron Asheton.

Jaan Uhelszki: Journalist. *Creem* magazine.

Pete Cavanaugh: Disk jockey, promoter. WTAC, booked shows in areas north of Detroit.

Punch Andrews: Promoter, manager. Bob Seger's manager from almost the beginning. Andrews also promoted and booked Detroit's Hideout teen clubs.

Jeep Holland: Founder, A-Square Records. Manager, Rationals, SRC, and host of others. Deceased.

Robin Seymour: Disc jockey, television personality. Host of *Swingin' Time*, DJ at CKLW. Introduced Stevie Wonder, Bob Seger, Glenn Frey, and Ted Nugent to local television audiences.

Art Cervi: Talent coordinator, *Swingin' Time*, Bozo the Clown in Detroit.

Jerry Wexler: Record exec, producer, considered by some the man who made Aretha Franklin. Deceased.

Scott Morgan: Musician. Guitarist, vocalist, the Rationals, Sonic's Rendezvous Band.

Deniz Tek: Musician. Guitarist, Radio Birdmen.

Scott Richardson: Musician. Vocalist, Chosen Few, Scott Richard Case, SRC.

Steve Forgey: Musician, scenester. Guitarist.

David Teegarden: Musician. Drummer, Teegarden & VanWinkle, Bob Seger, Silver Bullet Band.

John Sinclair: Band manager, starmaker, inmate, actvist. Managed the MC5 and headed the White Panther Party.

Iggy Pop: Musician. Vocalist, the Stooges, solo.

Gary Rasmussen: Musician. Bassist, the Up, Sonic's Rendezvous Band, Iggy Pop.

S. Kay Young: Photographer.

K. J. Knight: Musician. Drummer, Ted Nugent and the Amboy Dukes.

John Finley: Musician, scenester. Guitarist, the Lourds (pre-Amboy Dukes Nugent band). Deceased.

Rusty Day: Musician. Vocalist, Ted Nugent and the Amboy Dukes, Cactus. Deceased.

Ted Nugent: Musician. Guitarist, the Lourds, the Amboy Dukes, solo. Also known as the Nuge and the Motor City Madman.

Dennis Thompson: Musician. Drummer, MC5, New Order.

Jon Landau: Music writer, producer.

Jac Holzman: Record exec, Elektra.

Frank Bach: Musician. Vocalist, the Up.

Bob Sheff, aka Blue Gene Tyranny: Musician. Keyboardist, the Charging Rhinoceros of Soul, the Stooges, Laurie Andersen, John Cage.

Rick Kraniak, aka Rick K: Promoter.

Leni Sinclair: Photographer. Coauthor of *Detroit Rocks! A Pictorial History of Motor City Rock and Roll 1965–1975*.

Gary Grimshaw: Photographer. Coauthor of *Detroit Rocks! A Pictorial History of Motor City Rock and Roll 1965–1975*.

Sigrid Smith: Ex-wife of Fred "Sonic" Smith.

Fred "Sonic" Smith: Musician: Guitarist, MC5, Sonic's Rendezvous Band. Deceased.

Sun Ra: Musician. Composer, pianist, synthesizer. Sun Ra Arkestra, solo. Deceased.

Dennis Dunaway: Musician. Bassist, Alice Cooper.

Norm Liberman, aka Panama Red: Musician. Vocalist, the Frut.

John Kosloskey, aka Kozmo: Musician. Bassist, the Frut.

Neal Smith: Musician. Drummer, Alice Cooper.

Pete Woodman: Musician. Drummer, Popcorn Blizzard, Floating Circus, Bossmen.

Susie Kaine: Musician. Keyboardist, Popcorn Blizzard, Floating Circus.

Jack Bodnar: Scenester.

Bill White: Musician. Bassist, Ted Nugent and the Amboy Dukes.
Rick Stevers: Musician. Drummer, Frijid Pink.
Donny Hartman: Musician. Guitarist, vocalist, the Frost.
Michael Lutz: Musician. Guitarist, bassist, vocalist, Brownsville Station, Ted Nugent.
Shaun Murphy, aka Stoney: Musician. Vocalist, Wilson Mower Pursuit, Stoney and Meatloaf, Bob Seger, Silver Bullet Band.
Marvin Lee Aday, aka Meatloaf: Musician. Vocalist, Floating Circus, Popcorn Blizzard, Stoney and Meatloaf, solo.
Dave Palmer: Musician. Drummer, Ted Nugent and the Amboy Dukes.
Greg Arama: Musician. Bassist, Ted Nugent and the Amboy Dukes.
Al Jacquez: Musician. Bassist, vocalist, Savage Grace.
Bobby Rigg: Musician. Drummer, the Frost.
Patti Quatro: Musician. Guitarist, Pleasure Seekers, Cradle.
Suzi Quatro: Musician, actress. Bassist, Pleasure Seekers, Cradle, solo. Played Leather Tuscadero on seventies sitcom *Happy Days.*
Nancy Quatro: Musician. Vocalist, Pleasure Seekers, Cradle.
Johnny Badanjek: Musician. Drummer, Mitch Ryder and the Detroit Wheels, Detroit, the Rockets, Ronnie Montrose, Nils Lofgren, Alice Cooper, Edgar Winter.
Ray Goodman: Musician. Guitarist, Mitch Ryder and the Detroit Wheels, SRC.
Gary Quackenbush: Musician. Guitarist, SRC.
Billy Goodson: Scenester.
Glenn Frey: Musician. Guitarist, Eagles. Sang backing vocals on Bob Seger's hit "Ramblin Gamblin' Man."
Wayne Kramer: Musician. Guitarist, MC5, Gang War, Was (Not Was), solo.
Becky Tyner: Wife of Rob Tyner.
Bill Graham: Iconic music promoter, stable of venues that included the original Fillmores. Deceased.
Michael Davis: Musician. Bassist, MC5, Destroy All Monsters. Deceased.
Steve Mackay: Musician. Saxophonist, Charging Rhinoceros of Soul, the Stooges.
Arthur Kane: Musician. Bassist, New York Dolls.
Jim McCarty: Musician. Guitarist, Mitch Ryder and the Detroit Wheels, the Rockets, Cactus.
Lester Bangs: Journalist, *Creem* magazine. Deceased.
James Williamson: Musician. Guitarist, Chosen Few, the Stooges.
Dave Alexander: Musician. Bassist, the Stooges. Deceased.
Ron Asheton: Musician. Guitarist, bassist, the Stooges, Destroy All Monsters, New Order. Deceased.
Jimmy Recca: Musician. Bassist, the Stooges, New Order.
DJ Dianna, aka Dianna Frank: Scenester.
Niagara: Artist, musician. Vocalist, Destroy All Monsters, Dark Carnival. Girlfriend of Ron Asheton.
Tony DeFries: Head of MainMan, which briefly represented Iggy and the Stooges.
John Kordosh, aka John Amore: Musician, journalist. Bassist, the Mutants. Wrote for *Creem* early to mideighties.
Cathy Gisi: Journalist. Wrote for *Creem* mid- to late seventies.

Robert Matheu: Photojournalist. Shot for *Creem* and numerous other rock magazines. Author of *The Stooges: The Authorized and Illustrated Story* and *Creem: America's Only Rock 'n' Roll Magazine.*

Nikki Corvette: Musician. Vocalist, Nikki and the Corvettes, Nikki and the Stingrays, Gorevette.

Todd Rundgren: Musician, producer. Produced Grand Funk Railroad, *We're an American Band* and *Shinin' On.*

Art Lyzak: Musician. Vocalist, the Mutants.

Mike Rushlow: Musician. Bassist, the Pigs, the Boners, Rushlo-King Combo.

Bob Mulrooney, aka Bootsey X: Musician. Drummer, vocalist, Coldcock, Ramrods, Bootsey X and the Lovemakers.

Skid Marx: Musician. Bassist, Flirt, Seat Belts.

Nick Kent: Journalist. New Musical Express, The Face.

Dave Hanna: Musician. Guitarist, the Boners, the Ramrods, Space Heaters.

Scott Asheton: Musician. Drummer, the Stooges, Sonic's Rendezvous Band.

Barry Kramer: Cofounder, editor, *Creem* magazine. Deceased.

Ric Siegel: Journalist. Part of the crew that started *Creem.*

Greg Errico: Musician. Drummer, Sly and the Family Stone.

Peter Rivera: Musician. Drummer, Rare Earth.

Gil Bridges: Musician. Saxophonist, Rare Earth.

Alice Cooper: Musician. Vocalist, Alice Cooper, solo.

Bob Ezrin: Producer. Alice Cooper, Detroit, Kiss, Lou Reed, Peter Gabriel.

Glen Buxton: Musician. Guitarist, Alice Cooper. Deceased.

Mark Parenteau: Disc jockey. WABX.

Gail Parenteau: Promoter. Married to Mark Parenteau.

Michael Bruce: Musician. Guitarist, Alice Cooper.

Jim Kosloskey: Musician. Guitarist, the Frut.

Cindy Lang: Alice Cooper's girlfriend for a while.

Dave Marsh: Journalist, author. One of the first *Creem* writers, went on to join the enemy, *Rolling Stone*. Books include *Born to Run: The Bruce Springsteen Story* and *Before I Get Old: The Story of the Who.*

Tony Reay: Cofounder, editor, *Creem* magazine.

Charlie Auringer: Photographer. *Creem* magazine.

John Angelos: Musician. Vocalist, Ted Nugent and the Amboy Dukes, the Torpedoes. Deceased.

Gilda Radner: Comedian, actress. Detroit native, was among first cast of *Saturday Night Live*. Deceased.

Kim Fowley: Raconteur, musician, producer.

Ben Edmonds: Journalist. *Creem* magazine.

Bob Seger: Musician. Vocalist, guitarist, keyboards, Bob Seger and the Last Heard, Bob Seger System, solo, Bob Seger and the Silver Bullet Band.

Toby Mamis: Journalist, promoter. Now road manager for Alice Cooper.

Tom Weschler: Photographer, road manager for Bob Seger.

Dick Wagner: Musician. Guitarist, the Bossmen, the Frost, Ursa Major, Alice Cooper, Peter Gabriel, Lou Reed, solo.

Mark Farner: Musician. Guitarist, bassist, the Pack, Grand Funk Railroad.

Terry Knight: Disc jockey, manager, musician. Vocalist, the Pack, managed Grand Funk Railroad. Deceased.

Don Brewer: Musician. Drummer, Grand Funk Railroad, Bob Seger and the Silver Bullet Band.

Dave West: Equipment guy, made amps for Grand Funk Railroad.

Jim Atherton: Manager. Terry Knight and the Pack.

Dave Knapp: Terry Knight's brother.

Tom Wright: Photographer, promoter.

Michael Quatro: Promoter, musician. Vocalist, keyboard player, Michael Quatro Jam band, solo. Brother of Suzi and Patti Quatro.

Jerry Vile: Musician, journalist, artist. Vocalist, the Boners, editor of *White Noise* fanzine.

Bob Heath and Bill Spiegel: Radio producers for WLW in Cincinnati, helped make the Cincinnati Pop Festival go down in 1970. It was the first rock concert ever taped for future national broadcast, preceding ABC's *In Concert*, which debuted in 1972.

Tom Copi: Photographer.

Dallas Hodge: Musician. Guitarist, Catfish Hodge Band.

Steve Hunter: Musician. Guitarist, Detroit, Lou Reed, Alice Cooper, Peter Gabriel.

John Sauter: Musician. Bassist, Detroit.

Terry Kelly: Musician, Guitarist, Detroit Wheels, Cactus. Deceased.

Dave DiMartino: Journalist. Wrote for *Creem* in the late seventies and the mideighties.

Marcia Rabideau: One of the MC5 girls.

Richard Haddad, aka Shemp: Musician. Bassist, SRC. Deceased.

Mark Manko: Musician. Guitarist, Catfish, Detroit.

Bob Crewe: Producer. Mitch Ryder.

ACT II

Chris Panackia, aka Cool Chris: Soundman. Worked every venue in Detroit for thirty years.

Tom Gelardi: Capitol Records promo man. Known as the guy who tossed the Beatles first US single away and claimed "they'll never make it."

Cary Loren: Artist, musician. Guitarist, Detroit All Monsters.

Mike Skill: Musician. Guitarist and bassist, Romantics.

Gerald Shohan: Musician. Guitarist, Coldcock.

Johnny Thunders: Musician. Guitarist, vocalist, New York Dolls, Johnny Thunders and the Heartbreakers, Gang War, solo. Deceased.

Bobby Hackney: Musician. Bassist, vocalist, Death.

Mike Murphy: Musician. Drummer, vocalist, the Denizens.

Vince Bannon: Promoter, musician. Guitarist, Coldcock, the Sillies, booked Bookie's, City Club, and a number of other venues in the city.

Jimmy Marinos: Musician. Drummer, Romantics.

Don Davis: musician, producer, songwriter. Penned "Who's Making Love," which Johnnie Taylor turned into a hit. Head of production at Stax.

Doug Banker: Manager, promoter, musician. Manager of Ted Nugent.

Gloria Bondy: Scenester, musician. Sang backup for the Sillies.

Tim Caldwell: Scenester, psycho-intellectual.

Tex Newman: Musician. Guitarist, RUR, Shock Therapy, Country Bob and the Bloodfarmers.

Gary Reichel: Musician. Vocalist, Cinecyde.

Charlie Martin: Musician. Drummer, Silver Bullet Band.

Skip Knape, aka Skip Van Winkle: Musician. Keyboardist, bassist, vocalist, Teegarden & Van Winkle, Bob Seger.

Drew Abbott: Musician. Guitarist, Third Power, Bob Seger, Silver Bullet Band.

David McCullough, aka Dansir: Crew, Bob Seger.

Jamie Oldaker: Musician. Drummer, Bob Seger, Eric Clapton.

Craig Frost: Musician. Drummer, Grand Funk Railroad, Silver Bullet Band.

David Tedds: Fan, record industry guy. Executive producer of the Grand Funk Railroad reissues by Capitol Records in the early 2000s.

Linda Barber: Journalist. Wrote for *Creem* magazine in the seventies and eighties.

John Brannon: Musician. Vocalist, Negative Approach, Laughing Hyenas, Easy Action.

Cathy Gisi: Journalist. Wrote for *Creem* magazine in the seventies and eighties.

Susan Whitall: Journalist. Editor of *Creem* in the seventies and eighties.

Bill Holdship: Journalist. Wrote for *Creem*, *Rolling Stone*.

Mike Kelley: Musician, artist. Drummer, vocalist, Destroy All Monsters. Deceased.

Jack Smith: Artist, photographer, filmmaker. Considered by many as the father of performance art films for his 1963 miniflick *Flaming Creatures*, which predated and influenced Warhol and Waters. Deceased.

La Monte Young: Artist, composer, musician. Cited by Lou Reed in his liner notes to Metal Machine Music.

Jim Shaw: Tastemaker extraordinaire. Deceased.

Sue Rynski: Photographer.

Larry and Ben Miller: Musicians, Destroy All Monsters. Brothers of Mission of Burma's Roger Miller.

Harold Richardson: Musician. Guitarist, Gravitar, Easy Action, Negative Approach.

Freddie Brooks: Scenester. Briefly managed Sonic's Rendezvous Band.

Lenny Kaye: Musician, journalist. Guitarist, Patti Smith Group. Wrote the liner notes for psyche comp *Nuggets*.

Patti Smith: Musician, author. Vocalist, Patti Smith Group, solo. Married to Fred "Sonic" Smith from 1980 until Fred's death in 1995. Books include *Just Kids* (2010).

Jim Olenski: Musician. Guitarist, Cinecyde.

Peter James: Musician. Guitarist, Ramrods, Nikki and the Corvettes.

Michael Profane: Musician. Guitarist, the Sillies.

Steve King: Musician, producer. Guitarist, the Pigs, the Boners, Ramrods, Rushlow-King Combo, producer of Eminem.

Andy Peabody: Musician. Vocalist, Coldcock.

Paul Zimmerman: Scenester, journalist. Editor of *White Noise* fanzine.

Steve McGuire: Musician. Bassist, the Traitors.

Jack Tann: Producer. Worked with Don Was at Sound Suite. Was and Tann formed the Motor City Revue, a fairly failed stab at marketing the emerging punk rock scene in the late seventies.

Lenore Paxton: Musician. Jazz pianist, vocalist.

Scott Campbell: Musician, promoter: Vocalist, the Sillies. Booked and ran sound at Bookie's.

Rick Metcalf: Cartoonist, scenester.

Frank Gagen: Musician, club owner. Leader of a local big band, also owned Frank Gagen's, a supper club that eventually became Bookie's.

Bookie Stewart: Bought Gagen's in the early seventies. Deceased.

Michelle Southers: Scenester.

Kirsten Rogoff: Musician. Keyboardist, Algebra Mothers, the Sillies.

Tesco Vee: Musician, journalist. Vocalist, Meatmen, Blight. Cofounder, *Touch and Go* magazine and Touch and Go Records.

Rich Cole: Musician. Bassist, Romantics.

Bill Kozy: Musician. Guitarist, Meanies, Speedball.

Irene DeCook: Fashion designer. Created leather outfits for the Romantics. Also appeared as Irene the Leather Weather Lady in Howard Stern's book *Private Parts* after the two met during Stern's time in Detroit.

Joel Zuckerman and Arnie Tencer: Managers of the Romantics.

Wally Palmar: Musician. Guitarist, vocalist, Romantics.

Gary Buermele, aka Gary Brimstone, aka Brim: Drug dealer, hanger on. Deceased.

Jerry Nolan: Musician. Drummer, New York Dolls, Johnny Thunders and the Heartbreakers. Deceased.

Billy Rath: Musician. Bassist, Johnny Thunders and the Heartbreakers, the Stooges.

Walter Lure: Musician. Johnny Thunders and the Heartbreakers, the Waldos.

Keith Jackson: Musician. Guitarist, the Gerbils, Shock Therapy.

Katy Hait: Photographer, musician. Vocalist, Sillies.

Sirius Trixon: Musician. Vocalist, Motor City Bad Boys.

Diane Koprince: Chili Sister.

Brian Mullan: Promoter, scenester.

Glenn Johnson: Musician. Drummer, Mr. Unique and the Leisure Suits.

Johnny Ramone: Musician. Guitarist, the Ramones. Deceased.

Dave Rice: Musician. Guitarist, L-Seven, the Linkletters, Algebra Mothers.

ACT III

Larissa Strickland: Musician, scenester. Vocalist, L-Seven, guitarist, Laughing Hyenas. Deceased.

Chris Moore, aka Opie: Musician. Drummer, Negative Approach.

Rob Michaels: Musician. Vocalist, Bored Youth.

Marc Barie: Scenester.

Sherrie Feight: Musician. Vocalist, Strange Fruit, Spastic Rhythm Tarts.

Andy Wendler: Musician. Guitarist, the Necros.

Corey Rusk: Musician, record label owner, promoter. Bassist, Necros. Took over Touch and Go Records in 1981 and turned it into one of the largest independent labels in the world. Booked the Graystone Hall, the Freezer, and numerous other venues in Detroit.

Hillary Waddles: Scenester.

Gloria Branzei: Scenester.

Jon Howard: Scenester.

Cary Safarian, aka Scary Cary: Promoter; Managed Graystone Ballroom. Currently in prison.

Rob Miller: Scenester, owner and cofounder of Bloodshot Records.

Mike Hard: Musician, actor. Vocalist, God Bullies, Thrall, Brainsaw.

John Speck: Musician. Guitarist, vocalist, Hoarse, the Fags.

Doc Dart: Musician. Vocalist, Crucifucks.

Scott Schuer: Musician. Guitarist, L-Seven.

Margaret Dollrod: Musician. Vocalist, guitarist, Demolition Doll Rods.

EWolf: Photographer, musician. Drummer, Angry Red Planet, Dirtbombs.

Ken Waagner: Promoter, manager.

Charlie Wallace: Musician. Vocalist, effects, guitarist, ADC, Fractured Cylinder.

Norm Zebrowski: Musician, Scenester. Vocalist, Disinfect.

Lacy X: Musician. Vocalist, Son of Sam.

Rachel Nagy: Musician. Vocalist, Detroit Cobras.

Kevin Monroe: Musician. Bassist, Laughing Hyenas, Mule.

Mike Danner: Musician. Drummer, Laughing Hyenas, Big Chief.

Preston Long, aka P. W. Long: Musician. Vocalist, guitarist, Wig, Mule, P. W. Long's Reelfoot, solo.

Jim Magas: Musician. Vocalist, electro manipulator, Couch, cofounder, Bulb Records.

Dave Feeny: Musician, producer. Keyboardist, guitarist, Hysteric Narcotics, the Orange Roughies, Blanche, founder, Tempermill studio.

GG Allin: Musician, performance artist. Deceased.

Jim Kimball: Musician. Drummer, Laughing Hyenas, Mule, Jesus Lizard, Denison Kimball Trio.

Peter Davis: Booking agent, Creature Booking.

John Szymanski, aka John Hentch: Musician. Keyboardist, guitarist, the Hentchmen.

Mick Collins: Musician, producer. Guitarist, vocalist, the Gories, Blacktop, the Dirtbombs.

Jason Stollsteimer: Musician. Guitarist, vocalist, Baby Killers, Von Bondies, the Hounds Below.

Dan Kroha: Musician. Guitarist, vocalist, the Gories, Rocket 455, Demolition Doll Rods.

Peg O'Neill: Musician. Drummer, the Gories.

Alex Chilton: Musician, producer. Guitarist, vocalist, Box Tops, Big Star. Deceased.

Dave Buick: Musician, founder of Italy Records. Bassist, the Go.

Tim Warren: Founder, Crypt Records.

Tav Falco: Musician, actor. Vocalist, Tav Falco's Panther Burns.

Meg White: Musician. Drummer, White Stripes.

Troy Gregory: Musician. Bassist, guitarist, vocalist, Witches, Dirtbombs.

Karen Neal, aka Queen Bee: Musician. Bassist, Inside Out, Thrall.

Andrew WK: Musician, producer. Vocalist, keyboards, Wolf Eyes, solo.

Twig Harper: Musician, various instruments with Scheme, Mini-Systems, Nautical Almanac.

Aaron Dilloway: Musician. Guitarist, tape manipulator, madman, Wolf Eyes, Galen, Universal Indians.

Pete Larson: Musician. Cofounder, Bulb Records.

John Olson: Musician. Electronics, Wolf Eyes.

Rusvelt: Owner of Blondies.

Steve Nawara: Musician. Guitarist, Electric Six, Detroit Cobras, Rocket 455, the Go, Ko and the Knockouts.

Greg Schmitt: Musician, photographer.

David B. Livingstone: Musician, producer. Guitarist, God Bullies.

Bob Madigan: Musician. Vocalist, Slaughterhouse, Cum Dumpster. Deceased.

Kevin Reis: Musician. Bassist, Laughing Hyenas. Deceased.

Anthony DeLuca: Musician. Drummer, Swirlies, Blake Babies.

Jack White: Musician, producer. Vocalist, guitarist, keyboardist, White Stripes, Raconteurs, the Dead Weather, solo.

Bobby Harlow: Musician. Vocalist, the Go, Conspiracy of Owls.

Tom Potter: Musician. Guitarist, vocalist, Bantam Rooster, Dirtbombs.

Neil Yee: Manager, booker, Gold Dollar.

John Krautner: Musician. Bassist, guitarist, the Go, Conspiracy of Owls.

Chris Fuller: Manager, Electric Six.

Matthew Smith: Musician, producer. Vocalist, guitarist, Outrageous Cherry.

Martin Heath: CEO, founder, Lizard King Records.

Ben Blackwell: Musician. Drummer, the Dirtbombs.

Timmy Vulgar: Musician. Guitarist, vocalist, Clone Defects, Human Eye. Timmy's Organism.

Ko Melina: Radio personality, musician. Bassist, guitarist, vocalist, Ko and the Knockouts, the Dirtbombs. Has show on *Little Steven's Underground Garage*.

Dan Trager: A&R, Sub Pop, signed the Go.

Jim Diamond: Producer, musician. Bassist, Dirtbombs, owner of Ghetto Recorders.

Joe Burdick: Musician. Bass player, vocalist, the Dirtys.

Marc Watt: Musician. Guitarist, the Dirtys.

Eddie Sights, aka Eddie Baranek: Musician. Guitarist, vocalist, the Sights, Ko and the Knockouts.

Tyler Spencer, aka Dick Valentine: Musician. Vocalist, Wildbunch, Electric 6.

Marcie Bolen: Musician. Guitarist, Von Bondies, Slumber Party, Silverghost.

Larry Hardy: Founder, In the Red Records.

Long Gone John: Founder, Sympathy for the Record Industry.

Violent J: Musician. Insane Clown Posse.

Shaggy 2 Dope, aka Joseph Utsler: Musician. Insane Clown Posse.

Kenny Olson: Musician. Guitarist, Kid Rock, Twisted Brown Trucker Band.

Mike E. Clark: Producer. Insane Clown Posse, Kid Rock.

Jeff Ehrenberg: Musician. Drummer, Starlite Desperation.

Gregg Kostelich: Founder, Get Hip Records.

Rick Rubin: Weirdo, record producer.

Note: Some people on this list may not be noted as deceased but indeed are no longer among us. If their status was unavailable, though, we optimistically erred on the side of life.